Presented to
Mrs. Rivka Katz

who made special education in our Yeshiva
a "SPECIAL EDUCATION"
and who made the Resource Room
a "RESOURCE ROOM"
for all students and educators.
From:
The Faculty and Administration of
Yeshiva Tifereth Moshe /DRC
June 2004

ArtScroll Series®

Rabbi Nosson Scherman / Rabbi Meir Zlotowitz
General Editors

THE HOUSE

Published by
Mesorah Publications, ltd

OF
RIZHIN

CHASSIDUS AND THE RIZHINER DYNASTY

RABBI MENACHEM BRAYER

PREVIEW EDITION
February 2003

Published and Distributed by
MESORAH PUBLICATIONS, LTD.
4401 Second Avenue / Brooklyn, N.Y 11232

Distributed in Europe by
LEHMANNS
Unit E, Viking Industrial Park
Rolling Mill Road
Jarow, Tyne & Wear, NE32 3DP
England

Distributed in Australia and New Zealand by
GOLDS WORLD OF JUDAICA
3-13 William Street
Balaclava, Melbourne 3183
Victoria, Australia

Distributed in Israel by
SIFRIATI / A. GITLER — BOOKS
6 Hayarkon Street
Bnei Brak 51127

Distributed in South Africa by
KOLLEL BOOKSHOP
Shop 8A Norwood Hypermarket
Norwood 2196, Johannesburg, South Africa

ARTSCROLL SERIES®
THE HOUSE OF RIZHIN
© *Copyright 2003, by* MESORAH PUBLICATIONS, Ltd.
4401 Second Avenue / Brooklyn, N.Y. 11232 / (718) 921-9000 / www.artscroll.com

---

ISBN:
1-57819-794-5 (hard cover)
1-57819-795-3 (paperback)

Typography by CompuScribe at ArtScroll Studios, Ltd.

Printed in the United States of America by Noble Book Press Corp.
Bound by Sefercraft, Quality Bookbinders, Ltd., Brooklyn N.Y. 11232

לזכר נשמת האי גברא יקירא איש החסד והמעש

ר׳ אליעזר בן ר׳ אברהם בצלאל ע״ה

נלב״ע בעש״ק ג׳ כסלו תשס״ג

In honor of the memory of

MR. LEO GRAHAME ע״ה

of London
noted philanthropost and supporter of
Torah and chesed institutions
in Israel and England.

After entering the Rizhiner
family through marriage,
he became a strong supporter of
the House of Rizhin and
a founding pillar of the renowned
Rizhiner Yeshiva in Jerusalem.

Dedicated by his wife

GUGGY;

children
JUDITH AND GEOFFREY PREGER,
NAOMI AND JEFFREY GREENWOOD,
JOANNA AND AVRAHAM KUSHNIR,
ALAN AND GOLDIE GRAHAME;
GRANDCHILDREN AND GREAT-GRANDCHILDREN.

THE HOUSE OF RIZHIN

For nearly 200 years, "The House of Rizhin" — encompassing the *chatzeiros*, the Chassidic courts, of Rizhin, Sadagora, Buhush, Leova, Shtefanesht, Chortkov, Boyan, Husyatin, and Kopitchnitz — has been at the epicenter of Torah, *chassidus*, *emunah*, and *chessed*.

Why *"The House" of Rizhin?*

That house was, and is today, home to generations of Jews. It exudes warmth, spirituality and sustenance. The stones of each Rizhiner edifice came together to form more than merely buildings. They formed a foundation of Jewish life.

The holy Rebbes who held court in these Houses of Rizhin were pillars of strength who kept their communities strong through the wars and programs of Eastern Europe; the immigration and resettlement in the United States before, during and after the Second World War; and the continuation of the Rizhiner legacy in Israel and around the world.

The Tzaddikim of the Rizhiner dynasty give "The House of Rizhin" its eternal resonance.

In this book, the stories of this House come alive, sparking the light that has illuminated each House of Rizhin for two centuries.

Come, let us enter …

ON THE COVER

The renowned Beis Medrash Tiferes Yisroel in the Old City of Yerushalayim. Surrounding it are the beautiful shuls of Sadagora, Chortkov, Husyatin, and Boyan. At he bottom right is the Rizhiner Yeshiva in the new city of Yerusalayim, founded and built after the Beis Medrash in the Old City was destroyed.

AUTHOR'S PREFACE TO THE PREVIEW EDITION

THE PUBLICATION OF THIS VOLUME IS FOR ME A MAJOR MILESTONE in my life. As one whose roots go back many generations to the Holy Rizhiner זצוק״ל and whose origins are intertwined in many branches of his illustrious offspring, it is a special זכות, a privilege, to bring the story and the teachings, the glory of the past and the unfolding of the future, to the Torah public, both those who are close to Rizhin and those who may learn about its greatness for the first time by reading this book.

Both my parents — R' Yosef זצ״ל and Rebbetzin Blima Malka ע״ה Brayer — were Husyatiner chassidim. My paternal grandfather, R' Mordechai Dov זצ״ל, was born in Husyatin (where his father R' Sholom Zalman זצ״ל was killed on *Kiddush Hashem* wearing his *tallis* and *tefillin* in the Husyatiner *kloiz*) and married in Rizhin where he became Rav and where my father was born. In later years they both became *rabbanim* in Shtefanesht, being appointed to that position by the Shtefaneshter Rebbe himself. My father visited the Pachad Yitzchok, the first Boyaner Rebbe, as a young man. (His birth certificate was changed then to list the town of Boyan as his birthplace, instead of Rizhin, in order to avoid being drafted into the anti-Semitic Russian army.) All the above cities are branches of the Rizhiner dynasty with which the reader will become familiarized in the later chapters of this book.

My bond with Rizhin strengthened and became a קשר של קיימא through my marriage to my dear אשת חיל, the daughter of the Boyaner Rebbe זצוק"ל of New York, and our younger son carries on not only the name but the principles of Boyan, as the present the Boyaner Rebbe שליט"א. Rizhin and Boyan course through my veins, so that, for all the scrupulous efforts to preserve the authenticity and accuracy of the events and teachings recorded in this book, there is an enormous sense of personal mission.

This volume begins with the origins of Chassidus. It includes novel Torah thoughts and comments, orations, and stories about the life and activities of some of the greatest *tzaddikim* in the history and development of Chassidus. The first era recorded here tells us of the Baal Shem Tov and his successor the Great Maggid of Mezritch, the Malach, R' Sholom Shachna of Prohobisht, and finally, the central figure of this book, R' Yisroel of Rizhin. The next era recorded here tells of the Holy Rizhiner's sons and their offspring, culminating with the life of the Boyaner Rebbe of New York.

The collections of Torah discourses by the Rizhiner and his sons are published for the first time in English to enable the reader to acquaint himself with the pearls of wisdom given orally by these *tzaddikim*, which have been preserved devotedly by the chassidim, either in print or through transmission from parent to child, from teacher to disciple.

Shlomo Hamelech tells us זֵכֶר צַדִּיק לִבְרָכָה, *the mention of the righteous is for a blessing (Mishlei 10:7)*. Ibn Ezra comments that the verse refers to the remembrance of the *tzaddik* after his death. According to chassidic tradition, when the Baal Shem Tov left this world on Shavuos, he ascended to the heavenly sphere and encountered *Mashiach*. The Baal Shem Tov asked, "When will you come to redeem us?"

Mashiach replied, כְּשֶׁיָּפוּצוּ מַעְיְנוֹתֶיךָ חוּצָה, *"When your wellsprings spread out"* (see Baal Shem Tov's letter to his brother-in-law, R' Gershon Kitever). Thus, every effort of the chassidic *tzaddikim* to disseminate Torah study and *Ahavas Yisroel* are important and productive stops in accelerating the Messianic era. It is my sincere hope that this volume will be seen in that light and that it will succeed in at least some degree in spreading the teachings and principles of these very great teachers of our people.

ACKNOWLEDGMENTS

I am deeply grateful to the many people — too numerous to mention — who have contributed encouragement, information, advice and material help to make this book possible. I am indebted to the elder chassidim, not only for the knowledge that they kindly shared with me, but for their living example of the legacy of Rizhin, the legacy that I have feebly tried to capture between the covers of this volume.

This volume is dedicated in memory of Leo Grahame ע"ה. He joined the House of Rizhin through marriage, but he became an integral part of it. His warmth and generosity earned him the respect and gratitude of all who knew him. It is a fitting that Mrs. Guggy Grahame and her family have chosen to honor his memory through this history of Rizhin.

My dear friend R' Shimon (Steve) Adelsberg, who has always been close to Boyan and whose help made the publication of this book possible. Rabbi Meir Zlotowitz is an old and dear friend, who graciously offered to include this book in the ArtScroll Series, which has revolutionized Torah study and Jewish life. Rabbi Nosson Scherman's friendship and courtesy, and his assistance in editing the work, have been very important. I am grateful to them both. Reb Sheah Brander's high standard of elegant graphics brings glory to the cause of Torah. He, Reb Eli Kroen and Reb Hershy Feuerwerker have made the physical beauty of this book worthy of its great subjects.

Reb Yisroel Friedman of Manchester assisted in the editorial work and provided new material. Mrs. Judi Dick edited and made extenisve and perceptive comments, and Mrs. Faygie Weinbaum proofread. Mrs. Esther Feierstein, among others, typed and offered suggestions. Mrs. Tzini Fruchthandler and Menucha Mitnick had the complex task of typesetting the book. Reb Avrohom Biderman labored magnificently to shepherd the work from manuscript to publication. He was assisted by Leah Seeve and, in the book's early stages, by Mrs. Zissel Keller.

To them and all the others who were involved in making this book a reality. I can only offer my humble thanks. May the *z'chus* of the *tzaddikim* mentioned in these pages be a source of blessing to them all.

I am grateful to מנב"ת, my wife Malka תחי׳, for more than I can put into words. Our children, grandchildren and great grandchildren are a constant source of *nachas* to us and of כְּבוֹד שָׁמַיִם. May they enjoy from their offspring the same *nachas* they give us.

Finally to the Creator of all and Source of everything for His infinite blessing, my deepest, most heartfelt thanks. May we, among *Klal Yisroel*, soon see the open manifestation of His mercy with the coming of מָשִׁיחַ צִדְקֵנוּ, בִּמְהֵרָה בְיָמֵינוּ אָמֵן.

Rabbi Menachem Brayer

5 Adar I 5763
Yahrzeit of my father-in-law, the late Boyaner Rebbe זצוק"ל

TABLE OF CONTENTS

PART I: ROOTS

PART II: R' YISROEL OF RIZHIN

PART III: THE RIZHINER'S CHILDREN

INTRODUCTION

THE HOUSE
OF RIZHIN

CHASSIDUS HAD ITS BEGINNINGS IN THE SOUTHEAST OF
Poland-Lithuania, mainly in the regions of Podolia and
ORIGINS Volhynia, in the 1730's-1740's in what
were dark times for Polish Jewry — in
the aftermath of the Cossack revolt and the savage pogroms of
Chmielnitzki, in 1648-49; the Tatar incursions from the Crimea and
the war with Moscow (the Republic of Muscovy), bringing mas-
sacres and vast destruction to the Jewish communities in Poland and
in Lithuania. The Jewish people were brought to the nadir of suffering by the false messianic promises — the ignominious debacle of
the deceptive messiahs Sabbetai Tzvi (1637 — 1676) and Yaakov
Frank (1726-1791), and the period of depression and disillusion that
ensued. It appeared as a movement of awakening — both radical
and conservative in nature, emotional and intellectual in orientation

— an awakening of the Jewish masses brought on by the ascent of the Baal Shem Tov and the Maggid of Mezritch and their followers.

In its earliest form Chassidus was based largely on kabbalistic teachings, but it neutralized the messianic element, removing it from its position of primacy and replacing it with emphasis on the personal. Chassidus taught that the way to bring *Mashiach* (the Messiah) and the redemption of the world was to concentrate upon the salvation of the individual soul. The Baal Shem Tov himself was the inspiration for the tendency to accelerate the arrival of *Mashiach* through personal improvement. In a letter to his brother-in-law, R' Gershon of Kitev, in 1751, he writes about his verbal exchange with *Mashiach*, during a spiritual ascent, עֲלִיַת נְשָׁמָה on Rosh Hashanah, 1747, when he asked *Mashiach*, "When will the master come?" To which the response was: "When your wellsprings (of learning) will be acknowledged and revealed to the world ..."

The Baal Shem Tov tried several times to emigrate to the Holy Land but his plans did not materialize. However, his disciples made *aliyah* and contributed to the renewal of the Yishuv.

What were the basic principles of Chassidus? Total reliance on faith and tradition, revelation and devotion; *d'veikus* (cleaving to Hashem), living one's religion and actualizing it as a personal and communal experience. Add to these: meditation, introspection, genuine brotherly love and mutuality, and pursuit of the loftiest levels of perfection as a means of bringing divinity into everyday life. Joy and absolute faith in the Rebbe were the principles that the chassid lived by, and all the qualities mentioned made up the fabric of the true chassid.

Chassidus teaches that man can indeed have an intimate relationship with Hashem, as long as he acknowledges and enters fully into the filial-parental relationship with Him. In the words of R' Elimelech of Lizhensk — quoting his Rebbe, the Maggid of Mezritch — "A man should call out and cry out to the Holy One, Blessed is He, 'Father!' until He becomes his father" (*Eser Oros*, p. 28). Thus, *tzaddikim* would cry out in their prayer, "Oh, *Tatte zisse* (sweet Father)." R' Elimelech actually taught his son, R' Elazar, this practice, and explained it with a parable.

A father and his son were traveling a long distance in a carriage. As they were passing a forest upon whose trees sweet fruit was growing, the child was permitted by his father to get down and pick some. Although they had a great distance left to travel, the father could not get his ravenous son away from the fruit. The son went deeper and deeper into the forest. Before he was out of earshot, his father told him that he should keep crying out, "Father, father," to which he would respond, "My son, my son." As long as he would hear his father answering him he would feel safe. Once he didn't hear his father answering him, he would know that he was lost in the forest and he should run until he found his father again.

(*Divrei Shmuel* by R' Shmelke of Nikolsburg, *Bechukosai*)

The term "chassid," as it is used in the Bible, implies a perfect man, a man of great spiritual stature who endeavors to fight the *yetzer hara*, evil inclination, and enhance the relationship between man and Hashem and between man and man.

In the eyes of the Baal Shem Tov, the main purpose of Chassidus is to prevent others from stumbling.

Chassidic literature is replete with man's actions and problems on earth, seeking to guide him to loftier realms of spirituality. The literature points to the last five of the Ten Commandments which deal with relations between man and his fellows — and which are parallel to the first commandments, dealing with relations between man and Hashem. This implies the importance of human relations and love for one's fellow man. The saga of Chassidus — in the form of sayings, novellae, comments and teachings — has been passed traditionally from master to disciple. It is no less than the oral Torah of Chassidus — a vast and unique literature, devoid of "pilpulistic" material and hyperbole.

The chassidic movement was able to draw the Jewish soul out of its lowly state, uplifting it after the period of great disappointment and disillusion brought about by the downfall of the false messiah, Sabbetai Tzvi, and the disastrous conclusion of his mystical activities, which led to his conversion to Islam.

The *tzaddik* is the charismatic leader of the chassidic community and is called fondly, "Rebbe." This term refers to the saintly men, performers of good deeds. Reb Nachman of Breslov and Rabbi Yaakov Yosef of Polonoye, the "Toldos" (d. 1782), both referred to the *tzaddik* as the *neshamah* (soul) of the Jewish people, who was dedicated to Torah and to serving Hashem in an exceptional way. It was Reb Elimelech of Lizhensk who claimed that the *tzaddik* achieved a synthesis between being the leader of the community, who was concerned with the day-to-day needs of his people, and the devout *tzaddik* who was always bound in his *d'veikus* (intense closeness) with Hashem. Thus, he was involved with nurturing the spiritual needs of his people.

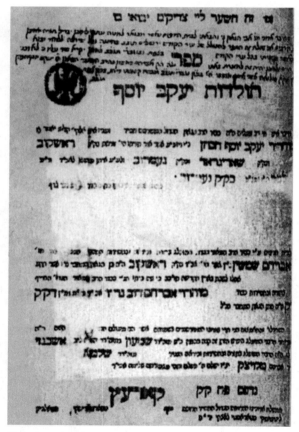

Title page of Toldos Yaakov Yosef, by R' Yaakov Yosef of Polonoye

Humility is the hallmark of the true *tzaddik* who grieves over his distance from Hashem and is always striving for more and more closeness with Hashem.

The *tzaddik* is able to achieve high spiritual levels and is endowed with supernatural feelings — stemming from his prayers. Reb Nachman states, "Only *tzaddikim* can perceive the true essence of prayer." The *tzaddik's* concern for the spiritual needs of his chassidim and the totality of Israel is called *kelillus Yisroel.* Reb

Elimelech feels that even though there are differences of opinion among the *tzaddikim*, there is still a commonality in their holiness. The *tzaddik* possesses *ruach hakodesh*, or spirit of holiness, because he has achieved the highest level, the *shefa*, or channel of providing the Divine Presence, by *hamtakas hadinim* — the complete sublimation of evil turning *din* (judgment) into *chessed* (lovingkindness).

The major function of the *tzaddik* is to increase the *shefa*, acting as a helper of the Jews by inspiring Hashem's grace toward Israel.

The *tzaddik* — the righteous man — serves as the paradigm of all chassidic values. He fulfills a leading role and acts as the dominant force in the Jewish community. He undertakes many missions and is constantly engaged in the battle against the *yetzer hara*. The *tzaddik* brings his chassid closer to Hashem by guiding him and showing him how to conquer the *yetzer hara*.

Said R' Nachman of Breslov: "The letters of the word רֶבִּי, 'Rebbe' form an acronym that can either spell out ראש בְּנֵי יִשְׂרָאֵל, *Rosh Bnei Yisroel*, a leader in Israel, or רַע בְּעֵינֵי ה', *ra b'einei Hashem*, evil in the eyes of Hashem."

Needless to say, skeptics were legion about the honesty and real motives of the Baal Shem Tov and his new movement, especially the learned Lithuanian rabbis, who suspected that he might be a new Sabbetai Tzvi or Yaakov Frank.

The common man, who had been totally neglected because of his ignorance and spiritual poverty, now came to find solace and acceptance in the chassidic camp, where everyone can approach Hashem and be close to Him through a great variety of ways. "In all your ways know Him and He will smooth your paths" (*Proverbs* 3:6) — this was the slogan of Chassidus. It preached this verse and actually made of it a new way of worshiping Hashem.

It was quickly brought home to its adherents that neither Kabbalah nor philosophy is the path that leads to Hashem; it is the practice and the experiences of everyday life. One does not have to bring man into heaven but heaven into man. Chassidus changed the dry and formalistic mode of worship into a deeply emotional, even ecstatic, experience. Man need not isolate himself and escape from society or from material endeavors, as long as the core purpose of his ideation is to cleave to Hashem. The idea of *d'veikus,* or "communion with Hashem," stems from the Biblical injunction, "But you who cling to Hashem, your G-d, you are all alive today" (*Deuteronomy* 4:4).

Chassidus did not uproot any of the old halachic traditions, nor did it change any of the fundamentals of worship. What it did was to transplant things from one place to another and to preserve the essence of the rituals in a manner that both enhanced them and made them more meaningful.

Chassidus aimed to change the concepts underlying everyday life — enjoining its adherents to live in common fellowship and loving mutuality under the leadership of the *tzaddik,* whose soul is in a state of connection with all souls.

Baal Shem Tov's letter to R' Yaakov Yosef of Polonoye

A *misnaged* once asked Reb Moshe Midner, "What is it that Chassidus innovated and what changes did it bring about? All it did was to transpose the walls of the *beis hamidrash* by moving the east wall to the west and the west wall to the east." Reb Moshe replied, "That is not so. Chassidus changed about not only the walls of the *beis hamidrash,* but also the walls of the heart. It brought about a revolution in the mind."

Everyone comes down into the world in order to fulfill a certain mission and to bring about an improvement of some kind. Chassidus revitalized the concept of personal providence (*hashgachah pratis*) — the principle that Hashem exercises personal supervision over man and nature, even in the details of existence — as a principle of faith and of *kavannah* in prayer and in the fulfillment of mitzvos.

"Know yourself" is another basic principle, requiring introspection and courage. Chassidim bewail the fact that the *Shechinah* is in *galus* (exile). For the essential *galus* is the *galus* of the mind. As the Baal Shem Tov explained: Man is where his heart is — where the essence of his being dwells. Reb Simchah Bunim of Pschis'che (1767-1827) said: Man should always be dressed in a garment with two pockets: one pocket on his right side in which he should place the adage, בִּשְׁבִילִי נִבְרָא הָעוֹלָם, *The world was created for me*, and another pocket on his left side, in which to keep the verse, וְאָנֹכִי עָפָר וָאֵפֶר, *What am I but dust and ashes!* Chassidus teaches that man must be proud as a monarch and humble as dust and ashes.

Chassidus gave new meaning to many Biblical sayings, imbuing the words with new connotations. The Baal Shem Tov, for example, interpreted the verse, ה' צִלְּךָ, *Hashem is your shadow* (*Tehillim* 121:5), to mean: Hashem acts with you as your shadow acts with you, requiting you measure for measure, according to your acts.

Essentially, a story has to be lived and experienced. A story is a projective means to achieve *teshuvah*. Chassidus placed the highest value on the telling of old stories. Said the Rizhiner: "Telling chassidic stories is the magical key to unimpaired faith." Said the Chozeh of Lublin: "The light of these narratives is as great as the light of the Torah." A good story is not about miracles, but about אַהֲבַת יִשְׂרָאֵל and this is the greatest miracle of all.

Many authors on Chassidus have researched the Rizhiner's multi-faceted personality, as well as his paradoxical style — some from within the chassidic camp, others from the secular world of the *maskilim*, "enlightened ones." Some historians question the extravagance of his royal lifestyle and the exquisite affluence of his surroundings; others, his singular style of leadership and the idolizing respect he inspired in the masses. Abundant are the tales and legends describing his piety and humility, the singular path that he hewed to in worship and behavior as a Rebbe. All this mysterious phenomenology in the world of the *tzaddik* requires the researcher to separate fact and factual documentation from fiction, reality from idealization. In order to present an authentic biography of the Rizhiner, one has, in the manner of a dialectician, to cull material from all available sources.

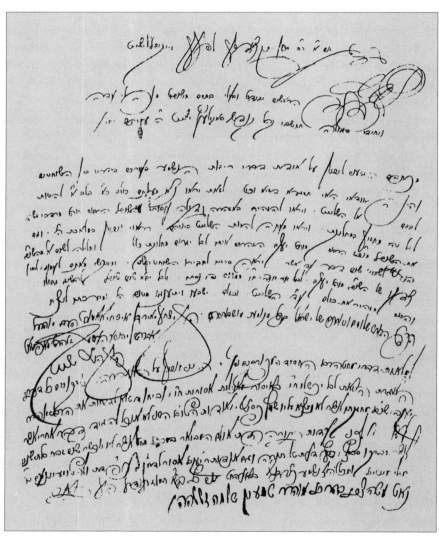

Letter signed by the Apter Rav and his talmid the Savranier Rav

Some students of 19th-century Chassidus, and of the Rizhiner in particular, relied on spurious sources, undocumented accounts and hearsay. Such is the case with the oft-quoted Polish Graf, Xaveri Korczak Branicki, in his book, *Brama Pouty* (in French, *La Porte de Pénitence*, Paris, 1879), in which he sets out to describe the Rizhiner, whom he visited in his magnificent palace.

Some historians question the authenticity of such a visit. A source that is authentic for purposes of analysis is the approximately forty letters of the Rizhiner, together with the many other letters and imprimaturs available today, all bearing his heavily stroked signature and from which may be gauged the extraordinary influence and sway that he exercised throughout the Eastern European Jewish communities.

It must be made clear — the Rizhiner wrote no books. The content and the drama of his life were written by his erudite chassidim.

The present work's claim to authenticity derives from the fact that it is based upon an oral tradition transmitted to the author by elderly chassidim, as well as upon several manuscripts obtained from the rich heritage of the House of Rizhin-Boyan. Given that the bulk of this source material was written in Hebrew, it is only to be expected that translation into English will lose some of the flavor of the original. Nevertheless, the inner spark of the material remains undiminished. It is this rich fount of knowledge that we present to the avid reader of chassidic folklore as he or she enters the orchard of Chassidus to partake of its tasty fruit. In truth, one feels a deep nostalgia for the mystical and romantic world of the European *shtetl* which, in the wake of the Nazi *Shoah*, exists no more, leaving us orphaned in a cold, passive and indifferent world. It is the intention of the author to enlighten the spirit of the reader, directing him to ever higher levels of aspiration and opening for him the gates of a heavenly "World to Come."

The stories and anecdotes, as well as the Biblical exegeses of the Rebbes of the House of Rizhin, remain loyal to the chassidic tradition, which is not to change the text of the original, delivered orally or in print. As the Rizhiner emphasized: "Be careful not to underestimate the homiletic tale."

Chassidus was a movement of spiritual renewal. It taught the Jew who could not see beyond his material concerns a lesson in piety and humility, the meaning of prayer and the joy of performing the commandments of the Torah and the Rabbinic decrees — and concern for one's fellow Jew.

The Rebbe is an integral part of the individual chassid's life. In a certain sense, chassidic philosophy is a type of oral law, whose authors were more interested in "doing and actualizing" than in writing down their teachings. Their impeccable conduct and impeccable actions became the models and guidelines for their followers, and out of reverence for their Rebbes the chassidim oftentimes named the Rebbe's works — as recorded by their disciples — after the character traits (*middos*) symbolic of their behavior and lifestyle. All such works were influenced by the *Zohar* and the Lurianic Kabbalah, which reinterpreted kabbalistic concepts, such as *tzimtzum, eser sefiros, sheviras hakeilim,* and gave a new meaning to the *tzaddik* concept.

The yawning gap that had developed between the learned class and the common people, between the Jewish masses and their leaders, was a basic factor in the evolution of Chassidus, which sought to narrow this gap — this *peirud* (cleavage) between the intellectual, ruling elite and the plebeian class within the Jewish communities.

On the wave of hope and renewal that it generated, Chassidus spread throughout Eastern Europe, including Galicia, Central Poland, Belarus, Ukraine, Romania, Hungary and even farther afield, where the majority of Jews embraced the chassidic way of life.

To the chassidic movement belongs the distinction of being the first organized and legitimate trend in Judaism since the era of the Second Temple — a movement with its own *modus operandi* functioning within the ambience of the Orthodox world and its traditionalism.

The clear message of the movement, beyond its total commitment to Torah study as the focus of the intellectual life, was its emphasis on devotional prayer and introspection as the method of choice with which to approach the Almighty. Thus, the Baal Shem Tov stressed that *tefillah* was the elemental, ecstatic avenue to Hashem. Moreover, the doctrine of *d'veikus* is to be actualized in all of man's daily activities — not only in prayer — for "faith is the cleaving of the *neshamah* to Hashem."

Said R' Yaakov Yosef of Polonoye, "*D'veikus* is the one mitzvah in the Torah which includes everything." *D'veikus* is basically achieved during prayer by using the right *kavannos* — the inner kabbalistic meaning of the words through which one ascends the ladder to the *Shechinah*.

D'veikus, according to the chassidic tradition, is the inspiration for the hallowing of all life and the consecration of man to the Divine, permeating with holiness all the activities of his everyday life. It is the beginning and the end of all religion — that Hashem is One and His Name is One.

It has been said that in chassidic writings one need not turn many pages to find Hashem, because you meet Him on every page.

PART I:
ROOTS

CHAPTER I

CHASSIDIC PERSPECTIVES

PERFORMING A MITZVAH WITHOUT *KAVANNAH* IS MEANINGLESS. The true reason for the fulfillment of mitzvos is not to receive a reward, nor even to find grace in the eyes of Hashem, but to become a "chariot" through which to reach and to love Him. So it is with the study of Torah — it is neither to gain knowledge nor reward from Heaven but to learn from one's study the real meaning of *avodas Hashem lishmah* (service of Hashem for its own sake).

I

SINCE CHASSIDUS BELIEVES THAT ALL IS IN HASHEM AND THAT THERE IS NO place devoid of Divinity, לֵית אֲתַר פָּנוּי מִנֵּיהּ, and given that the *Shechinah* is the Source of joy — it follows that the performance of mitzvos should especially be experienced with שִׂמְחָה, *joy*. Joy is the expression of chassidic fervor, of its suprarational and ecstatic optimism, which is faith in the Almighty that all His actions are good, and the be-

II

lief that man can achieve closeness to Hashem through joy. Indeed, the Psalmist exclaims, *Worship Hashem with gladness, come before Him with joyous song (Tehillim* 100:2). Nevertheless, joy is to be combined with awe and respect for Hashem, which is essential for spiritual growth.

III IT WAS PART OF THE CHASSIDIC MISSION OF R' AHARON OF KARLIN (1736-1772) to spread Chassidus in Lithuania, and to be the pioneer of chassidic music.

Atzvus, or melancholy, is considered by R' Aharon to be the worst of transgressions, one which leads to other transgressions. For the *Shechinah* does not dwell in a place, or milieu, of sadness and depression; rather its element is the joy a Jew feels in the performance of a mitzvah. In the words of the Baal Shem Tov: "No child can be born except through pleasure and joy." By the same token, if one wishes his prayers to bear fruit, he must offer them with pleasure and joy. Enthusiasm, exhuberance and joy are the best antidote to melencholy and despair (*Keser Shem Tov,* Lemberg, 1858).

Letter by R' Aharon of Karlin

IV THE BAAL SHEM TOV SAID: "HE WHO LIVES IN JOY DOES HIS CREATOR'S will." The Baal Shem Tov would dance to attain spiritual enthusiasm, *hislahavus* and *d'veikus*. He considered the dance of a Jew before his Creator as *tefillah*, based on *Tehillim* (35:10), *All my bones shall say: Lord, who is like You?* He considered dancing a vehicle to lift up holy sparks (*Keser Shem Tov*, p. 329). Many *tzaddikim* would sing during prayer and Torah study, humming melodies that lift up the soul. Indeed, the *niggun* (melody) in Chassidus is considered a part of Divine service, full of deep meaning and ecstatic attachment to Hashem. The Baal Shem Tov stated that through music one can reach joy and *d'veikus* with the Infinite One, Blessed is He. His grandson, R' Nachman of Breslov, developed a complete theory, showing the sublime value, and spiritual effect of the religious *niggun*. R' Aharon of Karlin, R' Zusya of Anipoli, the Baal HaTanya, the Shpoler Zeide, and many others would sing and dance as part of their service to Hashem.

Joy achieves the forgiveness of sins, said R' Pinchos of Koritz, since it comes from a higher world, the world of Divine light.

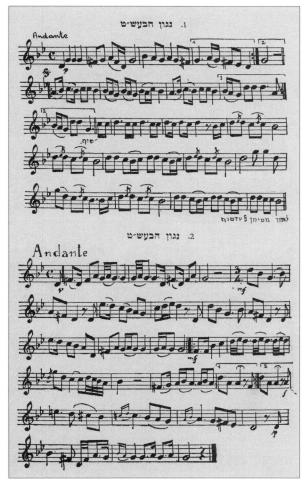

Niggun HaBaal Shem Tov

Sadness, said the Breslover, leads to contention, and joy leads to peace. Repentance, said the Karliner, comes essentially out of joy and delight.

Music plays a very important role in Chassidus. It is the *niggun*, a chassidic mode of worship with original tunes of great depth, vitality and inventiveness, basically textless, that were used mainly during Shabbos and Yom Tov prayers, as well as at the *tisch* (literally, *table*. It refers to the gathering of the chassidim at the Rebbe's table for inspiration and teaching), of the

The Tomb of R' Nachman of Breslov in Uman

Tomb of R' Pinchos of Koritz

Rebbe. The *niggun* most commonly sung at the *tish* is particularly noted for its focusing on *d'veikus,* or it is sung as a march in brisk tempo (allegro) — or as a *freilichs,* a joyous *niggun.*

Most *niggunim* are composed at the various courts and by the various dynasties of Rebbes, many of them overlapping thematically and melodically. Chassidic melodies have become very popular, have so far entered the mainstream that they are sung or played at weddings and other joyous occasions.

Title page of Sefer Likkutei Shoshanim by R' Pinchos of Koritz

The *niggun* in Chassidus is a form of Divine service, expressing the love of, and yearning for, Hashem; — Who created harmony in His world — and to bind oneself to Him with cords of love and joyous song. This phenomenon has its roots in the Talmud: *What is the source of joy and happiness — this is song (Arachin* 11a).

R' Zusya of Anipoli, in his great love for Hashem, served Him with song. Rav Nachman of Breslov suggests that the essence of *d'veikus* is through melody (*Likkutei Eitzos,* Bnei Brak, 1974; p. 4, *Neginah*).

Nowadays we live in a multicultural so-

ספר

מדרש פנחס

עם

גבעת פנחס

המדרש פנחס הם דברים עמוקים, שבעתים מזוקקים, יצאו
מפי קדוש ד' איש אלקים, רבינו פנחס מקארץ זצללה"ה,
וכבך נורע דרכו בקודם, כי בכל שיחותיו הסתיר סודות
נוראים והזין דאורייתא!

גם דבריב נוראים מו:צדיק הקדוש ה' רפאל מבטריטש זצ"ל
"תלפידרו, וגם הנרגות מדרב הצדיק מ"ה שמואל וואלצים זצ"ל:
ורא ה ה דבר תדק, חלק סני, בשם ,

גבעת פנחס

וזא חידושי תורה, מהרב הצדיק ,רחש ה' הג"ל, 'רבינו פנחס
מקארץ זצללה"ה, סנדפסו אך פעם אחת לפני מ א ה סנה בראש
ספר ,וצוה הכהן' מהגאון הק"דש סוה"ר אדרן סמואל ובהן צל"ה.
גם הדפסנו דבר חדש בראש הספר תולדה קמנא ויקרה סנדלח
קדושתו סל ה"ץ הקדוש רבינו פנחס מקארץ זצללה"ה. מאת
מח"ג הגרו"ל הספירסם כו' מ"ה צבי יחזקאל מיכלזאהן סליט"א,
בועד הרבנים דווארסאו

בילגורוי

בתולאה ובדסוס י' נתן נטע קרוננברג
סנת ,,גבעת פנחס מנחם טוב מאה" עפ"ק

MEDRASZ PINCHOS
Druk. N. KRONENBERG,
BIŁGORAJ, Wojew. Lub. (Poland) 1929

Title page of Sefer Midrash Pinchos by R' Pinchos of Koritz

Title page of Sefer Devarim Nechmadim by R' Pinchos of Koritz

ciety, in a time of soul-searching, when values seem to be in constant flux, and we know as a certainty that unless man is more than man, he is less than man. Fortunately, one can warm up his soul by connecting himself to a Rebbe, drinking from the rich chassidic fountain and living a life of devotion and purity. The melodies and songs of love of Hashem which encompass this mystical movement will touch his own soul and it too will break into song.

Said R' Menachem Mendel of Vitebsk (1748-1787): "A Jew should rejoice that he has an opportunity to sing to Hashem, rejoice that he is a Jew, and rejoice that he is able to pray, to study and to perform Hashem's will."

The Maggid of Mezritch gives a classic example of this attitude of joy. When a king is present at a celebration, he is accessible to many people who would otherwise be denied admittance to the palace. Likewise, when we serve Hashem with joy He is more approachable (*Toras HaMaggid MiMezritch*, Berlin, 1923). The *niggun* opens the gates of heaven, melancholy closes them.

Said the Chozeh of Lublin, "I prefer a simple Jew who prays with joy to a sage who studies with sadness."

V CHASSIDUS INTRODUCED GENUINE *KIRUV* — OUTREACH TO UNEDUCATED Jews who had basically been ignored by the educated *talmidei chachamim* — and gave to the proletarian and the dispossessed a place in the socioreligious mosaic of Eastern Europe. It was a rebirth of the authentic concept of *ahavas Yisroel* — through the removal of the barriers of prejudice and discrimination by Jew against Jew.

VI A BASIC CONCEPT IN CHASSIDUS IS THE STATE OF *HISLAHAVUS* — THE SOUL aflame with yearning to attach itself to Hashem, — the true goal of worship.

Descent for the sake of raising and uplifting the sparks, and denigration of elitist intellectuality, are major components of the chassidic agenda as found in its homilies and Biblical exegeses. Chassidic lore has it that with the death of the Baal Shem Tov in 1760, in Mezhibozh, the *Shechinah* moved its mantle from Mezhibozh to Mezritch, where thirty-nine renowned scholars gathered around their master, the Great Maggid, for twelve years. When the Maggid died in 1772, these thirty-nine scholars became the founders of major chassidic dynasties. They infused reality and experience with G-dliness, now reflected and actualized in every human activity. Its preachers carried a clear message of the Torah: Living its legacy is our only option if we are to actualize the Torah, which applies to every person and to every time.

VII THE RABBIS CALLED PRAYER *AVODAS HALEV* (SERVICE OF THE HEART). There is a story about a chassid who came to R' Simchah Bunim of Pschis'che and complained that whenever he *davened* he got a headache from his deep concentration. "What does *tefillah* have to do with the head?" R' Simchah Bunim asked in surprise. "*Tefillah* is the service of the heart, not a labor of the head."

VIII R' PINCHOS OF KORITZ IS QUOTED AS SAYING: THE WORLD IS FILLED with Hashem's light, but there is a screen that prevents us from seeing it, similar to the clouds that obscure the light of the sun. [The prosecuting angels and the *kelipos* (shells) are a barrier interposing itself between us and Hashem when we try to reach Him, just as the shell of a nut prevents one from enjoying the taste.] And when we *daven*, it is through our words of prayer — which are called *ruach*, spirit, as it says: *The spirit of Hashem spoke through him* (*II Shmuel* 23:2) — that the "clouds," or obstructions, are dispersed. This is also one of the reasons for our swaying during prayer.[1]

The 19th century witnessed the arrival of a new comet, a source of light that was to produce beacons of its own — R' Yisroel of Rizhin and his children, the dynasty of *Tiferes She'b'Malchus*, the Splendor of Royalty, as the House of Rizhin was called.

---

1. It is the custom in Rizhin, however, not to sway during *Shemoneh Esrei*, but to pray in an erect, forwardly inclined position, expressing both royalty and humility. This is because Rizhin emphasizes the inwardness — the *p'nimiyus* (פְּנִימִיוּת) — of prayer, which is a mode of quiet worship.

CHAPTER II

THE HARBINGER OF GOOD NEWS

"A GREAT MIRACLE HAPPENED THERE," IN MEZHIBOZH, IN THE years 1700-1760, the years when a superior man, R' Yisroel Baal Shem Tov, walked the face of the earth. A like miracle occurred in Mezritch, in the years 1760-1772, when there resided, in the seclusion of his room, R' Dov Ber, an invalid, formerly a wandering preacher. To the tapping of his crutches there replied, as if in echo, the beating of the hearts of his many followers, all gathered round him to learn Torah, Chassidus and a new way of life.

THE CHIEF MASTER

It may well be that the latter miracle was even greater than the first!

The legend that surrounds the Baal Shem Tov is the stuff of dreams. He descended to this world like a heavenly ray, as an envoy sent to us from the upper spheres. All his actions resemble those of one who is not of this world, even if, at first glance, he seems to be involved with the world, dealing fastidiously with the simple folk, wandering in the fields, listening to the songs of the birds and the secret language of the grass and trees, treating the whole of creation with mercy and love: doing good deeds for the poor, teaching children, healing the sick, occupied ceaselessly with the mitzvah of פִּדְיוֹן שְׁבוּיִים, redeeming those held in captivity. But the abiding impression, the image of him engraved in our hearts, is of one who dwells "above."

Through the multitude of stories in praise of the Baal Shem Tov, we follow him on his many travels, marveling as we contemplate the miracle of קְפִיצַת הַדֶּרֶךְ, *k'fitzas haderech*, the shrinking of distances so that he could travel great distances as if they were but short trips. This miracle was wrought on his behalf as he speeds to succor souls abandoned to extremity and desolation. The appearance of the Baal Shem Tov in our lowly world is, in and of itself, a supreme wonder, and this has a paradoxical effect, in that his wisdom and his deeds lose the power to astonish us, for what can be more wondrous than something wondrous by its very nature?!

It would seem that the more unparalleled the miracle the more it appears to us as the most natural of things. Hence, anything arising out of that miracle, in any and all of its ramifications, appears to us in the guise of the natural, offending our faculty of reason not at all.

Tombstone of the Baal Shem Tov

Such is not the case with the Maggid of Mezritch, the lines of whose countenance show no heavenly cast and in whose ways there is nothing that calls attention to itself. No denizen of the world of legend he — but of the world of cold, pure and fastidious reason. He is nothing if not human — a teacher, preacher, exegete, and chronic invalid to the bargain! Not a single miracle do we find attributed to him by his disciples, not one — much less stories of legendary doings. But — consider this amazing fact. Out of the power and the charisma of this man was born the whole complex phenomenon of Chassidus. It was his merit that the Torah should be transmuted, as if by alchemy, into lightness, *joie de vivre*, an elixir of life. He looked into it and fashioned the living tree of Chassidus. Not content simply to take the teachings of the Baal Shem Tov, found, as it were, in scattered verses here and there, and to make of them a scroll, a sealed record, he also established the community that accepted upon itself in quintessential fashion the principles that it embodied: to learn and to teach, to observe and to do. And such acceptance was of the essence, for the creation of a community to function as the receptacle and the vehicle for that Torah was a desideratum, equal to the receiving of the Torah itself. For what is the value, what is the potency, of a Torah whose letters fly up into the vault of heaven for want of a point of reception, an anchorage in the world of men? Torah is light, but the community that holds fast to it is a mirror to reflect it back upon its hidden parts, and to spread the illumination of its revealed face to places hitherto sequestered from its rays.

BOTH THE BAAL SHEM TOV AND THE MAGGID PRESENT US WITH A RIDDLE. Although they differ from so many points of view — in personal

A SECOND GENESIS

style, in disposition, in most of the early indications — they are in essence united, since both drink deeply at the fount of wisdom. Through this shared attribute one may approach the mysteries of their vision and the esoteric aspects of their work.

They also share something more immediately apparent. They had no precursors, their appearance took the world by surprise, and they embarked upon their careers complete, not as apprentices but as masters. They worked as messengers from above, drawing authority from the blessed source in their soul. They spoke, not in borrowed tones, but with a strong and authentic voice. They came before us not as searchers but with their spiritual discoveries in hand: the Baal Shem Tov, as a herald, and the Maggid, as a guide, both of them figures of trust and valor. They are "men of creation," progenitors.

A hint of this can be found in the account of the fire that broke out in the house of the Maggid's father. The flames devoured all the family's meager possessions and turned into ashes the irreplaceable record of the family tree. When his mother wept and mourned more for the burning of the records than for the loss of the house, little Dov Ber sought to console her: "Be comforted, my mother; with me will begin a new family tree."

The inevitability of the Maggid's succession to the leadership of the chassidic movement was rooted in his very conception of leadership, with the profound attention it paid to matters of pride and humility.

> *Chassidic tradition tells us that before the Baal Shem Tov died his disciples asked him, "Master, how can you leave us?" He replied: "There is a bear in the forest." They all agreed that it*

Burial place of the Baal Shem Tov and that of his disciple, R' Wolf Kitzes

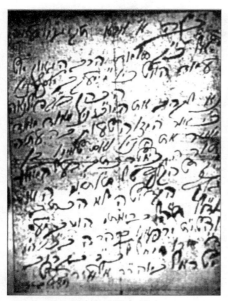

Manuscript of the Baal Shem Tov

was R' Dov Ber who possessed all the qualities necessary for their future leadership.

The Baal Shem Tov had stipulated before his death that his successor must know how to break and subdue the attribute of pride and haughtiness. The Maggid redefined the issue with his teaching that the tendency to pride can never be eradicated, but must be striven against all the days of one's life.

Although there were not miracles without number in the court of the Maggid, the extreme holiness of his way of life could not help but introduce alteration into the laws of nature.

When the Baal Shem Tov died, R' Pinchos of Koritz (1728-1790) remarked: "When the king dies, no one is allowed to wear his crown, not even the highest minister of the realm, but it is placed on a pedestal, out of reach of all. But in this case we see that R' Dov Ber has totally subdued his pride — such a man may wear the crown."

The accession of R' Dov Ber marks a watershed in the history of Chassidus. He is at one and the same time disciple and rabbi. The nucleus is that of the rabbi, but the power and the energy by which this divides, replicates and grows is unique to him. He does not go one step without innovating something. Even a statement of the Baal Shem Tov takes on new life when he gives voice to it. In the words of R' Yaakov Yosef of Polonoye, "The Divine Presence passed with pack and staff from Mezhibozh to Mezritch." Or, as R' Yechiel Michel of Zlotchov (d. 1781) said: "The sources of wisdom that formerly flowed to the Baal Shem Tov now flow to the Maggid."

In the world of practicalities, the Maggid accomplished more mightily than the Baal Shem Tov. The Baal Shem Tov attracted to himself the light of emanation. The Maggid brought it into "doing," the world of action. It is possible to say that, but for the fact that Divine Providence had prepared a courageous disciple for the coming of the Baal Shem Tov, one to do his word in the face of the forces at work in the world, the appearance of the Baal Shem Tov in our world would have been the equivalent of a celestial event merely, the breathtaking spectacle of a comet traversing the nighttime sky, feeding the sense of wonder, and then gone from the eye, gone from the heart. Nevertheless, those with an eye to see, a mind to record and a heart to retain, indeed saw and retained, and all with awe, even with terror. But they were ever few. R' Dov Ber, the Maggid of Mezritch, came and — to pursue the analogy — arrested the comet in its flight and made it a shield and a servant to the distressed community of Israel.

The heart quails at the very thought of penetrating the palace of the Baal Shem Tov and of removing the veil from his mysterious image. Nevertheless, the leaping of the man of secrets over the order of nature is beloved to us, and we cannot forbear to search for a hint of a solution, be it only a solution to the riddle of the great influence the Maggid's study hall exerted upon the congregation of his students ... and students' students, and thence to the widening future congregation of those who thirsted, and still thirst, for the light of Chassidus. It is a wonder in and of itself that his disciples — almost all of whom were, and were descended from, intellectual and spiritual giants, deeply versed in the wisdom of Torah and intense in the fear of Hashem — formed a tight circle around this poor, sickly, lame teacher, who was not even the official rabbi of a city, nor a person of rank, whose reputation as a Torah giant did not precede him. Of course, G-d-fearing Jews were always capable of serving as rabbis for the sake of heaven, and not for receiving any sort of compensation. In any event, an "eighth of an eighth of materialism" is mixed into every good and righteous act, because if there is no "flour," that is, physical sustenance, there can be no Torah (*Avos* 3:17). But the disciples of the Maggid received nothing in compensation for their closeness and devotion to their Rebbe but persecution and every form of pressure, shame, condemnation and execration, hunger and privation,

Title page: Kisvei Kodesh, a collection of teachings by the Baal Shem Tov, the Maggid of Mezritch, R' Levi Yitzchok of Berditchev and R' Yisroel of Kozhnitz

and uncertainty as to what the next day would bring. They served their Rebbe with fervor and self-sacrifice, and for their pains they were mocked and even exiled from their homes and dismissed from their rabbinical posts. They were even subject to excommunication, and sometimes imprisonment and corporal punishment.

It is an amazing thing. The disciples of the Maggid stood fast in protecting their Rebbe from the blows rained down upon them from without. Even more amazing is the fact that they were so internally united, attached to one another and all of them together to their Rebbe. Go out and see for yourself what was accomplished in the study halls of Torah throughout the years and among all the people. The era of their blossoming was extremely short. Their "springtime" passed as a shadow and flew away as a dream.

If the conflict between father and son is the way of the world, all the more so is it the case between teacher and student as children and students grow up and seek their own ways in their chosen fields. The victors emerge from this conflict with the strength that fosters growth and development. But there are less pleasant manifestations of this phenomenon as well. Representative of it is the student who turns against the teacher and falsifies his "Torah" by means of a distorted exegesis whose principle is "to discard the meat and consume the shell," or who works to undermine what has worth and supplant it with what does not. In their efforts at gaining renown and influence for themselves, there are students who fight over the Rebbe's coat and end up apportioning a piece of it to X or to Y, or cutting for him a branch from the living tree of the Rebbe's teachings, until his Torah is fragmented into a number of "*Toros*," pitting one against the other. You may counter that there are study halls which rose to greatness as centers of real influence in the history of ideas and religious education and infiltrated themselves into the lives of the masses, as well as wielding authority at the religious-institutional level in their country of location. Yes, this has happened, but more often than not it was not so. All too often, a study hall attained power because there was a naked sword at its disposal — a means of power to force acceptance of its doctrine. The "book without the sword" often failed. Even if it succeeded in winning over the minds of the few, it did not educate, let alone penetrate the minds and hearts of the masses. As Midrash states: *"The Sword and the Book come down from Heaven bound together"* (*Vayeira Rabbah* 25:5).

But here, from Mezritch, comes a Jew, an invalid, poor, modest and unassuming, and proves that one can awaken, restore and greatly influence minds and hearts, establish a congregation, and beyond that, a permanent popular institution wherewith to unify the lowly and the great into one group with hearts and minds bound together. He does it not by means of superior strength, nor even with "spirit" in its commonly accepted connotation, which has an inevitable component of secularism. Rather this Jew of Mezritch exudes the gentle persuasion of some hidden light of heavenly wisdom and with a special indefinable grace, that defies analysis and most probably cannot be cultivated or taught, and of which the ultimate source is *chessed Elyon*, Divine benevolence.

In view of its overuse, it seems to us wiser to eschew use of the term *chessed Elyon*, or Divinely given grace. At the same time it is clear that no benefit will rebound to Torah through our naming the performer of good deeds "magician," itself a hackneyed expression. In the realm of Chassidus one is not, thank Hashem, reduced to using terminology that is the stock-in-trade of the contemporary culture. The explanation we are attempting will be finer and closer to the truth if it draws from the vocabulary of the chassidim and says: The Maggid influenced through the power of purity and holiness, belief and enthusiasm, through the power of truth quarried and carved out from the life of truth. But there comes a point when it is no longer possible to foster a bond to holiness through the use of its own proper terms. Just as the nullification of Torah is sometimes its basis, so at times, a fence is made around holiness by hiding one of its aspects.

> The Maggid once said to his disciples: "I shall teach you the best way to say Torah: You must cease to be aware of yourselves. You must be nothing but an ear that hears what the universe of the world is constantly saying within you. The moment you start hearing what you yourself are saying, you must stop."

The title "master of mysticism" seems well suited to the wise man of secrets and great guide who stood at the cradle of Chassidus and made of it a vessel brimming over with life, supercharged with sparks of wisdom and truth. R' Dov Ber was also a master with regard to the superiority of his preparation, which enabled him to don a veil — that is to say, his power of concealment.

The fundamental truth with regard to those who do deeds for the benefit of the masses is that they have two faces, or rather a face and a mask. No one can exert influence unless he presents a double image. Did not the Baal Shem Tov — just like Moshe himself — go through most of his life in disguise? Mysterious people are, by their very nature, figures on a stage.

When, on occasion, we are apprised by the disciples of the Maggid of the fear that they felt upon seeing their Rebbe's face or hearing his voice, we are forced to conclude: Here is proof, if more proof were needed, that the Maggid was a spiritually elevated personality. We do not hear that he *imposed* authority in any way. No, they were in awe of him; consequently they stood before him like subjects before their monarch. This is a paradox, for where in the system of Chassidus do we find this quality of royalty? Quite the opposite was taught by the Maggid! "Kingdom" is, in fact, one of the more lowly qualities as it has nothing of its own, since it depends for its power on the existence of servants and followers. Nevertheless, it was he who instituted the quality of "Kingdom" in the distressed Assembly of Israel, a people without a land to call its own. He was not a Rebbe to chassidim but a Rebbe to Rebbeim.

> Said R' Shneur Zalman of Liadi: "Elsewhere one learns how to master the Torah. In Mezritch, you learn to let the Torah master you." (The Torah teaches one to become a Torah himself.)

Under the leadership of the Maggid, the number of chassidim grew in many countries beyond Volhynia and Podolia, especially in Lithuania, the stronghold of the *misnagdim*. When asked what he considered his main accomplishment, the Maggid replied, "I found a light in the forest, and all I did was open the door." Indeed, the Maggid was the last universally accepted leader of the movement. The Maggid had 300 disciples, thirty-nine of them were Rebbes in their own right, leaders and many were founders of dynasties.

R' Dov Ber was born in 5464 (1703) or 5470 (1709) in the city of Lukatch, in Volhynia, to a family which — tradition has it —

HIS LIFE traced its origins to R' Yehudah HaNasi. As a young man he studied in the yeshivah of the *Pnei Yehoshua* in Lvov. He married the daughter of R' Sholom Shachna of Turtshin, and set up home there, earning his livelihood by teaching. From there he moved to Koritz and then to Rovna, Kreepa, Mezritch, and back to Rovna. During his years of wandering, he supported himself by preaching — in this way acquiring the sobriquet "The Maggid." In 5517 (1757) when he was in his middle 40's, he set eyes upon the Baal Shem Tov for the first time.[1] "וְהָיוּ עֵינֶיךָ רוֹאוֹת אֶת מוֹרֶיךָ"

R' Dov Ber was a profound scholar who had mastered Talmud and Codes, and a great and G-d-fearing man who worshiped his Creator through fasts and penances. Hearing reports that the Baal Shem Tov was a miracle-worker who was pointing to a new path in the service of Hashem, one that shifted the emphasis from fasting to joy, he passed a negative judgment on the man and all for which he stood. With the passing of time, when he saw that many people continued to follow the Baal Shem Tov and sing his praises, he decided to visit him to see for himself what nature of a man he was. He hired a wagon and went to Mezhibozh. At the first meeting, the Baal Shem Tov plied his distinguished guest with small talk about wagon drivers, and tales of horses, dead and left to rot. The Maggid began to regret having come such a long way, and at so much expense, only to have his ears filled with such trivia. He left the Baal Shem Tov and returned to his inn. At the stroke of midnight, when the wagon driver was making preparations to return home, the servant of the Baal Shem Tov came with an urgent request that the Maggid make his way to the house of his master without delay. He complied and when (as told in *Shivchei HaBaal Shem Tov*) he arrived, the Baal Shem Tov asked him if he was versed in Kabbalah. The Maggid answered in the affirmative, whereupon the Baal Shem Tov asked him for an explanation of a passage in the mystical book *Eitz Chaim.* He was

---

1. The account of the Maggid's first visit with the Baal Shem Tov has several versions.

at a loss to explain it properly. The Baal Shem Tov then explained the passage, in which the names of several angels are mentioned. The Maggid was later to report that no sooner had the Baal Shem Tov uttered the names of the angels than the house filled with a great light, and something resembling a funnel of fire lit up around his mouth as he spoke. It was as if the angels actually appeared in front of him.

At that moment, the Maggid understood that his former method of study had been form without spirit, and all his worship of the Creator lacking an "extra soul." R' Dov Ber ordered the wagon driver to return to his city without him. He stayed some time in the house of the Baal Shem Tov and learned Chassidus

Siddur of the Baal Shem Tov

from him. In a matter of a few weeks, R' Dov Ber had become a close disciple of the Baal Shem Tov, and with the demise of the latter was chosen to become the leader of the חַבְרַיָא, *chavraya*. Unlike his predecessor, R' Dov Ber did not undertake many journeys. Instead, he established his home in Mezritch, where disciples flocked to him. His custom was to remain secluded in his room and only the select among the disciples earned the right to enter his presence. At the climax of the dispute between the chassidim and the *misnagdim* — in the year 5533 (1772) — when the chassidim had finally achieved equality of numbers, R' Dov Ber said to his disciples: "I see that your victory is near at hand, and that with every conflict that erupts between yourselves and the *misnagdim* it is you who will prevail more and more — but you will pay for victory with 'the head.' "

The disciples understood their Rebbe's remark to mean that their leader would soon pass away. Shocked, they remained silent.

CHAPTER III

THE MEETING OF GIANTS

T HE MAGGID OFTEN FASTED UNINTERRUPTEDLY FROM SHABBOS TO Shabbos, a regimen that took a serious toll on his health. Once R' Mendel, a disciple of the Baal Shem Tov, came from Bar to Turtshin and stayed at the home of the new *parnas*. The Maggid lived in a small house nearby. R' Mendel entered the study hall of his host's home and overheard the Maggid learning with his student. His words were pleasing to him but when he drew near, he saw that the Maggid was unwell. He said to him, "Has not his honor heard that there is a Baal Shem Tov in the world? The Rav should go to him for a cure." Answered the Maggid, "It is better to trust in Hashem than in man."

When R' Mendel came to the Baal Shem Tov, he spoke the praises of the Maggid and said, "I was in the city of Turtshin and saw a holy vessel."

The Baal Shem Tov understood immediately and said, "I saw him a few years ago and I yearn for him to come to me."

The account of the Maggid's first visit to the Baal Shem Tov is found in several versions. According to the one we follow here, his relatives induced him to go.

When he came to the Baal Shem Tov, he found him sitting on a bed meditating. *"Shalom aleichem,"* he said, and then asked him to heal him. The Baal Shem Tov replied in a scolding tone, "My horses do not eat matzos!"

At this the Maggid was overcome with weakness and broke out into a sweat. He went out and sat on the porch to rest. He saw a young fellow passing and called him over, saying, "Please go to the Baal Shem Tov and ask him why he is not fulfilling the verse, *And you shall love the stranger"* (*Devarim* 10:12). This young man was R' Yaakov of Anipoli. Moved by the Maggid's request, R' Yaakov went to the Baal Shem Tov but, at the last minute, his courage failed him. Intending to sneak away, he went to the other side of the house. On the point of doing so, he called to the Baal Shem Tov, "A man stricken with melancholy is sitting at the front of the house. He asked me to ask his honor why he does not fulfill the verse, *And you shall love the stranger."* And then he was gone. Immediately the Baal Shem Tov gathered a *minyan* (quorum of ten men), went out to him, appeased him and sought to heal him with words.

R' Gershon of Pavlutz reported that the Baal Shem Tov would visit R' Dov Ber for a week or two, sit across from him and recite *tehillim*. Afterwards, the Baal Shem Tov said to him, "At first I wanted to heal you through prayer, because that is a lasting cure, but now I will have to use physical cures on you."

He set him up in an apartment and allotted him 12 gold coins a week for his living expenses.

R' Yaakov and R' Eliyahu, another chassid, would, visit R' Dov Ber regularly, at times engaging deeply with him in the intricacies of *Gemara* and *Tosafos,* as he did not have the strength to go to the Baal Shem Tov. A little later when he was on the road to recovery, R' Dov Ber would visit the Baal Shem Tov and eat at his table.

Beis Midrash of the Baal Shem Tov

On one occasion, R' Dov Ber fainted and it took them until noon to revive him. The Baal Shem Tov went to the *mikveh* three times. He also sent word to a rich man three *parsaos* away and bought a precious stone from him for 30 red coins. He crushed it and gave R' Dov Ber to drink. Afterwards R' Yaakov and his friend came to visit him. They asked him, "Why did you faint?" He greeted their question with silence. They then asked the people in the house if R' Dov Ber had gone out that night. They answered that, yes, he had gone out for awhile and then returned to the house — and at that point his fainting attack had begun. They turned to R' Dov Ber and asked him where he had gone. He replied, "The Baal Shem Tov sent his *gabbai* to me at midnight and he took me to him. I found him sitting in a chair, dressed in a coat of wolf fur and with his head supported by a small pillow. He asked me, 'Have you learnt the wisdom of Kabbalah?' and I replied, 'Yes.' A book was sitting before him on the table and he commanded me to read to him from this book. The book was made up of brief passages, and each passage began, 'The Ari said, Matatron, the heavenly minister of the interior, said to me!' I read a page or so, and the Baal Shem Tov said to me, 'It is not so, I will read to you!' and he read to me. While doing so he began to tremble. He arose and said, 'We are dealing with *maaseh merkavah*, and I am sitting!' So he read standing. I did not see him any more. I only heard voices and saw lightning and fantastic flaming torches. This lasted about two hours. I became very frightened and out of this fear my fainting fit began ..."

"This experience was like the receiving of the Torah. For such I have heard from the pious Rav of Polonoye, who received 'Torah' (soul) from the Baal Shem Tov, with voices for his thunder and lightning. He would also say, 'With all kinds of instruments, as is mentioned in the Holy *Zohar*.' I did not see this description of "all kinds of instruments" in the *Zohar* in reference to receiving the Torah. But, I did hear from the Rav, 'Just as Israel received the Torah collectively, so the Baal Shem Tov received the Torah in isolation.'"

The Baal Shem Tov's circle asked him about a certain passage in the *Zohar*, which he explained to them. They asked the same ques-

Letter by the Baal Shem Tov's grandson, R' Boruch of Mezhibozh

tion of the Maggid and the explanation was identical in all respects to that of the Baal Shem Tov. This they reported to the Baal Shem Tov, and he replied, "Do you think that he acquired the Torah on his own?"

When the Maggid left the Baal Shem Tov, the latter blessed him. Immediately, the Baal Shem Tov put forward his own head so that the Maggid might bless him, but he refused. The Baal Shem Tov then took the Maggid's hand and placed it on his own head and then the Maggid blessed him (*Shivchei HaBaal Shem Tov*).

The Maggid's relationship with his master was very intense. It was said that they were mutually dependent. The Baal Shem Tov taught the Maggid the secrets of the Torah, the book of Raziel the Angel, as well as the cosmic power of the *Aleph-Beis*, the secret traditions of cosmology and the language of the birds and the trees.

> *Rabbi Shneur Zalman said that when the Maggid spoke, it was the voice of the Shechinah that spoke through his throat, while he was in a state of detachment from the world.*

The Maggid was eventually to introduce the systematic study of Kabbalah into the chassidic system.

OUR MASTER OF THE CLOAK

THE BAAL SHEM TOV AND HIS DISCIPLE, THE MAGGID, MADE KNOWN TO us many matters originating in the heights of the world of grace. However, so little is known to us of these exalted beings — of their human feelings, even of their very features, and the day-to-day conditions of their world. And, most important, of their unique spiritual powers, which made them magnets both to the elite and to the common people.

It never entered the thoughts of chassidim to compose biographies of their Rebbeim, neither did they make icons or images of them, or indulge in iconography in any shape or form. However, they were sure to commit to memory every utterance of the Rebbe, to contemplate his every attribute, to observe his holy manner, to take example from the details of his conduct and to run to hear Torah from his lips. In a word, they conducted them-

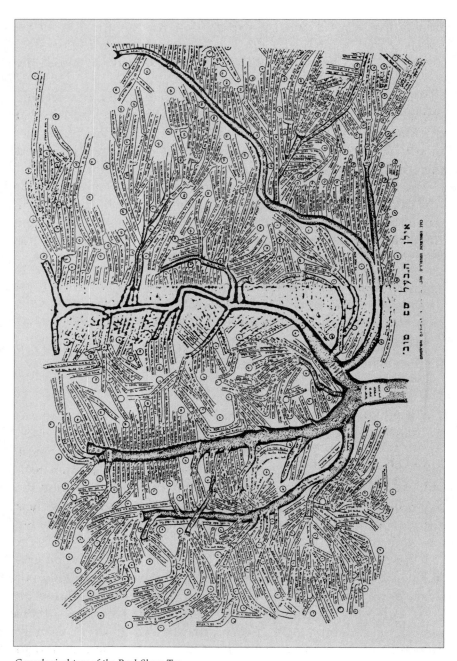

Genealogical tree of the Baal Shem Tov

selves according to the oft-quoted saying of R' Leib Sarah's, who, on his journey to his Rebbe, the Maggid of Mezritch, professed to come "not to hear Torah from his mouth," but rather to see how his Rebbe "tied his shoelaces in holiness and purity." Their real goal was to capture, in the more concrete sense of the term, the living personality of their Rebbe, not even through the spyglass of refined materialism.

The reason for this, it seems to us, lay in the particular sensibility that has always characterized Judaism, a sensibility that finds repellent the image or picture that comes to serve in place of the living man, and substitute, as it were, for his living presence. Chassidus shrank most of all from so-called representational art. Chassidus is, by its very nature, excitement, ceaseless movement, enthusiasm, infinite transformation, endless climbing, ascents of the soul. It does not recognize death. The Rebbe does not "die" in the sense that his spiritual life and accomplishment end. Rather, he is liberated (*niftar*), summoned to the heavenly yeshivah; thus his ideals and teachings remain alive. Chassidim looked for the "point" and ran away from the "line." The point is the spiritual essence of its world, it is not spelled out and defined in words, and you can comprehend it only through miracle or revelation. The line exists and stands. Therefore, they did not write biographies of their Rebbes and did not connect line to line to create a profile.

We who warm ourselves by the light of the first wise men of Chassidus yearn, because of habits ingrained in us by a secular culture, to give their images concrete form. We yearn to assign to each one of them his unique visage, the better to concretize our conception of his spiritual riches — wherein, for the most part, we labor in vain. The written sources are poor and there is no sure support in the oral tradition. Much error has crept in; for every ray of light which shines out on us from the cracks of the past, a bank of clouds comes and obscures it. Yet, what we lack in the concrete and the exact we are compensated for by the glory of the "lower cloud," which hovers over and permeates the hints of utterances and fragments of deeds. That which the story hides the legend explains, such as *Shivchei Baal Shem Tov* (Praises of the Baal Shem Tov). Wonders upon wonders are mentioned there, which shimmer like drops of light over the plains of the miraculous, and it is these in particular that magnify for us the Baal Shem Tov, exultant and holy in his lovingkindness.

At the sound of the name of the Baal Shem, we are transported to a world of galloping steeds, their bells jingling as fields and forests pass before us in a blur, the distances miraculously shrinking. Shepherds and their flocks are caught up in this stupendous journey; springs bubble over, kids bleat; the cycle of life renews itself with vigor, mountains dance like calves; the entire world is rejuvenated and shouts with joy; the heavens and the earth sing out. The Baal Shem Tov himself roams over the upper world, we the lower one, parallel to him, jumping on mountains, skipping over the hills. In the merit of the eternal life of the holy Baal Shem Tov, we taste more deeply of the transient world.

And what, at first glance, could be more strange, than that the successor of the Baal Shem Tov — the one upon whom his crown was placed, this architect who built a

Title page of the Baal Shem Tov's will

popular movement out of the rarefied soil of individuals — should be this R' Dov Ber. This man who in his very nature and demeanor was the diametric opposite of the Baal Shem Tov: a man who kept to his room, holding himself aloof from worldly matters; a man apart, whose haunts were neither the roads nor the fields; his preoccupation, neither shepherds nor their flocks. This was the man destined to become the shepherd to the flock of the Baal Shem Tov — its teacher and guide.

In fact, it was not so strange. The Maggid's power was self-evidently great, for the reason that, unlike the Baal Shem Tov, he did not wear farmer's furs but the cloak of a *talmid chacham*. The latter has several explanations, among them the symbolic.

The cloak was the Maggid's "idea." Not only did he wear white clothes and was crowned "*Admor,*" but he also enclosed the holiness, the enthusiasm and the wisdom within a frame. He made a fence around the wondrous. The Baal Shem Tov was the sun, which spreads its rays on everything. The Maggid, his disciple, was, like every disciple, the moon. In reality, however, the power of the moon was greater than the sun in terms of harnessing spiritual power and concentrating it in one place. Moshe takes out (from Egypt) and Joshua brings in (to Israel). We interpret the word מַכְנִיס not only in the sense of, "bring in," but also as מְכַנֵּס, "gathers," packs tightly, concentrates. The Rebbe disseminates, diffuses; the disciple gathers, packs tightly, concentrates.

The Rebbe is like a living stream. Streams, however, do not attract intense scrutiny because, like the rays of the sun itself, they are ever before us. Beneath the rays of the moon, however, the soul awakens from its slumbers to thoughts of self-evaluation. The Baal Shem Tov was a living stream. Came the Maggid and made Chassidus a walled garden, a retreat.

What *was* the mysteriousness of the Maggid, so unlike that of the Baal Shem Tov, with his miracles and his wonders?

It seems to us that it resided in the supernal levels of understanding that he communicated to his students in his study hall. Here, the emphasis passed from the miraculous to the personal act; to inwardness, contemplation of first causes — of the miracle that is implicit in the natural world.

The *"doodele"* niggun of R' Levi

There are no accomplishments without the play of surface forms. The Baal Shem Tov appeared to us in farmer's garb. The Maggid's disguise, so to speak, was the mantle of kingship, the voluminous robes of the sage.

Go and inquire and you will see that the science of camouflage, of the masquerade — that is, concealment of one's true nature — is the mother of all spiritual concepts and levels.

Of that science, and of that art, R' Dov Ber was a master. So much so that he appears before us in a costume fabricated out of every one of his utterances. Every one of his gestures contributes to the total effect.

Looking at him through this eyepiece, we come to some conception of the way in which he won so many hearts — those of his brilliant disciples among them. In truth, the latter were hesitant to explain to themselves by what supernatural arts it was that their Rebbe came to wield such influence over them that they became as putty in his hands. They searched in vain to explain the inexplicable. More than they spoke they mumbled, and to the extent that they explained, they continued to obscure. Alternatively — to put it another way — "they revealed one *tefach* (handbreadth) and hid two more" (*Nedarim* 2b).

One disciple put it clearly: "When we traveled to the Maggid, immediately upon entering the city limits we felt that our heart's desires had been fulfilled. When we gazed upon the radiant countenance of our Rebbe a peace beyond compare took possession of our souls."

R' Levi Yitzchok saw in the face of the Maggid brilliance, splendor and majesty, arrayed like the colors of the spectrum in the rainbow arc, until fear and trembling possessed him and he fell back, recoiling from that splendor.

Countless are the volumes that his disciples were inspired to fill with the praises of their Rebbe, nor can we form even the minutest conception of the truth that they try to convey. For the truth is that the magnetic force of any personality defies analysis.

Suffice it to say that a warm heart is the key to the secret chambers of knowledge. With it, we gain access even to those matters for whose exalted substance the cold of space is the only "preservative."

Perhaps the white cloak that the Maggid wore in the "courtyards" of the chassidim may be said to be a symbol, even though it was not his invariable practice to wear it. Look at his attributes — patience, lucidity of thought and a logical method of purity and refinement. Out of such materials, R' Dov Ber made something seminal, whose germ was ever enthusiasm and great yearnings. He is both north and south — the gaunt figure of privation, the primal sea, incubator of fervent hearts — the archetypal sage. He is the fount of secret wisdom at which the generations of initiates slake their thirst. Against "all this," there is, at one and the same time, the man: totally revealed, patient, softspoken. To all appearances, no more than a rabbi, a teacher of Jewish law, who sits in a yeshivah — not an *Admor*, regally apart, seated at a festive *tisch* (table). Such was the phenomenon of R' Dov Ber — one who subdued within himself the wholesome impulse to ecstasy. Such was the effect upon his disciples that their fervor knew no bounds at the wonder of it. Where the Baal Shem Tov was all irrepressible motion, a lightness and cavorting of the soul, the Maggid was stillness, the reining in and containment of forces, the effect of which was so awesome that his disciples reeled before its power. He seemed to them the complete person: one whose essence is concealed, warm on the inside and cold on the outside, a great heart enclosed within a great mind, passion and dialectic intertwined.

He is good and his raiment is good — to paraphrase the *Zohar*. The author of *Chiddushei HaRim* has explained for us the verse in *Tehillim* (23:5): *Set before me a table, against my oppressors*. Every righteous person has a certain kind of dress — the world turns its gaze upon him and his dress deflects the evil eye from his essence. The Holy *Yud* (Jew) of Pschis'che wore the clothing of a learned man. R' Simchah Bunim of Pschis'che (d. 1827) made intelligence his clothing. King Dovid's words, "Set before me a table, against my oppressors," can also be explained: "Let everyone who wants to give me the evil eye and bring troubles upon me see only my table, that is, my clothing, my exterior, and not my essence."

A personal impression of the Maggid is found in *Lebens Geshichte* (Berlin, 1798) a book by the Kantian philosopher, Solomon Maimon (1754-1800).

He describes a Sabbath with the Maggid in Mezritch.

I found there a great number of worthy people who had come from various places ... At last the great man appeared, his charismatic form all clad in white satin (the color of grace in Kabbalah). He gave everyone there "Sholom." All sat down at the table ... All during the meal, a solemn quietude prevailed. After the meal, the Maggid sang his Sabbath niggun, while each of us was required to say a verse from the Holy Scripture, and everyone did so. Then the Maggid preached, and the text of his sermon consisted of a combination based upon all the stated verses, while he worked them together with such tremendous skill that it appeared as if they were a whole to begin with. What was still more strange: Each of the guests felt that there was something in the sermon that fit his own case exactly!

The Maggid wore the cloak both literally and symbolically, in that he displayed severity of intellect and coldness of logic, the better to conceal his warm heart and fervent soul from the eagle eyes of the shells (קְלִיפּוֹת, *klippos*). This was consistent with his own teaching that one must search out the spark hidden in the ashes. Therefore, upon him devolved the privilege of serving as the archetype for the chassidic movement, which is, in its very essence, a flame of eternal life amid the temporal. Chassidus appears austere to the eyes but rich brocades bedeck its soul. The Baal Shem Tov had the visionary aspect of a *seraph* riding the heavens in a chariot of fire, its silken, fiery streamers brushing the face of earth. However, it is to be doubted if in the gorgeous fabrics of the Baal Shem Tov, there was from what to weave a *tallis* to cover the masses of Israel. It was the destiny of the Baal Shem Tov to be a miracle-worker, a legend, a re-membered radiance, a once-living flame now extinct. Then came R' Dov Ber to frame the legend in the bricks and mortar of logic, and to make it a vessel for real life. And a complete vessel it was, because its artificer was, in the most comprehensive sense, a wise man, a sage.

Come and see how lofty are the ways of Divine Providence, working from level to level. It creates souls and clothes them in flesh and bone. Thus, it causes legend to precede the life of action. Dreams are cyclic and repeat themselves. Similarly, good news comes twice. We blow the shofar and blow again. First, the prince of the nation — its guardian angel — blew the shofar of the Baal Shem Tov, to whom all eyes would turn, as he walked in the fields, the forests and all the public places. Afterwards, he blew the shofar of the Maggid, whose element was the private domain. Sequestered within the four walls of his dwelling place, he assembled, ordered and established a popular movement.

R' Dov Ber had authority, although he was never formally invested with it. Like his predecessor, he was born with scepter in hand. These are the crowned heads, in the primal sense, of the most exalted kind. For those with an eye to see, a nimbus surrounds them always, each with its distinctive properties, whether of outspread wings, or of majestic rays and countenance. In the gait of the Baal Shem Tov, in the gait of the Maggid, there is a world of evocation: the murmuring of animals, the rush of constellations. The knocking of the Maggid's crutches has the power to summon up pearls of wisdom — at their sound the disciples stand in breathless anticipation of the words he will speak to them. When they tell us of their crippled Rebbe hobbling among them, in the darkness of the night, to find the one who is reviewing the words that he heard from the Rebbe today, in order to press the chassid to rest from the labors of the spirit and the mind — for in every spiritual attachment of the disciple there is the stealing of sleep — we sense that all the souls breathe in unison and all the minds think in unison, and that all partake of a wonderful unity.

The wisdom of holiness is not learned, not passed down. It is not the result of planned or gradual growth. Consequently, we search out its sources. There is a process of a different order at work here. Rather than reaching for wisdom and plying it like a craft, a human being gives himself over to it. It is an act of self-abandonment performed, it should be understood, with all requisite preparation and with the fullest consciousness of what he is about. The principal features of wisdom are humility, nullification of the self, conquest of the self; a gathering of the powers of the soul in order to penetrate to wisdom's innermost chamber. Silence and abnegation, as the Maggid not infrequently remarks, are one's allies in the quest.

However, even this wisdom, which we characterize as the reward of silence and of "doing without," even this wisdom is of legendary

Title page of Sefer Ohr HaMeir by R' Zev Wolf of Zhitomer

stature — lest you should think it commonplace. For the Maggid, whose signature it is — for all that logic and method distinguish him from the Baal Shem Tov — the Maggid, too, is obscured by a dark cloud. Granted that he is the foremost leader of the congregation, that he is Rebbe and guide, exegete and explicator, organizer and unifier of enormous skill; yet, still, we stand dumbfounded at the scale of his achievement. We do not understand how a man, with one head and two hands, could simultaneously embody the truth of the structure. How he could establish a palace on high for generations, and join together, in one congregation, great souls, isolated, singular, ever striving, consumed by longings, each one drawn to the will of the Creator, running like a doe, but together, linked hearts, private souls bound to the all-inclusive soul. Consider: The building of a congregation is a work of construction achieved by only a few architects in history.

R' Dov Ber, the Maggid of Mezritch, merited seeing his work meet with success after success, while his students marched in step with him, holding the line of wisdom, which conquers through self-conquest.

> Said the Baal Shem Tov: "When the Maggid came to me he was already a pure golden candelabra. All he needed was for the candles to be lit."

However, the Maggid is the prime vessel. This is not to say that a secondary vessel is not an original. It is not correct to say, "This one is first." There is a first before the first, as well. The order of things is not significant, only their depth. The first degree is befitting the one who extracts things from their source. This need not be the Rebbe. The Rebbe finds — that is his metier. He locates the treasure and sends his disciples in search of it.

Said one of his disciples, "When we traveled to the Maggid, upon entering the city limits we immediately felt that all our desires were fulfilled. If, nevertheless, yearnings troubled us, from the point at which we crossed the threshold of his house, they lost their hold on us completely. If anyone remained in a state of agitation, as soon as he looked at the radiant figure of our teacher, he achieved inner peace."

The Maggid laid the foundation of the chassidic movement. To his many disciples he was a devoted teacher. The Maggid's soul was pure marble, his every word profound and warm — the warmth of Torah in cold vessels. For the Maggid was not an effervescent personality. Indeed, he remains an enigma.

SAID THE MAGGID TO RABBI ZUSYA, HIS DISCIPLE, "I CANNOT TEACH you the ten principles of service. But a little child and a thief can

THE TEN PRINCIPLES
OF THE MAGGID

show you what they are. "From the child a person can learn three things:

- He is merry for no particular reason.
- Never for a moment is he idle.
- When he needs something, he demands it vigorously.

The thief can instruct a person in seven things:

- He does his work by night.
- If he does not finish what he has set out to do in one night, he devotes the next night to it.
- He and those who work with him love one another.
- He risks his life for slight gains.
- What he takes has so little value for him, that he gives it up for a very small coin.
- He endures blows and hardship, and it matters nothing to him.
- He likes his trade and would not exchange it for any other."

CHAPTER IV

THE AUTHENTIC
TEACHER AND
TRUE REBBE

THE FIRST REBBE IN CHASSIDUS, THE "ARCHETYPE," WAS R' DOV
Ber of Mezritch. The Baal Shem Tov was not a Rebbe in the traditional sense, although the title Rebbe befits him from all
points of view. However, he transcends such categories. The Baal
Shem Tov is a sun that heats souls that they in turn may reflect light
like precious stones.

It is not correct to say that the group around the Baal Shem Tov
consisted of his disciples. They are as nothing compared to the great
eagle that hovers high above them. One of them, it is true, seems to
us like a wing of the Baal Shem Tov. He never becomes, though, like
an entity unto himself. From this, we are able to deduce the nature
of the true Rebbe — he who educates, guides and raises his disciples
to the point where they are able to make a place for themselves as
individual personalities.

Manuscript of the Maggid with his signature

However, we cannot leave things there — this matter of Rebbe and disciple calls for greater clarification, for it is the veritable cornerstone of the edifice of Chassidus. What better place to raise it than here, where our subject is the Maggid of Mezritch himself: the foremost of the *tzaddikim* in the love of Chassidus, the Rebbe *par excellence*. Gaze upon him. Penetrate to the essence of the Rebbe and you will find the Maggid standing before you.

To understand the nature of the Rebbe, we have also to understand the nature of the disciple. Is it the role of the latter to innovate, to complement his master's teachings, to "add the personal touch"? Is it to stand in the master's shadow or to expand boundaries established by him, to find his place in the sun? Is it even, so to speak, to wrap himself in the Rebbe's *tallis* and make of his Torah a forgery and perversion — as some have been known to do!

Title page of *Sefer Maggid D'varav L'Yaakov* (first printing). The final letters of the words of the title are enlarged to spell the name of the Maggid, דוב, Dov.

R' Shneur Zalman of Liadi (Baal HaTanya)

In fact, it is by scrutinizing the relationship of the Maggid with his disciples that we may, perhaps, come to a true understanding, a correct notion.

R' Shneur Zalman, who was wise in matters of definition, once said, "My teacher, the Maggid, of blessed memory, was the complete man." What does that mean? Perhaps the perfect man inhabits every kind of terrain, is master of all the levels of mysticism, ruler over all the qualities? It is not so. The complete man carries, as his obligation, the roots of all souls; he lives with the power of multifarious concepts; he hears the sound of the heavenly chariot from afar. This is not to say that the roots of all souls lying deep within him have all attained the level of his own or that he is at home with this or that quality alone in all worlds. Nevertheless, he has in his soul many gates, many entrances. A man with many gates and many levels is potentially the complete man.

Then with main force he founds for himself a yeshivah with students; behold, he is a teacher with Divine grace.

The Maggid did not seek to create replicas of himself; he used his great power to mold each student in his own mold, to develop his powers according to his own way and the root of his soul. It could be that some quality, concept or point of view reaches in the student a level of crystallization greater than in the Rebbe himself. Where the Rebbe's work may be likened to the rough copy, the student's work, building upon it, has the look of the finished copy. The Rebbe etches and the student engraves. He is not completely like his Rebbe, in whom many principles come together harmoniously. The student is an inheritor, a separate personality, albeit trained and developed in the "courtyard" of the Rebbe.

THE PASSING OF THE MAGGID

ON 18 KISLEV, 5533, ONE DAY BEFORE HIS DEATH, THE MAGGID SAID TO HIS students and close associates, "My sons, seek unity among yourselves. Through this unity, you shall overcome everything. You shall ascend and not descend, G-d forbid. The Torah alludes to this: וְהוּא בְאֶחָד וּמִי יְשִׁיבֶנּוּ, *He is unique, and who can contradict Him? ... (Iyov* 23:13).

So saying, the Maggid fell silent, his eyes closed. He seemed to be dozing. R' Zusya entered the room on tiptoe. The Maggid aroused himself and asked, "Who has come?" "Zusya has come," answered R' Shneur Zalman.

Tombstone of the Maggid of Mezritch
(erected after the Holocaust)

The Maggid pointed toward Zusya with his long hand, which trembled from weakness, like a broken branch hanging limp in the wind. R' Zusya approached the bed. The Maggid took R' Zusya's right hand, put his left palm on it and whispered in a faint but clear voice, "You were mine, Zusya, in this world, and there, too, in the other world, you will be with me of my company."

While speaking to Zusya, and of Zusya, the Maggid lifted his head from his pillow, thereby settling himself somewhat, the better to focus on Zusya. His head fell on the pillow by itself when he finished speaking. His gaze, however, remained fixed on Zusya's face. The memory of the gaze hovers in space and is attached to Zusya like an embrace.

"And where is Menachem Mendel?" asked the Maggid, awakening from a light sleep. The voice was now weaker and less distinct.

"Menachem Mendel of Vitebsk (1748-1787) is not here," answered R' Shneur Zalman. "And R' Yehudah Leib HaKohen of Puma is here?" asked the Maggid. The effort that it took to pronounce the words was so great that the letters were all but swallowed up by the faintness of his voice, which, for a moment, sounded like the grunt of a dying man.

"R' Yehudah Leib is here," answered R' Shneur Zalman.

The former approached the bed. Again the Maggid raised his head above the pillow and, to everyone's amazement, moved his hand slightly. He took R' Yehudah Leib's right hand and caressed it with his left palm. His lips spoke firmly and clearly, "Yehudah Leib, you are a Kohen. כִּי שִׂפְתֵי כֹהֵן יִשְׁמְרוּ דַעַת, *For the lips of the Kohen should safeguard knowledge* (*Malachi* 2:7). You will be of my company."

Now the Maggid turned his attention to R' Shneur Zalman and said, "Shneur Zalman, give me your hand. You will be alone. You are independent. You have your own way. You will need a great

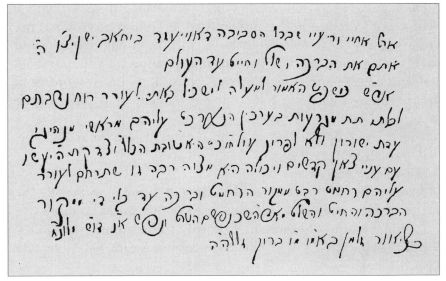

Handwriting of the Baal HaTanya with his signature

deal of Divine help. I will long for you very much and, G-d willing, I will save you from all your troubles."

After taking, as it were, a tender leave of all his other disciples, he asked, "Where is Avrohom? Where are you, Avrohom, my son? I do not see Avrohom, my son."

R' Avrohom, his son, known as the *"Malach"* (Angel), was not constantly at his father's beside, as were nearly all the Maggid's other disciples. Even in the latter days of his father's illness, the Malach would shut himself up in his room. Avrohom was not of this world. Therefore he was always involved in the circle of the rays of the sun of death. Death did not appear to him as a gate to the World to Come. Is there a world other than the World to Come? Now, summoned to his father for the last time, he stepped slowly, as if not called at all, his eyes shut even as he walked, like a sleepwalker. The habit of many years, to walk with eyes closed lent his gait the tremulous, hesitant quality of a bird. He was always deep in concentration — not only in his thinking but also in his listening, as if he were aware of the clatter of wings above his head. The clatter of the wings of the Angel of Death in the room of one approaching death did not change his manner or affect his composure.

He came near to his father's bed. The Maggid spoke with a clear voice in tones of encouragement. "Avrohom, Avrohom, my son — do not stray from your holy path. I am not commanding anything of you, but I will request one thing of you, my son. Speak to your fellow men. Only open your lips — your words will shed light. For too long have you been silent. It is only a little thing that I ask!"

The Maggid did not remove his gaze from his son for a long time, as if waiting for a response.

The *Malach* was silent.

Afterwards, the eyelids of the Maggid filmed over with the beams of deep sleep. His lips whispered in this world no more.

Within a matter of hours the heavenly court summoned R' Dov Ber. The head was gone. The legend of wisdom was over (19 Kislev, 1772).

It did not end. Its days are as the days of the world.

ספר

אור האמת

אמרי צדיקים

כשמו כן הוא **אור** המאיר לעולם כולו בכבוד
תורתו תורת **אמת** כולל **אמרי צדיקים**
אמרות טהורות מקדוש ה' מכובד מופת הדור
והדרו נזר הקודש רבן רבן של כל בני הגולה **אור**
העולם גדול מרבן שמו מהור"ר **דוב בער**
זצוק"ל זי"ע **המגיד ממעזריטש** אשר
כתבם עלי ספר תלמידו הגאון **אור** ישראל
וקדושו פאר הדור מו"ה **לוי יצחק** זצוק"ל
בעהמ"ח ספר **קדושת לוי** האב"ד דק"ק
בראדיטשוב וליקוטים נחמדים משאר צדיקי
עולם זי"ע ועכ"י.

הובא לביה"ד ע"י ר' משה מרדכי בא"א מו"ה חיים ז"ל מויג'ווקע
שנוא בן הרב הצדיק הר' צבי חסיד מיאמפפאלע פאדאל

בזיטאמיר

לפרט פרנסה ברוח ובכבוד

הוצאת "יהדות"
שנת תשכ"ז לפ"ק
בני־ברק, ת"ו

Discourses fo the Mezhritcher Maggid

Chapter IV: The Authentic Teacher and True Rebbe | 73

He was buried in Anipoli. Chassidim say that R' Dov Ber changed places of burial with R' Yaakov, the Baal Shem's student, from Anipoli, who died in Mezritch.

R' Dov Ber wrote no books, but his disciples recorded his talks, orations and discourses, and R' Shlomo of Lutzk published them in book form. In 5544 (1784), the book *Maggid D'varav L'Yaakov,* and in 5564 (1824) the book *Ohr Torah,* arranged according to the order of the weekly Torah portion, appeared. Selections of the Maggid's *Toros* appeared as *Likkutei Yekarim* (1792), and *Ohr HaEmes* in 1799 and *Likkutei Amarim* in 1781.

R' Dov Ber was extolled by his disciples as a holy master. He was revered in chassidic history by the unique title of "The Great Maggid."

Of the many voices raised in praise of him, we quote the following:

✑ R' Zev Wolf of Zhitomir:

Once, on Friday, the Great Maggid [of Mezritch] sat in his room, which was next to his *beis midrash* (study hall) and re-

IN PRAISE OF THE MAGGID

cited the Torah portion of the week — Torah twice, Targum (Onkelos' translation) once. A number of the students, myself among them, were sitting in the *beis midrash* when suddenly a great light shone upon us. In that instant, the door of the Maggid's room opened and his fiery countenance greeted our eyes. This rare vision caused us almost to go out of our minds. R' Pinchos of Frankfurt and his brother, R' Shmelke of Nikolsburg, and R' Elimelech of Lizhensk and his brother, R' Zusya of Anipoli, all fled. R' Levi Yitzchok of Berditchev fell into a state of ecstasy and rolled on the floor under the table. Even I (who am so unused to any emotionalism) clapped my hands in uncontrollable excitement (*HaMaggid MiMezritch,* p. 69).

When R' Pinchos (1731-1777), the author of *Hamakneh* and *Haflaah,* came to Frankfurt to become the rabbi there, they received him with great honor, were solicitous of his every need and escorted him to his inn. One of the guests at the inn was a *parnas,* a formidable opponent of the chassidim, who asked him mockingly, "Did not his honor say that he cannot travel so quickly from Frankfurt to his Rebbe, the Maggid, in far-off Mezritch?"

R' Pinchos answered him, "On the contrary, I am sorry that when I was in Poland I did travel to him. Now I regret it."

The *parnas* said to him, "As it happens, I am a merchant, and am quite sure that my class is not susceptible to feelings of remorse. Yet I am happy to note that his honor regrets his travels to that Rebbe."

"His honor misunderstands," explained R' Pinchos. "It is indeed true that I regret riding there, for I should have gone to the great Maggid on foot!"

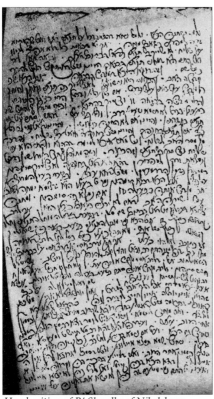
Handwriting of R' Shmelke of Nikolsburg

✑R' Shmelke of Nikolsburg:

Before I went to study with the Maggid of Mezritch, I would mortify my body for the sake of my eternal soul. Now I have seen and learned that the soul can endure the body without having to separate from it. Thus it is written, *And I will set My abiding Presence among you and My soul shall not abhor you* (*Vayikra* 26:11).

✑R' Zusya of Anipoli:

I once had to bind the world to my master, the Maggid, because it was a time of distress, Hashem have mercy on us, and there was a need to elevate the world.

I came before my master and said to him, "Rebbe, you are the righteous one of the generation." Immediately the Maggid rose to

Tomb of the Maggid of Mezritch and his disciple R' Zusya of Anipoli

his feet and exclaimed, "Master of the Universe, my sin is too great to bear."

R' Leib Sarah's:

I traveled to my teacher, the Maggid, not to hear Torah from his lips, but rather to see how he tied his shoelaces in holiness and purity.

The Baal Shem Tov: (1700-1760)

I know that this bear (*dov*, in Hebrew, a bear) is not swift because of his limp, but he has broad and ample hands to bring the hearts of the students under the wings of Chassidus.

R' Shneur Zalman of Liadi: (1745-1812)

Concerning my master, the Maggid, R' Dov Ber, the Torah says, *We will make man in our image and likeness,* for he was the complete man, although he was infirm. The complete man moves his limbs and the world moves in response, as it states in the *Zohar,* "Righteousness is the right arm, might is the left." His left foot could not move, lest it bring down the quality of might (*gevurah*) upon the world.

He also said, "In the house of our teacher, the Maggid, they would draw up the holy spirit in 'buckets,' and the miracles were left under the table — no one had time for them."

❧ The Maggid of Kozhnitz (1737-1814):

Before I was granted the privilege of coming before my master and Rebbe, the Maggid of Mezritch, I had learned 800 works of Kabbalah. When I came to him, I saw that I had not yet begun to learn.

❧ R' Levi Yitzchok of Berditchev (1740-1809):

Once, at the time of the Minchah prayer, I saw on the Maggid's face radiance similar to that of the colors of the rainbow. Fear and trembling seized me and I collapsed in a heap on the floor. Others held me up, but they did not know why I had fainted.

When my master saw my trembling, he turned his face to the wall and leaned his head on it for two or three minutes. He turned his face again and I saw nothing further. When my master passed away, I again saw the selfsame radiance, and in this way I merited to comprehend his Torah.

❧ R' Zev Wolf of Zhitomir (d. 1800):

I saw on more than one occasion that when he opened his lips to speak words of Torah, it appeared as if he was not in the world at all, and the Omnipresent spoke from his throat.

❧ R' Avraham of Kalisk (d. 1810):

When we were with the *Admor,* the Maggid discussed one topic for a long time. If we had only come to hear this topic, it would have been enough. We heard it in purity until he finished and then moved on to a second topic.

❧ R' Shlomo of Lutzk (d. 1813):

We despair of conveying the greatness and the holy level of the Rebbe, our master and teacher. Even if we were to tell of them, who would believe in the wondrous miracles that he performed, or the efficacy of his prayer ... *And he decided*

Tomb of R' Levi Yitzchok of Berditchev

and he arose. "You shall decree a thing, and it shall be established for you" (*Iyov* 22:28). Indeed, with our own eyes
we saw, we understood on how high a level he was. He
was humble of manner, unimposing of stature, the fear of
Hashem never left his face, and the sublime honor of
Hashem hovered above him all day long.

IN THE TOWN OF MEZRITCH THERE LIVED A WEALTHY AND SCHOLARLY young man. One day, he thought to himself: "People come from

A MAGGID STORY

far and wide to seek guidance from the famed Maggid, R' Dov Ber, while I who live in the very same town have yet to sample his wisdom. Shouldn't I go to him and seek the truth?"

Accordingly, the young man set off and visited the chassidic master, at once discovering that a new world had opened up for him — a world in which everything is imbued with purpose. And so he soon became a devoted chassid of the Maggid.

But in proportion as his spiritual life improved, his material fortunes plummeted. His business went from bad to worse and he soon found himself in the ranks of the poor. At first he held himself back but eventually he mustered courage to approach his master.

"Rebbe, why is it," he asked, "that from the time I became your disciple I became a poor man?"

Niggun of "Tzur MiShelo" by R' Avraham of Kalisk

"They say you are something of a scholar," replied the Maggid, "so I have a Talmudic question for you. The Gemara says (*Bava Basra* 25b), [When facing east in prayer] 'One who desires wisdom should turn his head toward the south; one who desires riches, toward the north.'

"But what if one desires both wisdom and riches? North and south are at a great remove from each other.

"I see that you are silent," continued the Maggid, "so I will answer the question myself. When a person humbles himself before Hashem and man, and negates himself, he no longer takes up space in the world. He can now be north and south at the same time!"

Said the Maggid: "Hashem has done us a great favor, in that our very soul does not fly out of our body when we pray."

He also said, "One shall cease to have thoughts related to the body, thoughts rooted in the lower emotions — of lustful desire, pride and so on. Then the soul is entirely in the spiritual world, and even the senses are largely 'shut off,' leading to a stripping away of material existence.

"You should find delight in Torah study such that the desire of your soul increases and your bodily senses cease to function. Your soul should cleave to the Torah until you cease to be aware of the things of this world … I have heard of many sages who had such *d'veikus* to the Torah that they lost awareness of this world altogether" (*Reishis Chochmah, Shaar HaAhavah*).

Chassidic tradition has it that when the Great Maggid became known throughout the Jewish world, he *davened* with the most abject sincerity, "*Ribbono Shel Olam,* please tell me, what sin have I committed that I am being punished with this terrible punishment?"

They asked the Maggid: "The Psalmist declares (85:12): *Truth springs out of the earth.* Why aren't people always truthful?" He replied, "People are too lazy to bend down and pick up the truth where it lies at their feet." He also said, "Sometimes a man must search to find a single spark."

Of *teshuvah* he said: When a person repents and directs his love toward Hashem, he thinks to himself: "Why did I expend my love on physical things alone. Isn't it better for me to love the Root of all roots?" — his love is then rectified and he draws the sparks of holiness out of the husks (*Imrei Tzaddikim* 24d).

Of humility he said: One cannot constantly be in a state of awe before Hashem's greatness. Whenever anything holy is removed, it leaves a mark. The mark left by awe and reverence is humility.

For Hashem, he said, past and future are exactly the same. He delighted in the deeds of the righteous in the far distant future and therefore constricted His Essence. This constriction (צִמְצוּם — *tzimtzum*) was a result of Hashem's love for Israel (*Maggid D'varav L'Yaakov*).

A person *davening* in a place where there are idle words, he said, can elevate them if they are words of spiritual joy. Their elevation results in great joy on High, giving rise to much enthusiasm. But if they are words of sadness, they are very difficult to uplift.

When a person does not believe with absolute faith that through his words and attachment to Hashem he can accomplish such things, then nothing at all is actually accomplished on High (ibid. §188).

CHAPTER V

R' AVROHOM THE MALACH
(1740-1777)

WHEN THE MAGGID DIED, HIS DISCIPLES BEGAN TO analyze every detail of his actions, in order to make of them the guide for their future conduct. As if to point out the futility of their efforts, R' Shneur Zalman of Liadi reminded them of the visits that the Maggid would make to a nearby pond, whose purpose no one understood: "Our master the Maggid would go to listen to the frogs singing the praises of Hashem," he said.

The great Maggid was full of enthusiasm and unfulfilled longings for the Holy Land. He said, "All this world draws its life from Zion, which is the essence of the world and the lifeblood of the entire universe."

As mentioned above, when the Maggid was a child, a fire destroyed the *yichus* scroll containing the genealogy of his father's

Niggun for "Azamer BiShvochin" by R' Avrohom the Malach

house, which had been traced back to King Dovid. The Maggid's mother was very upset, and he comforted her, saying, "With me will begin a new family tree."

In truth, the young speaker prophesied and indeed knew what he was prophesying. The Maggid of Mezritch was indeed meritorious and many great generations came forth from him. Their mission consisted of raising the status of Israel, with regal pomp and glory, in order to restore Israel to the splendor of the days gone by. He opened a new page in the history of Israel, not only in terms of the chassidic movement, that he founded, but also through his sons and grandsons, who were linked in a great chain of eminent leaders who strengthened the faith and hope of the Jewish masses for the longed-for day to come. The dynasty that one of his grandsons founded is known to us by the name of *Malchus Beis Rizhin,* the "Kingdom of the House of Rizhin."

On the original tombstone of the Maggid it stated: "Here lies buried the Rabbi, the Maggid of Mezritch, רַבָּן שֶׁל כָּל בְּנֵי הַגּוֹלָה, the head of the entire Diaspora, our teacher, R' Dov Ber, son of R' Avrohom, who died in the year 5533 (1772), on the 19th of Kislev."

THE GREAT MAGGID WAS SURVIVED BY A SON, R' AVROHOM THE MALACH, the son of the Maggid's first wife. His second wife always com-

MOTHERS AND HOLINESS

plained that she had no children. Once she said to him, "What possible vexation could it be to you if we were to have another Malach?" The Maggid answered that he had no power to bless her with a child; only her *tefillos* and piety could accomplish that. He told her a story about his first *rebbetzin*.

Once she had to go on a mission at night to purify herself, and all she had was a few small coins. To make matters worse, she got lost on the way and wandered off the snow-covered path. She went around in circles for hours in the cold, wintry night before she found the house she was looking for. The woman caretaker shouted at her for waking her and refused to let her in.

Suddenly a beautiful horse-drawn carriage drew up and four wealthy-looking women stepped out. The caretaker was happy to see such distinguished people and she invited all of them in including the *rebbetzin*. The four strangers paid all the expenses and then brought the *rebbetzin* home in their carriage. They even gave her a warm cloak to protect herself from the cold and wind.

The Maggid concluded, "You should know that these four women were our Matriarchs, Sarah, Rivkah, Rachel and Leah. My son the Malach was born that year."

R' Avrohom, the Malach, was so named because, as a result of his leaning toward asceticism, he often seemed not to exist in the physical world at all.

Everyone referred to him as the Malach because he was as holy and pure as an angel of Hashem. It is told that one of the sages of his time was more than a little scandalized that he should be called the Malach, since he was born of woman. This sage came to R' Avrohom on the eve of Tishah B'Av and saw that he sat on the ground the entire night with his head between his knees; and in the morning, at midday, there was a puddle of tears around him. The man then understood that not for nothing did they call him the Malach.

Devout and dedicated as he was to the service of Hashem, R' Avrohom the Malach rarely ate and in due course became very weak. Once his father — whose natural tendencies were in the same direction — sent him a message, urging him to take better care of his health. The Malach answered, "I do not have to listen to my father when it conflicts with my obligation to Hashem in Heaven."

Once, when he was in the midst of his prayers, it was noticed by those standing near him that he had become painfully weak. His

MORE ANGEL THAN MAN

friend, the Rav of Liadi, asked that they remove from him the *tefillin* of Rashi and replace them with the *tefillin* of Rabbeinu Tam. As they did so, his strength returned.

The Maggid had organized his disciples *b'chavrusa*, in pairs, to have them learn together, and he assigned R' Shneur Zalman of Liadi to his son, R' Avrohom the Malach. They began to learn

Tomb of R' Avrohom the Malach in Hvastov

Mesechta Beitzah. After the Liader had fully explained it, the Malach said that the word *beitzah* stood for twelve different representations of Hashem's Name. He then continued to explain the hidden meaning of the Mishnah. From that point on, the Malach learned the revealed Torah from his friend, while he in turn taught him its kabbalistic meaning.

HOW ARE WE TO MEASURE THE GREATNESS OF R' AVROHOM, THE MALACH? His source of knowledge was his father — the Maggid. He wrote a

BY WHAT YARDSTICK

book called *Chessed L'Avrohom* which dealt with Kabbalah. His father's disciples accepted him as their leader; however, he died not long after moving to the city of Hvastov, only four years after his father's *petirah.*

R' DOVID MOSHE OF CHORTKOV ONCE TOLD THE FOLLOWING STORY about his great-grandfather, the Malach. The Malach went to

LESSON FROM NATURE

Kreminitz to visit his father-in-law, R' Meshulam Feivish HaLevi Horowitz, the author of *Mishnas Chachamim* on Mishnayos. The whole town turned out to greet him, and to see what a holy man he was. However, the Malach did not so much as look at them. Instead, he was looking out of the window at a very tall mountain. All the assembled were hoping to hear words of Torah from him, but he continued to gaze silently at the mountain. In the group was a very distinguished and learned man who did not understand why the Malach was acting so tactlessly toward those assembled. This man showed great pride in his learning. He turned to the Malach and asked him what was it that he saw in the mountain — a thing made out of earth alone. The Malach replied that he was looking at the mountain with astonishment, because it was so difficult to understand how a mound of plain simple earth could become so great and haughty a mountain. The man began to tremble at the answer.

R' Yisroel of Rizhin thus related of his great-grandfather:

My maternal grandfather, R' Feivish of Kremenitz, the author of *Mishnas Chachamim*, was a Torah giant. Whenever he encountered a difficult passage in his learning, he would fast and the explanation was revealed to him from Heaven. Once he was studying a Talmudic portion and was deeply puzzled by the explanation of the *Ran*. He fasted, as was his custom, and the proper answer was accordingly revealed to him from Heaven. R' Feivish was then an opponent of my paternal great-grandfather, the Maggid of Mezritch, insofar as he was called "the Rebbe." He decided to travel to the Maggid and to ask him the question on the *Ran*, and if the latter were able to answer his question, then indeed the name "Rebbe" was befitting to him. And so he did. He took under his arm his *sefer* containing the *Ran* and went to Mezritch.

When he arrived at the Maggid's home, the *gabbai* whose job it was to screen visitors refused to allow him entry. The ensuing dispute reached the ears of those inside the room where the Maggid was sitting. Immediately, the Maggid himself opened the door to see what the commotion was all about. At once R' Feivish seized the opportunity to enter.

Said R' Feivish, "I have heard that they call you 'Rebbe.' Therefore, I came to ask you the explanation of a certain difficult passage in the *Ran*." The Maggid took the *Ran* and perused it, and after the briefest of pauses gave him the true explanation. Then and there R' Faivish admitted that the name "Rebbe" indeed was fitting for the Maggid. And from this meeting a close relationship developed between the two. Eventually a marrige took place between R' Feivish's daughter and the Maggid's son. The offspring of this marriage was my father — R' Sholom Shachna." Thus did the Rizhiner end his tale.

Concerning the *shidduch* between R' Feivish and the Malach, we hear the following:

After the passing of the Malach's first wife, his father, the Maggid, sought a second partner for him. The idea of a match with R' Meshulam Feivish was proposed to him. The Maggid sent two respected messengers to Kremenitz on this important mission. They took a large heavy wagon and left for Kremenitz. When they arrived at the Rabbi's house they were told that he was engaged in study in the *beis medrash*. They first began to negotiate with his wife, and afterwards they sought his opinion. R' Meshulam Feivish agreed to the *shidduch* and pressed for the writing of the *tenaim* (marriage contract) right there and then.

When they reached the paragraph relating to the date of the wedding the messengers said that it would be impossible to postpone the marrige, and they immediately requested that the bride — Gittele — come with them.

R' Feivish and his wife claimed that, according to rabbinic law, one must give a girl twelve months to prepare herself for a wedding. Moreover, the entire matter had come as something of a surprise — something which naturally enough required the proper preparation.

The messengers responded that the preparation of a trousseau was of no importance in this case, and that they desired that she travel immediately with them to Mezritch.

It was finally decided that the bride should travel to the wedding in the company of her mother, the *rebbetzin*, since R' Feivish was unable to travel at that particular moment.

ADVOCATE FOR LIFE

THE WIFE OF THE MALACH ONCE HAD A DREAM THAT SHE HAD ENTERED A palace where she found the Divine Tribunal sitting in session. They ruled to take her husband away from her, but she shed hot tears before them and presented many arguments in her attempt to dissuade them. She had the same dream on the second and the third nights, but told no one. On the third night they told her that they had accepted her arguments and that they would extend her husband's life another twelve years. The following day she told this to her father-in-law, the Maggid, and he told her that she had done very well, that she was blessed because through her pleadings she had extended the life of his son another twelve years. And so it was.

From this match of the Malach, the son of the Maggid, and the daughter of R' Meshulam Feivish, was born R' Sholom Shachna, and his brother R' Yisroel Chaim.

The Maggid once appeared in a dream to his daughter-in-law (the wife of his son R' Avrohom the Malach) and told her that her husband should move into her room, or at least she should move his books from his room into her room. In the morning she came to inform her husband of this. He would not listen to her, however, because his father had not told him but only her. In the end, his room with all his books burned during the night.

Several years after the death of the Maggid, his son R' Avrohom the Malach traveled to the city of Hvastov where he accepted the position of Rabbi. He then sent a messenger to bring his wife. That night, when the messenger arrived at her home, she had a dream in which her father-in-law, the Maggid, came to her and told her not to travel in these wagons to Hvastov. In the morning she accordingly refused to travel. This caused confusion among her proposed companions, the *tzaddikim*, R' Zusya of Anipoli and R' Yehudah Leib HaKohen of Puma, because they wanted her to travel with the messenger to join her husband the Malach. Nevertheless, she remained adamant in her refusal. Not many days passed and the Malach, R' Avrohom, fell ill and died and a messenger was dispatched to his wife to inform her of his death. The *tzaddikim*, however, did not want her to know as yet, and they hid his death from her. They did, however, tell her son, R' Sholom Shachna, who was very young at the time, so that he should say *Kaddish*.

His mother, however, noticed something unwonted in her son's behavior, in that he was getting up very early in order to go to the synagogue to say *Kaddish*, something she knew he had never done before. One day she followed him and stood outside the wall of the *beis midrash* in order to hear him say *Kaddish*. She was not able to confirm this until after the prayers were concluded. She then asked her son why he had hidden from her the fact that he was saying the mourner's *Kaddish*. Now it was no longer possible to hide the truth from her.

After the *shivah* days were over, she traveled to the town of Hvastov to take possession of all her husband's effects. She was received there with great honor. They prepared a special meal for her at the inn where she was lodging. But she refused to accept any condolences from the people. At the third meal of Shabbos, nearly every inhabitant in the town was present. As they sang the customary Shabbos *zemiros*, her soul was very bitter and very sad, and she sat on her bed with the wife of the innkeeper. Suddenly, and without transition, she was dreaming, and found herself in a great palace. The door opened, and her husband, R' Avrohom the Malach, came out. His face was lit up and he seemed to be very happy. Behind him came many old and wondrous-looking people. All of them sat around the table and he said to them: "During my lifetime I denied my wife many things that she was really entitled to and I want to beg her forgiveness before you." His wife replied, "You are forgiven

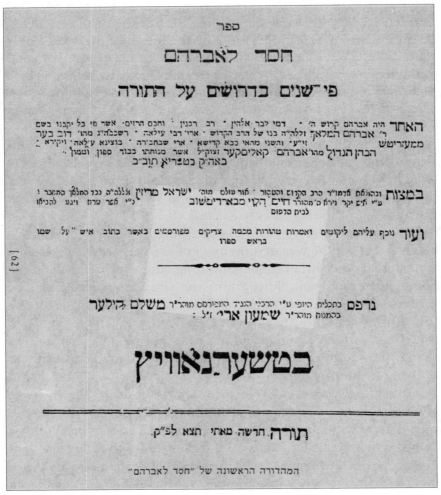

Title page of the sefer Chesed L'Avrohom by R' Avrohom the Malach

wholeheartedly." The Malach said the Torah allowed for his wife to remarry since she was very young. "However, if she should choose not to remarry, I shall take care of her needs."

She awoke from the dream, her face no longer sad because she had been comforted by his words. On her return home, marriages were arranged for her children, while she was able to maintain herself with honor and respect, and in truth she wanted for nothing. On occasions when she needed advice, the Maggid would never fail to appear to her and advise her as to what course of action she should take.

Time passed and the wife of R' Nochum of Chernobyl passed away. R' Nochum would have been pleased to take the Malach's widow as his wife. He spoke with her son R' Sholom Shachna, who was also his son-in-law, and he acquiesced because his mother was still young. R' Sholom Shachna was sent to speak to his mother. On his way to her, R' Sholom Shachna had a dream, and beheld a great palace standing before him, and his father, R' Avrohom the Malach, appeared at the door of the palace with his two hands resting on the roof and was shouting, "Who has the nerve to enter into this palace!" Immediately R' Sholom Shachna awoke and understood the meaning of the dream. He returned to his house and refused to make the trip.

The final resting place of the Malach is in the town of Hvastov.

CHAPTER VI

R' Sholom Shachna
of Prohobisht
(1771-1813)

R'Sholom Shachna was born in 5531 (1771), less than two years prior to the passing of his grandfather, the Maggid. R' Sholom Shachna was about 6 when his father passed away leaving a young widow and two orphan sons. Since the widow decided not to remarry, she brought her two orphaned children to the *tzaddik,* R' Shlomo of Karlin (1738-1792), who took the responsibility of educating and marrying them off. She herself went to the Holy Land. There she refused to reveal her identity and supported herself on her earnings as a laundress. She passed away in Israel and was buried in Tiberias. It was not until R' Sholom Shachna, the great Maggid's grandson, however, that the unique brand of what would be the Rizhiner Chassidus took shape.

He settled in the town of Prohobisht in the Ukraine with the commitment to fostering a national and spiritual renaissance of the

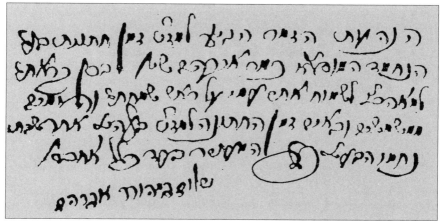

Signature of R' Sholom Shachna of Prohobisht

Jewish people, on the model of the scope and authority of the *Reish Galusa*[1] in Babylonia.

R' Sholom Shachna belonged to the category of righteous leaders who could not simply follow the steps of their forebears but were born to innovate; he functioned on a more elevated spiritual level. That which he received from his forefathers, the pioneers of Chassidus (in general), he desired to expand and perfect through his own resources. His grasp of Chassidus springs away from the restraints and routines that began to establish themselves among his contemporaries; routines against which he passionately rebelled. After the passing of the Maggid, Chassidus stood at a crossroads, with each of the Maggid's disciples adding his own interpretations and approaches to conventional chassidic thought and practice. R' Sholom Shachna likewise added his own approach, a spiritual path that was an outgrowth of his own personal qualities. R' Sholom Shachna introduced a rare quality of royalty — *malchus* — which he passed on to his son Yisroel, the founder of the Rizhiner dynasty. The son expanded this quality and raised it to its highest levels of *tiferes she'b'malchus*, regal splendor.

R' Sholom Shachna's revolution against the chassidic trends of his time was the product of many factors and values. He refused to

---

1. The title *Reish Galusa*, Head of the Exile, was held by the head of the Jewish community in Babylonia, who was referred to as the Prince of the Captivity, or Exilarch.

take into account the material means and miracles used by the *tzaddikim*, such as those of his wife's grandfather, R' Nochum of Chernobyl. He wished to help all Jews, rich and poor alike. His means lay in the spiritual and mental realms. The righteous man, who himself stands at a lofty spiritual height, and whose soul lights up the world from end to end, must be capable of descending to the spiritual depths of the humblest and weakest soul, in order to lift that soul to the light. Thus, he sees nothing extraordinary in the Talmudic statement of Shmuel that "the paths of the firmament are as bright and clear to me as the paths of [my city] Nehardea" (*Berachos* 58b). "It is much more difficult to descend to the roots of the nether world," said R' Sholom Shachna. There is a mission to raise the lower world from darkness to brighten and illuminate it like the heavenly glow. This task falls upon the righteous man, the *tzaddik,* whose roots are close to royalty, and whose soul is linked to the souls of the Jewish monarchs from generation to generation.

R' Sholom Shachna took cognizance of the fact that he traced his lineage to the House of Dovid and that his soul was of the spark of King Dovid; hence, like Dovid, he perceived his mission to be humble.

In the house of R' Shlomo of Karlin the two orphaned sons of the Malach grew to manhood. R' Yisroel Chaim, the firstborn, was later to become the son-in-law of the Karliner, and the latter sought a suitable match for R' Sholom Shachna, the younger son. For this purpose he sent two messengers to a certain city, and charged them prior to their departure, "On your way to that town you will have to pass through the town of Prohobisht, where R' Nochum of Chernobyl (1730-1797) lives. When you pass through I warn you not to tarry there, but to continue onwards to your appointed destination."

The messengers departed, arriving at Prohobisht on a Friday. They remembered the command of their master and did not remain in the town but rather continued on their way, hastening to reach the next town in order to spend Shabbos there.

At the exact time when the messengers passed through the town of Prohobisht, however, R' Nochum woke from his afternoon nap. In his sleep, he had seen himself in the upper world where he heard them saying, "R' Nochum, now the time is ripe to make a match between your granddaughter and the grandson of your teacher, the Maggid of Mezritch." Immediately he saw there the Malach, father of the groom. They shook hands and the *shidduch* was confirmed. R' Nochum woke up and "behold it was a dream." He asked his people, "Did you just see a wagon passing through this town?" to which they replied, "Indeed we did see a wagon and in it two men passing with great haste through the town." The *tzaddik* immediately commanded that people be sent to overtake the wagon and return it to the town. Those entrusted with the task overtook the wagon on the outskirts of the next town and insisted, in the name of the *tzaddik*, that the men return to Prohobisht to spend Shabbos there. When the men reached the house of the *tzaddik*, he told them his dream and that the *shidduch* had already been completed between him and the groom's father in the upper world. When the men saw that *the matter stemmed from Hashem* (*Bereishis* 24:50), they remained in Prohobisht for Shabbos and on Sunday they returned to R' Shlomo of Karlin and told him the story. Once R' Shlomo heard that the match was concluded in heaven, he brought himself to accept the idea and R' Sholom was taken to Prohobisht to the home of R' Nochum to become the groom of his granddaughter, Chavah, his daughter Malkala's child. After the wedding R' Sholom Shachna remained in the home of his wife's grandfather, R' Nochum of Chernobyl.

Like his father, R' Avrohom the Malach, R' Sholom Shachna was accustomed to solitude, and he ate and drank a bare minimum. He was fond of saying, "A person should always eat and drink little, and even though there is no proof to the statement, there is a sign supporting it. A camel eats little and lives long. A horse eats much but his days are short." It was only with special permission that one could come before him.

After R' Sholom Shachna settled in Prohobisht, he began to actualize his long-contemplated goal, the formation of a new image of chassidic leadership. He had something which his predecessors apparently lacked, which was precisely a new approach in Chassidus. He differed outwardly from contemporary chassidic leaders in his style of dress. In preference to wearing white clothes, as was common among most *tzaddikim*, he ordered stylish woolen clothes sewn with buttons. Woolen garments were in general suspect of *shaatnez* (the Torah prohibits the mixing of wool and linen in the same garment), and the chassidim were stringent in their avoidance of them. Even buttons were considered an innovation. He was fastidious both in his wardrobe and in the matter of the length of his *peyos* (sidecurls), taking pains that they be no longer than required ritually. He created a magnificent environment for himself, maintaining a beautiful home, with a large garden. His royalty reflected itself in the nobility of his outward appearance as well as in his radiant composure. It appeared clearly that the purpose behind this new spiritual path was his recognition and faith that his soul was infused with the regal spark of the soul of King Dovid.

A chronicle of the refined habits and the daily routine of R' Sholom Shachna is included at the end of *Chessed L'Avrohom*, the work of his father, R' Avrohom the Malach. In it we find how R' Sholom Shachna himself justified his luxurious wardrobe:

> "And when you will wear comely garments you will say, Behold I invite my body to wear comely garments in order to fulfill that which is stated, *Prepare yourself for the coming of your G-d, Israel* (*Amos* 4:12). For when one goes before the king, one must wear clothes of distinction; how much more so before the King of kings, the Almighty, but not, Heaven forbid, in order to take pride in them. It is also written, in the name of the Maggid, that if one were to stand before a king, he would certainly fear to think alien thoughts and desires; how much more so before the King of kings, the Almighty. Know that you always stand before Him ..." (based on *Tractate Derech Eretz*).

The realization that he was descended from King Dovid influenced him in this regard, as did the teaching of R' Shlomo of Karlin with whom he studied in his youth. The latter (murdered by Polish farmers in the year 5552/1792) was a disciple of the great Maggid. He used to say, "The greatest sin of a Jew is that he forgets that he is a prince." R' Sholom Shachna never forgot that he was a prince, and with every step he tried to insure that this fact be recognized and remembered. He conducted himself in an independent manner, without regard to what others might think. He functioned as a free man, an independent thinker and creator of an original viewpoint in Chassidus, and thus he is remembered.

R' Sholom Shachna's princely behavior inspired respect in the Jewish world. R' Boruch of Mezhibozh, the grandson of the Baal Shem Tov, said concerning him that his reality was unique in his generation. In chassidic circles, there was amazement that in such hard times for Israel, in the tyranny of Czarist Russia, he managed to establish a royal house, almost entirely without moral support or material help from external sources.

It is told that the *tzaddik* R' Aryeh Leib of Bender (d. 1859), brother of R' Moshe of Savrani, was an enthusiastic follower of R' Sholom Shachna and and was very attached to him. Each day before praying, he was accustomed to praise the Rebbe. And if no one appeared to whom he could sing R' Sholom Shachna's praises, he would instead cry out, with his *tallis* on his shoulders, "The Rebbe, R' Sholom Shachna, the Rebbe, R' Sholom Shachna, the Rebbe, R' Sholom Shachna!"

The greatly revered Shpoler Zeide (d. 1811) held R' Sholom Shachna in great esteem. It is told that when the building of the synagogue in Shpole was completed, the "Zeide" sent an invitation to R' Sholom Shachna of Prohobisht to dedicate the house of prayer, and he was placed at the forefront of the dignitaries. The Shpole himself served the guests, dressed in a white apron like a *Kohen Gadol* (high priest), and afterwards went out to dance before the Rebbe, R' Sholom Shachna, and said, "It is fitting and appropriate that when the father is an angel and the mother an angel that such a son should be born to them…"

From then on, R' Sholom Shachna followed his path without interference. Even then, while at the home of his grandfather-in-law in Chernobyl, there gathered about him young scholars of his own age who venerated him and bound themselves to him, for he combined Torah, wisdom and Chassidus with a delightful and aristocratic spirit. All his energies were devoted to restoring the glory of the House of Dovid. His behavior was that of a crown prince, whose children would follow him in the line of kingly succession.

R' Sholom Shachna was not able to learn much from his father, "the Malach," who died at a very young age, yet he inherited from his father the inclination and the courage to walk in new paths. R' Sholom Shachna's path was clear before him, although none of his predecessors had walked it. In spite of its many risks, it was his highway.

The question that most concerned him was: Why had this exile been so long? He sought the answers as to how to hasten the redemption of a nation rotting in the waste and refuse of exile. Clearly, one must first uplift the nation from the waste heap, but how could this be done?... He recalled the teaching of his master R' Shlomo of Karlin, who had said:

> *If you desire to raise a man floundering in the refuse heap in the mud, do not think that you will be able to remain above and that it will suffice to throw him a rope. No, you will have to descend completely into the refuse and the mud, and hold him and yourself and pull both of you up into the light ...*

He felt that there was a way to help people without recourse to the methods that the *tzaddikim* of his generation had adopted. Once he was traveling with his grandfather-in-law, R' Nochum, when they arrived at a inn. The innkeeper's wife was in the throes of severe labor pains. The innkeeper besought the elder *tzaddik* to help relieve the pregnant woman of her pain. R' Nochum commanded that four items be prepared: an empty room, a *mikveh*, a new table and 160 copper coins. When R' Sholom Shachna saw all of this preparation, he removed himself from the scene and did not return until everything was over. Upon his return, his grandfather-in-law chided him, "My son, it would have become you to remain inside and learn from me the method of *pidyon hanefesh* (redemption of the soul). Why did you leave?" He replied, "I have no desire to learn such a method, for should one of the items be lacking, it would be impossible to perform a *pidyon hanefesh* in any way. I would rather be able to bring about salvation through all things, small and large, without any 'soul redemption,' without the loss, G-d forbid, of even one Jewish soul."

Eventually the time came for R' Sholom Shachna to leave the household of the Chernobyler and make his own way. So R' Nochum went to Chernobyl and R' Sholom Shachna remained in

Prohobisht where he began to serve as the chassidic Rebbe. All types of Jews came to him, great Torah scholars, ordinary householders, the wealthy, but mainly the poor and simple folk. He conversed with each visitor in a manner understandable to that person. He evaluated everyone fairly, bringing out the true inner self of all.

It is told: Once he was standing near the window in his room. In the room, among all his followers, there was a rich man. The Rebbe gazed out the window and told the rich man, "I have already inherited the entire city of Uman; indeed the whole city is now coming to see me." At that juncture six Jews, whose clothes evinced their poverty, arrived from the city of Uman. They presented R' Sholom Shachna with an "introductory letter" signed by ten men — these six present, and another four who could not meet the costs of the journey. The six produced "soul redemption" (money), each one the same amount, including funds for the absent ones. R' Sholom Shachna was overjoyed to see them and welcomed them. The rich man who stood there saw the entire occurrence and broke into laughter. When the men left, R' Sholom Shachna asked the rich man why he had laughed. He answered, "Why should I not laugh? When the Rebbe announces that he has inherited the entire city of Uman I thought that many wealthy men would come, and here I see but six poor people came." R' Sholom Shachna said to him, "Believe me, these men are better able to discern right from wrong than the whole city of Uman ..."

THE WAY TO DIRECT YOUR MIND...

THE WAY TO DIRECT YOUR MIND TO HASHEM AND HIS SERVICE IS THROUGH *kavannah*, meditation from the heart, which helps man accept fully upon himself the awe and love of Hashem. Meditation from the heart and *d'veikus* are means to separate yourself from this materialistic world and to be constantly aware of the presence of Hashem.

The Gemara states, "The early chassidim used to wait one hour before *davening*" (*Berachos* 30b). What did they do during this hour? They prayed in order to be able to perform their prayers with the proper *kavannah*. This particular preparation before the daily prayers was intended to achieve the right attention and full concentration during the regular prayers.

Said the Maggid of Mezritch, "In Chassidus, Torah and prayer are complementary. One should study Torah as a preparation for *tefillah* and after prayer, go and study Torah again" (R' Mordechai of Kremenitz, *Tzava'os Vehanhagos*, Bnei Brak 1977, l.c.138).

Once R' Sholom Shachna found himself in the home of R' Pinchos of Koritz. The *tzaddik* invited him to dine. R' Pinchos always stored garlic on a high post on the ceiling beam. R' Pinchos climbed up on a bench in order to retrieve some garlic. R' Sholom Shachna sat and watched as the *tzaddik* climbed up, wondering why such an elderly man as R' Pinchos would bother to climb so high solely to obtain some garlic. The Koritzer was conscious of R' Sholom Shachna's wonder and said, "I am but climbing up to Hashem, may His Name be blessed." R' Sholom Shachna said to him, "And I — from my very place — am with Hashem."

These words — "The place where I am, there is Hashem" — have become an aphorism among the chassidim. These were not empty words of arrogance or power-seeking; rather, they encapsulated the essence of an entire *weltanschauung* (worldview), the fruit of his continuing contemplation, his thoughts and ideas. It is clear that he arrived at this conclusion concerning the relationship between man and his Creator on the basis of his chassidic way of thinking. According to this outlook, man, alone created in the image of Hashem, becomes a harmonious creation — "all of whose outward movements are but manifestations of his inner soul, and he himself (man) is but a part of a life spirit that breathes life into all the essence which Hashem has wrought through His Spirit." This feeling is the heritage of the higher individual — the *tzaddik* — and therefore the *tzaddik* must take extreme care that all of his actions are directed to this goal (the harmony of creation) and not its opposite, chaos. A *tzaddik* must rule over all of his actions and never do anything that is wasteful of him or his powers. He explained the verse (*Chabbakuk* 2:4), *And the righteous person shall live through his faith*, to mean, the *tzaddik* who believes this in himself, he shall live. He consequently established for himself a set of values in prayer, in eating, drinking, for dress and for all other things pertaining to daily life, in order that everything further that cosmic harmony.

R' Sholom Shachna was filled with love of mankind. We find in this connection the following passage in his remarks regarding a valid religious outlook:

> "One should be careful to observe the passage, *I will teach the sinful Your ways* (*Tehillim* 51:15), in order to take them out of the wrong paths and bring them to the sanctity which will bring pleasure to the eyes of their Creator. Also, one must be careful to observe the commandment of, *And you shall love your fellow as yourself* (*Vayikra* 19:18).
>
> "*Hashem's portion is His people* (*Devarim* 32:9), for in essence all Jews are of one root; only in their physical existence do they differ. Thus, he who hates one of them hates them all, and he who loves them becomes one with them, both with their bodies and their roots in the heavens above …"

He was asked, "How is it possible to love an evil man?" He answered, "Is it not true that each man's soul is but a portion of Hashem above, and is it not a pity that the holy spark of Hashem within him is captured in that which has been shattered …"

He empathized in a deep and humane way with the souls of those who suffered, who were sick and in pain, and with the sinner. He understood the spiritual trials of the great and the lowly alike. It is indeed interesting to study his outlook on sin and the concept of *teshuvah* (repentance). Once it happened that a woman, through accident and lack of caution, asphyxiated her baby while sleeping with him in the same bed. The Rabbis of the generation imposed upon her the penance belonging to one who is in the category of a negligent murderer and decreed that she leave her home and wander from place to place, each Monday and Thursday, until her sin should be forgiven. In the course of her wanderings, she chanced upon the city of R' Sholom Shachna, and upon meeting him told him the story of her sin and the penance imposed upon her. She asked him when her sin would be forgiven. R' Sholom Shachna told her, "Return, daughter, to your home, eat and drink each

Monday and Thursday, beautify yourself and cease your fasting." He subsequently explained his statement: "It is well known that the proper repentance is *teshuvas hamishkal,* the repentance that fits the crime, and according to the severity of the crime is the severity of the repentance.

"Of what sin was this woman guilty? She caused the loss of a soul from Israel. If she returns to her home and eats and drinks, she will be pleasant in the eyes of her husband and will be able to rectify her transgression by giving birth to another child in place of the deceased. This is in fact the fitting repentance for her for she has already received her punishment at the hands of those who judged her. But if she continues to wander and fast and mortify herself, she will become unwelcome to her husband, nor will she any longer be able to live with him, thus making it impossible for her to properly atone for her sin and rectify the damage."

On this basis, R' Sholom Shachna interpreted the psalm (51:1,2), *... a psalm of Dovid, when Nosson the prophet came to him after he had come to Bas-sheva* — Dovid returned to Hashem and said this psalm to Him with the same passion with which he had gone to Bas-sheva. That is why Hashem forgave him instantly.

The paths of the soul of man shone for R' Sholom Shachna as brightly as the paths of heaven. He understood the depths of the soul of the most insignificant man, crying out for redemption. Likewise he comprehended the struggles of a great man, fighting his evil inclinations. He envisioned man freed from the burden of materialism and physical reality that pulls him downward, and he searched for the means to raise up, as in the story of the wagon driver who came to complain of his sick calf, when in truth he meant to pray for the uplifting of his soul to a higher level. R' Sholom Shachna dreamt of redeeming the entire Jewish nation from the burdens of exile. He visualized the kingdom of Israel and saw himself as standing in the first rank of its leaders.

He directed his heart toward a redemption that he saw as flowering not out of "doing justice" but out of practicing *rachamim,* mercy. *The world will be built out of mercy (Tehillim* 89:3) — that was his slogan. The sinful world will be restored and the sinner redeemed through a redeemer whose defining quality will be that of mercy. This idea we gather from his response to R' Boruch of Mezhibozh, the grandson of the Baal Shem Tov. It is told that when R' Boruch, known for his pedantic exactitude, suggested to R' Sholom Shachna, "Both of us will rule the world," R' Sholom Shachna answered, "I alone can rule the world." With this he enunciated not only his faith in his personal qualifications but more fundamentally, his repudiation of R' Boruch's approach of ruling harshly, with justice and exactitude. Thus we can understand the story told by his grandson R' Dovid Moshe of Chortkov, heard from his father the Rizhiner.

Once R' Sholom Shachna had a mystical experience. His spirit went from temple to temple until he came to one that was decorated with jewels from top to bottom, resplendent in glory. In this temple stood a table and a chair. On the table lay a crown studded with precious stones and pearls, the splendor of which could not be adequately described, and on the chair that was beside the table sat a great *tzaddik*, whose name he did not wish to reveal. R' Sholom Shachna realized that this wondrous crown lying on the table came from the Torah and mitzvos performed by the great *tzaddik* sitting on the chair. Because in life he ruled the world with exactitude, he did not merit wearing the crown upon his head. Afterwards, R' Sholom Shachna awoke and sent for his son R' Yisroel, the future Rizhiner, who was at that time still a young boy. R' Sholom Shachna told his son what had transpired, and he added: "I am telling you this story for there shall come a time when it will stand you in good stead ..."

R' Sholom Shachna passed on his vision of redemption to his children. He firmly believed that from them would descend the leaders of Israel until the advent of the *Mashiach*. He would say of the passage. "To the many offices, and endless peace" (*Yeshaya* 9:2): "Before the coming of *Mashiach* there will be many governments, 'many offices,' many leaders and spokesmen for the Jews, but 'no end to *sholom*,' to my descendants there will be no end, for there will always be *tzaddikim* descended from me until the end of days ..."

His grandson, R' Nochum of Shtefanesht, tells, moreover, of how R' Sholom Shachna wrestled with the Angel of Death in order to learn from his hand the secret of the End of Days and the coming of *Mashiach*. The following story demonstrates R' Sholom Shachna's determination to hasten the End of Days and to bring near the future redemption:

When the Jews sinned and exile was decreed for them, Hashem summoned the Angel of Death to tell him that the Jews were given into his hands to suffer in exile for a thousand years. The Angel of Death demurred. Hashem asked him why. He answered, "I have already seen the bitter ends of Pharaoh and of Nebuchadnezzar." Hashem rejoined, "Behold, I have placed them in your hands for a thousand years." Still, the Angel of Death remained adamant. Hashem then said, "Here, I am giving you one special *yichud*, union, upon which the future redemption depends, and no angel or *seraph* will be able to disclose it. The only way that it will be revealed is if some man born of woman will be able to divine the secret, and then the redemption will come. But the secret of this union is placed in your hands, and no angel or *seraph* can reveal it."

The Angel of Death overflowed with happiness at the thought that the Jews would be permanently in exile. Yet, when the light of the holy teacher, R' Shimon bar Yochai, and his colleagues began to shine, and when they began to try hastening the redemption, they asked for advice as to how to attain the secret of the "union," but met with little success. Afterwards the Holy *Ari*, R' Yitzchak Luria, arose and he shook whole worlds in his fierce determination to discover how long and extensive would be the suffering of the Jews in exile. The heavens told him that there was one "union" upon which the future redemption depends: a secret that can never be revealed, only discovered. If a person were to discover this "union" on his own, then the redemption could come about. The holy *Ari* separated himself from the concerns of this world and devoted himself completely to finding the secret of this "union." He eventually passed away without having discovered it.

The search continued and continued in succeeding generations until the Baal Shem Tov, and after him our grandfather the Maggid, R' Dov Ber of Mezritch, who also met with no success, for he was very sickly. The quest was passed on to his son, the Malach, but in his days no gains were achieved, until finally the search was continued by his son who was our grandfather, the Rebbe R' Sholom Shachna of Prohobisht. And when R' Sholom Shachna reflected that so many great *tzaddikim* before him had tried unsuccessfully, he attempted a form of espionage. To this end, he dressed in the manner of worldliness and materialism, so that no one would discern any holiness of service of Hashem within him, and that even the Angel of Death would count him as one of his own. He succeeded in befriending the Angel of Death and in attaining his confidence, so that the latter lowered his guard before him and revealed to him all of his secrets — including the secret of the "union." Our grandfather began to delve into this "union" and the redemption started to spark. Once the Angel of Death realized what was happening, he shook the world to find the culprit who had revealed the secret, asking all of the angels. Finally, the angel Metatron came and laughed at him, saying, "Look! A man born of a woman has brought out this secret from your very hands, through a ruse."

Immediately, the Angel of Death came to our grandfather, R' Sholom Shachna, with the intention of killing him. Once again, our grandfather chose the way of trickery in order to fool the Angel of Death. He went to the marketplace where he bought a fowl from a certain non-Jewess, and he took the money from his own hand and placed it in hers. When the Angel of Death saw this, he could not believe that our grandfather had betrayed him, but he still asked why he busied himself with the secret of this "union." Our grandfather responded, "Look, you can readily see for yourself that I am one of your own, since you desire that Israel remain permanently in exile; I too desire it." But when the Angel of Death saw the light of the redemption waxing stronger day by day, he knew he had been betrayed, and he returned to our grandfather and said to him: "I will remove my attention from the whole world just to deal with you and your children if you do not tell the truth."

Then our grandfather was distressed, and he promised that he would no longer engage in study of the "union." "But," he told the Angel of Death, "to my descendants, I will extend the Holy Spirit from under the very Throne of Glory, and they will not fear you; they will renounce their bodies from the day of their birth."

R' Sholom Shachna wanted to hasten the *keitz* (end of the Diaspora) and to deceive the Angel of Death by way of his actions — he changed his mode of dress and behaved in ways that would incite opposition and complaint, but in truth this was an overt ritual on his part in order to hide his inner holy way. He remained unsuccessful, but he passed this secret to his son — Yisroel of Rizhin.

Three sons were born to R' Sholom Shachna: the eldest, R' Avrohom; the second, R' Yisroel; and the third, R' Dov Ber, who was the intended son-in-law of R' Levi Yitzchok of Berditchev, but died in childhood.

R' Sholom Shachna died at an early age, as had his father the Malach. He left his eldest son, the 16-year-old Avrohom, and his second son R' Yisroel, an orphan of 6. His spiritual inheritor was his younger son, R' Yisroel, founder of the Rizhiner dynasty.

After the passing of the Chozeh of Lublin (5575-1815), one of the Lubliner chassidim came to R' Yisroel in the second year of his ascendancy. R' Yisroel asked him, "Were you able to attain a close relationship with the Rebbe of Lublin"? The chassid answered that for eighteen years he had been a regular house guest of the Chozeh of Lublin. R' Yisroel asked him to tell a story about his Rebbe. The chassid said, "Every Shabbos at the third meal the Lubliner would count the names of all of the righteous men in the world and say, 'This *tzaddik* is lighting up this palace, and this *tzaddik* is brightening that palace.' And if any *tzaddik* had passed away, he knew of it. In the week that your father, R' Sholom

Tomb of the Chozeh of Lublin

Shachna, passed away, the Lubliner said, 'Woe! Woe that the holy *tzaddik*, R' Sholom Shachna of Prohobisht, has passed away. But I am comforted, for he has left two sons, the elder who will brighten his own palace, and the second, who has no special place set for him, for he is endowed with the soul of King Solomon.' " When R' Yisroel heard these words, he wept, saying, "It appears that he was a true prophet."

The Rebbe, R' Tzvi Hirsch of Rimanov, asked the Rizhiner why his father R' Sholom Shachna had chosen for himself such a new and dangerous path in the service of Hashem. He answered, "The Baal Shem Tov passed on to the father of our family, the great Maggid of Mezritch, a jewel, the true way of Chassidus. The Maggid hid this jewel within a fortress of Torah and prayer. But the 'thieves from above,' Samael, the Evil One, and his robbers who prey constantly upon those who serve the *tzaddik* of the generation, crept into the fortress and tried to destroy the jewel. R' Avrohom, the Malach, came and re-polished the stone, building for it a fortress of holiness and purity on the foundation of his fasts and suffering. But even there the thieves entered and tried all manner of contrivance to destroy the jewel. My father, of blessed memory, rose and found an alternative course. He hid the jewel in a garbage heap of self-elevation, glory and honor, and it has been in a safe place ever since. The 'sons of the dark path' can never know that under this garbage heap lies such a precious stone."

The *tzaddik* R' Moshe of Savrani and the Rizhiner had a disagreement regarding certain matters. The Savranier came to the Rizhiner to placate him, as he had been requested by the *Oheiv Yisroel* ("Lover of Israel"), the Rebbe of Apt. The Rizhiner asked, "Do you believe that the essence of the *tzaddik* is bound up with the Creator ceaselessly?" "It is possible," answered the Savranier, with some hesitation. "It was so with my grandfather, the holy Malach," cried the Rizhiner. "That's why he did not live long in this world," observed the Savranier. "And thus was my father, R' Sholom Shachna, too," added the Rizhiner. "And he too did not live long," added the Savranier. "What are you speaking of — longevity?!" the Rizhiner could not restrain himself. "Do we come into this world to shrivel up? They came, performed their service and returned to their source."

Thus did the Rizhiner evaluate the brief lives and works of his fathers.

R' Sholom Shachna passed away the day before Succos, at the young age of 42. Thus concluded the pioneering trials and tribulations of R' Sholom Shachna's short-lived career. He left his heritage and new chassidic *anschauung* to be actualized and enhanced by his charismatic younger son, R' Yisroel, the progenitor of the House of Rizhin.

R' SHOLOM SHACHNA ONCE REMARKED: "THE TALMUD TELLS OF THE WISE Shmuel who was well versed in astronomy, and who once declared:

ASTRONOMIC EXPLORATION 'The paths of the firmament are as bright and clear to me as the streets of Nehardea' (his city) (*Berachos* 58b). Now, if only we could say the same about ourselves, that the streets of our city are as clear and bright to us as the paths of the firmament! For to allow the hidden light of Hashem to shine out in this lowest world, the world of matter, that is the greater achievement of the two!"

ONCE, ON THE EVE OF ROSH HASHANAH IN THE *KLOIZ* (SMALL CHASSIDIC synagogue), while R' Nochum of Chernobyl was reciting Minchah

THE LIFTING OF SOULS with great ecstasy, his grandson-in-law, R' Sholom Shachna, who would recite this *tefillah* at the *amud* (reader's lectern), suddenly felt a spiritual depression. All the people around him were praying with great *kavannah*, while he needed all the strength he could muster just to utter one word after the other, and to grasp the simple meaning of each word. He felt very concerned and dejected. After Minchah services, R' Nochum said to him: "My son, how your prayer took Heaven by storm today! It lifted up thousands of excommunicated souls."

CHASSIDUS REMINDS US THAT ALL OUR ACTIONS AND MITZVOS ARE TO BE preceded by the *LeShem Yichud* instituted by R' Yitzchak Luria, a kab-

ON INTENTIONS PRIOR TO MITZVOS balistic formula expressing the intent that the mitzvah be performed in a manner most pleasing to Hashem. R' Elimelech of Lizhensk (1717-1786) advises: "In everything you do, whether Torah, prayer or mitzvos that require action,

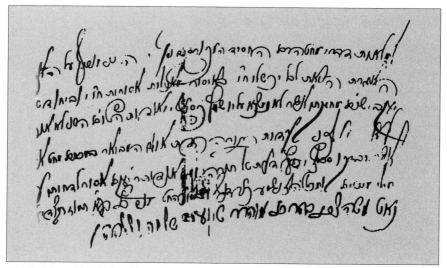

Handwriting of R' Moshe of Savrani

accustom yourself to say beforehand, 'I am doing this for the sake of the unification of the Holy One, Blessed is He, and His *Shechinah*, and to give pleasure to the Creator, Blessed is He' " (see *Tzetl Katan*, #4).

There are chassidim who say general intentions before any thing they do. Such was the custom of R' Tzvi Hirsh of Zidichov who uttered unifications even before a drink of water (*Ateres Tiferes* p. 7).

It is common to meditate a preparatory unification before performing a mitzvah with thought, speech and deed, as found in the writings of R' Sholom Shachna of Prohobisht. He designates and advises such an intention, to be said loudly before a meal, stating: "I am eating in order that I may have energy to do Hashem's commandments." He similarly advises that before donning nice clothes one should not have motives of pride but say, "I am putting on these nice clothes to fulfill the verse: *Prepare to meet your G-d, O Israel*" (*Amos* 4:12). And when you put on warm clothing on a cold day, say, "I am putting on these warm clothes to keep my body healthy for the service of Hashem."

Meditations, or unifications, performed before or during the actualization of a mitzvah refer to Hashem as the prime source of energy, as it were, which directs the limbs, the brain and the senses of the body to do the will of Hashem. Therefore, one would say, "My will is to do Your will, O Hashem. I am making myself a chariot for the *Shechinah*" (*Seder HaYom*, loc. cit.).

EFFECTIVE CONFESSION

R' SHOLOM SHACHNA OF PROHOBISHT URGES THE PIOUS JEW AS FOLLOWS: "You should make your request to Hashem, but before you conclude the *Amidah* and say, 'Who hears prayer,' you should make a last, general confession, for if you confess and abandon your wrongdoing, you will receive mercy from Above ... At the conclusion of the *Amidah*, when you bow, the *kelipos* see that you have come before the King of all kings, Blessed is He, and have exited from His presence. Then they begin making many accusations. At that point, you should make a full confession out loud so that you cut off all accusers, since he who confesses and accepts the punishment is released" (*Seder HaYom* in *Dvir Yaakov*, p. 6).

ONE OF R' SHOLOM SHACHNA'S CHASSIDIM HAPPENED TO BE PRESENT when R' Shneur Zalman of Liadi visited the town on a Shabbos and

THE HOLY RUG said Torah with intense emotion. But suddenly it seemed to the chassid that the Liadier grew less fervent, that his *drashah* (homily) appeared to lack the passion that he evidenced earlier. The next time the chassid came to his Rebbe, R' Sholom Shachna, he mentioned the incident, and clearly stated his surprise. "How can you comprehend or judge such matters!" said the Prohobishter. "You haven't studied enough to do that. But I shall tell you: There is a very high and holy *madreigah* (rung) — and he who reaches it is freed of all earthly matters and can no longer kindle the flame."

After R' Sholom Shachna's demise, his wife, Chavah, went to the Apter Rav to receive condolences. The Apter told her, "It is similar to the plight of an unfortunate merchant who must abide four or six weeks, while others purchase all their needs in two or three days," meaning that some people can accomplish their Divinely assigned task on earth in relatively short lifetimes!

PART II:
R' YISROEL
OF RIZHIN

RIZHIN DYNASTY

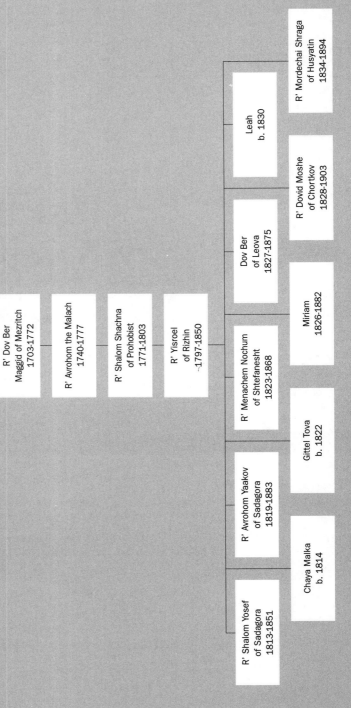

R' Dov Ber
Maggid of Mezritch
1703-1772

R' Avrohom the Malach
1740-1777

R' Shalom Shachna
of Prohobist
1771-1803

R' Yisroel
of Rizhin
~1797-1850

R' Shalom Yosef
of Sadagora
1813-1851

R' Avrohom Yaakov
of Sadagora
1819-1883

R' Menachem Nochum
of Shtefanesht
1823-1868

Dov Ber
of Leova
1827-1875

Leah
b. 1830

Chaya Malka
b. 1814

Gittel Tova
b. 1822

Miriam
1826-1882

R' Dovid Moshe
of Chortkov
1828-1903

R' Mordechai Shraga
of Husyatin
1834-1894

CHAPTER VII

THE EARLY YEARS OF RABBI YISROEL OF RIZHIN

LEGEND RAISED R' YISROEL UP ON OUTSTRETCHED WINGS TO LOFTY HEIGHTS to which no previous chassidic rabbi had been raised, save the Baal Shem Tov himself. He was born on the night of Rosh Hashanah, in the year 5557 (1797), in the province of Prohobisht in the district of Kiev, Russia. His father was the *tzaddik* R' Sholom Shachna, son of R' Avrohom, the Malach, son of the Maggid, R' Dov Ber of Mezritch, a disciple of the Baal Shem Tov, who was the founder of the chassidic movement. His mother was the granddaughter of R' Nochum of Chernobyl, a *talmid-chaver* of the Baal Shem Tov.

Legend encompassed him from "cradle to grave" — for surely clouds bore him aloft to his final resting place. Chassidim explain the verse in *Tehillim* (68:19): *You ascended on high, You have taken captives, You took gifts of man.* When Moshe went up to heaven to receive the

Tablets, he brought down from there a present — holy souls that had been imprisoned since the days of Adam in the hands of Satan, as a type of pledge to appease him, so that he would desist from incriminating mankind. Since all the angels of heaven gave presents to Moshe, the Satan also came of his own accord and brought him a gift of these holy souls. And these were: R' Shimon bar Yochai; Yitzchak ben Shimon and the Ari Hakadosh; R' Yisroel Baal Shem Tov and R' Yisroel ben Sholom Shachna. And all of them are alluded to in the initials of the word *shevi* (שֶׁבִי, *captivity*). According to the chassidic tradition, before he died the Baal Shem Tov said that forty years after his passing, he would return to the world, and one great *tzaddik* hinted that in order to understand that שבי alludes to the Rizhiner, one needs to write his name in Hebrew: ישראל בן שלום, Yisroel ben Sholom. They told wonders about the boy Yisroel — his righteousness, his wisdom, the depth of his perception, about his being an *ilui* (genius), not only in Torah, but also in his level of *yiras shamayim* (fear of Hashem).

When R' Avrohom Yehoshua Heschel of Apt, the *tzaddik* of the generation, saw R' Yisroel's mother was expecting, he described her as a holy ark wherein was contained a *sefer Torah*. The Apter Rav said of him, "He did not forget any of his learning from the womb, and as the Torah is written above, black fire on white fire, so is it always before the Rizhiner."

His great-grandson R' Nochum Dov once said: "Avrohom our father became aware of Hashem when he was 3 years old. The Rizhiner knew him when he was born, except that he did not have complete understanding then. When he saw his mother on the bed, he said, 'Hashem created this.' Afterwards, when he saw the house, he said that Hashem created this also. Once when he was a little boy, like all the other children, he made a small garden to play in. His brother, R' Avrohom, said to him, 'My beloved, you should know that it is almost Shabbos.' The boy raised his eyes to heaven and answered, 'Yes, I know.' His brother asked him how he, Yisroel, knew this. He answered, 'Don't you see that the sky is changing?' At that time, R' Yisroel was not yet 3 years old."

Once, when R' Yisroel was 5 or 6 years old, his father entered the boys' room, as was his custom, to see his children. There he found his younger son walking back and forth alone, clapping his hands, crushing his fingers and crying out. "Why are you weeping, my son?" he asked. The boy stopped for a moment and said, "Father, I was just thinking of all the times I lifted my hands today, but not for the sake of Heaven."

It is told that R' Shneur Zalman of Liadi, founder of the Chabad movement, once had to pass through Prohobisht. The *rebbetzin* of Prohobisht, Chavah, came with her two sons to the Rav of Liadi. R' Shneur Zalman was impressed by both of them, and especially the younger, who asked him a question that the Rav of Liadi remembered for the rest of his life, and used to repeat on different occasions. It was a difficult question: When we read the first verse of the *Shema*, we must say it with such dedication that we would be willing to sacrifice our lives. How, then, can we immediately afterward say, *v'ahavta* (and you shall love), which is the epitome of existence and being? He was 7 years of age when he asked this question of the Rav of Liadi, who was impressed, not only by the question, but also by the youth's understanding of the profound answer which he offered based on the *Chabad* approach.

The wisdom of the Rizhiner, as a popular leader to his devoted following, expressed itself in his pithy talk and agile mind. He knew how to embrace whole systems of thought in one sentence or a short story (where the tendency of Chabad for instance was to expound at length, although the profundity of its ideas and the broadness of its horizons did not penetrate so well the minds of the readers or listeners as did the Rizhiner's concise statements, preceded by a parable which he put across with such laconic incisiveness).

R' Sholom Shachna of Prohobisht passed away the day before Succos (1803), survived by two sons, R' Avrohom, called the Small Malach after his grandfather, R' Avrohom the Malach, and R' Yisroel, who at that time was 6 years old. On the eve of Succos, R' Avrohom entered the succah and sat in his father's seat. Thereupon he assumed the mantle of leadership. Among those present was one fervent follower of his father who was indignant that R' Avrohom had assumed the position of leadership so soon after his father's death. Furthermore, he felt that, considering R' Avrohom's youth, he should not have assumed leadership without the consent of the great men of his day. The chassid did not accept R' Avrohom as his rebbe. After Succos he returned home with the thought of attaching himself to another *tzaddik*. After a number of days, he found himself again passing through Prohobisht. He said to himself, since I am already here, I will go and visit the son of my teacher and Rebbe. The chassid went to R' Avrohom's house and stood silently.

R' Avrohom began to tell a story. There was once a king who wanted to build a great and beautiful palace. He hired a team of artisans who designed and built it. The palace incorporated many different designs. When the work was complete, the king invited all his subjects to see the palace. He decreed that whosoever should discern an imperfection would be rewarded from the king's treasury. Among the many qualified people who came to the palace was a villager. He noticed a mural which portrayed a man whose appearance was similar to his own. The man was holding a cup of wine in his hand and drinking from it. The villager exclaimed, "I have found an imperfection in this painting! A drunk cannot keep his hand steady a moment, but here I see that he is not shaking at all." The king commanded that he be given a reward. The villager was overjoyed with this and said that the following day he would come again to try and discover another imperfection. The following day he entered the palace and noticed a crown. He said, "Here, too, I have found an imperfection." The king thereupon commanded that the villager be given one hundred lashes. The villager cried in protest: "Yesterday I was rewarded; today I am given lashes?" Came the reply, "You are a villager and you understand inebriation, but from where did you become knowledgeable concerning crowns?"

When he completed his story, the R' Avrohom extended his hand to the chassid and said, "Have a peaceful trip home."

R' Avrohom was strangely happy on the eve of Succos, the time of his father's death. His mother was disturbed and inquired as to the reason for his happiness. She said, "Even a simple man with a simple father would not be so happy after his father's death." R' Avrohom replied, "If you were to see where my father is presently you would also be happy." R' Avrohom wanted to enter the succah with his younger brother on that Succos eve. Before making his entrance he said, "We must first go to our mother and wish her a good *Yom Tov*. When he came to his mother he said, "Hashem will have a new guest and we must send Him something in honor of His guest. I will make *Kiddush* for Him." He then entered the succah and recited the *Kiddush*.

The author heard from his father, the late Rabbi Yosef Brayer, Rav of Shtefanesht and a native of Rizhin, who heard from his father, Rabbi Mordechai Dov, Rav of Rizhin, that when on the first night of Succos the young Rizhiner entered the succah, packed with chassidim, he was dressed in a very thin robe. The weather was freezing cold and all the assembled were shivering. The young Yisroel turned to the massive crowd and said, "*Yidden* (fellow Jews), why

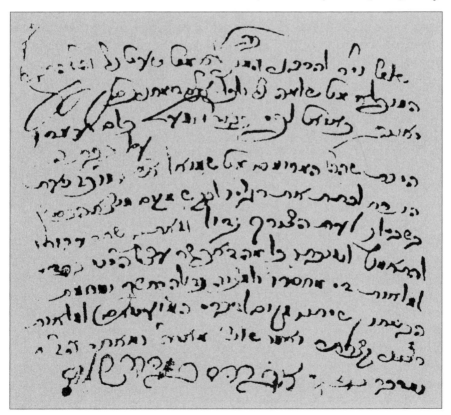

Signature of R' Avrohom, brother of the Rizhiner

are you trembling? Don't you feel how the walls of the succah are warming us?"

After the passing of his father, the 6-year-old orphan was taken to the synagogue every day by his teacher in order to recite the *Kaddish* (mourner's prayer). Once, when he began to recite the *Kaddish*, another boy also began reciting the same prayer for his own father. When the boy heard the young R' Yisroel reciting *Kaddish*, he stopped his praying out of respect for him. The Rizhiner then stopped his recitation and ran out of the synagogue. The teacher followed him and rebuked him, "See how the son of a simple man recited the *Kaddish*, while you, the son of a *tzaddik*, did not." Immediately he answered, "What was I to do? My father came to me in the middle of my prayer. The other boy stopped out of respect for my father. My father told me that the other boy's father came to him and complained to him that my father did not need the recitation of the mourner's prayer to save him from judgment, while he did need the *Kaddish* of his son to save him from the judgment of the world of truth. Why then did my son cause his son to stop his recitation of the *Kaddish*? My father instructed me to leave the synagogue in order that the other boy be permitted to complete his prayer."

The young Yisroel was looked after by his brother, Avrohom. As children do, little Yisroel liked to lark around and it often seemed that he was ignoring the lessons of his teacher. All words of rebuke were to no avail. At last, the teacher became very upset because he felt he was being paid for nothing. He therefore decided to discuss his charge with R' Avrohom in the hope that R' Avrohom might persuade his younger brother to mend his ways. After registering his complaint he was instructed by R' Avrohom to summon the child. When the child appeared, R' Avrohom confronted him with his teacher's complaint. R' Avrohom then laid his arm on the table and rested his head on his arm in the posture of one who is asleep. The child then went and stared out of the window. The two brothers did not speak for a while. The teacher stood between them, nonplused at this strange state of affairs.

Afterwards, R' Avrohom said to the teacher, "You have much merit in that you have taught my brother and me. If not for this you would have been lost to both worlds for admonishing my brother, who is a prince in Israel. You must be aware that in our family a child is taught only the *aleph-beis*. Everything else he is taught by Heaven. Therefore, how can you possibly accuse my brother of not wanting to learn? If not for your great merit, you would have been lost to both worlds. Now this merit protects you."

In the town of Prohobisht, there was a woman of doubtful reputation. A rumor that she had visited the home of the mayor in the evening created an uproar in the town. She reported to the mayor that the townspeople were making life miserable for her. She blamed her situation on R' Avrohom, as he was the leader of the Jewish community. She therefore requested that the mayor arrest R' Avrohom and have him beaten. She suggested that R' Avrohom not be arrested during the day, because the Jews would not permit it. The mayor's servants arrested him before daybreak and R' Avrohom was incarcerated in the early morning. When the townspeople became aware of R' Avrohom's plight, they caused an uproar, exerting such great pressure that R' Avrohom was released. Sometime later, that same woman took ill, and her relatives came to R' Avrohom, requesting that he pray for her recovery. R' Avrohom then said to Hashem, "This woman tried to cause me harm, so I am unable to petition for her recovery. Please heal her without my prayers."

WHEN R' YISROEL WAS ONLY 7, HE WAS BETROTHED AND WAS TAKEN TO Berditchev for the celebration of the *tenaim* (engagement) to Sarah, daughter of R' Moshe, who was

MADE IN HEAVEN then Rosh Yeshivah of Berditchev and afterwards Rebbe in Botoshani, Romania. His mother came with him to Berditchev to sign the *tenaim,* since his father had died. R' Levi Yitzchok of Berditchev ordered all of the city teachers to appear with their students and welcome the groom. The chassidim recalled that he said that whoever would welcome the young *chassan* (groom) would remember for the rest of his life that he saw the face of an angel of Hashem. For a distance of about half a kilometer the students lined up on both sides of the road, in the middle of which

The old shul in Botoshani, now an old-age home

passed the wagon bringing the youngster. Instruments played and all came out to see the young groom and to welcome him.

THE PRECIOUS STOREHOUSE

THE BERDITCHEVER THEN BLESSED HIM AND SAID TO HIS MOTHER, "Rebbetzin, you will guard well this precious storehouse, about which it is often said, *Yisroel, in you I will be glorified* (*Yeshayah* 49:3).

When, some years later, the Rizhiner was imprisoned, he said that to the best of his knowledge he had never committed a transgression save that during his reception in Berditchev, when he was a child, he had experienced a sense of superiority and pride.

With all his wealth and splendor, there was little that excited the Rizhiner or ruffled his calm. "I was 7," he said, "when I visited Berditchev, where I was received with such a demonstration of love that nothing impresses me any more."

The wedding took place nine years later in the city of Ustik, for the bride lived there. (After the wedding, he lived apart from his wife for several years.)

After his brother died childless in 1812, R' Yisroel began to assume the leadership of the fold, at the age of 16. He still had no children. His mother, Chavah, was widowed. Like her oldest son, her youngest son Dov Ber (who had been bethrothed to the daughter of the Berditchever Rav,) died very young, before he married. She traveled to the elder of the *tzaddikim*, the Apter Rav, and pleaded before him, "Is Hashem bringing about the end of the holy house of the Maggid, Hashem forbid?" The Apter promised her that her son, Yisroel (the future Rizhiner), would yet have sons and daughters. And, indeed, this prophecy of the Apter was fulfilled, and the Rizhiner had six sons and four daughters; his mother lived to see a third generation in her lifetime. She derived much *nachas dikedushah* (spiritual satisfaction) from this illustrious son and his children, but also a good deal of pain and tribulation, as the reader will discover.

A year before her demise R' Sholom Shachna's widow, Chavah, the mother of R' Avrohom and the Rizhiner, was stricken with an intestinal disease, to which she eventually succumbed. On the third day of mourning, R' Sholom Yosef, R' Yisroel's *bechor* (firstborn), said that now he understood what had been unclear before. His father, the Rizhiner, had always been able to effect a cure for everyone's illness, but his *tefillos* on his mother's behalf had been to no avail. He now heard from his father that when his grandmother had come to heaven, she had requested that she be taken to the place of her husband, R' Sholom Shachna. She was told that this was an impossibility because her husband was on a very high celestial level and could not tolerate the air of the world from which she had just come. When this became known to R' Sholom Shachna he pleaded on her behalf. Because she had been afflicted with the aforementioned illness during her last year on earth, she was permitted to join her husband. (The illness had helped to cleanse her of any worldly impurities.)

When R' Yisroel, now aged 16, became Rebbe, crowds of chassidim flocked to him. Even *rabbanim* and *admorim* admired him. R' Yisroel moved to the town of Rizhin and there built for himself a veritable palace, decorated and furnished with much glory and splendor. He lived in opulence. The table he kept, the carriage and four white

אָדָם ... יוֹשֵׁעַ ...

חֶעיוֹל מק׳ אפט״א

בחרב החסיד והעניו

שלשלת יוחסין מ׳

שמואל זר נפ׳ ה״ניסן

הק״ש ה׳

ולעת זקנותי התקע

אשדלו של תורה פה

מד׳ בין ולמ׳ ...

Tomb of Apter Rav in Mezhibozh

horses with harness and upholstery, the attendants, the brilliance of his court, his very regal demeanor — all was consonant with his status as prince and ruler. And yet there was no one to raise so much as an eyebrow at the luxury and splendor in which this *tzaddik*, R' Yisroel, lived. The contrary was true. The chassidim, his followers and even the *tzaddikim* of his day saw in the palatial scale of his house a living proof and a great sign of his regalness and exalted holiness. They all loved him and venerated him. They said that he did not, G-d forbid, benefit personally from the wealth and honor, rather his entire purpose was to raise the stature of the *tzaddik* of the generation as a reflection upon earth of the Divine principle of *malchus Yisroel* (sovereignty of Israel), Israel's immortal kingdom. His privileged status was unique. His new path, so different from that of his predecessors, was never questioned. It was *derech hamelech* (the manner of the king) and undisputedly, Rizhin represented *malchus*. And all in order to magnify the honor of the Creator, כְּבוֹד מַלְכוּת שָׁמַיִם.

On one occasion, when R' Yisroel appeared in a kaftan cut according to the latest style (which was a daring innovation), the Apter Rav exclaimed: "This is the king of Israel whose holiness illumines my eyes. I have never yet seen the entire Torah, the

Title page of the first edition (תרכ"ז 1863) of the Sefer Oheiv Yisroel

Babylonian and the Jerusalem Talmud, *Sifra, Sifri, Tosefta*, embraced within one mantle as I see in R' Yisroel, not to mention the writings of the *Ari*, which are fluent in his mouth more than the prayer *Ashrei* in our mouths." Such plaudits naturally removed all doubt as to his greatness.

The Apter also said the following concerning the Rizhiner: In *Tehillim* 72:7, the Psalmist states, יִפְרַח בְּיָמָיו צַדִּיק, *the tzaddik will flourish in his time*. Rashi explains that the word *tzaddik* means Yisroel. It was to R' Yisroel of Rizhin that Rashi was referring.

The first time that R' Tzvi Hirsch of Rimanov met the Rizhiner, he was amazed. How can a person to whom is directed all the honor in the world be concerned only with the honor of Heaven? This will not be understood till the coming of our Redeemer. He also said, "The Rizhiner took his direction from the angel Chanoch and I took mine from my father."

From R' Yisroel of Grublinka we learn that by the time the Rizhiner was 18 years old, his every action was for a G-dly purpose. Even the blinking of his eye and the slightest movement of his limbs were in Hashem's service.

Great people, among them the Rabbi of Dinov, said that his fame is alluded to in the initials of the Hebrew word *Bereishis* — *Ohr Toras Yisroel ben R' Sholom* — "Light of the Torah, of our teacher, Yisroel, the son of R' Sholom."

R' Dovid of Butchuch, author of *Daas Kedoshim*, said the purpose of the work of the Maggid, his son the Malach and his grandson, R' Sholom Shachna from Prohobisht, was to bring R' Yisroel into the world.

In his orbit, in the Ukraine and Volhynia, no one was antagonistic to Chassidus. R' Yisroel put an end to any dissension, with the result that Chassidus entrenched itself there for a period of one hundred years. This spanned a period of time of from five to six generations among the people.

There was a celebrated chassidic wedding in Ustila, in 1813. R' Yisroel was 16 years old at the time. The *chassan* was R' Don, son of R' Yitzchok of Radzevil and grandson of the Zlotchover Maggid. The *kallah* was the daughter of R' Yosef of Heinbisho and a granddaughter of the Apter Rav, the acknowledged dean of the Rebbes. The wedding was attended by a hundred rebbes and rabbis, among them the leading *tzaddikim* of the generation. When R' Yisroel's *gartel* (ritual belt) came undone and dropped to the floor, a 70-year-old man — the venerable R' Avrohom Yehoshua Heschel of Apt — bent down in the presence of all the guests, picked it up and put it round

R' Yisroel's loins, saying, "Heaven has granted me the honor of rolling the Torah scroll." All those who witnessed this were amazed. The Apter Rav, the renowned author of *Oheiv Yisroel,* said, "It is brought down in *Midrash Aggadas Bereishis,* that in the future it will be thought a wonder that someone who had never studied would be found sitting among the Patriarchs. And Hashem said, 'These merited only because they listened to Me during their lifetime.' " The Apter then grasped his beard and said, "I swear that this *Midrash* was referring to him."

The Apter Rav once asked R' Yisroel what had moved him to choose a new way in life, one unknown to his forefathers. He preceded his query with the assertion that it was not his intention to criticize him or to offer him instructions; he was merely prompted by curiosity. Whereupon the Rizhiner replied:

> "The Gemara identifies humbleness and wisdom as virtues not to be separated one from the other. Moshe was the humblest of all men, hence he was the wisest of all men. King Shlomo is famous as the wisest of all men, consequently he was the humblest of all men. Now if that be so, how is it that the Torah stresses Moshe's humbleness and Shlomo's wisdom? The answer is: because the Gemara distinguishes between a religious leader and a king, as we read: if a Rabbi forgoes the honor due to him he is forgiven, but if a king forgoes the honor due to him it cannot be condoned. Moshe was the religious leader of all Israel — he therefore was within his right if he chose to be humble, but Shlomo was king of Israel, and he could be given no such latitude. I am impelled by heavenly injunction to choose the path of authority and power and have no right to avoid it."

CHAPTER VIII

R' YISROEL'S IMPRISONMENT

R'YISROEL'S STANCE IN CHASSIDUS AND AS A G–D-FEARING man was one of moderation and self-control. His praying lacked visible animation. He did not practice asceticism. Nor did he allow himself to be viewed applying himself to study; nevertheless he let slip here and there a profound Torah thought. However, some fragments of his conversation and sayings that were passed down to us orally, as well as those published by others, are striking for their sharp wit and wisdom. The name of R' Yisroel of Rizhin was praised even by gentiles. High officials used to visit him. Despite this, he felt all alone when tragedy befell him and his family, and they were sentenced to prison by order of the Czar. The story of his imprisonment follows:

It was the winter of the year 1838, a tragic one for the Rizhiner. An incident that happened in the district of Ushitzi-Podolia in Russia brought about his imprisonment. Two Jewish informers made their living by profiteering, informing on their fellow Jews to the officers of the Russian government, and by trading in the black market. Eventually, they began to attack entire communities with extortion, threatening to hand over to the government lists of the "missing people." These were the Jews who were not listed in the official Russian census of the population. Many did this to escape the mandatory twenty-year conscription into the Russian army. Poor Jews who barely made a living tried to avoid the heavy taxes by not being listed in the census. These Jews were known as the "invisible souls."

All the bribe money in the community could not satiate the informers' arrogant demands. The regime of Czar Nicholas I (1825-1855) had issued a decree that a man could be imprisoned in Siberia even if he had not committed a crime. Any information and slander was enough to bring terror on the community. The slanderers' first victims were those who had evaded conscription in the district of Volhynia and Podolia. The heads of these communities convened an assembly to decide which action to take against those traitors. The elderly R' Michael Auerbach of Dunayevtzi was also a participant, since the two slanderers worked primarily in his town. It was decided to secretly execute these two villains as there was no other way to protect the Jewish community against them. The informers were put to death. The discipline of the community was so strong that no one said anything; even the families of the dead informers acted as if they knew nothing about it. The episode would have passed without incident, except that a third informer named Koenigsberg of Diesna heard about it and informed the police and the governor of Podolia.

The latter ordered several investigations and transferred the entire case to the Governor General of Kiev, Count Guriev, who sent a report to the Czar in St. Petersburg. The Czar showed interest in the case and ordered Count Guriev to carry out a special investigation. At the Governor General's order, hundreds of Jewish suspects were brought to the city of Dunayevtzi and imprisoned in a deserted convent, protected by a high wall. Each prisoner was placed in solitary confinement, so that he could not communicate with others. Every day, the number of prisoners increased. Among them was the venerable R' Michael Auerbach of Dunayevtzi. All of his books were sent to the censor in Vilna who, in turn, extracted all the passages in the Code of *Choshen Mishpat* concerning "informers" and translated them into Russian.

Before he was imprisoned, the Rizhiner was summoned to Berditchev for an investigation. When the Apter Rav was informed about it, he immediately dispatched two important men to Berditchev to petition the government and said, "Be informed by my grave warning that I am *mafkir* (divest myself of) all of my worldly goods for the sake of this *tzaddik*. Therefore, you should know how to behave." The Rebbe concluded, "Many troubles have passed over my head. In me is fulfilled the verse, *Seven times a tzaddik falls* (*Mishlei* 24:16). May the blessed Hashem grant that the conclusion of the verse, *and rises,* may also be fulfilled in me. I pray to Hashem that the streams of water continue to flow, as is found in the Holy *Zohar.*"

The Governor General hesitated to detain the Rizhiner. He knew that the Rebbe was considered to be the saintly leader of the masses. But certain prisoners had confessed under torture and implicated others. The influence of the Rizhiner became so obvious to the Governor General that he finally decided to imprison the Rebbe.

The authorities came for him on a Friday, but he was not at home because he had gone to the *mikveh* in honor of the Shabbos. Upon returning from the *mikveh*, he learned that they were ready to take him into custody. He showed no anguish or fear. He asked for some water, washed his hands outside, and offered them to the gendarmes to be tied. He then climbed on to the wagon that would take him to the prison in Kiev. When his family and friends encircled him before they separated, he comforted them, saying that he was not better than his forefather Dovid Hamelech who suffered persecutions at the hands of kings and their officers.

The Rizhiner viewed his imprisonment as a Divine test, which he accepted with humility. Once, he said that he was always wondering about the Talmudic explanation of the verse in *Koheles* (4:13), *From a king, old man and a fool,* which refers to the *yetzer hara* (evil inclination). "King" he understood, since the *yetzer hara* is strong and rules over man. The name "old" was understandable for it incited man from the day of his birth, while the *yetzer tov* (inclination for good) arrives on the scene only at the age of 13. But why call the *yetzer hara* "fool," when he demonstrates such cunning in inciting man to evil? When he was sitting in jail, the *yetzer hara* visited him, and the Rizhiner told him that he, himself, was imprisoned and forced to sit there. The *yetzer hara*, however, came of his own free will. There is no greater foolishness than that.

Czar Nicholas listened to the voice of his secret informers, to the effect that the Rabbi of Rizhin was establishing a kingdom for himself and criticizing the government. He ordered the *tzaddik* to be brought into his presence. At the sight of him the Czar concluded that the *tzaddik's* eyes were "the eyes of a rebel."

Initially, the Czar decreed house arrest in Kaminetz. Afterwards, he imprisoned him in Donevitz for a period of seven months; and finally, when the people had made an attempt to ransom him with an offer of a substantial sum of money, he ordered him to be thrown into a prison cell in Kiev for a period of fifteen months, pending his decision whether to exile him to the Caucasus or to Siberia. This was the merciless autocrat from whose dungeons no prisoner ever escaped, as it is said concerning Nevuchadnetzar: ... *who never released his prisoners to go home* (*Yeshayah* 14:17).

While sitting at the table during Shabbos, R' Leibish of Opalas said: "The Jewish kingdom is falling." The people around him did not understand what he meant. Afterwards it became known that the Rizhiner had been incarcerated.

When the guards came to take him to prison, the Rebbe got up and told a story about a king who was childless. In his old age, he was blessed with a very beautiful daughter who was treasured by both king and queen and given everything according to her station. When she reached marriageable age a groom from the upper echelons of society was chosen for her. She married him and conceived soon after. The king and queen, however, did no know how they would cope with the pain that their daughter would experience during labor. It then occurred to them that their daughter was wise enough to understand that they would not be able to tolerate her anguish and that she would therefore not cry out in her pain. The girl, in fact, did suffer in silence in order to spare her parents pain. At the very climax of her labor, however, she could no longer remain silent. She cried out, and her parents became confused. They took a stick and hit her on the head because she had not waited the extra moment before crying out. In this way R' Yisroel explained his incarceration …

Once the Rizhiner and R' Mottel, the Chernobyler Rebbe, spent Shabbos *Parashas Mikeitz* in the same town. The Rizhiner then quoted a verse from the previous week's portion, *And Yosef was taken down to Egypt (Bereishis* 39:1). "This means Kiev," he said. The Rebbe of Chernobyl then answered, "I forgive you because I am old and my strength is no longer with me." This occurred approximately ten years before the Rizhiner was imprisoned in Kiev.

As he left for prison he was whispering verses from *Tehillim.*

As they reached the town of Vielipoli, Shabbos was almost upon them. Word spread throughout the town that the Rizhiner had been taken prisoner. The Jews of Vielipoli, including those heads of the community who were his chassidim, bribed the guards so that the *tzaddik* would not have to travel on Shabbos, and so the Rizhiner remained imprisoned in the town until Sunday. Finally he was brought to the prison in Kiev and placed in solitary confinement. All the twenty-two months that he was in prison, he did not complain about anything, resigning himself to whatever fate decreed with a quiet optimism.

Gittele, the daughter of the Rizhiner, once told a story about the prison's courtyard, a place where the Rizhiner would sit. There was a source of water there. Once, on Shabbos, it had proved impossible to bring the Rizhiner his *Kiddush* wine and challos because the water had overflowed. They were very concerned, because fasting is prohibited on Shabbos. Toward evening the water subsided; they brought him his *Kiddush* wine, challos and the rest of his food. The Rizhiner then said that it might have been better if the water had not subsided, for he would then have had to fast all of Shabbos. This would have created a tumult in the heavens above. It is possible that then all his troubles would have ended, but now that the food had been brought to him he had no choice but to eat.

Once, on Friday, in jail, he remained in his *tallis* and *tefillin* until evening. When he saw the sun setting he hurriedly removed them and sanctified the day. In great haste he lit the candles for Shabbos. Suddenly the guard entered, put out the candles and began to yell. The Rizhiner concentrated for a few moments; the guard returned and relit the candles for the Rizhiner. He turned and asked his servant if he knew who this guard was. It turned out he was a guard of the Czar of Russia. "He had a great deal of effrontery to put out the candles; however, in spite of all this, he was afraid of me and had to return to relight them."

Somehow, in a way inexplicable to us — and, as it was rumored, with the intervention of the Prince Vorontzeff-Dashkin — the governor of the state of Kiev received an order to free him. This took place on Shushan Purim, in the year 1840. But, while clearing the Rizhiner of murder — the charges brought by the informers — the Russian government still claimed that he wanted to seize control of the Jewish population in Russia and oppose the Czar.

When he came out of prison he walked to and fro in his room, saying: "Why do they call me Rebbe, if no one above listens to me?" On his return home he continued to be under daily police surveillance. As it became increasingly difficult for his chassidim to visit him, the Rebbe decided to attempt to escape to freedom across the Russian border.

Upon the advice of his followers, R' Yisroel decided to move to Kishinev, in Bessarabia, where the district officer was more lenient. Later, his family was permitted to join him in Kishinev. Nonetheless, he was constantly watched by the police.

When the chassidim found out from inside sources that the Rebbe was to be banished, they intervened with the governor of Kishinev, who was heavily bribed. They obtained for the Rebbe an exit permit for Moldavia. Two Jews guaranteed to the authorities that the Rebbe would return in time to Kishinev, as required by the relevant Russian law. With two escorting *gabbaim*, he secretly left Kishinev and arrived by carriage at the Moldavian border of Romania. Just as he left Kishinev, the orders came from St. Petersburg for his arrest and deportation.

The Czar's edict did not accuse him of having royal pretensions. Instead it claimed, cunningly, that as R' Yisroel Friedman was a holy man of Hashem, the multitudes that flocked to him for his blessing interfered with his peace of mind and disturbed his worship of Hashem. Therefore, the government of Russia had decided, in the interests of his welfare, to send him and his entire family to a remote place in Russia where it is prohibited for any other Jew to live. There, the holy Rabbi would have a place of refuge and find peace. The government allows him to take ten men with him so that he can pray with a *minyan,* also a *shochet* (ritual slaughterer) will go along so that he will be provided with all his needs for sustenance, in order that he may worship his G-d. All other Jews are to be prohibited from visiting him.

However, when this deportation ordinance arrived, the Rizhiner was already far away in the Moldavian capital of Iassy. Afraid of being punished for giving an exit permit to a man in exile, the governor of Kishinev turned to the Russian consul in Iassy and asked him to imprison R' Yisroel and extradite him to Kishinev. Friends of the Rebbe in Kishinev sent messengers to Iassy to inform the Rebbe of this order of extradition. When all this became known to his chassidim in Moldavia, they procured a travel pass from Moldavia to Austria for the Rebbe.

Chassidim from both countries showed great and boundless self-sacrifice as they arranged for his escape. Among the Rebbes of Galicia who saved him were his friend and admirer, R' Meir'l of Premishlan, who sent a porter to help R' Yisroel cross the border under conditions of mortal danger.

The porter's name was Nosson Shimon Horowitz of Suceava and he was the man that R' Meir'l of Premishlan had sent. Nosson Shimon was a non-observant Jew who had traveled to R' Meir'l of Premishlan in order to be a penitent. The *tzaddik* had told him that there was a secret task for him to perform, a great mitzvah, to save the life of a holy and righteous Jew. Since Nosson Shimon lived near the border and knew all the paths, he would carry him on his back and this would be his repentance for his sinful past. Nosson Shimon agreed, promising R' Meir'l to carry out his request.

At midnight, the Rizhiner and a few of his chassidim started out on their hazardous journey. It was a cold winter night and danger was lurking all around. When they approached the border, Nosson Shimon lifted the Rizhiner upon his shoulders and entered the frozen, icy river. Midway, he stopped and would not continue until the Rebbe promised him forgiveness for his sins and his share of *Olam Haba* (the World to Come). Having no choice, the Rizhiner agreed — with the proviso that he indeed repent as he was called to the Torah on Shabbos. Upon his return to R' Meir'l, he was greeted with admiration and blessed by R' Meir'l with a *mi shebeirach* that his barren wife, Rachel, would soon bear him a son. From then on he became R' Meir'l's fervent admirer.

As the Rizhiner crossed the river into Austrian territory he took the golden *yarmulka* (skullcap) from his head and three tears fell into it, and from then on he did not put it on his head while he was in that country. No longer was he *Reish Galusa* (Exilarch), a position of which his golden *yarmulka* was the symbol.

After they crossed the river, from Russia into Austria, they found two men with a wagon waiting for them. They first reached the small town of Campulung in the Carpathian mountains in Bukovina. But the Rizhiner could not remain there, for it was too close to the border, and there were not even ten Jews for a *minyan*. He then sent word to his *mechutan* (relative by marriage), R' Chaim of Kossov, and his friend, R' Shmelke, the son of the *tzaddik*, R' Moshe Leib of Sassov in Kolomaya, and asked them to send him a *minyan* of men for the daily prayers. Immediately they dispatched a *minyan*, one of whom was R' Shmelke.

From Campulung they brought him to Skolya, where the great Rabbi, R' Shlomo Drimmer — the author of *Responsa Beis Shlomo* and *Yashresh Yaakov,* on *Yevamos* — a Kossover chassid, greeted the Rizhiner with great respect. The Kossover Rebbe with his 14-year-old son, R' Mendel (who later became the Rebbe of Vizhnitz), also came to visit him in Skolya. R' Mendel became engaged to Miriam, the daughter of the Rizhiner. But the *tzaddik,* in continuous transit, still had no idea where he would finally settle.

After his escape from Kishinev, the governor placed a domicilliary arrest on his family to prevent them from escaping. The Rizhiner's eldest son, R' Sholom Yosef, was forced to write a letter to his father, asking him to return to Russia quickly, lest the entire family be exiled to Siberia. This hand-written, signed letter was handed to two chassidim who vouched for its safe delivery. At the same time, the *rebbetzin* sent him a letter by special messenger, warning her husband that the letter sent to him by his son had been written under coercion. She urged him to run further away from Russia, to France or England, but under no circumstances was he to return home.

While still in Skolya the Rizhiner found out that the Czarist government was trying to have him extradited to Russia. He became a hunted man, and an international cause celebre. The chassidim of Galicia, Austria, Bukovina, Romania and Hungary tried by all means to help save the Rebbe from exile. They turned to the great nonchassidic rabbis in the hope that they might also intercede with the authorities on behalf of the Rizhiner. The *tzaddik* R' Moshe Teitelbaum of Uheli was asked to write a letter to the famous *gaon* the Chasam Sofer, that he intercede with the authorities on behalf of the Rizhener. In his letter asking the Chasam Sofer to help save the Rizhiner, Reb Moshe wrote that thousands of Jews were heartbroken on account of the Rebbe's plight. Governors, ministers and clergy became involved.

The chassidim also turned to Rabbi Dr. Mannheimer of Vienna, who had connections with Prince von Metternich, the Austrian foreign minister, to intervene on behalf of the Rebbe. Since Dr. Mannheimer was unacquainted with the chassidic movement, he turned to the well-known *maskilon*, Yitzchok Miezes of Cracow, and asked him his opinion on the matter. Miezes answered in a letter that Chassidus is of great ethical value, and cited many examples of chassidic works.

The Austrian government turned to the Rabbi of Cracow, R' Berish Meisels, who was also a member of the Austrian parliament, inquiring about the Rizhiner. Two of the Rizhiner's chassidim from Strelisk, one of them R' Ephraim Lemberger, went to Cracow to speak to R' Meisels and plead the Rebbe's innocence. They told him that the Rizhiner was a true *tzaddik,* in total control of himself. Whereupon, R' Meisels asked them: "How can you prove it"? They answered: "Never in his life did he bend his head as much as a hairsbreadth toward the spoon during the meal." These words were greeted with boisterous laughter, and R' Meisels said, "Nothing in the world can be learned from that. Besides, who cannot do such a thing?" At that time, the rabbi sat down to eat and said that he, too, was capable of performing this feat.

When the rabbi began eating, unconsciously, he slowly bent his mouth down to the spoon. He tried for a few moments to prevent this action, but could not. The rabbi admitted to the chassidim that they were right. R' Meisels then reported to the government, praising the Rizhiner and interceding on his behalf.

When Dr. Mannheimer asked Prince von Metternich for refuge for the Rizhiner, the prince advised the Rebbe to acquire some property. This would afford him immunity, as a property owner, against any possible harassment that might befall him in the future.

The Rizhiner chassidim then began to search for ways the Rebbe could earn Austrian citizenship. It so happened that in Sadagora, next to Chernovitz, a 10-year-old child by the name of Yisroel Donenfeld had disappeared almost forty years earlier. Witnesses were brought to testify that this boy, the son of a poor family, had made his way to the Ukraine to his "uncle," R' Sholom Shachna Friedman in Prohobisht, where he grew up in his house and adopted his uncle's surname, Friedman. The Rizhiner, who was about 50 years old, presented himself as Yisroel Donenfeld, who was returning to his native town after forty years of absence. Eight men testified that he was born in Sadagora. On the basis of this evidence, the Rebbe was then issued citizenship papers. When the baron who owned the town heard about the Rebbe's persecution at the hands of the Russians, he invited him to live in Sadagora under his protection. Upon the advice of the Kossover Rebbe and R' Meir'l of Premishlan, he accepted the offer of the baron and settled in Sadagora. It is told that Reb Meir'l of Premishlan wrote to him, when he was still living in Skolya, hinting, as was his custom, through such questions as "Did you see the *samech?*" — an allusion to the first letter of Sadagora — "in which will you reside?" Meir'l is telling you this is not Skolya, but rather Sadagora."

It was General Gabriel Spleney, the first Austrian administrator of Bukovina, who in 1790 encouraged Jewish settlement in Sadagora, granting it the status of a free residential district. Thus, Sadagora became the second largest Jewish community after the neighboring city of Chernovitz.

The Austrian government paid no attention to further demands of the Russian government for the extradition of the Rizhiner, for he had been declared a native Sadagoran and was under the government's protection. Still, in accordance with the peace treaty established by the Congress of Vienna in 1815, the Russian government demanded the return of the fugitive Rebbe. Pressure was exerted from all sides. The family in Kishinev was threatened with exile to Siberia if the Rebbe did not return. The predicament the Rizhiner found himself in was extreme. Nevertheless, he placed his trust in Hashem and decided to remain and wait for his salvation. The chassidim bribed the governor to reply to the Russian government that even if the Rebbe was a native of Russia, as the Russians claimed, the demand did not specify his crime or the reason that he should be confined. R' Friedman had, furthermore, come to Austria from Moldavia. Therefore this case was not covered under the treaty of 1815. This letter of the governor was sent to the Office of the Imperial Cabinet in Vienna, whose response to the Russian government stated that there was no legal basis for his extradition that would oblige Austria to send him back to Russia.

The Austrian government took the Rizhiner under its protection. He was given honorary citizenship on the condition that he acquire some property, as well as show that he had a sum of 20,000 crowns for his support. His chassidim brought him the whole sum, and also bought him the Zlati Potik estate near Sadagora.

Several years before the Rizhiner settled in Sadagora, Reb Mendele of Kossov spent a Shabbos with him. Before he left the town, he blessed its inhabitants, saying: "I hope to Hashem that Sadagora will become נַחֲלָה לְיִשְׂרָאֵל עַבְדּוֹ, *an inheritance to Israel, his servant* (an allusion to *Tehillim* 135:12)." Now Yisroel of Rizhin had found his place in Sadagora where the whole community had helped him during the investigations and became his chassidim. Even the gentiles in town testified that he was a native of Sadagora so that he might become a citizen. One of them testified that he remembered R' Yisroel very well. As a wild youth, Yisroel stole apples from his orchard and when his uncle sent him to Russia, he was glad to be rid of that vandal. Two other non-Jews asked to see the Rizhiner so as to be able to identify him as the man whom they had known in his youth. When he came out of his room, both of them exclaimed, "Of course we know this man."

He arrived without his family in the winter of 1842 before Purim, but the Rebbe did not accept Austrian citizenship, choosing rather to become a citizen of Turkey, which had jurisdiction over the Holy Land.

His citizenship read, "a citizen of Jerusalem." His sons and all his descendants continued to be listed as Turkish citizens.

The wedding of his daughter Miriam, set for after Shavuos, drew nearer. The bride was waiting with the rest of the family in Russia, being without a permit to leave Russia. The Russian demand for the extradition of the Rizhiner was still in effect. On the Shabbos after Shavuos, the *forshpiel* (pre-nuptial feast celebrated by the calling of the *chassan* to the Torah) took place, as is customary before a wedding. Thousands of chassidim came to participate in the Rizhiner's *simchah*. Since the families could not get out of the house to the synagogue because of the crush of the crowd around it, as everyone was pushing to see the Rebbe and his son-in-law, the Rizhiner suggested that the *chassan* have an *aliyah* in the house. As he always kept a small *sefer Torah* and a *minyan* with him in the house, they prayed inside and read the Torah while the crowd stood outside and prayed. As the crowd refused to disperse, the *mechutanim* remained in the house the whole day, with their meals passed to them through the window.

The next day, the Rizhiner arranged a *seudah* in honor of the *mechutan* and the *chassan*. Before *Birchas HaMazon* (Grace after Meals), he said, "It is a mitzvah to praise the *chassan* before the *kallah* and the *kallah* before the *chassan*." He then began to praise his daughter as "a beautiful and pious *kallah*" (*Kesubos* 17a). Then he faced the *chassan* and blessed him without placing his hands on his head, as was the custom of other rebbes. The *mechuteneste* (chassan's mother) protested and asked the Rebbe to place his hands on the head of the *chassan* and bless him, for the *tzaddik* of the generation is like the *Kohen* offering *Birchas Kohanim* (the Priestly Benediction). The Rizhiner answered that there was no need for it.

"The mouth is holier than the hands," he explained. "It is written quite explicitly in our Torah in the *Birchas Kohanim*, *So shall you bless the Children of Israel, saying to them* (*Bamidbar* 6:23) — by mouth, not with the hands" (*Sifrei, Sotah* 38a).

During the ritual, the Kossover Rebbe asked his *mechutan* why he hardly ever ate the food placed before him. The Rizhiner answered that it was very simple: "Before I came into this world, I made a pact with my body that I would only associate with it if it agreed to exist with the most minimal of bodily requirements. The body agreed to this and has to keep this condition."

The Kossover then put down his spoon and stopped eating. "And why doesn't the *mechutan* eat?" asked the Rizhiner. "Did his body also agree to something at the time of birth?"

"Not necessarily," answered the Kossover. "On the contrary, I usually eat all that my body requires. At this moment, however, something which has puzzled me my whole life has become clear to me. On Friday night, when the Jew comes home from the synagogue led by two Shabbos angels (*Shabbos* 119b), he welcomes them by singing *Sholom Aleichem,* and then immediately sends them off and sings to them *Tzeis'chem lesholom* (depart in peace). I never understood why he sends them away so abruptly. Now I understand. A person is not able to eat in the presence of angels, who do not taste anything."

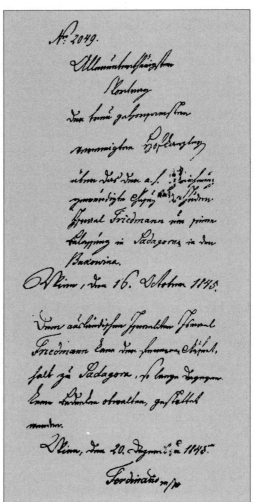

The Rizhiner's letter requesting that the Austrian emperor Ferdinand allow him to settle in Sadagora and approval of the emporer (From the royal archives of Austria)

R' Menachem Mendel of Vishnitz

After the feast, the Rizhiner accompanied him as far as the Russian border. They sat in the forest, and drank *l'chaim*. The chassidim sang and danced around them. Before taking leave, the Rizhiner asked the Kossover to climb onto the wagon and he would recite after him *Birchas Kohanim*. After doing so, he turned to the *chassan*, with tears in his eyes, and said, "It is known that a *chassan* is like a king, and especially in this family, who are descendants of kings, generation after generation. So I bid you to decree that I and all the Children of Israel will be spared all hard and bad decrees." The *chassan* answered *amen*.

THE LEGAL INVESTIGATIONS AGAINST HIM IN RUSSIA CONTINUED. He missed his family, his homeland and his chassidim. He once mentioned to friends that he wanted to ask Sir Moses Montefiore of London to intercede with the Austrian emperor or with the minister Prince von Metternich to influence the Russian Czar to stop his persecution.

QUARRY OF THE CZAR

HOWEVER, WITH TIME, HE BEGAN TO ESTABLISH ROOTS IN SADAGORA, feeling that he was safe there and knowing that Hashem had a reason for his exile and sufferings. When the Austrian government refused to extradite him to Russia, his chassidim proclaimed that the Rebbe's wishes were being granted. "If our Rebbe would have agreed to live in

HASHEM'S STANDARD BEARERS

Russia," they exulted, "we know that Hashem would have fulfilled his wish there, too." He answered them, "Yosef the *Tzaddik*, while living in Egypt, sent a message to his father, Yaakov, to the land of Canaan saying: *Hashem has appointed me master of all Egypt* (*Bereishis* 45:9). When the holy Patriarchs lived in the land of Canaan, they spread the Name of Hashem everywhere but Egypt, where the Hashem's Name was not yet known. When Yosef told his father, 'And you shall tell him thus,' he was quoting Hashem. In other words, Hashem is saying to Yaakov: 'Your son, Yosef, appointed Me, Hashem, Lord over the whole of Egypt' — that Yosef made Hashem G-d over the Egyptians when he made it known that there was a G-d in the world. And so it is with me," concluded the Rizhiner, "my holy fathers lived in Russia and made the Divine Name known, and I have come to spread His blessed Name here, too."

IN THE SUMMER OF 1842, THE CZAR AUTHORIZED THE RIZHINER'S FAMILY to leave Russia after divesting them of all rights to visit or return

TO SADAGORA   there. And so the Friedman family arrived in Sadagora during the week of *Parashas Shoftim*, in the late summer of 1842. His mother, Rebbetzin Chavah, passed away two years after joining her son in Sadagora (1844). The Rizhiner did not walk in the funeral procession. When R' Meir'l of Premishlan was told of this, he explained that a king does not follow in the aftermath of a coffin (*Sanhedrin* 20a).

In the vicinity of Sadagora he built a palace more beautiful than the one he presided over in Rizhin. The palace is still seen by visitors to Sadagora, by the many chassidic pilgrims who visit the Rizhiner's grave there. The synagogue was large enough to accommodate 3,000 worshipers. Chassidim came in droves from all over — Galicia, Russia and Romania. They crossed the border, sometimes at risk of life and limb, and came to Sadagora. Soon, his *hoif* (court) returned to its ancient honor and splendor.

Thenceforth, R' Yisroel adopted moderation in all the outward forms of life. However, the number of his admirers grew unabated, through the appeal of his marvelous activities and his

Partial photo of the Rizhiner's stately residence in Sadagora

matchless personal conduct. His prestige and charisma was enhanced immeasurably by the fact that eminent *tzaddikim*, from near and far, whose followers numbered in the thousands, honored and respected him.

CHAPTER IX

THE RIZHINER'S CHASSIDIM

RABBANIM AND *REBBEIM*, EVEN *MISNAGDIM* AND *MASKILIM*, AND common folk — Jew and gentile, young and old alike — flocked to Sadagora to catch a glimpse of the young

RABBANIM AND RABBEIM master. To mention only some: R' Yitzchok Zev Soloveitchik, father of R' Yosef Dov Ber of Brisk, vis-

ited the Rizhiner on a special mission. R' Yitzchok Zev's grandfather, R' Chaim of Volozhin, had sent him to have the Rizhiner intercede with the authorities through his influential chassidim to substitute the "army ordinance" against the Jews with a per capita tax.[1] R' Shlomo Drimmer of Skolya, author of

---

1. Based on a personal communication from R' Y.B. Soloveitchik to the author.

סדר

מעמדות

נחלקת לשבעה ימי השבוע ּ מסודרת נס־דר יפה ֶ כאשר
הבדיר הגאון הגדול המקובל האלקי כמוהר״ר ישעיה
הורוויץ ס׳ל וצ״ל ּ בחבורו ספר של״ה ּ ואתריו קם הגאן
בעהמ״ח ספר תבואות שור ומילא את המעלה מה שקיצ־ בעל
השל״ה הרח״ב וביאר באר היטב ומה שחסר זה גילה זה :

עוד הוספתי כור אמירת נשורת לותן מניפה ר״ל מיחכד ומחזור עפ״י הגאון
המפורסם נוליגת קדישא חים הלקיס קדים ע״י תוס׳ אברהם
יהושיע העשיל נ״י התב״ד נק׳ אפטא ׳ונג״ע ליתן מזבן נק׳ מעזבון :

כ״מ ינגזר חיבח גוי וכרזמה רכיינה על אימית שיו בזמנים
הקודסים אבל האוסות שביסנינו ּ בצלרם אנחנו מסתוכפים
ומרתה־ק לדרוש שלום וטוכתם כרב־ז יכ כי בשלום יהיה לכם שלומ׳

ע״י הרבי מנח   כרשיון   כולצנור הקדושׄ ּ
צבי   נשמה ּ
זאב   נכרכני כ־ב־ד   דוו־ל:א ּ
מהור״ר דוך רנין   תקע״ו :
פיין

במאהלוב

בשנת   תקע״ז   לפ״ק

תחת ממצלת אדוננו סניסר אומפעפריסוויעלנוסי דפריה וכו׳ כ וייב וויבן ראכיא־ל׳
סיתפיסּו אלכסנדר פּאוולאירטש כ׳־ו ּ וב יוסא הגסם
ונתסיסקי כ־לכיד־ר הויכב תינעפטיוזסיע ד ה ר

Title page of Seder Maamados including the Korbanos to be said in time of plagues

Beis Shlomo and *Yashresh Yaakov* on *Yevamos*, in his responsum (*Yoreh Deah* No. 125) to the Rizhiner, addresses him with great respect. R' Yosef Landau of Iassy, author of Responsa *Birchas Yosef,* calls the Rizhiner, "The luminary of Israel and its holiness."

R' Shlomo Kluger of Brody mentions the Rizhiner with honor in his Responsa, *HaEleph Lecha Shlomo, Even HaEzer* No. 118. R' Dovid Ortenberg of Berditchev, author of *Tehillah L'Dovid* on *Shulchan Aruch,* was a fervent chassid of the Rizhiner. R' Yaakov Orenstein of Lvov, author of *Yeshuos Yaakov,* though a *misnaged* to Chassidus, met with the Rizhiner and accorded him great honor.

R' Reuven of Odessa was a renowned chassidic follower of the Rizhiner, as were R' Sholom of Kaminka, R' Yehoshua of Ostrov, the Zolkover Rebbe and R' Tzvi of Tiberias, grandson of the Baal Shem Tov.

R' Chaim Halberstam of Sanz, the great chassidic sage and Rebbe, author of Responsa *Divrei Chaim,* held the Rizhiner in great esteem and twice made the journey to Sadagora. On his first journey he was asked by his coachman to stop on the way to rest awhile, to which the Sanzer replied: "How can one stop and waste time to rest when one travels to such a saint? ..."

MANY *TZADDIKIM,* THEMSELVES GREAT REBBES, VISITED AND ADMIRED the Rizhiner. These included the following: R' Yitzchok Meir of Ger, the Chidushei HaRim, visited

••• AND TZADDIKIM Sadagora in 1844. R' Tzvi Hirsch of Rimanov, though older than the Rizhiner, nonetheless praised the young master and they subsequently became *mechutanim.* R' Tzvi Hirsch twice visited Sadagora (1843, 1844) and was highly impressed with the "new" path of the young chassidic Rebbe. The Apter Rav, the *tzaddik* and elder of the generation, exalted the unique leadership and qualifications of the young prince, R' Yisroel. R' Aron Leib and his son R' Meir'l of Premishlan were considered close friends and adherents of the young R' Yisroel. Their friendship was known to all. R' Naftali of Ropshitz, the well-known sage, was another admirer who frequented Rizhin.

THE REBBE OF LUBAVITCH, THE *TZEMACH TZEDEK*, ALSO VISITED SADAGORA and remained in close contact with the Rizhiner, united

THE TZEMACH TZEDEK

with him in the struggle against the anti-Semitic ordinances of Czar Nicholas.

R' Mordechai of Nadvorna, Reb Nechemia'le, son of the holy Yud of Pshis'che and his son R' Elimelech of Grodzhisk, the Ostrovtzer Rebbe, R' Moshe of Kobrin, the elder R' Yitzchok of Vorki, R' Shlomo of Tulchin, R' Moshe of Savrani, a close friend of the Rizhiner; R' Rephael of Bershad, R' Yehudah Hirsch of Strettin and most Ukrainian and Polish Rebbes accepted and respected the great grandson of the Maggid of Mezritch — R' Yisroel — a unique phenomenon in chassidic history. Among his many admirers was R' Mendel of Kotzk,[2] who took it very much to heart when the Rizhiner was arrested in 1838. Chassidim knew that the Rizhiner was constantly opposing his Russian anti-Semitic adversary, Czar Nicholas I, in ways known only to kabbalists. The Kotzker used to wonder

Niggun of Deveikus by the Tzemach Tzedek

---

2. See *Emes VeEmunah*, 1971, pp. 53 and 906.

The beautiful Beis Midrash of the Rebbe of Sadagora

greatly about the Rizhiner's daring and public opposition to the powerful Czar (*Shem MiShmuel, Shemos* 2, p. 153), and for his not acting in a more secretive way (*Emes VeEmunah*).

AMONG THE MANY DIGNITARIES VISITING THE RIZHINER WERE GREGOR Nikolayev, admiral of the Russian Black Sea Flotilla. He was the

••• AND DIGNITARIES

husband of the famous "Muma Leah" of the wealthy Raphaelovich family of Odessa, a "chassidah" of the Rizhiner, who interceded on behalf of the Jewish community in Russia, especially against the edict of Czar Nicholas. This barbaric edict was promulgated on August 26, 1826, its purpose being to draft very young Jews into the Russian army for a period of twenty-five years. This terrible ordinance prompted the leading rabbinic authorities of that time to rise up as one man against the Czar's decree — the Rizhiner foremost among them, all of them voicing dire predictions about the total assimilation of Russian Jewry.[3]

---

3. See introduction to *Teudah b'Yisrael*, 3rd ed., Warsaw, 1879.

Another of the Rizhiner's visitors was Field Marshal Baron Vitgenstein (1769-1842) who, at the urging of the Rizhiner, intervened several times on behalf of the Jews.

Prof. Edward Mayer, who extols the young master in his book *Die Juden In Unzerer Zeit* (Regensburg, 1842), describes his own visit to the Rebbe in 1826.

FOR A PERIOD OF TIME R' YISROEL REFUSED TO ACCEPT THE OFFICIAL TITLE of Rebbe. Day and night he secluded himself in his room, immersed in learning and solitary

DRAW BACK IN ORDER TO LEAP FURTHER

meditation. His soul was somehow absorbed in the remote and distant world of spirituality, as all the while he smoked his long pipe. He spoke little, never mentioning his troubles. Publicly he always appeared with a bright face of inspiration and calm, with an aura of gladness, even. Looking deep into the heart of his fellow-suffering Jews, he never divulged his own pain to others. Only rarely did an account of his traumatic experience in prison surface.

During his first year in Sadagora, he told one of his chassidim that just as they had arrested him without any investigation, so they had released him without investigation. When, in contrast, R' Shneur Zalman of Liadi, the Baal HaTanya, and founder of Chabad, was taken to St. Petersburg to be investigated, it was with fifteen other *tzaddikim*, including R' Sholom Shachna, the Rizhiner's father. All the *tzaddikim* in the world prayed to Hashem for them, and He saved them. One Thursday night R' Sholom Shachna had a vision of a rainbow of bright colors. It is written in the *Tikkunim* (*Zohar*), "When the bright rainbow will appear, you should hope for *Mashiach* to come." When the *tzaddik* got up from his bed and saw that a general salvation had not arrived, he understood that this was only a private salvation. He said that surely they had killed ... (he deleted the word "Czar" because of the censor). After a few days word came that the Czar had been assassinated. The edict for the investigation of the *tzaddikim* was rescinded. The Rizhiner said that the *tzaddikim* prayed for him, too — the prayers of the *tzaddik* from Premishlan were especially felt in prison.

THE COURT OF THE RIZHINER IN SADAGORA WAS FILLED WITH BEAUTY and honor, and the spirit of gladness and happiness hovered over

THE GLORY RESTORED

it always. Despite their suffering the Jews of Galicia would put aside their troubles and with joy and love they came to the Rebbe's *hoif* in Sadagora. There, close to the Rebbe — a loving and caring father who knew how to uplift their spirits and infuse them with fresh hope and encouragement — they felt at home. The Rebbe's magnetic power was beyond imagination. The journey to Sadagora was, for the chassidim, a true pilgrimage reminding them of the *aliyah l'regel* (pilgrimage) to the Holy Temple in Jerusalem. From all over, Jews of every stripe, the simple and sophisticated, the rich and the poor, all flocked to Sadagora. From the Holy Land, *shadarim* (emissaries) came to the Rizhiner to obtain hope and support, for the Rebbe had become the active *nasi* (president) of the Russian and Galician *kollelim* (chassidic communities in the Holy Land).

His representative in Jerusalem was his devoted chassid, R' Nissan Beck, who would visit him yearly and report to the Rebbe regarding all his projects in the Holy Land. In the year 1844, the Rizhiner sent him, together with R' Landau of Romania (Moldavia), as delegates to Sir Moses Montefiore of London. They asked him to intercede with the Czar to allow Russian Jews to collect money in the name of the Fund of Rabbi Meir Baal HaNess, to support their poor Russian brethren who had settled in the Holy Land.

In the year 1848, with the French declaration of rights and equality for all people, including the Jews, the Jewish *maskilim* (intelligentsia) rejoiced, believing that the true redemption for the Jewish people had finally arrived. The Rizhiner, however, said that this was not yet the ultimate redemption of Israel. For one who is in servitude, with his arms and legs in shackles, cannot attain his ultimate true existence. The shackles must be removed so that he can return to the land of his fathers and to his Holy Temple. A government must permit the Jews to return to the land of their forefathers. They will then rise to the moral demands of Judaism, and then all the promises of the prophets regarding the complete Redemption will be fulfilled. This is the meaning of

כִּי עֵת לְחֶנְנָהּ כִּי בָא מוֹעֵד, *For it is time to ask for mercy, for the time has come* (Tehillim 102:14). The word *chaninah* (mercy) comes from the root חָנַם, *chinam* — מַתְּנַת חִנָּם, *matnas chinam* (an unearned gift). That is, before the time of complete redemption, Hashem, in his mercy, must give Israel something: the ability to be redeemed

Signature of the Rizhiner

naturally, without terrible suffering. But if He waits any longer, "behold, the time has come" — our Redemption will finally come, but there will be no more time for *chaninah* (a merciful redemption)." If it is without G-d's mercy, the Redemption may well be accompanied by severe privation.

BENDING WITH THE WIND

WHEN THE *MASKILIM* DECLARED WAR ON THE CHASSIDIM, ALL THE Rebbes of Galicia gathered at Sadagora to plan what action to take against these Jewish slanderers. The Rizhiner's *mechutan*, Reb Chaim of Kossov, opened by asking if they were so helpless that the *maskilim* could treat them like chickens going to *kappores* (slaughter before Yom Kippur). With foresight, the Rizhiner answered him in his characteristic homiletic fashion:

White chickens once held a meeting to work out a way to prevent the selection of white chickens for *kappores*. A young chicken proposed a rebellion. Listen to my advice: Let us doff our white jackets and get mixed up with the crowd, so that we will no longer be so conspicuous. The young roosters jumped up and said that they must go out and openly protest against this custom. Afterwards, the eldest rooster of the group rose and ruled, "We should fly through the chimney and, as our feathers will blacken, they will no longer recognize us."

"So it is with us," said the Rizhiner. "I advise that we take off our white garments and come and mix with the rest of our people. In that way we will become less visible and will be able to bring counsel and salvation to the masses."

THE ANTIDOTE FOR MELANCHOLY

"IF A JEW HAS PAIN IN HIS LITTLE FINGER," HE ONCE SAID, "HIS PAIN REACHES the very core of my heart." In a conversation years later with a Rizhiner chassid, his son, R' Dovid Moshe of Chortkov, said: "You knew my father when he lived in Sadagora and wore the black *yarmulke* (skullcap) on his head and was a little melancholic, but you never saw him when he still lived in Rizhin with the golden skullcap on his head." The chassid replied: "I am amazed how it was possible that your revered father could ever be enveloped in melancholia. From his own mouth we always heard him say that melancholy was the worst possible characteristic of the *sitra achra* (lit. the 'other side,' the Satanic dimension), and he who falls into it has forgotten Hashem Himself, Heaven forbid."

"Yes, it is so," replied the Chortkover. "And from this fact, itself, it is apparent that it is so, for only in his later years when my father

Proclamation appointing Sir Moses Montefiore as president of the holy places in the Holy Land

was at his highest level was he capable of lowering himself to the level of melancholy, in order to retrieve and elevate the forsaken souls that had fallen there."

AFTER SUPPRESSING THE POLISH REVOLT IN 1830, CZAR NICHOLAS turned his attention to the Jews. Inasmuch as he did not hesitate to **CZARIST** snatch children away from their mothers' bosoms and forcibly conscript them in his army **OPPRESSION** for twenty-five years, Christianizing them or sending the objectors to the steppes of Siberia to face certain death, he was surely delighted to lay hands on the leaders of a Jewish movement with the power to unite and fire far-flung communities.

In the same year a general ban was proclaimed against the *tzaddikim*, which metamorphosed, thanks to the power of the

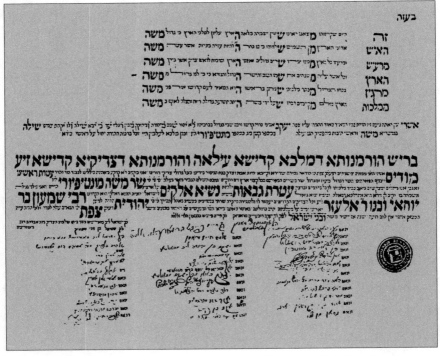

Proclamation appointing Sir Montefiore in charge of Rabbi Shimon bar Yochai's tomb

judiciously distributed rubles, into a prohibition merely against a change of residence without a special permit. Later on, the authorities forbade the use of the ancient Polish garb as "Jewish insignia." The crypto-anti-Semites had more of an instinct for what was of the essence in the burgeoning Jewish religious consciousness than did the so-called intellectuals of the time.

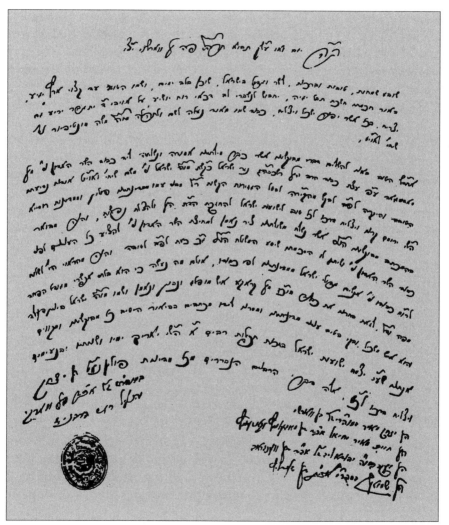

Letter of R' Yitzchok of Vorki and other Polish Rebbes to Sir Moses Montefiore

FOR THE SAKE OF TRUTH WE HAVE TO STATE THAT THE STRICT AND BRUTAL Czar Nicholas I, who threw mercy out of the window in his hatred and hostility toward Judaism, nonetheless, out of a ruler's pride, abhorred lies; by virtue of this he eradicated once and for all, by governmental decree, the notorious "blood libel."[4]

BLOOD LIBEL AND THE CZAR

It happened once that the false accusation of ritual murder reared its malevolent head, but Czar Nicholas I was unimpressed, giving the charge no credence whatsoever, on the grounds that he was daily regaled with slander against Judaism from pseudo-Jews, and that had there been one iota of truth to the accusations, there would have been something to substantiate them in the records of his own agencies.

To make assurance doubly certain, the Czar inquired of the clergy what they had to say regarding this matter. He also gathered together all the Jewish apostates in the country, who all swore, by their allegiance to the New Testament, that this charge had no basis in truth. Just as in old Poland, the work of the Jesuits, who were responsible for the spread of these accusations, was frustrated by a decree of the rulers, so in Russia, too, the Czar put an end to the anti-Semitic propaganda of the Church. Notwithstanding all the persecutions that they underwent, the Jews, who quickly forget the injustices done to them and remember forever manifestations of kindness, preserved their allegiance to that mighty dictator.

CAPTIVE CHILDREN

THE ABDUCTION OF TENDER JEWISH CHILDREN BY THE RUSSIAN RULERS, to subject them to years of training, army service and ultimately conversion to Christianity, was considered by our people, even by the standards of the Middle Ages, to be an act of unheard-of cruelty. R' Yitzchok of Vorki, disciple of R' Simchah Bunim of Pshis'che, was looked up to as a great religious leader by masses of followers in Poland. He exerted himself unsparingly to have the abominable edicts of Czar Nicholas I rescinded, among them the notorious edict that enforced military service upon Jewish youth, subsequent

---

4. An obscene libel, going back centuries, according to which the Jews tortured and then used the blood of gentile children for the dough of the Passover matzos.

to which efforts would be made to convert them to Christianity. R' Yitzchok came to Sadagora to enlist the help of the Rizhiner. He was advised to seek out the influential R' Yitzchok Bienenfeld in Cracow, and have him visit Sir Moses Montefiore in London, in the hope that the latter might be able to intercede with the Czar on behalf of Russian Jewry in the name of the English government. The Rebbe of Vorki traveled to Cracow and beseeched R' Yitzchok Bienenfeld to go as an emissary to Sir Moses Montefiore. As a result of this action, Sir Moses Montefiore did visit Russia and made an effort to improve the lot of the Jews there.

Thus Sir Moses Montefiore, glorious defender of Judaism and close friend of Lords Disraeli and Palmerston, the leaders of Parliament, succeeded in obtaining a mandate from the English government to visit St. Petersburg on behalf of the Jews. Lord Disraeli had this in mind when he expressed his wonderment at the capability of the Jews, despite their severe treatment by the government, to find a way to navigate the devious ways of politics.

Sir Moses Montefiore's personal intervention with the Czar was crowned with success and the Jews of Russia and Galicia were spared ultimate extinction. History records with pride the important part played by the Rizhiner in helping this vital Jewish cause.

On Purim 1855, Czar Nicholas I died, four years after the demise of the Rizhiner, a foremost victim of his persecutions.

CHAPTER X

THE RIZHINER: THE MAN

IN THE SPIRITUAL TEMPLE THAT ENSHRINES THE SOULS OF THE GREAT
rebbes, there is prepared a chair for R' Yisroel of Rizhin, perhaps
higher and loftier than the seats of all the pious men of his gen-

**THE HIGHEST
PEDESTAL**
eration. He was esteemed not only by
great numbers of his followers, but
also by chassidim of other dynasties
who acknowledged his greatness. Many chassidic dignitaries
placed him on the highest pedestal, among them such great men as
R' Meir Yechiel of Mogelnitza and R' Moshe of Kobrin, who was
embellished with the title of Holy Angel. Even Rebbes heading great
communities of chassidim used to set out on foot on a pilgrimage to
him, in order to be near him and hear his pleasant talk.

The fact is, there was no pious man in his generation who did not
have opponents to criticize his conduct, but no one criticized the

Rizhiner. It was a foregone conclusion and accepted by all that he was superior. And when R' Chaim of Sanz, himself an eminent Rebbe, a great, erudite and G-d-fearing man, was asked what induced him to pay a visit to the Rebbe of Rizhin, his answer was that the latter was comparable to the mountain of Moriah. Although the revelation did not take place on it, as on Mount Sinai, yet the Holy Temple was erected on it, because in that place Yitzchok son of Avrohom stretched out his neck for the sake of Hashem's Blessed Name. He said further: "The Rebbe of Rizhin stretches out his neck every hour of the day for the sake of Hashem." The Apter, the oldest of the virtuous men of the generation, held him in the highest esteem, asserting that his soul had been taken from the temple of "a bird nest," *kan tzippor* — alluding of course to the Temple of *Mashiach*.

Surprisingly enough, the Rizhiner gave no opportunity to his chassidic followers and admirers in general to marvel at his miracles and wonders, because he performed none; legendary stories were not told about wonders supposedly performed by him. He was not a miracle-worker and yet he was called a miraculous man. This is indeed the only "wonder" in the life of R' Yisroel of Rizhin. Men great in Torah, Chassidus, fear of Hashem, virtue and exemplary conduct stood in his shadow, while his renown spread far and wide. He was his era's undisputed beloved leader. He was both the beginning and the conclusion of an era.

How are we to resolve this enigma unless we allow that every once in a while Providence places in our midst one so extravagantly graced with the rarest of virtues and qualities — an act of bounty of the Divine treasury — that even the loftiest voices of his generation are hushed in universal veneration and wonder.

His generation was not worthy of a leader like this. As he once observed, "I have a complaint about my parents — why they should have set me down in a low generation like this!" Those of his generation who came to stand in his shadow failed to understand his way and were unable to learn from his allusions and gestures. They needed a leader and counselor who would explain to them his intent in explicit terms, who would teach them like a rabbi explaining difficult concepts to his students, but the holy

Rebbe was mystical and hidden, beyond their sphere, and they could not wrest from him his secrets.

The Rizhiner did not have disciples in the way of the Baal Shem Tov and the Maggid, students who would spread his thoughts to the outside and would put them into action, in speaking, writing and printing, to teach them to all Israel.

On his desire to establish a system of Chassidus in matters between man and his fellow man, he likened his task to that of one traveling a road full of holes, thorns and thistles, in the midst of the darkest night, and lightning strikes time after time to light the way. A foolish traveler looks to the sky which is rent by lightning and in the process falls into one of the holes; the wise man uses the lightning to look at the road in order to avoid the pitfalls. Chassidus is the lightning to show the way in the world of action.

THE APTER RAV ONCE ASKED THE RIZHINER IF HIS FATHER HAD ALSO borne himself in such a regal manner. He answered that his father

THE HIGHEST AND THE LOWEST

was in the category of a father, and was not required to stand on ceremony. He, however, was in a category of royalty and a king must always stand on ceremony.

The charisma of the Rizhiner — that priceless pearl that he polished into such radiance that other gems were obscured and, as it were, annihilated in its light — was the true source of his elevation. Grace and charm were not only in his facial features, but in the amiability of his speech, in the beauty of his form and in all his aristocratic ways. He was descended from the royalty, as it were, of Chassidus, rendering him an outstanding personality, Chassidus' favorite son.

In the book *Divrei Dovid* by R' Dovid Moshe of Chortkov, we learn that his father the Rizhiner knew everyone's thoughts. Once he and his father were riding together; he thought of something and the Rizhiner told him what he was thinking about. He knew the thoughts of all who stood before him. We call this clairvoyance, and he possessed it in full measure.

He once said to those sitting around him at the table, "Why do you come to me? What do you see in me? I am the worst of the worst!" In reference to this, he once said, "I am able to live alone on an island for one hundred years without any *seforim*, and worship Hashem without the slightest interruption."

R' Yisroel traveled to Karlin, by way of Pinsk, for his son's wedding. He stopped the wagon in the middle of the town, opened the door and beckoned to those outside to gaze upon his face, saying , "All those who see my countenance will not see Hell."

Once he was considering the great men of his time as if they were limbs of *Mashiach.* "This great man is the head of *Mashiach,* and this great man is the hand." He concluded, "I am the rock that is silent." At another time he said, "Woe is to the stone that has no one to understand its value."

The author of this work heard from his revered father-in-law, the late Rebbe R' Mordechai Shlomo Friedman of Boyan-New York, that his great-grandfather, the Rizhiner, "was incomprehensible. At times he spoke of himself as 'very high,' and at other times he perceived himself as 'very low.' However, never challenged, he enjoyed the approbation and acceptance of the entire world."

MOMENTOUS DEMANDS

HE STEPPED INTO THE SHOES AND INTO THE INHERITANCE OF *TZADDIKIM* who had a happy spirit and joyous heart. As sons and grandsons of saintly men who walked the earth, the new heirs would often be grim of countenance, under the pressure of the grief and weight of their descent from lofty spheres. It was as if they were dressed, not in the raiment of golden genealogy, but fettered with thorns and briars. It was as if their forebears were of an inflexible cast, demanding of them incessant growth and steady, fearless labor until the departure of their souls.

However, whether one had the benefit of a joyous legacy, joyous accession or a negligible family descent it was imperative that they create something new, to add a definite measure of one's own merit, commensurate with the legacy of their forefathers' merits.

Such men of noble truth either abandon the path of their fathers to blaze a trail of their own — a process entailing great hardship (every newly chosen road throws up adversity, the more so when the new road runs counter to the imposition of birth) — or they collapse ineffectually beneath the intolerable burden of their genealogy. Their fathers' magnitude infects them with dread and paralysis, with the result that, on the one hand, you have daring, and on the other hand, repressed offspring. And still, the degree of daring demanded that they rise relentlessly, exponentially.

R' YISROEL OF RIZHIN WANTED TO BE AN EXAMPLE FOR THE MASSES. He wanted them to be congenial and well mannered, to carry themselves with dignity and speak with decorum, in order that the Name of Heaven should become beloved through their behavior, as our Sages have said (*Yoma* 86a). But the opportunity was denied him. The chassidim said, "Only he and his aristocratic household were obliged to behave in a regal manner, because they were of the House of Dovid, but not his generation of chassidim ..."

HIDDEN EXAMPLE FOR THE MASSES

R' Dovid Ortenberg, of Berditchev, heard the following from the Rizhiner: "What do you think — *tzaddikim* do not know how to learn Torah?! The truth is that Torah teaches a way of life; how to worship Hashem. The study of Torah is a mantle to the Torah. Therefore one who is secluded with the King is secluded with His own mantle."

He once sent for his carriage and left orders that no one should follow him. When he went out to the carriage, the Rabbi of Romania stood there. He gestured to the Rabbi of Romania to approach him. The Rizhiner then said, "Rabbi of Romania, you are a world traveler, this is what I want you to say: 'The Rizhiner's carriage is worth so much money and the horses are worth so much money, and the Rizhiner has never benefited from anything in this world, regardless of how little or how much it may seem. Who knows how much the breadth of a hair really is? לֹא נֶהֱנֵיתִי מֵעוֹלָם הַזֶּה אֲפִילוּ כְּחוּט הַשַּׂעֲרָה." He then repeated this statement.

Other men of his caliber spent days in fasting, cried at the dearth of Divine Inspiration, felt humble and degraded their own world, full of shame and self-contempt at being steeped in sin and transgression. They were strict and exact with themselves, sometimes even chagrined at the presence of the impure thoughts, or at a tinge of alien intention.

AND, LO AND BEHOLD! IN THE MIDST OF THIS COMMUNITY OF DEPRESSED and distressed chassidim and righteous men there appeared a

THE SOUL OF A BIRD jewel of aristocratic descent, self-confident, overtly happy, cheerful, a rigorously dialectic and reforming soul. Rumor spread far and wide that he was a very important figure in the upper spheres and that his soul had been created for soaring flight. Were not these rumors in actuality the truth? Was not the sound of legend the reverberation of reality? He wanted the best for Klal Yisroel and advocated and pleaded with Hashem like the Berditchever and Shpoler Zeide. As the defender of his people before the A-mighty G-d, he vindicated the cause of man. The Rizhiner's soul was quintessentially that of a bird, a light-winged bird. What others obtained with endless hardship, with self-flagellation, with breaking of the evil inclination, with asceticism, with tears and self-abasement, he acquired with a light touch, with a pleasant smile, with mirth, with a witticism, with a beautiful phrase, and all of it, as it were, touched with genius, for "out of delicacy came forth much astuteness." Wealth and pleasure — things which were barred to others — were permitted to him.

In the realm of ethics there are combinations of reckoning that do not chime with common sense. What is stringent in the case of one is deemed light with regards to another; a slight aberration for which one is adjudged guilty is, in the case of another, reckoned as virtue. A light-headed chassid is completely unqualified, whereas a *tzaddik* is a granite foundation, though he too may sometimes be acting as one light of heart.

The Rizhiner himself once tossed off a seemingly trivial comment, as was his wont. "Why do we feed birds cereal on *Shabbos Shirah* — the Shabbos when the song of Moshe is read at the Torah reading in the synagogue?" The following parable will explain:

Once there was a king who had a huge palace containing many apartments for the accommodation of his ministers, their assistants and his associates. Each apartment was a minipalace in itself, and in each palace there were musicians and singers to entertain guests with music and song. The king had a special palace housing the most talented instrumentalists and the best instruments. But the king's greatest pleasure was the chirping of one bird, and he enjoyed its singing above that of all the singers and players. This tiny creature delighted the king throughout his life.

The moral lesson of the parable is this: the Israelites are nicknamed *kan tzippor*, a bird's nest. When the Jewish multitudes left Egypt, there were a select few especially great people, symbolized by this bird. This symbolic bird also found a resting place among

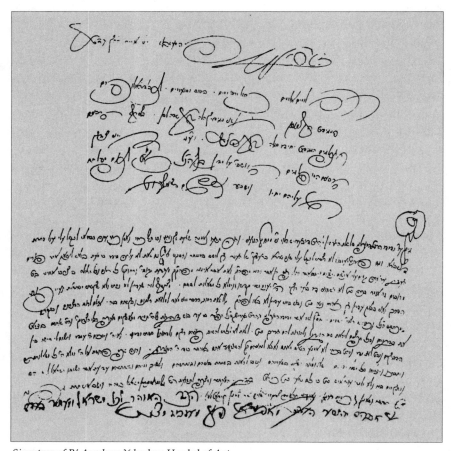

Signature of R' Avrohom Yehoshua Heschel of Apt

them, and the Sea of Reeds was divided for the bird's sake, too. And when all the angels and *seraphim* were singing in the presence of the Holy One, Blessed is He, no chanting was as sweet to Hashem as that of the bird that accompanied the Israelites on the Exodus and was singing along with them. For this reason we feed the birds cereal on *Shabbos Shirah* — to commemorate the bird and its singing.

Surely within this parable and its moral lesson there is hidden another parable and a great lesson. And this is the Rizhiner himself, in the image of this singing bird. There is no doubt whatsoever that this is so. And to this his own very being attests: that the Rizhiner was like a bird of *Gan Eden* (Paradise).

Once, when a terrible decree of the Czar was issued against the Jews of the Ukraine, the Apter proclaimed a public fast day. On the same day, however, R' Yisroel invited his band of musicians to entertain him. When the Apter found out about it, he was not angry, nor did he grumble. On the contrary, he began to relate the greatness of the Rizhiner, and he exclaimed, "The *tzaddik* of Rizhin has fulfilled the verse 'When war comes into your land, you shall blow the trumpets and be saved from your enemies.'" "Everything is forgiven and permitted to him. One should not try to find fault with the *tzaddik* of Rizhin, whose little finger is broader than our loins." The Apter Rav also said: "We with our white beards stand abashed and ashamed in the presence of this young man, the greatness of whose stature one cannot imagine, much less attain."

OF WHAT DID HIS UNIQUENESS CONSIST AND WHAT ACCOUNTED FOR THE unprecedented esteem in which his contemporaries held him? In

HIS SECRET terms of all conventional notions of the *tzaddik*, as defined by the highest levels of integrity, of scholastic profundity and breadth of vision, of wonder-working, or originality of interpretation, of extreme self-sacrifice and love of one's fellow Jew — in all such terms, the picture he presents is not an overwhelming one. In his conduct he never waged open war against the evil inclination by means of adjurations and the like (as other *tzaddikim* were wont to do).

But perhaps this riddle may be approached from a different point of view, which is that there is a higher crown than that of the *tzaddik* of the generation and the prince of the people; and that is the crown of the generation's man of truth. All crowns are destined to disappear, save the crown of the man of truth. This will endure forever. All other great men were great in their time, but the man of truth truly belongs to all generations, to eternity.

He was responsible for earthly inspiration insofar as he raised the esteem of Chassidus in its time, and gave it wide circulation among the noblemen of the world.

NEW HEIGHTS BEFORE THE SUNSET

THE CENTURY-LONG ASSAULT OF THE *MISNAGDIM* AND *MASKILIM* AGAINST Chassidus continued unabated, with no quarter given, even during the time of the Rizhiner and his descendants. We may quote the Psalmist and say, Chassidus was a *stone the builders rejected* (*Tehillim* 118:22). Why? Because its opponents were unable to surmount the obstacles separating them from its brightness, purity, depth, charm and kindness, the core of its magnificence. The Rizhiner was fashioned from that core. Evidently he assumed that there was no kingdom without a crown, that a crown was unthinkable without a royal court, and with the latter came, naturally, chamberlains, stewards, lackeys — an entourage. He raised the stature of Chassidus to royal heights. From this viewpoint he is the head of a dynasty, not a follower like his grandfather, the Maggid, nor a leader of a group of followers, like all the other chassidic Rebbes. At the third generation, high rank ceases altogether, whether it be of wealth or of wisdom. After the Rizhiner there begins the sunset of the Chassidus of service. Chassidus of a lighter caliber comes to the fore. It is quite possible that because he made his appearance during the decline of Chassidus that there blazed up in him all the rainbow colors in one last dazzling display.

He moved in other worlds. He sought solitude and lived his own life of contemplation. His primary aim, we may say, was to restore to its original splendor the outer crown of Jerusalem and

Judaism, and its traditional culture, which had suffered for so long a time through all the Diaspora restrictions and struggles; the excessive scholasticism, the one-sided mysticism. He was no less than just in proclaiming that he and R' Menachem Mendel of Kotzk (1787-1859) were poles apart. For, indeed, they were diametric opposites. In Kotzk, there was a stoicism that made naught of the entire world, deprecated involvement in temporal affairs and ignored the accepted modes of life. Rizhin, in contrast, fostered neat dress, careful grooming, along with dignified demeanor and deportment. Nevertheless, for all its outward ostentation, Rizhin insisted on abstention from pleasures from childhood on, which led to personal austerity even in the consumption of food.

He inherited, and transmitted to his children, the ascetic path, eschewing the custom of yore of a prolonged fast succeeded by a gluttonous meal. Oftentimes he sorrowed over the fact that the older style of eating with austerity and self-restraint had passed away.

Once, two men who were not his followers came to him. They remained for two Shabbosos and upon their departure, they queried, "Why is it that when we go to our Rebbe and we stay for just one Shabbos, we receive from him enough Chassidus to last us an entire year, while here we have remained two weeks and we do not have enough Chassidus for even one day?" The Rebbe responded that the situation was comparable to that of one who sits on the top of a mountain, enjoying an abundance of all good things, and beneath the mountain sits a mass of starving and impoverished wretches. Should the one on high go down to those below? He cannot possibly forge an association with such low wretches. The ones below certainly cannot ascend to him. The only recourse for them, then, is to go to someone down below who sits on the ground, but who thinks that he sits on the mountain.

Followers of another Rebbe once came to spend Shabbos with the Rizhiner. On Friday evening, they heard his *divrei Torah* and they were of one mind that the Rizhiner did not approach their Rebbe in Torah scholarship. On Shabbos morning, they heard his Torah again at the table and they said that this time it was better than on the previous day, but it still did not equal the Torah of their Rebbe. At the *shalosh seudos* (the third meal), they again heard his Torah and concluded that it was as good as their Rebbe's. After Shabbos, when they entered his room to bid him farewell, the Rizhiner acknowledged that he had said all sorts of words of Torah on Friday night and on Shabbos morning, and only at the third meal had he said Torah that was comparable to their Rebbe's. He compared this phenomenon to that of a king who built a large tower which was exceedingly difficult to climb. The king decreed that whoever could scale the tower would receive his daughter's hand in marriage. Many tried to do this, but none succeeded. Finally, there was a man who stood and cried and beseeched the king and with his pleading was able to influence the king to raise him to the top of the tower and give him the princess's hand in marriage. But this man, once atop the tower, could no longer descend. So it is with your Rebbe, who rose up to the heights on the wings of his tears and *Tehillim*-saying. Now that he has attained this highest level, he can no longer descend, and he must perforce say only great words of Torah, he can no longer descend to the more humble levels of Torah!

R' Reuven of Odessa went to visit the Rizhiner. On the way, he passed through the city of Lemberg and stopped in to see the Gaon of Lemberg, R' Yaakov Orenstein, author of *Yeshuos Yaakov*. As was to be expected, they engaged in *divrei Torah*. When R' Yaakov heard that he was going to visit the Rizhiner, he asked him how it was possible that he should go and visit a person who was not a Torah authority. R' Reuven answered that once when he had been with the Rizhiner, a tearful woman came in to see him. She asked that the Rizhiner give her a blessing, pleading with him to promise her that Hashem would grant her a male child. The woman remained unconvinced and continued to cry tearfully. In order to pacify her, the Rizhiner swore that in a year's time she would give birth to a male child. In order to give credence to his oath, the Rizhiner cited the Talmud, *Yevamos* 121a: the case where a woman's husband had drowned and she was permitted to remarry because of the application of the principle of *rov* (majority): "Even in matters of life and death, we apply the principle of *rov* — that our Sages have told us that most women become pregnant,

and give birth. Therefore, it was permissible to make this oath." R'
Yaakov then countered with a *Tosafos* in *Yevamos* 37, that states that
if a woman has not given birth for many years, the principle of *rov*
does not apply to her. When R' Reuven presented this objection to
the Rizhiner, the Rizhiner answered with a different explanation of
Tosafos, and the discussion vindicated his Talmudic knowledge.

AFTER THE PASSING OF RAV DOV BER, THE SON OF R' SHNEUR ZALMAN OF
Liadi, his chassidim decided to travel to Rizhin in order to determine

LIADI AND RIZHIN
whether they could attach themselves to the Rizhiner. However,
they were accustomed to words of Torah based on the Chabad approach, whereas it was the custom of the *tzaddik* of Rizhin to say but
few words of Torah, in conformity with the idea that the glory of
Hashem dwells in secret. Hence, when these chassidim came to
Rizhin, they did not find what they sought. When they came to him
for a blessing at their departure, the Rizhiner said to them, "It is written: *And Moshe said to Hashem, 'Behold, when I come to the Children of
Israel… and they will ask me: What is His Name? What shall I say to
them?' (Shemos* 3:13)." According to the simple explanation, this verse
is impossible to understand. Is it possible that Moshe, soon to become the leader of all the Israelites, still did not know the Name of
Hashem? Even had he been in Egypt until then, it would still be impossible that he should not know the Name of Hashem. Rather, the
truth is that not only Moshe, but the rest of the Israelites also, knew
the Name of Hashem. So the verse, *And they will say: What is His
Name?* means, they will anticipate me and tell me the Name of
Hashem, which they have known for many years; but what shall I,
Moshe, say to them? Hashem answered and said, 'I will be what I
will be.' The two words אֶהְיֶה, *I will be,* amount numerically to 21
times 21, which is the numerical value of אֱמֶת, *truth,* and indeed, the
seal of G-d is truth (*Shabbos* 58a) (חוֹתָמוֹ שֶׁל הקָ"בה אֱמֶת)."

Once, a certain learned scholar from Poland traveled hundreds
of miles on foot to hear his words of Torah, arriving at Sadagora for
the Lag b'Omer *seudah*. This gentleman took a seat directly behind
the Rizhiner, for he desired to hear him well. To his dismay, the

Rebbe said very little. The man's disappointment was keen indeed, having invested so much time, energy and money for so scant a return in rare and inspiring words of Torah. In this mood of bitter rejection he remained until the time for *Birchas HaMazon* (Grace after the Meal). After *Birchas HaMazon*, the Rebbe arose from his place in a tone of wonder and question quoted the verse, *For he is an angel of Hashem, Master of Legions, and Torah will be sought from his mouth* (Malachi 2:7)? "Is it not enough," he asked, "that the Rebbe appears to be an angel? Is it also necessary that Torah be sought from his mouth?"

When the Rizhiner visited the city of Lvov, for medical treatments, he was welcomed by the brilliant R' Mordechai Zev Itinger. The Rizhiner asked him to be seated and told him a story, as was his custom. When he had finished, R' Mordechai told him that, while the story was nice enough, he preferred to hear some words of Torah.

The Rizhiner responded with a parable: King Shlomo said, *For Hashem is in the heavens and you are upon the earth; therefore let your words be few* (Koheles 5:1). What is the interpretation of this verse? If the intent is that a man should limit his speech and take care not to prattle, because *the whole earth is filled with His glory* (Yeshayah 6:3), then it should have stated, "For Hashem is in the heavens and the earth, therefore let your words be few." Why also did Shlomo emphasize "and you are on earth"? The answer is that Hashem is the Creator and the relationship between the creatures and the Creator is one of a son to his father. Just as it is natural for a son to love his father, so it is natural for His creatures to love and fear their Creator. Yet, since man is in this world, the Creator gave him the Torah, as our rabbis of blessed memory said, "I created the *yetzer hara* and I created the Torah as a remedy" (Kiddushin 30b) in order to remind man and to teach him that there is a Creator to be loved and feared. But if "you are on this earth" and remember and know that there is a Creator, then it is enough for you to speak little and there is no need to overindulge in words of Torah. R' Mordechai Zev was so impressed by the Rizhiner's words that he later commented: "Such *divrei Torah* can only be said by someone who is not a regular human mortal."

INDEED, THE ESSENCE OF HIS INFLUENCE UPON HIS FOLLOWERS LAY, NOT in saying words of Torah at the table, as was the custom of the

POWER OF A STORY

other Rebbeim, but rather in the nature of the individual relationships that he had with each of them. He would devote many hours of the day to receiving them; he would listen to their requests, questions and worries, and would respond to each one appropriately; sometimes with a succinct and clever saying and sometimes by way of parable or story with a pertinent moral. He explained this chassidic custom of telling stories and leading simple discussions with his followers in this way.

After the sin of Adam, many holy sparks fell into unclean containers, and it is incumbent upon everyone to rescue the sparks from their unclean shells and to return them to their origins. And the means for doing this is the Torah. Still, even in eating and drinking, if one eats according to the commandment of the Torah and makes the proper blessings on the food before and after eating it, one can also rescue the sparks and also repair them. However, there remain sparks which have descended to places where even Torah and prayers can no longer reach them, and these apparently cannot be replaced. It was for this purpose that Avraham our Patriarch discovered a new method of repairing those things that are beyond the realm of Torah and prayer, and this was through ordinary conversation. When Eliezer wanted to remove Rivkah from the place of impurity (Haran), he saw that, purely by means of Torah and prayer, he would be unable to do so, and he would have to rely upon stories and "idle chatter." Therefore he said, *I cannot, until I have spoken my piece* (*Bereishis* 24:33). *I cannot* — I cannot go about this according to the commandments of the Torah alone, *until I have spoken my piece* but rather on the basis of conversation and "idle chatter." And this is what Rav Acha said, "Better is the chatter of the servants of the fathers than the Torah of their sons" (*Bereishis Rabbah* 60:11).

The Tzemach Tzedek of Lubavitch (1799-1866) once sent one of his followers, R' Yitzchok of Homel (1799-1866), to the Rizhiner on a matter of community welfare. When R' Yitzchok was there he found himself in the company of two chassidim who had come to seek endorsements for their books from the Rebbe. One of them, a great Torah scholar, had authored a halachic treatise; the other had written a book of stories about *tzaddikim*. He saw that the Rebbe gave first his endorsement to the latter and was greatly surprised that this should have been given priority. The Rizhiner explained himself: "Even Hashem followed this practice. In the beginning of the Book of *Bereishis*, Rashi says that Hashem should have begun the Torah only from the commandment about the consecration of the month (*Shemos* 12) which contains the first commandment to the nation of Israel. Instead of this He began with stories, and we, too, follow this practice."

CHAPTER XI

HANGING BY A HAIR

A CHASSID OF R' CHAIM TIRER OF CHERNOVITZ, AUTHOR OF *Be'er Mayim Chaim*, came to see the Rizhiner. Since he doubted whether he would be able to see the Rebbe again, he requested that he tell him something that would always be of help to him. The *tzaddik* replied that he would. "Before the coming of *Mashiach*," he commenced, "Judaism will hang by a hair. It will therefore be imperative that Jews gather together each Shabbos and tell stories of the *tzaddikim*, to strengthen their faith. This is what the Torah hints at when it says, *Gather together and I will tell you what is to happen at the End of Days* (*Bereishis* 49:1). *Gather together* is to be taken in the literal and simple sense, that you should periodically make assemblies because יִקְרָא, "what will happen," implies קַר, "cold," that which will "freeze you" in the End of Days. People should gather to invoke the memory of the *tzaddikim* and thus warm themselves spiritually. The Rizhiner then made a threefold stipulation — with his visitor — that he should uphold, remember and transmit this advice.

Every once in a while, he would tell stories of the *tzaddikim* before the daily *tefillos*. Once, he became so immersed in this storytelling that it was already very late when he realized that he had not yet *davened*. Sharing this realization with his followers, he simultaneously disclosed to them that stories, like prayer, can bring one closer to Hashem. Thus, prayer is the realm of, *Praise the Name of Hashem* (*Tehillim* 113:1), while the stories of the *tzaddikim* are in the realm of *Praise the servants of Hashem*. We find psalms which begin with *Praise the Name of Hashem* before the phrase *Praise the servants of Hashem,* as in Chapter 135, but sometimes the Psalmist begins with *Praise the servants of Hashem* before *Praise the Name of Hashem,* as in Chapter 113, and if such is the case, then both are equal.

HIS SCHEDULE

HIS CUSTOM WAS TO SLEEP ONLY THREE HOURS A DAY. HE WOULD RISE early in the morning and sit locked in his room for several hours, studying Torah. He received guests from 9 o'clock in the morning until noon, and afterwards he would *daven*. There were however frequent periods when the Rizhiner refused to see anybody, even his closest family. During such times he secluded himself in his quarters in total communion with his Creator. After *davening*, he ate something and continued receiving visitors. A quarter of an hour of the day he would chop wood for physical exercise, on his doctor's advice. Between the afternoon and evening *tefillos* he would venture out in his coach. After the evening *tefillos* he received guests until midnight, so that his day was filled with Torah, prayer and communing with his followers.

Even on the holy Shabbos he slept little. The rabbinic dictum, שֵׁינָה בְּשַׁבָּת תַּעֲנוּג, "Sleep on Shabbos is a pleasure" (*Yalkut HaReuveni, Va'eschanan*), he interpreted as, "When one sleeps on Shabbos, the pleasure of Shabbos is what he sleeps away." He used to tell the story of Napoleon, who did not sleep for three days in a row after having been crowned emperor. The doctors warned him that he was endangering his life. He told them that they may have been right but that when he slept he ceased to be emperor.

When his followers asked the Rizhiner how he could extend the halachic time of *tefillah*, he explained that before the first sin, instigated by the serpent, there had been no time limit on *tefillah*, but that only after the sin, when the world became impure, did our forefathers have to establish special times for *tefillah*, thereby re-purifying the world during those times. At the Sinaitic Revelation, the impurities of the Jews fell away, and they rose above time, only to fall under its domain once again, when they sinned with the Golden Calf. Finally it was left to the Men of the Great Assembly to establish times for *tefillah*. But the soul of the *tzaddik*, which had no part in the sin of the serpent nor in the sin of the Golden Calf, is above time and can pray at the times when it feels spiritually prepared.

On another occasion, when the conversation turned to the subject of *tefillah* outside of the appointed hour, he compared it to the practice of the king who established times for his chiefs and princes to come before him with their needs and requests. Were someone to have come before him on matters vitally affecting the welfare of his kingdom, however, then any time would serve and the king would accept him with alacrity, with or without an appointment, since he comes not for his own but for the common-weal. "Since all my *tefillos* are directed only to the common good," the Rebbe said, "the King will grant me an audience at any time and be glad to receive me."

ONCE, DURING THE HIGH HOLY DAYS, SOME MEN WHO WERE STAYING with the Rizhiner noticed that he was not overly scrupulous regarding which hour he prayed, and they took to blindly following this practice. At the time of departure, he adjured them to pray at the appointed time, adding:

PARABLE TURNED AROUND

There was a man whose wife would cook bean soup every day for lunch. Once she was delayed and served him the food several hours late. Her husband, angered, said, "I thought that today you would surprise me and serve a different and better dish that might have required more time to prepare, so that I waited patiently until now; but for this bean soup that you serve me every day, I do not wish to wait even one minute more."

With this, the men, suitably chastised, left. On the road they stopped at an inn where they met an old man. In the course of conversation, they told him the story of the bean soup that they had heard from their Rebbe. The old man heard the story and said that only a husband who does not love his wife could become angry at her for such a thing. Whereas, if there were complete love between husband and wife, then, even if she were to take ever so long a time before serving him, her husband would not become angry!

When they returned to the Rizhiner the following year, they told him what the man had said. He listened and said: "That old man came to this world only in order to be מְלַמֵד זְכוּת (find something positive to say) on behalf of those who are late for prayer."

HE ONCE COMMENTED ON THE REASON WHY JEWS FIRST SAID AT THE Sinai revelation נַעֲשֶׂה, *We will do,* and then וְנִשְׁמָע, *We will hear*

INSTINCT FOR COMMANDMENTS

(*Shemos* 24:7). It is well known that a baby instinctively feels the hunger and knows that food will satisfy his needs without having to be taught that this is so. Such is our case. The 248 positive precepts and 365 negative precepts which are the spiritual sustenance of man correspond to the 248 organs and 365 sinews. Were it not for the fermenting yeast in the flour (meaning the *yetzer hara*) which holds him back, man would discern innately what he needs and what he does not need without the assistance of the precepts of the Torah. That is why our forefathers were able to observe the Torah before it was given, because from their own instincts they were able to tell what they lacked — as a newborn child knows that he requires food and drink. When Israel came to Mt. Sinai, their impurities were all purged; they themselves realized that they must take on the precepts even before they received the command to do so. Therefore, they said, "We will do," even before they heard what it was they were to do. Knowing this, we can grasp more clearly what we say in the Pesach Haggadah, "If you had simply brought us before Mt. Sinai without even giving us the Torah, it would have sufficed."

THE REBBE WOULD SAY THAT IT WAS APPROPRIATE FOR THE JEWS TO BE saved and granted all manner of good things even before the com-

IMPORTANCE OF WELL-BEING

ing of *Mashiach,* in order that they be able to distinguish between good and even better. When a man is released from prison, it is no great thing if he knows that freedom is something good. If the Jews were to taste the good life, then they would know that the Messianic age is even greater. He noted that the Jew seldom finds that he can serve Hashem in true holiness while he is embroiled in troubles. This ability arrives only from the other path. With respect to the path of holiness, we find that a Jew can best serve Hashem from a position of well-being. A proof of this concept is to be found in the passage in *Bereishis* 31:47. Yaakov and Lavan set up a pile of stones as testimony to their agreement to part from one another in peace. Lavan called it *yegar sahadusa* (יְגַר שָׂהֲדוּתָא). *Yegar* expresses the idea of fear and limitation, and this was only from the side of Lavan, from the other path. But Yaakov called it גַּלְעֵד, *gal eid,* which expresses the idea of happiness and joy, which comes from going on the path of holiness.

R' LEVI YITZCHOK OF BERDITCHEV ONCE RAISED HIS EYES TO HEAVEN AND said, "Master of the Universe, if You want to forgive the sins of

HASHEM'S TEFILLIN

Your nation, Israel, so be it; and if not, I will reveal the meaning of the Talmud statement, 'The *tefillin* of the Master of the World, what is inscribed on them? *And who is like Your nation, Israel?'* (*Berachos* 6a). And if you do not wish to forgive them, then the *tefillin* that You wear are defective."

The Rizhiner added to this the words of the Talmud, "When a man is in pain, the Holy Presence says, 'My head is heavy, My arms are heavy' (*Sanhedrin* 46a). The intent of the Talmud is that when a man is suffering because of his sins, then the *tefillin* of Hashem are defective and so He says, 'My head is heavy, My arms are heavy.' This is likewise the meaning of the *tefillah* in the *Selichos* services, *Do it for the sake of Your glory.* This is the glory of the *tefillin* of Hashem, as stated in *Ezekiel* (24:17), *Your glory is bound to You,* which indicates that 'Your *tefillin* are bound to You.' "

ONCE, A YOUNG MAN CAME BEFORE HIM AND PRESENTED HIM WITH A strict program he had written for himself through which he hoped

INDESTRUCTIBILITY to destroy his evil traits. The Rebbe asked him, "Evil traits you wish to be destroyed? With this program you might succeed to destroy your back or lips, but your evil traits can never be destroyed. Rather, you should pray and learn seriously and your evil qualities will disappear by themselves."

ON ANOTHER OCCASION, PEOPLE CAME BEFORE HIM TO COMPLAIN ABOUT their town *shochet* in whom they sensed a certain miserliness, in-

BREAD AND BUTTER WITH A SHARP KNIFE stanced by the fact that he never allowed poor guests into his home. The Rebbe said that it is found in various books that when one is born under the constellation Mars (in Hebrew, מַאֲדִים, *ma'adim,* red) he is destined to become a *shochet* or a *mohel* (expert in ritual circumcision), for he possesses the innate disposition toward bloodshed, the mark of a cruel nature. This man must sublimate his trait to holiness and use it positively to serve Hashem, steeping himself in mitzvos and good deeds, so that the trait will be transformed to spiritual strength and holiness. This is the meaning of the passage, *And Edom refused to allow Israel permission to pass through his borders, and Israel turned aside from him* (*Bamidbar* 20:21). The phrase, *And Edom refused,* refers to a man born under the sign of Mars. Who does not allow an Israelite to pass within his border? — one who lacks the quality of hospitality and displays cruelty toward his fellow Jew. Then *Israel turned aside from him,* so that the quality of mercy, one of the three traits, רַחֲמָנִים, בַּיְשָׁנִים וְגוֹמְלֵי חֲסָדִים, *mercy, shyness and kindness,* by which the Jews are distinguished, left him.

Several Jews from a certain city came to him with a grievance against their local *shochet.* It happened that a simple Jew of Rizhin, named Yossi, was also present. The Rebbe told Yossi to go to the city and visit the *shochet* in question. Yossi, though he knew nothing of *shochtim,* did as he was told. He went to his house, hitched up his wagon and rode to the city. This took place in the middle of winter, and there was a bitter chill in the air. He came to the city in the dead of night, shivering and hungry. He went to the home of the *shochet,* who received him cordially, brought him into the warm house, offered him an excellent meal and then prepared a bed for him. The next day, Yossi returned to Rizhin. The Rebbe asked him his opinion of the *shochet.* Yossi answered that he was no authority of *shochtim* but he was very impressed by his *hachnasas orchim.* The Rizhiner commented, however, that when somebody welcomes a guest into a warm home and places before him bread and butter with a sharp knife, it is a certain sign that he fears Hashem.

In that time, people were careful to appoint a *shochet* who was a scholar, G-d-fearing and of good character. Periodically, there were problems, and there were those who would besmirch the *shochet's* reputation baselessly, and seek out faults in him that never existed. In such times, the Rizhiner was often called upon to arbitrate, and he would try to restore peace between the respective parties.

In a letter that was dated 1827 (5587), addressed to the congregation of Vladovka with regard to a *shochet* whom the people wished to discharge, his initial stand was to defend the *shochet* and to admonish the people not to commit an iniquity by dismissing him. He advised them to pay close attention to the strength of his warning, that the *shochet* should in no way be harassed, and "far be it from any Jew other than the *shochet* to lift the *chalef* (slaughtering knife) in your city." With regard to their complaints against the *shochet,* an impartial arbitrator was sent from Rizhin to attempt some sort of compromise. This man was to examine both sides of the issue, and his decision would be final. Because of the Rebbe's faith in their honor, they congregation heeded his words.

ONCE, AS THE RIZHINER WAS PASSING THROUGH THE TOWN OF VLADOVKA, he spent several hours with the rabbi and chassidim of that town. At

HOLINESS IN SIMPLICITY one point, some chassidim excused themselves to go *daven*. The Rebbe told them that he had also not yet *davened*. Even so, they replied, a Rebbe can reach lofty spiritual heights, even in his idle chatter, but they were but simple folk. The Rebbe then turned to the rabbi and asked, "What is the law if one letter of a *Sefer Torah* is missing?" The rabbi answered that the *Sefer Torah* is *pasul* — invalid.

"And if one letter is missing from the Torah dealing with Yaakov's conversation with the shepherds? (*Bereishis* 29:4-9). It is, again, doubtlessly invalid," answered the rabbi. "And if a letter is missing from the Torah telling us what the shepherds told Yaakov?" the Rebbe persisted. "Once again, it is not valid," said the rabbi.

"Indeed," said the Rizhiner, "in Yaakov's speech to the shepherds there may have been spiritually creative thoughts, but in the shepherds' response to Yaakov, what kind of exalted thoughts could there have been? We must conclude that the exalted thoughts of the *tzaddik* can also be couched in the words of the simple folk with whom he speaks."

BEFORE ROSH HASHANAH, TWO IMPORTANT RABBIS AND ONE YOUNG scholar were seated before him. The Rebbe said, "Since three people

THE REBBE'S CONSENT can constitute a *beis din* (rabbinical court), I wish you to rule that the coming year will be a blessed and good year." One of the rabbis answered him that they could rule thus only on condition that the Rebbe consent.

The Rebbe was pleased with the rabbi's answer and replied that, when he was still in Rizhin, a certain individual became ill in a neighboring village. The man's wife went to the next city and declared before the rabbi that she had hitherto turned to him with all sorts of questions in matters of law, but now she would like him to rule that her husband regain his health. The rabbi agreed to convene a *beis din* for the purpose, on condition that the Rizhiner also agree to his words; and he explained himself in a letter to the Rizhiner: We read, *And now shall the power of Hashem grow strong* (*Bamidbar* 14:17). יִגְדַּל, *grow strong,* is written with a large *yud,* implying that to strengthen Hashem's healing power, one requires a large and great *yud* ("Jew" in Yiddish), a Rebbe.

It was Erev Rosh Hashanah, just before Minchah, when a group of cattledealers timidly entered the chamber of the Rizhiner to receive his blessing. They were uncomfortable, embarrassed and ill at ease for having arrived so late. "We had to conclude urgent business," they apologized, huddling in a group before the Rebbe. The Rebbe replied, "You need not apologize. You are fine Jews. Why do you think that in our High Holiday prayers we say that הַטּוֹב וּמֵטִיב לָרָעִים וְלַטּוֹבִים, 'Hashem is good and does good to the evildoers and the worthy'? Is it not odd that the prayer mentions the evildoers before the worthy? Why not the reverse?" The Rizhiner explained, "There are some Jews who begin preparing for Rosh Hashanah from Rosh Chodesh Elul, while still others only awaken to the significance of the approaching Days of Penitence when they begin reciting *Selichos,* the week before Rosh Hashanah. And there are those who must linger in the market-place until right before Rosh Hashanah. But when they remember that Rosh Hashanah approaches, they leave their wagons and hurry to the synagogue. Yet Hashem undertakes to show them mercy, just as He does to those others, and even ahead of them. Hashem says: Just as you hastened to shut your shops and close your business affairs in order to pray, so will I hasten to inscribe you for a good new year, for good life.

"These late-coming Jews, like yourselves, consider themselves evil and unworthy. But Hashem treats them with favor and in-scribes them for a good new year, even before He favors those who consider themselves as fine, upright Jews."

ONCE, SEVERAL VILLAGERS APPEARED BEFORE HIM, DISMAYED AT THE drought, and asked him to intercede with Hashem to bring rain. He referred them to the passage in the Torah which states that "If you will follow My ordinances, then I will bring the rains in their proper season" (*Vayikra* 26:4). One of them jumped up and cried, "Why does the Rebbe talk to us 'Torah,

COMMON FOLK, COMMON WEALTH

Torah, yes Torah, no Torah!' What we need is rain!" The Rebbe walked out and refused to talk to them. One of them ran after him and pleaded, "Rebbe, even in the Torah it is written (*Shemos* 16:4), לְמַעַן אֲנַסֶּנּוּ, *lemaan anassenu* (Hebrew, נֵס, *neis*, means a banner held aloft on a pole) — '*in order to raise you, whether you will follow My Torah or not.*'[1] If Hashem elevates His Jews, certainly our Rebbe should not be so severe with us." When the Rebbe heard this "original" interpretation from the innocent heart of a simple Jew, he returned and blessed them, "May it be the will of Hashem to hearken to your requests and grant that the rain fall in its proper season."

Not only did he bless the common folk, but there were those who he asked to bless him, for the blessing of a simple man is considered in the eyes of the Almighty as the blessing of the righteous. After having escaped from Russia, he traveled to the marriage of his son, R' Dovid Moshe of Chortkov, with the daughter of the Rebbe of Chernobyl. Since the bride was in Russia, the groom went there and the *tzaddik* of Rizhin was only able to accompany him as far as the border. On the way, he stopped in the woods between Husyatin and Kopitchinitz to rest and to recite the Minchah prayer. After praying, he told his servant to bring him wine. He then filled his cup and the cups of his wagoners, and he asked them to bless him with peace and *nachas* from his children for generations to come.

Such was the Rebbe's relationship with the common folk. From his most important followers, however, he demanded a high level of commitment to Chassidus. One of the basics of Judaism is love of one's neighbor. Although everyone must strive to love his neighbor to the best of his ability, the more elevated individual must reach the uppermost levels of self-sacrifice for his neighbor.

CHASSIDIM TELL A STORY OF HOW, ON ONE OCCASION, THE RIZHINER heard that his sons had had an argument. He sent his *shammas* to

NO ROOM FOR ARGUMENTS

call them to appear before him. When they entered, he said to them,

---

1. The explanation being that whether you follow the Torah or not, Hashem still promises to help you.

"Welcome, good Jews." He continued, pleasantly, "Sons, far be it from me to become part of an argument. Do the people of Israel have a dearth of troubles? We are still suffering today because of the differences between Yosef and his brothers. My sons, you are among the chosen tribes of Hashem. A separation among you is a catastrophe for *Klal Yisrael*, the essential unity of Israel."

The Rebbe explained the Biblical passage, *And you shall love your friend as yourself, I am Hashem* (*Vayikra* 19:18) with a story. There were two close friends, one of whom was accused of a capital crime, judged guilty and sentenced to death. A decree went out that all citizens were required to witness the execution. His friend came to the execution, and when he saw his friend led out to die, began to shout, "Let him go, for I am the guilty one and he is innocent!" The accused however was not about to allow his friend to be killed in his place and he told the hangman to ignore his friend who was lying in order to save him. The incident reached the ears of the king, who commanded that both men be brought before him. When they arrived, he said to them, "Tell me the truth, since only one of you could have committed this crime, why should the innocent one die?" One of them answered, "I know that my friend could not have committed such a crime, for I know his character and personality, and it is impossible that he should have done such a thing. Therefore, this must be a false accusation, and since my life is bound up with my friend's, it is better that I die and not see my friend's death. Indeed, I certainly deserve to die if I could come to such a point that I would see my friend put to death and do nothing." His friend responded in like manner. When the king heard this, he absolved both of them and requested that he be considered a friend of both of them. So it is that when men can reach such a degree of *And you shall love your friend as yourself*, then *I am Hashem* — G-d includes Himself in their comradeship.

CHAPTER XII

FROM THEIR BREATHS

ONE GENTILE BIBLICAL SCHOLAR ASKED THE RIZHINER WHAT the rabbis (quoted by Rashi) of blessed memory meant when they said that the עַנְנֵי כָבוֹד, "*Clouds of Glory* existed in the merit of Aharon alone" (*Taanis* 9a). The Rebbe answered him that when two friends love each other, then the breath that leaves their mouths joins together. Aharon, who loved peace and pursued peace, had the responsibility to insure mutual love among the Jews, so that there should be friendship and warmth within Israel. From their breaths, great clouds were formed; the "Clouds of Glory."

The Rizhiner was perceptive concerning the human personality and the difficulties facing the penitent soul, in particular. He would approach these people and make special efforts to bring them close, in order that they should take heart and not give up hope.

Once, the Rizhiner went to Odessa on the advice of his doctors, who insisted that he bathe in the Black Sea. He was told that the grandson of the Torah giant, R' Yaakov Emden — a man named Meir — lived there. Meir had lost his faith and had abandoned Judaism. He was living in extreme poverty. The Rizhiner invited him to live in Rizhin and offered to support him. Meir agreed and returned with

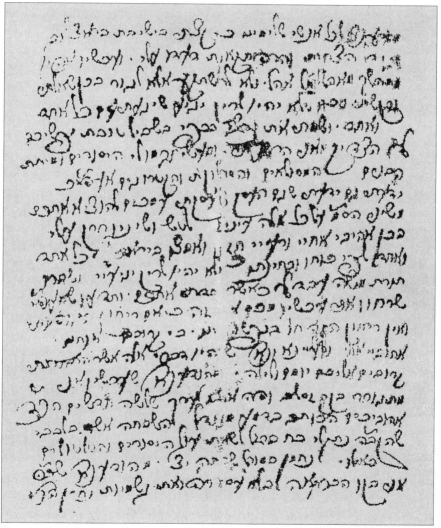

A portion of a letter written by the Rizhiner

the *tzaddik*, who provided him with all his needs. He eventually induced Meir to repent. One day, the *tzaddik* saw that Meir was deeply depressed and asked the reason for his sadness. If it was on account of his sins, he should know that penitence destroys sin. Meir answered that he was sad for he had sinned so much, and even after having repented, he still committed wrongs, so that he was sure that his repentance was unacceptable. The Rizhiner, in deference to Meir's preference for *pilpul*, answered him in scholarly fashion:

In the Rosh Hashanah service we say, כִּי אַתָּה סָלְחָן וּמָחֳלָן לְשִׁבְטֵי יְשׁוּרוּן "For You are the One Who forgives and pardons the tribes of Yeshurun." Now, would it not have sufficed for us to say, כִּי אַתָּה סָלַח וּמֹחֵל, "You forgive and pardon"? The Talmud (*Bava Metzia* 33a) discusses the commandment to help an animal that is laboring under too heavy a load, and lies on the ground. The Torah commands that if the animal is *lying under his burden, you shall certainly offer him aid* (*Shemos* 23:5). The Talmud differentiates between an animal that is רַבְצָן, "lying," and one that is רוֹבֵץ, "one who lies." Rashi explains the difference. "One who lies" implies an animal that *continually* lies under his burden. By adding the expression "one *who*," the meaning of the term changes and an additional meaning is added — that of continuity, permanence and repetition, i.e., the animal always shirks its burden. But *lying* implies sometimes, i.e., the animal is generally reliable; only sometimes does it fall under its burden. We similarly interpret that Hashem is "One Who forgives and pardons." Were we to say simply "forgive (סָלַח)" and "pardon (וּמֹחֵל)," we would mean that when a man sins sometimes, Hashem forgives him. However, "One Who forgives and pardons" implies that Hashem forgives constantly — even one who sins repeatedly, as long as he repents with a whole heart. This is, indeed, the meaning of "One Who forgives and pardons (כִּי אַתָּה סָלְחָן וּמָחֳלָן)" — that Hashem's forgiveness is constant.

Helping the confused to return to the right path was one of the missions of the Rizhiner. We are told that a certain man came to the Rebbe R' Mottel of Chernobyl with a list of sins that he had committed, requesting help to find ways to make amends. The Chernobyler had told him that he was too old to prescribe such a difficult penitence; the man should go to the Rizhiner, who was still young and would accept him as his responsibility. The man came to the Rizhiner and gave him the list of his sins. The Rebbe stared at the long list and said that this would be his penitence — everything holy, such as *tefillah* and even a simple blessing, he must recite only from the *siddur*, so that he become accustomed to patience, and not to be impulsive. R' Dovid Moshe of Chortkov related that this man in his later years was well known as a *tzaddik* and would even take *kvittlach* from his recipients.

ONCE A TRANSGRESSOR ASKED HIM, "HOW CAN I *DAVEN* TO HASHEM IF I have sinned so much?" The Rizhiner replied: "The Book of *Tehillim*

A NEW CREATURE

concludes with the following verse: *Let everything that has breath praise*

Early centers of Chassidus

Hashem (*Tehillim* 150:6). Our Rabbis, of blessed memory (*Bereishis Rabbah* 14:9), comment on this verse and state that man should praise his Creator for every breath he draws. For at every moment the soul desires to leave the body, but Hashem restrains it. And so man becomes a new creature from moment to moment throughout his life. Man can gain encouragement from this when the thought enters his mind at the time of prayer and worship, 'How dare you, so base a man, full of sin and iniquity, open your mouth to praise Hashem?' But he should then consider that at that very moment he has become a new creature and has not sinned in that moment, so that now he, too, can stand in Hashem's Presence and pray to Him."

Once, one of the Rebbe's chassidim became involved in a severe transgression. Naturally, he was too embarrassed to come to the Rebbe. After some time, though, the man's mind became more settled, and he wondered how long he could avoid the Rizhiner. Eventually, he gathered his courage, journeyed to Rizhin and apologized to the Rebbe for staying away so long as a result of his becoming involved in the transgression. The Rebbe referred him to the passage in *Koheles* (10:14): *If the overpowering wind shall come upon you, do not leave your place.* The *Targum* explains, "If the evil inclination seems to be gaining the upper hand, do not leave the good place where you have been until now, for the words of the Torah heal, and they can cause great debts to be annulled before Hashem."

In the court of the Rizhiner, all kinds of people met each other: Rabbanim, Rebbes, *shochtim*, scholars, *baalei teshuvah*, merchants, animal traders, wealthy householders, innkeepers, simple farmers and other common people, rich and poor, sick people, impoverished Jews, husbands asking for intercession for their childbearing or barren wives — in short, anyone requiring assistance and support. The Rebbe sat for hours every day listening, answering, comforting, encouraging and admonishing, and with all he dealt calmly, with love and deep wisdom. Everyone who felt the presence of the Rebbe seemed to have had a heavy stone lifted from his heart. Even those who did not believe in *tzaddikim* would speak of him in glowing terms.

Even gentiles would come to him to ask his advice, and he would relieve the worries of all; encourage, strengthen, gladden their hearts; and imbue them with belief and faith in Hashem. His honest words came from his heart, a loving and sometimes sorrowful heart, which carried within it the deep agony of the troubles of the Jews, individually and collectively, as a merciful father, broken over the pain of his children. That is why his followers loved and revered him and were ready to sacrifice their lives for him, just as he was ready to sacrifice his life for any Jew. They brought him gifts out of joy, and he deemed himself eligible to accept those gifts. He instructed his *gabbai* (secretary) not to accept any torn paper bills from any of his followers, for he saw in that a blemish in their affections, and he told his *gabbai* to tell them that their names were carved on his heart. Therefore, he merited that they give of their money with a full heart.

Among his followers there were those who came to benefit from his wisdom and there were those who were simply enthralled by the aura of royalty and charisma which surrounded him. He himself would catergorize his followers into three groups. One group was bound to him through Torah and *tefillah*; the second, by way of donations; and the third consisted of those who wandered into his court. The latter, he explained, were like matzah, which does not become *chametz* (leavened) as long as it is being steadily rolled. (In Hebrew, the word for "roll" and for "wander" is the same, לְהִתְגַּלְגֵּל — *l'hisgalgeil*.)

EVEN *MISNAGDIM* WOULD TURN TO HIM FOR ANSWERS TO THEIR QUESTIONS. It is told that once he had to pass through the city of Sunik and was

DEFINING ONE'S TERMS delayed there. The *misnagdim* bombarded him with questions, asking how it could be right that those who arise early in the morning to pray and afterwards learn Mishnayos while still wrapped in their *taleism* and wearing *tefillin* should be called *misnagdim* while the chassidim (Hebrew for pious ones) pray after the proper time and immediately afterwards sit down to drink whiskey. It should be the opposite, they protested. They, the *misnagdim*, should be called "pious" and the chassidim should be the opposition. The Rebbe's *gabbai*, R' Leib, could not restrain himself and retorted that *misnagdim* pray coldly, like the dead, and after the dead one learns Mishnayos, while the chassidim pray with fire and excitement like living men, and living men require some whiskey… So it is that they drink whiskey after praying.

The Rizhiner explained the answer that R' Leib had given was sardonic in nature, but the truth is that when the Temple was destroyed and sacrifices ceased, prayer was established in place of sacrifice as it states, וּנְשַׁלְּמָה פָרִים שְׂפָתֵינוּ, *And may our lips replace the bullocks* (*Hoshea* 14:3), i.e. our prayers stand in the place of sacrifices. Even the Talmud (*Berachos* 26a) says that "the services stand in place of the daily sacrifices." It is well known that having an improper intention with regard to eating the sacrifice can invalidate the sacrifice; similarly an improper thought can invalidate prayer. When someone stands in prayer the *yetzer hara* comes to him with all manners of tricks, underhanded diversions and sly means, in order to confuse his mind during the prayer service. The chassidim, therefore, managed to find a way out of this trap. Right after services they sit together and drink whiskey and bless each other with *l'chaim* — "to life" — and every man tells his friend what he lacks, so that his friend gives him a blessing that he should receive Divine help for his needs. Hashem accepts prayer in any language (*Berachos* 13a) and the *yetzer hara* has no power over it, for it seems to him as if they are wasting their time over whiskey since they talk in simple parlance and not in prayers. But, in reality, this is all a very profound form of prayer.

Once the *misnagdim* asked him to explain the rabbinic saying: "A scholar who has no ability to reason — a corpse is better than he" (*Vayikra Rabbah*). They asked him to give the simple explanation, rather than the homiletic and chassidic sense. He referred to the verse, *The faith of your times will be the strength of your salvations, wisdom and knowledge* (*Yeshaya* 33:6). The Talmud expounds that *faith* implies the Mishnaic order of *Zeraim*, the agricultural laws; *your times* indicates the order of *Moed*, dealing with such times as Shabbos and the festivals; *the strength* indicates the order of *Nashim*, and so on. *Knowledge* implies the order of *Taharos* (purity). Thus, a scholar whose reason is based on inadequate knowledge does not know the order that deals with purity, and even a corpse is better than he is.

He compared those who journey to the *tzaddikim* with the pilgrims who journeyed to Jerusalem in the time of the Holy Temple, say-

THREE CLASSES OF CHASSIDIM ing: "The three classes of people who journey to the *tzaddikim* remind us of the three levels of men in the time of King Yeravam, son of Nevat, who set up the golden calves and placed guards upon the roads to stop pilgrims from going to Jerusalem (*I Kings* 12:28-29).

To the first class belonged those who would fight the guards and were willing to risk their lives to get to Jerusalem; to the second belonged those who were not willing to go the Jerusalem even at the risk of their lives, but still did not want to worship the golden calves; and to the third belonged those who hearkened to the voice of Yeravam and did worship the golden calves. These three classes "wandered" and appear in this world, the "world of reparation." The first class have merited to be able to travel to a true *tzaddik* with ease. Those of the second class encounter difficulties and suffer, in the course of their journey to the *tzaddik*. But the third group has no merit to its name, and is not even bound up with a true *tzaddik*.

He knew how to console those whose enemies and oppressors made their lives difficult. Once, several Jews from a neighboring

GIVING CONSOLATION town came to him saying that they had been forced into exile. He insisted that they spend Shabbos at his home.

On Friday night, during the *zemiros* (songs sung at the Shabbos table), they all sang the hymn *Kol Mekadesh* (Everyone who sanctifies). When he reached the stanza, "Everyone who sanctifies the Shabbos appropriately without desecrating it, his reward will be great, as befits his deed, every man within his camp and each man by his flag," he turned to them and said, "Whoever observes the Shabbos properly and does not desecrate it can be sure that he remain at his own camp, standing by his own banner (*Bamidbar* 1:52), even when he is driven from his home."

A chassid, who had once been wealthy but had now fallen on hard times, complained to him that the eye of Hashem's protection had left him. The Rebbe told him, "The Torah states in the name of Balaam, *the man whose eyes are opened has said* (*Bamidbar* 24:3,15). Now, it is well known that there are three expressions for 'man' in Biblical Hebrew: גֶּבֶר, *gever;* אֱנוֹשׁ, *enosh;* אָדָם, *adam. Gever* implies the lowest level of man, one who has little faith in Hashem; one who does not believe in a 'seeing Eye' that watches over man and affects the actions of mankind. He believes that the world proceeds naturally, 'under its own steam,' and that everything that happens is mere coincidence. But 'he who sees the vision of the Almighty' — this is the level of *adam,* the man who believes in a higher power. Such a man is 'fallen and open eyed,' for even when he falls down, he remains steadfast in his faith that everything is under the influence of Hashem."

ONCE, A CHASSID ABOUT 40 YEARS OLD CAME BEFORE HIM, PRESENTING him with a *kvitel* of introduction which did not mention whether he

BLESSINGS FOR CHILDREN

had any children. The Rebbe asked him why he did not mention his children. If, indeed, he had any, then they should be mentioned in his *kvitel,* so that they might also be blessed. The man explained that R' Nachman of Breslov had been the *sandak* at his circumcision, and that great *tzaddik* had predicted that he would have no children. "That is why I did not bother to mention it in my *kvitel,*" he concluded. The Rizhiner told him, "If R' Nachman of Breslov told you that you would have no children, then rest assured that the Zeide of Shpole promised you children!" [It was well known that R' Leib, the Zeide of Shpole, continually took issue with R' Nachman], and I hereby join with him. As the Talmud states, "When an individual differs with the many, the verdict follows the many" (*Berachos* 9a).

R' Aharon of Cherson told of the time a man came to the Rizhiner and asked him to give him a *berachah,* blessing, that he might have children. The Rizhiner answered him, "I pass through the world of souls twice a day, and I see that after the year 1840 (5600), all the souls in the world will be flawed, yet if we are given them we have no choice, we must accept them. It is not our place to reject them." The implication was that he would indeed have a child and must be content without finding fault.

R' Aaron Karliner once told a story which he heard from his *mechutan*, the Rizhiner. There were two men living in adjoining cities. One was a great believer in *tzaddikim*, but his wife was not. The other did not believe, while his wife did. The believer took ill and requested that he be taken to a *tzaddik*. His wife wanted to fulfill her husband's wish and rented a wagon. On their way, they passed through the town of the other couple. When the wife of the man that did not believe saw that they were going to the Rizhiner, she decided to go with them, for they were also in some trouble — the lord of the manor was demanding taxes that they were unable to pay. When they came to the Rizhiner, each wrote his request on a piece of paper. However, the pieces of paper were transposed and the person who was sick submitted a request for money for the tax. The Rizhiner told the sick one that Hashem would help him, and the one who needed the money was advised to apply leeches to his back. The woman did not understand how leeches would help her pay her taxes, but she believed in the *tzaddik* and passed the message on to her husband. The husband became very upset, seeing no connection between leeches and the paying of the taxes. The situation was desperate, however, so he decided to try out the Rebbe's suggestion, and told his wife to put the leeches on his back. When the officer of the lord of the manor came to collect the taxes, he saw the man on his bed bleeding profusely. He went back to tell the lord, but the lord did not believe him, and ordered his servants to carry the bedridden man to him. He saw the man bleeding in his cot and asked him what had happened. The man, thinking quickly, said that he had gone to a distant town to borrow the money to pay the taxes. However, he was unable to rent a wagon and had to walk home. On the way, he was accosted by thieves, who stole his money and beat him up. The lord took pity on him and said that he, himself, would have to be responsible for healing the poor man, since he had gone to so much trouble for his sake. Furthermore, he would not have to pay taxes for the next three years.

The Rizhiner then said to the Karliner, "My *mechutan*, believe me, I had no idea what this woman wanted, nor how to grant her request. However, because of her great faith, she was helped by Hashem."

R' YISROEL BECK (FOUNDER OF THE FIRST PRINTING HOUSE IN THE HOLY Land, and father of R' Nisson Beck, a chassid of Rizhin who built

THE BEST DOCTOR

or provided the funds to build the Rizhiner's synagogue in Old Jerusalem), before going to Israel, went to the Rebbe to say good-bye. He asked the Rebbe if he might engage in dispensing kabbalistic "remedies" once he was in Israel, since the Talmud states that the best of doctors inherits hell (*Kiddushin* 82a). The Rebbe explained that when a doctor comes and tells a patient, "Take my medicine which I prescribe for your cure," he contradicts the benediction of the *Amidah*, which states, *Heal us, Hashem, then we will be healed* (*Yirmiyah* 17:14). Such a doctor leaves only seventeen of the eighteen benedictions of the *Amidah*, as in the numerical value of the Hebrew word *tov*, good — seventeen. It is of this type of doctor that the Talmud states, "The best of doctors inherits hell" (*Kiddushin* 82a). But if *you* will administer the medicine, you will not contradict the benediction, as you will surely know the influence of Heaven in the proceedings.

HE WAS OPPOSED TO SELF-MORTIFICATION (AS A MEANS OF ABSOLUTION from sin) and said that the way to serve Hashem was through *sim-*

NO SELF-MORTIFICATION

chah. One immersed in pain and sorrow could not properly serve Hashem. "Life was given in order for us to derive pleasure from it, provided one enjoys himself in a holy way, and not just in a materialistic manner. One must pursue the spiritual, and even in the pleasures of this world, one must seek the Divinity concealed within them."

He forbade his followers to afflict themselves. A certain chassid used to fast and vowed to abstain from food. The *tzaddik* told him that a Jew must eat and drink and pray and study, and endure the afflictions which are his lot. Before the Jew departed, the *tzaddik* told him to go in peace, but, if he continued his fasting, not to bother to return. The chassid asked him: How can one save himself after having sinned, if not through fasting? The Rebbe answered, "With this, you can be saved: Learn a chapter of the Mishnah or some *Ein*

Yaakov (*aggadah* of the Talmud), or a *daf* (folio) of the Talmud, and if, after having done this, you are still depressed, remember that you stand beside me and all will turn out for the best."

Once, in his youth, he had tarried at the sanctification of the new moon. It was a very cold night. The soles of his shoes were full of holes, and spots of blood marked his footprints, as the soles of his feet were torn by the ice. This resignation to and ready acceptance of pain might have been his equivalent, or substitution, for the systematic self-mortification practiced by his forebears. However, he was reluctant for this incident to be known lest others be tempted to emulate him with different kinds of self-affliction. He said, "There are young men who will never order their prayers to coincide with those of the general community, but who will try to elevate themselves spiritually through straining of the body and soul. I warn them against this and advise them not to overreach themselves, lest they take a sudden fall." All manner of extremism was alien to his teaching and to his nature.

With others, such deviations were regarded as the norm, so much so that public prayer was considered the business of the boorish and narrow-minded, a faraway echo from the ancient times, where an individual would erect an altar for himself, to satisfy his own caprices, acting as his own high priest. The natural result of the deviations he decried was that such people abandoned public worship in the presence of the Almighty, in the synagogue, which had preserved Judaism in the Diaspora.

THE REBBE, R' YEHOSHUA OF OSTROVA, WROTE IN HIS BOOK, *TOLDOS Adam* (*Metzora*): "The holy Rebbe of Rizhin, may the righteous be re-

A RECEPTACLE FOR THE SPIRIT membered for a blessing, spoke to me in my youth regarding physical remedies. I told him that, as far as I was concerned, spiritual health is more important, but he said that I was wrong. First, there must be a receptacle for the spirit and if, Hashem forbid, the body is not whole, then it cannot be a proper receptacle, so that physical health is of prime importance."

When his grandfather, the Maggid of Mezritch, forbade his son, the Malach, to afflict himself too much, he said to him: "Avrum'inyu, my son, a small hole in the body is accompanied by a large hole in the soul."[1]

The Rebbe would say that as long as a Jew held onto something of Judaism, one could not despair of him. He is like a bucket which falls into deep water but which has a rope attached. It can still be drawn up.

With regard to the ills that men suffer, the Rizhiner said that a man should conduct himself like a wall clock whose pendulum goes back and forth. Man should be like this; he should realize that life has ups and downs. As long as the affliction does not affect his spirituality he should be willing to accept it with love. But if he is spiritually afflicted, then he should pray to Hashem to save him.

THE FATE OF THE JEWISH CONSCRIPT

A WOMAN WHOSE SON HAD BEEN DRAFTED INTO THE RUSSIAN ARMY appeared before the Rebbe and cried that she would rather see her son in his grave than see him transgress the Torah, desecrate Shabbos, or eat nonkosher food. (It was common knowledge that the army of Czar Nicholas forced Jewish soldiers to transgress their religious beliefs, even to convert to Christianity.) The Rebbe told her that it is written (*Tehillim* 88:13), *Your mercy will be declared in the grave!* Would it ever occur to us to consider the grave a mercy? This can occur only if one's faith in Hashem has been destroyed.

He would encourage and try to influence the soldiers going into the army. It is told that when he came to live in Sadagora, two Jewish Russian soldiers made their way to him clandestinely from across the border. They presented him with a *kvitel* and 7 rubles of "ransom money," bitterly crying that they had been forced to desecrate the Shabbos and eat *treifah* (forbidden) food. He told them not to fear. When *Mashiach* comes, they would be among the first to greet him, even before all those who were righteous.

---

1. Heard from my revered father, R' Yosef Brayer *z"l* of Shtefanesht, Romania.

R' Yitzel of Lutzk was sitting at the table of the Rizhiner one Shabbos when only about eleven chassidim were present. The *tzaddik* said, "The days before *Mashiach* will come, it will be well with common people both with regard to material and spiritual matters, but not so for the refined, neither in material matters nor even in spiritual; by which I mean to say that they will be incapable of reciting even a single psalm from *sefer Tehillim*. The reason I tell you this now is so that you should not become discouraged. Be strong and of good heart for so it is and so it must be."

He remembered his followers and concerned himself with their affairs both while they lived and after they died. He felt himself responsible for their actions in this world and for their fate before the seat of judgment in the next.

IT IS TOLD THAT WHEN HE WAS IN THE TOWN OF SKOLYA, BEFORE establishing himself in Sadagora, one Friday, an hour before candle-

NICETIES OF LAW

lighting, he invited the rabbi of the town, the author of *Beis Shlomo*, to visit him. The rabbi came dressed in his Shabbos finery, but the Rebbe was still smoking his pipe. He told the rabbi the following story as he smoked:

In Russia there lived a Jew, a contractor for the government, who was both a scholar and a wealthy man. In the course of time the man became poor, but his friends lent him money to start up again in business. He traveled to Kiev in order to contract work in which he had already invested. The officials of the government were envious of this Jew, who managed to attract so much business with good and generous conditions. In order to insure that his new business would fail, they arranged it that he would have to pay the balance of the contract on Shabbos. If he did not pay then, the entire deposit would be forfeited. When the Jew found out what had transpired, he devised all sorts of schemes to avoid paying on Shabbos, but to no avail. He did not know what to do; whether to desecrate the Shabbos, or lose all of the money his friends had lent him and leave himself without an income. Finally, he decided to sign the document. He became wealthy from the business and paid of all of his debts. After a while he passed away and came to the next world to be judged on his desecration of the Shabbos. "That is why," said the Rizhiner to the rabbi of Skolya, "I have asked you to come here and decide the law as to whether compulsion with regard to money is legally considered a compulsion with regard to Shabbos as well."

"If according to your ruling, the halachah determines that he acted under duress and not of his own free will, he will have an easier sentence in the next world." The rabbi of Skolya realized that this was no regular question and he chose his words carefully. "Being so close to Shabbos, I do not have time to delve into this matter at great length," the rabbi answered. "But at first glance it appears to me that the dreadful situation of Jews in Russia under the wicked Czar is a redeeming factor insofar as we say that this Jew did not break Shabbos on purpose, but was rather a victim of circumstance."

Satisfied with the answer, the Rizhner bid him a good Shabbos and the Rabbi went his way.

CHAPTER XIII

SELF-EDUCATED

The Rizhiner never had any formal education. Strange is his contention that he was "never taught how to write." As is evident from his signatures, the Hebrew letters are always written in sharp strokes, decisive and authoritative, in forceful, energetic, bold script. He never wrote a complete letter or document. His custom was to sign his own and his father's name, leaving it to his *gabbai* to write the text — a custom adopted by his descendants, the Rebbes of the House of Rizhin.

The Rizhiner advanced the Chassidic movement after its formative period, when it identified with the Baal Shem Tov and the Maggid of

THE GREAT CONSOLIDATOR

Mezritch. He gave it a new direction, not always understood by the researchers of this second period of Chassidus.

His direct involvement with the spiritual life of the Jewish community in Eastern Europe, his deep personal concern and his sense of responsibility for the welfare of *Klal Yisroel* made him indeed the *tzaddik hador*, the righteous one par excellence of his generation.

A MAN OF MANY PARTS

IN ORDER TO GAIN A DEEPER APPRECIATION OF THE RIZHINER'S HOLINESS and deep devotion as "a *tzaddik* with a unique mission in this world," one has to understand the dicta and maxims found in his Torah discourses. One has to delineate the circumstances and dramatic biographical data in order to better comprehend his multifaceted personality. He was endowed with a strong, pragmatic sense and vivid imagination, unfettered spontaneity and perception. Above all, he was blessed with a healthy self-image and a warm and pleasant disposition — combined with a strong dialectical sense. All these qualities were integrated in one personality. No wonder that such a formidable gestalt[1] inspired the masses to flock to see and admire him, and draw warmth into their souls from the all-embracing heart of this *tzaddik*, who bore them, eaglelike upon his shoulders.

A peacemaker among various factions of chassidim, the Rizhiner gave liberally of his cognitive acumen to resolve conflicts, be they matrimonial, communal, economical, political or religious. Like Shmuel the prophet, the Rizhiner traveled extensively, and visited various towns and cities under his influence in Volhynia, Podolia, Hungary, Romania, Bessarabia and Galicia. His exposure to many different classes of people enriched his *savoir faire*, adding to his brilliant expertise in resolving the various problems brought to him. Not only Jews but also the gentile nobility requested his blessing and advice, impressed by his striving toward perfection in the service of Hashem. He made himself conspicuous by his active involvement as an intercessor for the Russian Jews, for whom he had felt a sentimental attachment since his youth. In his capacity as supreme religious authority over many provinces in Eastern

---

1. In psychology, an organized whole that is perceived as more than the sum of its parts (*Concise Oxford Dict.*).

Europe, many Jewish communities would seek his approval before engaging *rabbanim, shochtim, dayanim* and *melamdim.*

In the spirit of the adage that Hashem gave us the human body to be the vessel of the soul, the Rizhiner held that we should care for the body and respect it. As previously noted, he was opposed to asceticism is all its forms. His advice was to seek one's own good through optimism and faith in the Almighty, qualities that were indeed his hallmark.

THERE WAS A SAYING CIRCULATING IN RIZHIN TO THE EFFECT THAT "Rizhin is the chassidic kingdom in a perpetual state of celebration.

JERUSALEM OF THE CHASSIDIM

It is Jerusalem away from Jerusalem." After finally settling in his new home, the town of Sadagora, he made it a center of attraction, so much so that even the gentile population prayed for the Rebbe's well-being. R' Menachem Mendel of Kotzk remarked, "The most puritan of chassidim could no longer object to the Rizhiner's royal privileges. He had paid for them in full. Only one of Hashem's chosen ones becomes a target and victim of the Czar. Any man who suffers unjustly becomes Hashem's instrument."

THE RIZHINER WAS AN INSPIRATION TO THE CHASSIDIM. HE WAS KNOWN for his wisdom, not for his mystical powers. He shrank from the very

ACTIVISTS AND PRAGMATISTS

idea of meddling with the supernatural. When told of gangs of hoodlums attacking poor defenseless Jews in his town, he was not content with *davening,* but ordered the Jewish youth of the town to organize a self-defense group. He wanted his chassidim to be healthy and free of what in modern parlance would be termed "complexes." He urged them not to sacrifice the possible on the altar of the impossible, nor to trade an immediate for an abstract gain. He urged them to help one another, to raise themselves one step above the ground instead of trying to walk on air. He further encouraged his chassidim to keep their means as pure as their purpose.

In his ancestry, the Rizhiner seemed to embody the growth and development of the chassidic movement — after all, he was the great-grandson of the great Maggid. As one of the Rizhiner's grandsons explained, "The Maggid was the source of all *tzaddikim* in the world, from the time of Creation until the ultimate coming of *Mashiach*. He was the crown of the Torah and the crown of the kingdom, and his holy children are also the crown of the kingdom." The Maggid was the spiritual inheritor of the Baal Shem Tov, the man who filled his place and continued his work.

BETWEEN RIZHIN AND KOTZK

MANY ARE THE WAYS OF WORSHIP OF THE ALMIGHTY. AMONG THEM ARE two diametrically opposed approaches which held sway at the same time in Chassidus — the way of Rizhin and the way of R' Menachem Mendel of Kotzk (1787-1859). Each of them, the Rizhiner's in Ukraine, Romania, Galicia and Russia; and the way of R' Menachem Mendel of Kotzk in Poland emanated from the same source, the teachings of the Baal Shem Tov and the Maggid of Mezritch. But how different their paths. Rizhin with its royal splendor and aristocratic lifestyle, with masses of adherents and formidable weltanschauung[1] abhorred the ascetic seclusion and hermitlike withdrawal from the worldly pleasures as practiced in Kotzk with its introspective isolation. The sharp wit and sagacity of R' Menachem Mendel of Kotzk, mingled with his decision to withdraw from his own people for some twenty odd years — such behavior could not be accepted by the Rizhiner, scion of the great Maggid.

The Rizhiner represented, in the words of the Apter, "the soul of the soul, which incorporates all the souls of his chassidim." He also said of himself, "*Tzaddikim* are the letters, and chassidim are the vowels, of the Torah. The entire Torah is included in the first chapter of *Bereishis*. The entire world derives its abundant nurture from the Torah. The entire chapter of *Bereishis* is included in the word *Bereishis*. The letter *beis* is included in its own dot and I am the dot (the essence)."

---

1. German; means worldview.

Kotzk, on the other hand, tried to cleanse Chassidus of its admixture of worldliness and materialism. Kotzk demanded rigorous *mesiras nefesh* (self-sacrifice), total devotion and a restricted, spartan lifestyle of self-punishing abstention. This can be achieved by breaking down the "id" (animalistic forces of man) and the purging of man through self-denial, in order to elevate the spirit to the sphere of the Divine.

In Rizhin, you found emotional and social *kiruv* (outreach). Everyone was accepted and welcome to meet the *tzaddik*, the father who cares, feels and frets about his chassidim. In Kotzk, they did not welcome newcomers; one had to work very hard on himself, use introspection, live in poverty, detest all outward display of riches and joy. Kotzk is internalizing and self-sufficient. Rizhin is a pure blue sky without so much as a wisp of cloud to mar its clear firmament.

ON PARTAKING OF FOOD IN CHASSIDUS

ALL THINGS, INCLUDING FOOD, GET THEIR EXISTENCE FROM THE LIFE THAT Hashem put into them. This vitality is the "holy spark" from the *Shechinah*, that gives all things not only their existence, but also their attributes and qualities. Food too owes its existence to the holy spark within. The *Kesser Shem Tov* (Jerusalem 1968, p. 25) quotes the Baal Shem Tov: "It is an important principle that all your actions be for the sake of Heaven ... But the essence of spiritual perfection will be when the deed done for the sake of Heaven has an immediate connection with the service of Hashem, such as elevating the holy sparks within the food."

Rabbeinu Bachya ben Asher states that when one eats with holy thoughts and meditates on the *Shechinah*, "the eating itself as a bodily matter is transformed into an exalted service of the mind, being considered as a full service of Hashem, like all others, and is a mitzvah like all others" (*Shulchan shel Arba, Shaar HaKedushah* Chapter 15).

The Baal Shem Tov's colleague and disciple, the great Maggid, R' Dov Ber, declares: "I saw that everything that he, the Baal Shem

Tov, put into his mouth, food or drink, he elevated" (*Emunas Tzaddikim*, see *Ezekiel* 41:22, 23, and *Berachos* 5b).

Through the *d'veikus* — cleaving to the Almighty — achieved by meditation, we bring the act of taking pleasure from food into our relationship with Hashem.

In relating the pleasure of eating to Hashem through *d'veikus* by means of meditation, we are elevating the sparks of the food, and thereby incorporating them into the spiritual world.

The Rebbe Reb Zusya of Anipoli states, "When you eat you should meditate on Hashem's creation of Man for the spiritual purpose of eating: that he elevate the holy sparks to their source" (*Mazkeres Shem HaGedolim*, Bnei Brak, 1957).

WHEN EATING, THE RIZHINER NEVER LOWERED HIS HEAD TO THE PLATE, but sat upright and brought the spoon or fork to his mouth — and

TABLE MANNERS this became the custom of his chassidic descendants.

The act of eating is considered in the Rizhin tradition to be an *avodah* (form of Divine service). It was not so much intended to satisfy physical needs as to be a regular service of Hashem, a devotional act, similar to *tefillah*. *Tzaddikim* of the House of Rizhin meditate during their meals, which are saturated with salt (like the sacrificial meat of the offering in the Temple), while their ingestion of meat is frugal and very limited. Their meals are a ritual, an exercise in meditation, and they partake of their meals in awe and love of Hashem the Provider, in just the same manner that they perform their prayers (*Beis Rizhin*, Bnei Brak, 1987).

When R' Avrohom Yaakov of Sadagora (1820-1883) ate, it was no less evident to the eye that this was a service to Hashem than it would have been had he been praying. The Sadagorer explained this as follows: "You should believe with a complete faith that Hashem, Blessed is He, gives life and existence to everything, and that in everything there is to be found a sign of Hashem's energizing power — to vivify it, recreate it and cause it to flourish. Thinking about it while you eat, you join yourself with the life and the spark within the food, and in this way you are no longer benefiting from this world at all. As with R' Yehudah HaNasi, whose table was always blessed with the choicest food, but who said, 'I have not derived the least enjoyment from this' (*Kesubos* 104a); and, as we read concerning the seventy elders who ate at Mt. Sinai, *they ate and drank* (*Exodus* 24:11). Because, I tell you, through their eating and drinking they attached themselves to Hashem" (*Beis Yisroel*, Iassy, 1908). A similar idea is expressed in the *Or Haganuz LeTzaddikim* (Jerusalem, 1966): "If you eat something delicious, think that with this pleasure you are enjoying the radiance of the *Shechinah.*" However, when partaking of something pleasurable one should be guided by the Maimonidean principle of moderation and self-control.

It is told that one of the Rizhiner's chassidim saw in the Rebbe's courtyard one of his small children (the young R' Mordechai Shraga of Husyatin) holding a bagel in his hand and crying bitterly. The chassid approached him and asked why he was crying. The child replied that he was hungry. "Why don't you eat the bagel in your hand?" asked the chassid. The child replied, still crying, "My father said that when you crave too much for something you are not allowed to partake of it."

THE RIZHINER REMARKED THAT THE MAIN AIM OF THE DIVINE SERVICE IN Shlomo's Temple was the consolidation of public offerings in a cen-

THE GLORY THAT WAS

tral point to serve the unified Jewish people. In the Second Commonwealth, however, turbulent individuals were drawn by the light of the great seers and righteous ones of the period, and the charm of that brightness wrapped them to it like a moth into the flames — hence chaos and disorder rose to the surface. Everyone exalted himself: "I will be king" (אֲנִי אֶמְלוֹךְ), and nursed the ambition to carry in his pouch the scepter of leadership over the masses.

Where there should have been the recognition that hegemony over everything belonged rightly to Zion and Jerusalem, the heretical Tzaddokite clique adopted the slogan, *ubi bene, ibi patria* (wherever life is good, that is my fatherland). All this took place under the cover of a religious concept that throws overboard the performance of the commandments as defined by the Oral Law, while taking upon itself to "renew" the entire Torah from its inner depths and making it unstable, thus weakening the spiritual tie with all that is stated in Scripture and with Eretz Yisroel.

In Jerusalem was begun the erection of the magnificent great synagogue, *Tiferes Yisroel,* inaugurated by the Rizhiner. R' Avrohom Yaakov, his son and successor, completed the building. In tandem with this he threw all his energy into helping finance the settlement of Jews in the Holy Land. This he did with the help of his friends in Russia and Galicia, men such as R' Meir'l of Premishlan who, notwithstanding the difficult circumstances of his own family, collected each year for the Holy Land a sum of 702 ducats, an amount equal to the numerical value of the three letters of the Hebrew word Shabbos. The elderly *tzaddik,* R' Tzvi Hirsch of Rimanov, acted in a similar manner.

INNER FIRE

WITH THE RIZHINER, THE MINUTEST FLICKER OF THE EYE WAS A GESTURE to be read, an emanation of the soul. Shakings and quakings were not in his nature. His prayer, especially the *"lulav* shaking" at the *Hoshanos* ceremony, lasted for hours. His body was, as it were, a material casing for his thoughts: only to the discerning eye was revealed the radiance of the white fire burning beneath this surface.

The chassidim who came to the Rizhiner, after the passing of R' Uri of Strelisk, the Seraph, had been accustomed to *davening* loudly and with great enthusiasm. The Rizhiner once said to them: "If you are not capable of *davening* with perfect calm you do not belong in our midst."

HIS ASPIRATION

THE RIZHINER WANTED TO CREATE A NEW TREND IN CHASSIDUS, TO ADD A new dimension to it in addition to *yiras Shamayim* and *mussar* (fear of Heaven and the pursuit of ethical perfection). He desired that it also emphasize character training, conducive to socially acceptable behavior in the spirit of the Biblical dictum, דְּרָכֶיהָ דַרְכֵי נֹעַם, *Her ways are ways of pleasantness (Mishlei* 3:17) — to be pleasant in the eyes of Hashem and people alike. He wanted to remind his fellow Jews that they are *bnei melachim* (lit. the children of kings), princes.

He tried to restore the glory of *batei kenesios* and *batei midrashos* (synagogues and study halls) of the days of old. Some houses of worship in his days were lacking in style, aesthetics and general decorum. He built a model *kloiz* (house of prayer), in the style of an armory. The prayers there were recited harmoniously, with devotion and feeling, enhanced by the singing of a properly appointed *shaliach tzibbur* (cantor), possessed of a sweet melodious voice, in accordance with the *Shulchan Aruch* (Code of Jewish Law). What R' Sholom Shachna, his father, planned for many years and could implement only through hints and with difficulty, the young R' Yisroel brought to fruition with unusual vigor.

A NEW EPOCH

So it was that in Sadagora, a new chassidic lifestyle was instituted by the Rebbe. *Chazzanim* of repute intoned the ancient melodies, and readers, well versed in the *nusach*, the traditional style, preserved the pristine beauty of the Torah reading. No one felt impelled to disturb the solemnity of the moment with worldly talk — for all thought of the worldly was eclipsed in the presence of this singular radiant man.

THE REBBE'S TABLE

Exemplary calm and perfect discipline prevailed during the *tisch*, although these were gatherings of thousands. A special wooden construction, or *salash*, built in the form of an amphitheater, was erected for this purpose. So strong an attraction was exercised by his *hoif* (court) — together with his personality — that the overwhelming majority of his followers disregarded any danger or pain, in order to come, even from remote places, to his abode. To be sure, this was no easy thing, given the throngs of people to be contended with.

Once a chassid of Strelisk, Yossel Brodder, who had won prominence for his astuteness and sense of humor and consequently made himself a favorite of the Rizhiner [in the same way that his first Rebbe, R' Uri, was fond of him], asked, "Rebbe, why should it be that your chassidim suffer in this world and in the World to Come more than others do?"

"Why do you think?" the Rizhiner asked.

Yossel replied: "If a chassid visits one of the minor chassidic rebbes, something which has become *de rigueur,* his in-laws are happy, his wife bakes a cake and roasts a chicken and loads him with other provisions for his trip to the rebbe. The whole town turns out to wish him a *bon voyage.* When he arrives at his destination, the Rebbe receives him with outstretched arms, inquires about the welfare of his family, and honors him. Upon his return home he is given a joyous, rapturous reception.

"After a hundred and twenty years he appears before the celestial court. 'What kind of a man were you?' he is asked. 'I was a chassid,' is his answer.

" 'Tell us, who was the *tzaddik* to whom you attached yourself?' — 'Rabbi so-and-so.' Whereupon they scrutinize the register wherein all his deeds are written, and determine: 'If you ministered to that *tzaddik,* you could not have been a better man than you actually were — your place is in *Gan Eden.'*

"On the other hand, the man who sets out to visit you incurs the suspicion of his father-in-law that he, a young man, is preparing himself for a long journey. Because he tries to borrow money from his acquaintances, suspicion mounts; the father-in-law confiscates his *tallis, tefillin* and Shabbos apparel. Then he reveals his plans, demonstrating thereby his seriousness in the matter. He is refused his meals and has to sleep in the *beis midrash.* This drags on for about a month, until he manages to collect the small sum necessary for the trip to the Rebbe.

"He embarks, pursued by the curses of the townsfolk. It is a long and arduous journey. It takes him four weeks to cover fifty miles in a wagon. The remainder of the way he goes on foot. Finally, arriving at Sadagora, he has to wait a whole month before he is received by the Rebbe. Then a few more months pass before he is privileged to see him once more — only to receive a parting blessing. No compliments, no honor is bestowed upon him. Yet he is happy, having been privileged to gaze upon the Rebbe. Now the time comes for him to return home, and he has misgivings about the kind of reception he can expect to receive. He enters the town stealthily, again sleeps in the *beis midrash,* on a hard bench, for one whole month until his mother-in-law's wrath has passed. Then he is permitted to re-enter the house, only to be received with hatred and contempt. Shortly after, the miserable man again finds himself in the grip of nostalgia. And so on ad infinitum, until he is transported to the next world, the world of truth. There they pose him the question: 'Who was your Rebbe'? And when he mentions your name (the Rizhiner) they say to him: 'Is that so? And you had the impudence to spend your time in worldly matters! Your place is in *Gehinnom*!' "

"And now," asked the Rizhiner, "what is your answer to your question?"

Yossel answered, "I say that our *Gehinnom* is nicer than their *Gan Eden*."

A VISITOR ASKED THE RIZHINER WHY THE *TZADDIKIM* OF THE PREVIOUS generation had lived such austere lives. The Rizhiner answered

CONUNDRUM that, among the different types of people who bring gifts to the *tzaddikim*, three classes can be discerned. First there are the chassidim who want to come closer to Hashem. Then, the second class are simple people who come for a blessing, which is to meet their material needs. And the third class are sinners. The money received from the chassidim is given to charity and to buy *taleisim*, *tefillin* and *tzitzis*. The money received from the simple is spent on the Rebbe's personal needs. Finally, the money given to him by the sinners goes toward extraneous things, such as horses, carriages and residences. In the previous generation, there were fewer sinners, so that *tzaddikim* received very little money from the third category and as a consequence had but little to spend on horses, carriages and homes. But today, unfortunately, there are many more sinners. Therefore, *tzaddikim* are obliged to spend much more in the third category!

A MAN ONCE ENTERED THE COURTYARD OF THE RIZHINER AND NO ONE recognized him. Without asking permission, he entered and put

A HALF RUBLE down his gift of a half ruble, extending his hand to receive a blessing, and then made ready to depart. The Rizhiner said, "I want you to stay here with me." The man consented. When he went outside later, everyone was surprised by the favor the Rizhiner had shown him. The man said, "Don't think I am a great man; I am a simple man. My brother and I agreed whoever dies first would let the other know what was happening in the world of truth. These past twenty years that my brother has been dead he has told me nothing. During the last few days, however, he appeared to me in a dream and told me that until now he has not been permitted to disclose anything. He was not given permission to fulfill our agreement. He told me that on the day he died R' Sholom Shachna of Prohobisht also passed away. An announcement was made in heaven and the great sages came forward to greet him. Afterwards it was announced that all who had died on this day would be absolved from the *hibut hakever* (torments of the grave).[1] Then another announcement was made:

'Whoever saw his (R' Sholom Shachna's) holy countenance in this world will be absolved from the judgment of *Gehinnom*; whoever gave him money in this world will be absolved of all judgment.' When I heard these things from him, I began to cry, 'My brother, help me! Tell me what to do now that R' Sholom Shachna is no longer in this world; how will I also be found worthy?' Now my brother answered me, 'He has yet a son, the Rizhiner. Go to him and give him half a ruble and you will also have this merit, as if you had given it to R' Sholom Shachna, his father.' Therefore, I have come now and given a half ruble to the Rizhiner."

The Rizhiner said, "Because this man has such honorable thoughts in his head, I received him with honor."

"INSPIRE FEAR IN THE STUDENTS" (*KESUBOS* 103b) — THIS WAS THE ORDER R' Yehudah HaNasi gave to his son, his successor. The Rizhiner's **REBUKE** conduct was in accord with this tenet. *Better is open rebuke than hidden love (Mishlei 27:5).* The chassid un-

---

1. The pains that await the body after death, inflicted, according to tradition, by the *malachei chabalah*, the angels charged with that task.

derstands this to mean that rebuke that flows from love is more enduring than any other kind.

The Rizhiner's testimony about himself was: "I am a part of Israel's soul, despite the fact that I myself am a nobody; and wherever a Jew suffers, I feel it inwardly."

HE ALSO EXPOUNDED THE TALMUDIC STATEMENT, "MAN'S SUSTENANCE IS as difficult as the dividing of the Red Sea" (*Pesachim* 118a), as fol-

MAN'S SUSTENANCE

lows: Is it logical to say that any task is difficult for the Creator? Surely His power penetrates the entire cosmos! However, we find an answer to this in the verse: *And the sea, when the morning appeared, returned to its strength* (*Shemos* 14:27). On this the Talmud comments that the sea carried out the stipulation Hashem made when He created it. When the Sea of Reeds was created, Hashem stipulated that it was to change its nature and split so that the Israelites could pass through, and then return to its normal course. He showed the Sea of Reeds the souls of the Israelites, saying to it, "When they appear before you, you will have to make way for them." When, however, the Israelites who came forth from Egypt reached the sea — with their souls polluted by the hardships of slavery and bodies consumed by the dust and grime of work — the sea refused to split for them, saying that at its creation radiant souls had been shown to it, not these. It was, therefore, necessary to compel the sea to divide.

A similar situation obtains in the matter of man's sustenance. When man's soul descends from heaven, his sustenance descends along with him. They show the soul to the sustenance, saying: "You belong to this soul." But, descended to earth, the soul shrouds itself in black, and its sustenance fails to recognize it. The sustenance says: "This is not the soul that was shown to me." Here, too, force is necessary in order to bond them together.

CHAPTER XIV

RELATIONSHIPS WITH RABBINIC CONTEMPORARIES

R′ELIMELECH, THE SON OF R′ MEIR YECHIEL OF MOGELNITZA, was a renowned chassid of the Rizhiner and was ordained by him to become a rebbe. After the death of his father,

A WORD OF ENCOURAGEMENT

R′ Meir Yechiel, R′ Elimelech did not want to conduct himself as a chassidic rebbe. His brother, R′ Yaakov, was the Rebbe of the city of Blendov. R′ Elimelech lived in Grodzhisk, occupying himself with Torah, and also journeying regularly to Rizhin. The Rizhiner respected him greatly and asked him why he did not wish to function as a rebbe. The Rizhiner asked, "If a person came to you and you could help him, would you not do so?"

"I do not even know how to read a *kvittel*," cried R′ Elimelech. On the table was a *kvitel* with the name of Moshe ben Sarah. The

Rizhiner took the *kvittel* and gave it to him and taught him how to "read" it. Then the Rizhiner pleaded, "Let his honor return home and let him give aid and succor to his fellow Jews." On his return home to Grodzhisk, the news that he had agreed to accept *kvitlach* brought him large crowds. The first *Yid* to present him with a *kvittel* was a fellow by the name of Moshe ben Sarah! So R' Elimelech was in the end ordained to be a Rebbe and became the celebrated R' Elimelech of Grodzhisk. Even after becoming a Rebbe, however, R' Elimelech continued to travel to the Rizhiner, and he transcribed much of R' Yisroel's Torah (teachings) in his book, *Divrei Elimelech.*

WHEN R' YITZCHOK OF VORKI RETURNED FROM HIS JOURNEY TO Sadagora, his disciple and chassid, R' Shraga Feivel of Gritzah, asked

HIS GREAT LOVE

what distinguished the Rizhiner from all others. "I found in the *tzaddik* of Rizhin the attribute of *ahavas Yisroel* (love of one's fellow Jew), to an extent that I have seen nowhere else," R' Yitzchok replied.

The *tzaddik,* R' Yitzchok of Zidichov, before traveling to the Rizhiner, went to his father, the *tzaddik* R' Naftoli of Lizhensk, to ask his approval. His father said to him, "I agree that you should visit the Rizhiner Rebbe, but do not tell him who you are. Tell him that you are the son of Naftoli and no more." When R' Yitzchok came to Sadagora, he took his place in line with several hundred chassidim. As he passed before the Rebbe, he stretched out his hand, as was expected, but the Rebbe took hold of it and fastened his gaze upon him. He asked him his name. Was he not the off-spring of the *tzaddik* of Zidichov? The reply was in the affirmative. The Rebbe was delighted, told him that he knew his father, proceeded to tell him a story and, finally, asked him to re-late it to his father.

When R' Yitzchok returned from Sadagora and told his father the story and all that the Rizhiner had said, R' Naftoli replied, "If so, I am forced to go there." Of him the Rizhiner later said, "How can a man hide himself for so long? I only recognized him by the tip of his nose." And the Rizhiner asked if chassidim came to see R' Naftoli. They answered, "He does not allow them to come to him." The

Rebbe said, "Polish fools! They should break down the beams of the house to learn from him the way to worship Hashem."

SAGE ADVICE WHEN IT CAME TO CHOOSING A REBBE FOR A COMMUNITY, THE RIZHINER was often consulted. In the year 1848, R' Yechezkel Shraga, the son of R' Chaim of Sanz, was appointed Rav of Rozdol in place of his father-in-law, R' Yehudah Tzvi. His mother-in-law wanted him to follow in the footsteps of his father-in-law and assume the role of a chassidic rebbe. She went with her son-in-law to the Rizhiner to ask him to encourage the chassidim of her late husband to come to her son-in-law. The Rizhiner, however, told her that her husband's chassidim should go to the *tzaddik*, R' Yitzchok of Zidichov. The chassidim thereafter went to Zidichov.

A REVELATION THE *TZADDIK*, REB SHLOMO OF TULCHIN, WAS A FREQUENT VISITOR AT THE Rizhiner's *tisch*. One Rosh Chodesh, as he was leaving, the Rizhiner escorted him the full length of the corridor. He put his hand on the *mezuzah* and said to the Rebbe of Tulchin, "I, with my Torah, am not afraid nor embarrassed, even before the King *Mashiach*. Will he reveal a new Torah to us?" He placed his finger on his lips and continued, "G-d forbid! One of the Thirteen Principles of Faith is that the Torah will not be changed and there will be no other Torah besides that which we have. *Mashiach* will, however, uncover new explanations of the Torah, so that all scholars will bow before him. He will show them that they know so little that it will seem as if he brought a new Torah. My Torah and I, however, will not be humbled even before the *Mashiach*, because I did not receive my Torah from mortal men. When my father left this world, I was still a young child and had no teacher. I learned my Torah from the *Chai HaChaim* (the Life of Life) Himself, and no further revelations can be made concerning it."

In his old age, the Rebbe, R' Raphael of Bershad (d. 1816), a disciple of R' Pinchos of Koritz, visited the Rizhiner. The latter was very

A WORD TO THE WISE

happy to greet him and honored him in every way. After a while, the Rizhiner asked him to recount some Torah that he had heard from his master, R' Pinchos of Koritz. R' Raphael said in the name of his Rebbe, "*Mikveh* is the garb of *tefillah*." After R' Raphael left, the Rizhiner said to his sons, "Sometimes a man is given longevity only so that he will bring one maxim to the one to whom it applies."

The Rebbe, R' Moshe of Savrani, once visited the Rizhiner. The Rizhiner asked him what he did on Rosh Hashanah when many chas-

THE MIND OF THE TZADDIK

sidim came to visit him. The Savranier answered, "I review them all at a glance. And what does the Rebbe of Rizhin do with his chassidim on Rosh Hashanah?"

"All the souls of Israel," the Rizhiner replied, "are rooted in the heart of the *tzaddik*. When the *tzaddik davens* and pours out his heart like water, then, automatically, all his chassidim are remembered before Hashem."

When R' Moshe of Savrani died, on a Shabbos, the Rizhiner was sitting at his *tisch*, discussing the verse, *And Moshe went up to Hashem* (*Shemos* 19:3). He told the story of two watchmen in the forest. When one would call, his friend would answer his call loudly. Once, the watchman called and there was no response. He then realized that his friend had disappeared. The Rebbe had not yet been informed of R' Moshe's death.

Among the many friends and admirers of the Rizhiner was the Rebbe, R' Meir'l of Premishlan (1782-1850). All the time that the Rizhiner spent in jail, R' Meir'l did not sleep in his bed but on a plank, in order to participate in his sorrow.

The relationship between the Rizhiner and R' Meir'l of Premishlan was a long and intense one, dating from the Rebbe's days in Rizhin prior to his move to Sadagora. Once, when R' Meir'l returned from the *mikveh*, before Shabbos, he asked those around him, "Why are you looking at me? If you see a beam of light emanating from my face, that is from the Rizhiner Rebbe. That light emanates from his face." He would say, "R' Avrohom the Malach's main task was to bring a soul like that of R' Yisroel of Rizhin into the world. Such a noble soul could only be brought by an angel — a *malach*."

AMONGST THE *TZADDIKIM* WHO HAD CONTACT WITH THE RIZHINER WAS R' Menachem Mendel of Lubavitch (d. 1866), the author of *Tzemach Tzedek*. An edict had been issued in Russia

A DISSENTING VOICE

concerning the style of clothing that Jews were permitted to wear, banning the customary Jewish garb of Eastern Europe. The Lubavitcher Rebbe called a conference of the leaders of Jewry in Russia to protest the edict, even at the risk of life and limb, as the Law prescribes in times of *shmad*, when Jews are being forced to renounce their religion. They asked the Rizhiner, who then lived in Sadagora, for his concurrence. When the messenger came to Sadagora and communicated the decision of the rabbinic sages, the Rizhiner demurred, saying, "Yaakov, our father, accepted the *brochos* when he was wearing the clothes of Eisav. May it be Hashem's will that the blessings be fulfilled in our days, too, even when Jews wear the clothes of Eisav."

The Tzemach Tzedek

THE GREAT *TZADDIKIM* OF THE GENERATION followed him, even though they had their own followers.

FIRST AMONG EQUALS

Some of them came to Sadagora incognito, because of their humility. It is told that the *tzaddik*, R' Mordechai of Nadvorna, came to Sadagora and did not reveal himself to anyone. The Rizhiner would pass through an aisle of people as he left his sanctuary. With his eyes closed, he would bid *Sholom* to everyone. When he came to R' Mordechai of Nadvorna and touched his hand, he suddenly opened his eyes and asked who the young man was. "From Nadvorna," replied the young man. "Are you perhaps the son of R' Bertche, *zt"l*?"

"Yes," answered R' Mordechai. At the Shabbos meal, R' Mordechai was seated at the head of the table next to the Rebbe, who honored him and personally gave him *shirayim* (leftovers of the *tzaddik's* meal, customarily distributed among his followers) and said that the spirit of Hashem illumined his face.

NONETHELESS, IT IS IN RIZHIN ...

THE YOUNG SON OF THE YUD HAKADOSH OF PSCHIS'CHE WAS R' Nechemia'le. He was also one of the Rizhiner's chassidim, ordained and made a Rebbe by him. R' Nechemia'le was the son-in-law of the Rabbi of Volodirki-Kiev, near Rizhin. When he was still being supported by his father-in-law, R' Nechemia'le began to travel to Rizhin. The Rizhiner liked him a great deal and treated him like one of his sons. Even after the death of his father-in-law and his departure to Pshis'che to live with his older brother, R' Yerachmiel, R' Nechemiale often visited the Rizhiner.

Every young chassid that came to visit his brother, R' Yerachmiel, was persuaded by R' Nechemia'le to visit the Rizhiner. He was so attached to the Rizhiner that he used to say, "I know the great holiness of my brother, R' Yerachmiel; nonetheless, it is in Rizhin that I find the source of my soul."

DEALINGS WITH ELIYAHU HANAVI

ONCE, R' NECHEMIA'LE WAS DELAYED ON HIS WAY TO RIZHIN AND DECIDED to spend Rosh Hashanah in a small town. After Rosh Hashanah he pressed on, hoping to reach Rizhin in time for Yom Kippur. It was Erev Yom Kippur when he arrived in Rizhin. The sun was already setting, and he had no money left to buy a chicken for *kapparos*; nor was there an available *mikveh* for immersion.

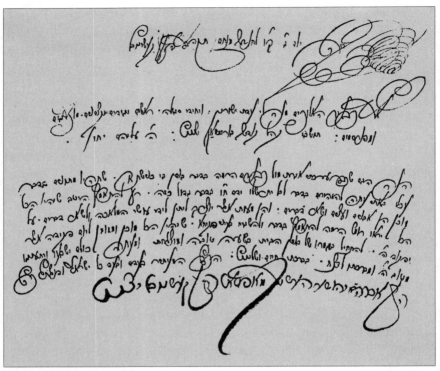

Letter written by the Apter Rav

He was distraught. Suddenly, he saw a river on the side of the road and he immediately immersed in it. A Jew approached on the road, holding a chicken. The Jew asked if he would like to buy the chicken, but he said he had no money. The Jew said to him, "I will give you the chicken on credit. When you get the money, pay me." R' Nechemia'le happily took the chicken and ran to the Rizhiner *kloiz* , getting there just before the Holy Day began. As he entered to greet the Rebbe, the Rizhiner said to him, "Nechemia'le, have you been doing business with Eliyahu HaNavi (Elijah the Prophet)"?

ONCE THE APTER RAV AND THE RIZHINER SPENT A SHABBOS TOGETHER, and R' Nechemia'le was among the chassidim. A youth of only

YEHUDI BEN YEHUDI 16, he stood behind the Rizhiner's chair.

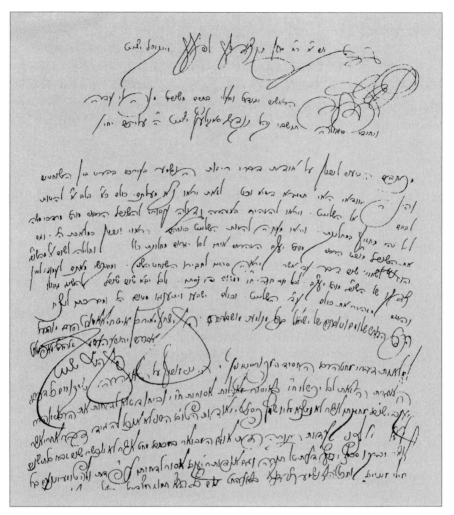

Manuscript written by the Apter Rav

The Apter Rav then asked the Rizhiner, "Who is the young man standing behind you?"

"He is the son of the Yud HaKadosh," answered the Rizhiner.

The Apter Rav turned his head to look at R' Nechemia'le and said, "The Yud HaKadosh was a *Yud* (Jew) and left behind a *Yud*."

When R' Nechemia'le was 20, the Rizhiner told him to settle in Bichov-Lublin and he ordained him to become a chassidic Rebbe.

R' MOSHE OF SAVRANI WAS KNOWN TO AVOID *KAVOD* (HONOR). ONCE R' Moshe visited one of the towns where he had many devoted

A WORD TO THE WISE chassidim. To pay him honor, they prepared a beautiful carriage, drawn by four white horses, to lead him into the town where the road was lined with people. As he sat inside the elegant coach, he felt very uncomfortable, because he was afraid that all the honor would go to his head and cause him to be guilty of *gaavah* (pride).

Sitting there, he asked himself, "What, after all, is a carriage? It's nothing without the horses that pull it, and the horse is nothing more than an impure animal. All that remains of it when it dies is a disgusting , malodorous carcass." Just the thought of the dead horse caused him to regurgitate.

Once when the Savranier came to see the Rizhiner, he related to him the experience of that trip. The Rizhiner said to him, "I think the *yetzer hara* of pride and haughtiness can be removed more simply. After all, what is there for man to be conceited about anyway?" He continued with the following parable: "A king's minister often walked through the streets of the capital. The citizens, mistaking him for the king, bowed low in respect. Once, however, the minister accompanied the king on a stroll. Passersby bowed to the minister, whom they knew, and ignored the king, not knowing who he was. The minister felt very uncomfortable, for he was fully aware that the people should be bestowing honor and genuflecting to the king, not to him."

The Rizhiner concluded, "So too, the honor given to us should really cause us shame and embarrassment."

THE RIZHINER OCCASIONALLY VISITED LEMBERG FOR MEDICAL REASONS AND each time he honored the rabbi of the city with a visit. R' Yaakov

BRICK, NOT IRON Orenstein was a gaon in halachah and was an ardent opponent to chassidim and Chassidic *rebbeim*. To the Rizhiner, however, he accorded the greatest honor. Once the Rizhiner asked the Rav of Lemberg, "What are the roofs of your city made of?" The Rav answered, "They are made of iron to protect against fire." "If that is the reason," retorted the Rizhiner, "you could have made them out of brick or tile." "Is this the man whom multitudes follow?" wondered the gaon. "I thought that he would want to show off his knowledge and sharpness of learning." The conversation reached the ears of R' Meir'l of Premishlan. "The *tzaddik* of Rizhin is correct," R' Meir explained. "Just as the roof protects the house, so the rabbi must protect the city, and his heart must be breakable like brick and not hard like iron."

On another occasion, the Rabbi of Lemberg blessed the Rizhiner at his departure: that he should have a safe trip and travel in peace. He added that Hashem should enable R' Yisroel to spread His word and knowledge throughout the land. The Rizhiner remarked: "Why does it state in *Yeshayah* (11:9), *And the entire earth will be filled with de'ah* (intelligence), *de'ah* rather than *chochmah* (wisdom)? When the *Mashiach* will come, all men and women will not be tested alike, but each will be differentiated from the other and judged individually. So it is written, 'And the whole earth will be filled with the knowledge of Hashem,' for if there is no *de'ah*, how can there be differentiation?"

DEROGATION — AFTERMATH

THE GAON, R' REUVEN OF ODESSA, A RIZHINER CHASSID, FREQUENTLY visited Lemberg. One visit for medical purposes coincided with a visit of the Rizhiner. When the Rizhiner visited the gaon of Lemberg, R' Yaakov Orenstein, the gaon's son asked the Rizhiner: "Does the Rebbe know that his chassid, R' Reuven of Odessa, is in Lemberg?" The Rizhiner replied, "Reuven of Odessa, yes, I know that he is ill and I have sent him 100 rubles." The son of R' Yaakov continued, "You refer to him as Reuven of Odessa without the title 'Rabbi.' His honor gave him 100 rubles and took away his title?" The Rizhiner remained silent and did not answer. When they served him wine, the Rizhiner drank just a little and gave the cup to the son of the Rabbi of Lemberg. The son took the cup and brought it outside to a guard, who was there to maintain order over the throngs who had gathered to see the Rebbe. When the

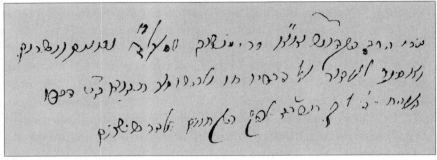

Signature of the Divrei Chaim, the Rebbe of Sanz

Rizhiner saw that the son gave his *shirayim* to a gentile, he felt offended. He stood up and bade good-bye to the gaon of Lemberg. That same year the son of the gaon passed away and the Rizhiner was imprisoned. The people said: "Two men of wisdom and learning could not get along in matters of halachah; one has died and the other has gone into exile."

AFTER THE DEATH OF R' URI OF STRELISK (1826), HIS CHASSIDIM CAME under the influence of the Rizhiner. When they came to him for the

A SECOND WIFE first time, the Rizhiner remarked, "Coming to a second rebbe is similar to marrying a second wife. As long as one remembers the first, he is unable to live happily with the second. Similarly, when one goes to a new rebbe, one must forget the first." Afterwards, he said, "My father once told me that there would be golden buttons on my clothing. Possibly, he was referring to the chassidim of Strelisk."

THE RIZHINER RESPECTED THE SANZER RAV AND TURNED TO HIM WITH A halachic question regarding the gentiles who worked for him on the

THE SANZER RAV Shabbos in the production of whiskey. The Sanzer replied that to answer this question, he must put aside all his other work and delve into the matter for two weeks. The Rizhiner invited him to his home to conduct his research there. In his Responsa, *Divrei Chaim*, Part I, *Orach Chaim* p. 7, the responsum, permitting the work via a sales contract, is to be found.

ONCE, THE SANZER RAV, WITH MANY OTHER WELL-KNOWN TZADDIKIM from Russia, was visiting the Rizhiner in Sadagora. At one point, the

A PROTEST Rizhiner turned to the rebbes and said, "Is this called free choice or free will? If there were chassidim who are as successful in their daily affairs as those who remain distant from Torah, this would be free will. But in fact we see that only people who are distant from Torah and Chassidus succeed financially, while chassidim and men of good deeds are starving. Can we call this *bechirah* (free will)?" After this he turned to the Sanzer and said, "I am protesting Divine injustice. What is your opinion, Sanzer Rav? Am I right or not?"

THE FIRST GERER REBBE, THE CHIDUSHEI HARIM (d. 1866), ADMIRED THE Rizhiner. He sent R' Eliezer HaKohen of Poltusk, the son-in-law of R'

THE CHIDUSHEI HARIM Yaakov Lorberbaum of Lissa, the author of *Chavas Daas*, to visit the Rizhiner, saying to him, "When you return home and describe his conduct to me, then I will go to visit him." While the Rabbi of Poltusk was with the Rizhiner, the wife of the Gerer Rebbe took ill. He then wrote to the Rabbi of Poltusk and asked him to give a *kvitel* for his sick wife to the Rizhiner, sending 18 rubles as *pidyon refuah,* a charity contribution for the merit of her recovery.

At a later time (1840) the Chidushei HaRim and his son-in-law R' Pinchos Menachem of Piltz traveled to the Rizhiner during the month of Adar. When they came to Sadagora, they told no one of their identity. When they came to the Rizhiner, he recognized them and spent a long time talking with the Chidushei HaRim. The Rebbe invited him to remain in Sadagora and gave him a special room in his mansion. The Chidushei HaRim remained there for two weeks, and every day they discussed Torah and Chassidus. To honor his distinguished guest, the Rizhiner called upon one of his foremost chassidim, R' Yitzchok, son of R' Yaakov of Stanislav, to join them. When the Chidushei HaRim returned from their first meeting, he commented: "We went with him through the whole of pardes (פַּרְדֵּס — garden: exegesis of secrets of Torah), but our friend, R' Yitzchok, was not able to keep up with us for the whole time."

Letter written and signed by R' Tzvi Hirsch of Rimanov

It is said that the Rizhiner asked the Chidushei HaRim, "Are there good roads in Poland?" "Yes!" the Gerer replied. "And who are the

PAVING ROADS contractors, Jews or gentiles?" the Rizhiner asked. "The Jews are the contractors," replied the Gerer. "No wonder," retorted the Rizhiner, "who knows better than the Jews how to pave roads…"

At the *Purim Kattan* meal,[1] the Rizhiner said to the Chidushei HaRim, "I will explain a Biblical verse in *I Shmuel* (15:13) to you. After Shaul's battle against Amalek, when Shaul disobeyed the command to kill all the Amalekites, Scripture states, *And Shmuel came to Shaul, and Shaul said to him: Blessed be you to Hashem, I have done Hashem's bidding.* This verse is quite difficult to understand. Shaul actually took pity on Agag (the Amalekite king), and did *not* do Hashem's bidding. How, then, could he say, 'I have done the bidding of Hashem'? It is possible to explain it thus: Shaul said to Shmuel, 'The fact that I pitied Agag led to the emergence of Haman, and because of Haman, the Jews upheld and accepted willingly and happily the Torah, which they had previously accepted under some degree of duress (*Shabbos* 88a). They upheld what they had already received, and therefore I expedited Hashem's bidding.' "

The Gerer then asked, "If that is so, what was Shaul's sin?" "Even so, Shaul sinned, for a king of Israel is not permitted to forsake his people and subject them to danger," the Rizhiner replied.

---

1. In a Jewish leap year of thirteen months, Purim is observed during the second month of Adar. The corresponding day in the first Adar is known as *Purim Kattan* (a small Purim) and is a time of a minor celebration.

CHAPTER XV

A STRONG FLAME

THE WELL-KNOWN TZADDIK, R' TZVI HIRSCH OF RIMANOV, (D. 1848) called by the Rizhiner "R' Hirsch the Great," at first associated with the Rizhiner as a friend and later as a *mechutan*

R' TZVI HIRSCH OF RIMANOV

(in-law). R' Hirsch sent his *gabbai*, the chassid, Rav Hirschel Itche's, to "look at the face of the glorious *tzaddik*, R' Yisroel of Sadagora." The Rizhiner asked him, "Where are you from?" "From Rimanov," replied the *gabbai*. "Is that where the great R' Hirsch resides?" asked the Rebbe. You know he is a fiery personality. I heard the *tzaddik* of Rimanov is a Kohen. Does he bless the assembled daily? Does he like to travel?"

The *gabbai* replied that R' Tzvi Hirsch traveled very little, only to obtain medical care for his feet. The Rizhiner commented, "What do you know about his travels? He goes on Shabbos and Yom Tov to places where angels dare not tread." The *gabbai* returned to Rimanov and told his Rebbe all he had seen at Sadagora. R' Hirsch took his *minyan* and set out for Sadagora with plans to reach it by *Parashas Chukas.* On the way, hundreds and thousands of chassidim greeted him. When he reached Sadagora, the Rizhiner came out to greet him joyfully. On their first meeting, they behaved as if they had been friends for many years. The Rizhiner then said, "To cleanse the soul and to raise it is not such a wonder, but how can you raise the body to such great heights?"

ON THE RARE OCCASSIONS WHEN R' TZVI HIRSCH OF RIMANOV CAME TO Sadagora, he treated it as a second home. On the eve of Shabbos, he

R' TZVI HIRSCH IN RIZHIN

would put on his white clothing, run to the *beis midrash* of the Rizhiner, and would shout out the prayer, *Hodu laShem Ki Tov* (*Tehillim* 107:1), together with the chassidim, who shouted in unison with him. The children of the Rizhiner went to their father and told him that R' Hirsch was praying loudly before the ark. Their father said to them, "Watch yourselves when speaking of such a holy man, for the holiness of the Shabbos burns so strong in him that he cannot control himself." Then the Rizhiner went to listen to the ecstatic prayers of R' Hirsch.

At the table, the Rizhiner ate little and left *shirayim* for his chassidim, but R' Hirsch ate all that was served to him. The children of the Rizhiner were intrigued at the fact that he ate so much. The Rimanover explained, "I eat for it gives me the strength I need, for upon me rests the burden of sustaining Israel."

After Shabbos, the Rimanover bade good-bye to the Rizhiner. The Rizhiner kissed R' Hirsch, but R' Hirsch did not kiss the Rebbe. When they asked R' Hirsch for his reason, he replied, "I do not know the secret of the kiss, for from heaven it was not revealed to me and from my holy teacher I never received it."

THE REBBE, R' HIRSCH, SAID OF THE RIZHINER, "I AM ASTONISHED THAT this holy man seeks so much wealth and receives all the honor from

A PARADOX

the world and still his only intention is to increase the honor of Heaven. It is a paradox that the Rizhiner adopted his *derech* (lifestyle) from Hanoch — the heavenly angel."

When the Rizhiner heard that R' Hirsch of Rimanov was a prodigious wonder-worker, he exclaimed: In your case, we were vouchsafed no sign, no explanations except as it is written, *You decree and it comes to pass* (*Iyov* 22:28).

ONCE, ON THE EVE OF YOM KIPPUR, AFTER HE HAD ALREADY MADE HIS permanent home in Sadagora, the Rizhiner was offered a place of

NOT BY MIRACLES refuge in Rimanov. He said: "For seven days Moshe refused to accept the mission to go to Egypt, for it involved miracles, and his wish was to achieve his goal in a natural way; and because the exodus from Egypt was achieved by means of miracles, the war with Amalek broke out right after the parting of the Reed Sea."

On many occasions the Rizhiner voiced his opinion on miracles. When the Gaon, Rav Sholom, the *av beis din* of Kaminka, was near him, the Rizhiner asked him what he was saying when his hands were on a sick person, praying for him to be healed, and whence did his power come? Rav Sholom answered, יִשְׁלַח דְּבָרוֹ וְיִרְפָּאֵם, *He will send forth His word and heal them* (*Tehillim* 107:20). The initial letters are *yud, dalet* and *vav*, which spell יָדוֹ, "his hand." On this the holy Rizhiner answered, " The final letters are *mem, vav* and *ches*, which spell מוֹחַ, "brain," an allusion that the true power is in the brain.

R' HIRSCH MADE THE FOLLOWING REMARK TO THE JEWS WHO INFORMED him of those chassidic leaders who, though not the inheritors of spe-

CLEAVING TO A STICK cial virtues, were yet proclaimed wonder-workers: "If thousands of Jews will attach themselves out of a sincere faith to a stick, the latter will perform wonders."

When the Rimanover returned home his chassidim asked him what he thought of the Rizhiner. He answered, "I do not know yet, for this time I only saw the tip of his nose, and if Hashem grant me life and I have the opportunity to see him again, I will see more."

When reciting Torah at his table, R' Hirsch of Rimanov defined his approach and that of the Rizhiner in this manner: He explained the verse, *The name of the first was Shifrah and the name of the second, Puah* (*Shemos* 1:15) as follows: "There are two types of *tzaddikim;* one who worships Hashem with *d'veikus* (cleaving), intensity of thought, without straining the voice and lungs. His actions show that he is worshipping, but he does it with modulated sweetness and melody. This type of *tzaddik* is exemplified by the name Shifrah. Then, there is a *tzaddik* who prays with such intensity and fear that he shakes the pillars of heaven and moves the hearts of those around him. A *tzaddik* of this type is called Puah."

THE FIRST VISIT OF R' HIRSCH TOOK PLACE IN THE SUMMER OF 1843, AND in 1844 he came a second time to Sadagora; but this time he came,

PROPITIOUS WORDS

not as a chassid, but as a *mechutan*. His only daughter, a 3-year-old, born in his old age, was engaged to the grandson of the Rizhiner, the 5-year-old son of R' Avrohom Yaakov. At the *tenayim* (engagement celebration), the Rizhiner said to R' Hirsch, "I want you to know that it is our custom before the engagement to tell the in-laws the qualities of the family and to describe our *yichus* (lineage). The founder of our dynasty was my great-grandfather, R' Ber; my grandfather was his son, R' Avrohom the Malach; my great uncle was R' Nochum of Chernobyl; and his son was R' Mottel." Then he turned to R' Hirsch and said, "Please now tell me of your family background." R' Hirsch answered him, "My parents left me an orphan at the age of 10, and I therefore did not know them too well. But I do know that they were wholehearted and righteous people.

"After I lost them, I was apprenticed to a master tailor. I studied the trade and became an honest laborer. One thing was explained to me: 'Try to fix the old, and be careful never to ruin a new garment.' " When the Rizhiner heard these last words of R' Hirsch, he stood up and said, "The *shidduch* (arrangement) is good on both sides." After the engagement, R' Hirsch returned home, but his happiness was short-lived. After a few months, the young groom suddenly took ill and died. When the period of mourning was over, the Rizhiner said to his son, R' Avrohom Yaakov, "From Heaven it was decreed that we should marry into the family of the *tzaddik* of Rimanov, and since the *shidduch* was not consummated, we will renew it and effectuate it for the second son. His name is Shlomo. As his name implies, he should be whole and healthy" (similarity of Shlomo and *shalem*, whole). This engagement with the son, Shlomo, was concluded without any fanfare.

R' MEIR'L OF PREMISHLAN WAS A TRUE ADMIRER OF THE RIZHINER, DESPITE the great differences that existed between them. R' Meir lived in great

LUXURY AND PENURY poverty, for he gave everything to charity, while in the court of the Rizhiner there was wealth and luxury. Even so, R' Meir showed great love and respect for the Rizhiner. "The differences between myself and the Rizhiner Rebbe," he would say, "is that of the Rizhiner it is said, *His wealth and glory are in his house and his righteousness stands forever (Tehillim* 112:3). Of me it is said, *He spends freely and gives to the poor, his righteousness stands forever"* (ibid. 112:9).

Once he sent a message to the Rizhiner, "The Rebbe of Rizhin travels the king's highway, and I travel only a simple path, yet we both arrive at the same destination."

IT IS TOLD THAT ONCE THE RIZHINER AND R' MEIR MET ON A ROAD, R' Meir in a simple wagon with only one horse, and the Rizhiner

SELF–SUFFICIENCY in a splendid coach with four horses. When they approached each other, the Rizhiner turned to R' Meir and said: "I travel with four horses, for if the wagon gets caught deep in the mud, we can get out again easily and quickly, but why do you travel with only one horse?"

"I have only one horse and it will not be able to pull the wagon out, so I am forced to be careful to avoid the mud," came the reply.

Once the Rizhiner told the following story:

Before my marriage, when I was still in my brother's house, I loved to go on trips. But I always tried to return home before nightfall, since my mother feared for my safety. Once it happened that a heavy rain overtook me on the road and I took refuge at an inn. The innkeeper had been a follower of my father, of blessed memory. When I entered his courtyard, the innkeeper approached me, and I could see that his countenance was both delighted and troubled. I asked him if, G-d forbid, something was the matter. He replied that he was very happy that his Rebbe's son had come to spend the night with him, but he regretted that he did not have an empty room for me, since a businessman from Brody had taken the last one available. I told him that I did not mind staying in the same room with the businessman. The innkeeper was thrilled, helped me down from the coach and brought me into the house. I lit my pipe and walked back and forth in the room, smoking. Then I saw the businessman, sleeping bare-headed on his back. He immediately awoke and began shouting to the servants, "Are my *varenikis* (dumplings) ready yet?" They brought him what he had asked for, and he ate a bowlful without washing his hands or reciting a benediction, and then he went back to sleep. I gazed at him, intent on discovering the source of his existence. I resolved to awaken him and talk to him. I touched him and he opened his eyes. He was puzzled and asked where I came from. I told him that I came from Prohobisht. He asked me if I knew the Rebbe there. I feigned ignorance and asked, "What Rebbe lives there?" He said, "Is it not the Rebbe, Rav Avrohomyu?" I said, "Is he really a Rebbe?" He grabbed a stick and began to chase me, trying to hit me. The innkeeper appeared and told him, "Before you stands the brother of this Rebbe."

When he heard that I was the Rebbe's brother, he did not know what to do. Out of his abject shame, and without further ado, he insisted that his coach be hitched up, and he left without saying farewell. After a while, when I had assumed the leadership, it happened that this particular Brody merchant had a legal dispute with a man from the town of Uman, who wanted me to decide the matter for them. The former chose to forfeit his money rather than appear before me, because of his embarrassment. "Do you see now," concluded the Rizhiner, "how far the concept of *emunas tzaddikim* — faith in the righteous ones, extends?"

ONE ATHEIST CHALLENGED THE RIZHINER: "WHY DO YOU WAIT FOR THE coming of *Mashiach*? Is it not written, *She has fallen and will no*

THE ATHEIST'S CHALLENGE

longer rise, the maiden Israel (Amos 5:2)?" He answered that the Rabbis understand this passage as follows: "She has fallen and will no longer fall. Rise, O maiden of Israel." The freethinker then said that he did not believe in the explanation of the Rabbis. Could the Rebbe not bring some proof from the Torah? The Rebbe responded that King Dovid had already written, *It is wasteful for you to rise up early* (מַשְׁכִּימֵי קוּם) *and sit up late (Tehillim* 127:2), and he was addressing this to those (atheists) who place the word קוּם, "rise up," early in the sentence (in *Amos*) rather than at the end of the sentence.

ONCE, DURING A WALK IN THE FOREST WITH A GROUP OF HIS FOLLOWERS, the Rebbe referred to the Talmud (*Makkos* 24a) which states that

... WILL LIVE BY HIS FAITH

Chabakkuk encapsulated the entire Torah in the single principle, *And the righteous person will live by his faith (Chabakkuk* 2:4). Chabakkuk was one of the last of the prophets. Certainly, he meant to prophesy for the generations preceding the coming of *Mashiach,* when the whole world would be defined by that one quality, *The righteous person will live by his faith* — faith in his leaders. In the generation prior to the coming of *Mashiach,* the situation will be such that everyone will do what is right in his own eyes. This does not mean simply that a great sinner will not be ashamed to sin before those who fear Hashem, but even if a Jew should want to say some words of Torah, he will have to look the length and breadth of the street to find someone who will not scorn and mock him. If a Jew will hold himself faithful at that time, this will certainly be the true choice, belonging to the category, מִי לַה' אֵלָי, *Whoever is for Hashem, let him join me! (Shemos* 32:26). At that time, if a Jew will arise in the morning and say *modeh ani* ("I thank You" — basic expression of faith said on awakening), even if he cannot distinguish between *modeh ani* (I thank) and לְפָנֶיךָ (You); and if he will wear a *tallis* and *tefillin*, understanding only that a head without *tefillin* implies an extremely low level, such a Jew will be considered important and welcome before the Creator. The Rebbe thrust both his hands into his garment close to his heart and asked, "Why? Because then there will be a true choice of the category, *Whoever is for Hashem, let him join me.* And of such a generation did Chabakkuk say, *And the righteous person will live by his faith.*"

Concerning the Rizhiner's approach to Kabbalah, we learn of this first through his grandfather's work, *Chessed l'Avrohom*, that he had preserved in manuscript and which was published immediately after the Rizhiner's death by two of his sons, who were equal to that spiritual legacy; and secondly, through a conversation he had with his son-in-law, R' Mendel of Kossov, son of R' Chaim, author of *Ahavas Sholom*, who asked the Rizhiner to devise for him a daily regime. Whereupon the Rizhiner inquired: "Do you study the *Zohar*?" "Yes," was the answer. "Do you understand it thoroughly?" "No, but it is assumed that its study is advantageous to the soul, even without a clear grasp of its contents." To this the Rizhiner replied: "To achieve this, it is imperative that the soul reside in man's body." (The soul is on the highest level, the mind the lowest and the spirit is in between, in relation to the study of the Doctrine of Secrets and its understanding.) Today, everything is in the category of the mind. It is, therefore, better to study *Ohr HaChaim* (the commentary on *Chumash* by R' Chaim ibn Attar), which is very beneficial to the mind.

R' REUVEN VALDEN PUBLISHED, UNDER THE TITLE OF *IRIN KADDISHIN* (Holy Angels), notes taken from the Rizhiner's teachings. He ex-

HOLY ANGEL pounded the song of Lemech, who spoke poetically to his wives Adah and Zillah (*Bereishis* 4:19-23) and asked, "What is the reason for including such a story in our Holy Torah?" And the answer is: The Torah is the stream of prophetic revelation, from the beginning of the existence of humankind. (The Gemara distinguishes between the teaching of Adam, Noach, Shem, Ever and that of our father

עירין קדישין תליתאה

דברים קדושים ונלהיבים נובעים ממעין קודש קדשים

מאורן של ישראל כ"ק מורינו ורבינו הקדוש צי"ע

מרוזין זצללה"ה ובנו **האר"י הקדוש** אדמו"ר

אביר יעקב טסאדינערא זצלה"ה

נעתקו מפי כתבים של הרב החסיד היקר פאר היחם

מו"ה **שמשון דוד** ז"ל מזאלישטשיק מחסידי

רוזין קדמאי ששמע מפה לאוזן אטרי קודש

הללו ונאספו ונסדרו ע"י הצעיר

באלפי יהודה וישראל

אלי' **מרדכי** לויפבאהן נ"י

מתגורר בק"ק מיעלעץ יע"א

דעת לנבון נקל שדברים יקרים באלה היוצאים מפי קדישי עליון איצ להמכסה. יען כי להם
דימי תהלה. אבל זאת אודיע נאמנה. כי אצלתי לי ברכה מבית ישראל הסמלאים
סקום אבותידם הכי שתתסכו בידי והשפיעו עלי משפעת קדשם אשר חפץ די בידי
יצליח יהיר שיחול עלי ועל כל הנלו"ם אלי' ברכת צדיקי ישראל אכי"ר:

Nachdruck verboten !

Verlag des Herausgebers: Markus Laufbahn Mielec (Galizien)

מיעלעץ תרע"ד

בדפים פ'. קאוואלעק (ע"י שוואנער & פרענקיל) הוסיאטין

Title page of Sefer Irin Kaddishin

Avrohom prior to the Revelation at Sinai.) The prophetic expressions in the Torah point out to us the stages of revelation's
development. Thus the first rung of the ladder of Divine revelation is eternalized with the ancient men in the form of poems

234 / THE HOUSE OF RIZHIN

stated by Lemech, Moshe and Yeshaya, beginning in the case of Moshe, with הַאֲזִינוּ, *Give ear,* and with Yeshaya with שִׁמְעוּ, *Listen* or *hearken.* Lemech uses both expressions. Moshe and Yeshaya, however, address their supplications to Heaven and earth, while Lemech spoke to his wives.

The heart of Moshe's poem comprises the idea contained in the verse, *He is the Rock, His work is perfect* (*Devarim* 32:4), and his chants about Divine Providence express the flows and rewards of religious recognition. Wondrous is the Rizhiner's faith, in that it bestows upon the complicated problems of Judaism a versatile yet hidden form, adapted as it is to all the varied organs of cognition. His faith is expressed in terms that do not oppress the weak, but illuminate the strong and independent mind capable of taking in the entire sweep of the horizon, and this it does with economy and succinctness of speech.

CONCERNING CHASSIDUS HE EXPRESSED HIMSELF AS FOLLOWS: IT IS A PATH under a dark sky, crowded and beset with obstacles and traps. At

ON CHASSIDUS times, brilliant lightning illuminates the darkness. When the lightning splits the sky, the ignorant man lifts his eyes heavenward; his legs buckle under him, and he falls into a pit. The intelligent man has his eyes open and watches where he sets his foot to avoid all the stumbling blocks.

This notion is entirely different from that of "correcting the performance" — the hiatus that exists between reality and fantasy, to which the author of *Kedushas Levi* constantly points. In his approach to "Love of Zion" the Rizhiner was also strikingly original.

R' YEHUDAH HIRSCH OF STRETTIN, DISCIPLE OF AND SUCCESSOR TO R' URI of Strelisk, taught that according to the system of R' Ovadiah of

THE HOPED- Bertinoro, in his commentary on the

FOR REDEEMER Book of *Rus,* the *tzaddik* of the generation, in every period, is deemed to be potentially the hoped-for *Mashiach,* provided the generation is worthy of this. And in his period this role was allotted to R' Yisroel, the Rizhiner.

IN THE YEAR 1848, WHEN IT APPEARED THAT THE STATE OF GENERAL upheaval was going to complete the revolution that started sixty

1848 — YEAR OF REVOLUTIONS

years before (which had, among other things, ended the power of the Bastille, symbol of oppression since the Middle Ages), it looked as though the Jews had attained the realization of their hopes and strivings.

However, similar to R' Meir of Apt, and to his responsa to the conditions in the Poland of his time, R' Meir'l of Premishlan also warned against "forcing the coming of *Mashiach*." The Rizhiner himself said: "The generation is not yet deserving of the Redemption; they demand repentance from a chained and enslaved people, deprived even of the strength to lift their crying voice to Heaven. Let them loosen their chains; give them a chance to return to their Land and establish anew the Sanctuary. At the beginning this will take place in a natural way, as was the case in the days of Ezra. Then the foundation will be laid for a perfect redemption."

The year 5608 (1848) was a year of fear and confusion. R' Hirshele Dubetzker stood at the entrance of the Rizhiner's prayer-room on Hoshana Rabbah of that year, and saw that when the holy Rebbe said the *Hoshanos*, "*Hoshana*, I pray, a soul in fright," with such feeling, his own soul was trembling. He poured out his soul in such trepidation that his teeth chattered, as if he already felt the trembling and trepidation of every single person. Finally, R' Hirshele was no longer able to stand near the doorway but sought to escape from the unbearable scene.

The year 5606 (1846) was a year of misfortunes, as R' Meir of Premishlan had foreseen. On Shabbos, *Parashas Emor,* 1846, during the Scripture reading, he expressed himself in the strange manner that was his hallmark: The year 1847 will bring fear; the year 1848 war; only the year 1849 will bring peace.

ON THE NIGHT OF THE LAST *SEDER* THAT WAS CELEBRATED IN HIS *HOIF,* ONE with the customary elevation of spirit and avoidance of strangers,

וְהִיא שֶׁעָמְדָה

the Rizhiner repeated about sixty times the verse in the Haggadah: וְהִיא שֶׁעָמְדָה ("and that same promise that Hashem made to Avrohom sustained both our ancestors and ourselves"), after which his face changed color so drastically that those around him took him for another man. At the conclusion of the *Seder* he said, "There will come a time when they will drive us out from their lands to Eretz Yisroel. To be sure, this will be a great shame, for following this dispersion, Redemption will begin in an analogous form. However, let happen what may, as long as we will be able to get out of their clutches. As for the rest — this will surely come by itself."

CHAPTER XVI

ON PURIFICATION

CHASSIDIM IMMERSE IN A *MIKVEH* (RITUAL BATH) EVERY MORNING before *davening* in order to be in a state of purity when they pray before the Almighty. Said R' Aharon of Karlin:

PROPERTIES OF MIKVEH "Immerse at least twice: once, to remove uncleanness, and again, to draw holiness upon yourself" (*Hanhagos Tzaddikim*, p. 3).

Ablution in the *mikveh* requires repentance for all one's transgressions. Said R' Sholom Shachna of Prohobisht: "On *Erev Shabbos* go to immerse in the *mikveh* with the *kavannah* (intention) that just as the water purifies your body on the material level, so on the inner, spiritual level may the water purify your soul" (*Seder HaYom*).

"Through immersion in the *mikveh* one becomes a new creation by confessing and casting the sins away through *teshuvah* and holy intentions" (*Kitzur SheLah*, 151).

However, true purification can be achieved through other forms of practice, such as the study of Torah, prayer, song and dance, and especially by *d'veikus* — engaging in intense meditation so as to cleave to Hashem.

It is told of R' Avrohom Kalisker that he used to dance and sing in order to create an inspirational mood for *tefillah*.

An alternative to ablution in the *mikveh*, when there is no *mikveh* or river to immerse in, was offered by the Chozeh of Lublin. "You can immerse yourself in the 'River of Fire' — the river of *d'veikus*" (*Eser Oros*, p. 98).

IN PRAISING THE RIZHINER R' MOSHE OF KOBRIN TOLD HOW HE WAS sitting next to the Rizhiner on Shabbos at *shalosh seudos*, when

THE RIVER OF FIRE

suddenly the Rizhiner said to him, "A Jew must learn how to immerse himself in the River of Fire!" And immediately, the Rizhiner bent over three times (as if immersing in the water), and when he straightened up, water was dripping from his *peyos* (*Beis Rizhin*, p. 206).

A chassid once approached the Rizhiner and complained about his own son-in-law, that he wasted his time before *Shacharis*. He didn't open a *sefer* to study Torah or go to the *mikveh* as other chassidim do. The Rizhiner asked him, "What does he do then?" The chassid replied, "He walks around singing your *niggunim* (melodies) to himself." "If so," said the Rebbe, "you should know that, just as the *mikveh* purifies, so my *niggunim* purify" (*Beis Rizhin*, p. 120).

THE HEBREW WORD הִתְבּוֹדְדוּת [*HISBODEDUS*] CONNOTES ISOLATING yourself in a secluded place where you can literally be alone with

COMMUNICATING WITH HASHEM

yourself and with Hashem. When you dedicate a specific interval of time to this type of meditation, even being silent in front of Hashem, you are with Him.

One can converse with Hashem, through self-reflection, meditation, introspective analysis, oral stocktaking, repentance and prayer.

Traditionally, *hisbodedus* is practiced before going to bed at night or at *tikkun chatzos* — the kabbalistic midnight lament for the destruction of the Temple.

R' SHOLOM SHACHNA OF PROHOBISHT TAUGHT: "YOU SHOULD SET yourself a special time to be with Hashem in the morning. So, when

SESSIONS OF SILENT THOUGHT
you awaken, if your mind is clear and bright, meditate on Hashem's greatness and on your own lowliness. It should be a meditation to stimulate yourself to love and fear Hashem, and to do His commandments. Such *hisbodedus* you should perform mentally, even verbally, in any language you choose." R' Sholom continues: "You should do your *hisbodedus* in the morning, and a second time before Minchah, so that during the same day you can correct where you have begun to go astray, then a third time before sleep, when you should assess the wrongs you did that day, G-d forbid, in thought, speech and deed. These three sessions of *hisbodedus* should be a fixed obligation, daily, on the pattern of your daily prayers" (*Seder HaYom*).

R' PINCHOS OF KORITZ IS QUOTED AS SAYING: "THE WORLD IS FILLED with Hashem's light, but there is a separating screen that prevents us

DISPERSING THE CLOUDS
from seeing it, similar to the clouds that block the light of the sun. And when we pray, our words of prayer — which are called *ruach* (spirit), as it says 'The spirit [רוּחַ] of Hashem spoke through him' — then the 'clouds' are dispersed. This is also the reason for our swaying during prayers, to symbolize the movement of the clouds."

WITH REGARD TO THE LOVE OF HASHEM, HE EXPLAINED WHY IT IS THAT IN the Siddur *Mishnas Chassidim*, the text of the evening service

GUARDING THE CRIB
reads, הַשְׁכִּיבֵנוּ אָבִינוּ, "Lay us down to sleep, our Father," rather than הַשְׁכִּיבֵנוּ ה' אֱלֹקֵינוּ, "Lay us down to sleep, Hashem our G-d," as

in other prayer books. He said that before Hashem, Who fills the whole world with His glory, it is disrespectful for man to sleep with outspread limbs, because of embarrassment before Hashem. But, if He is our "Father" and we are His children, then we can sleep like a son before his father. Furthermore, it is natural for a father to guard and watch over his son as he sleeps; that is why we request, "And spread over us the protection of Your peace."

THE *TZADDIK* SAW THAT THE NEEDS OF THE JEWS ARE MANIFOLD BUT their wisdom is limited. Accordingly, he made himself the inter-

DIVINE ADVOCACY

cessor. He would defend them as follows:

The Shpoler Zeide argued before Hashem, "Master of the World, because of Your claims over the Jews, must they suffer such a long exile? You say, שׁוּבוּ אֵלַי וְאָשׁוּבָה אֲלֵיכֶם, *Return to Me and I will return to you* (*Malachi* 3:7). You want them first to return to You, and then You will agree to return to them. But they argue conversely, הֲשִׁיבֵנוּ ה' אֵלֶיךָ וְנָשׁוּבָה, *Return to us, and we will return* (*Eichah* 5:21). Why, then, do You prolong the exile by waiting until they return to You? I swear to You by my beard and *peyos* (sidecurls) that they will not return to You in repentance until You first redeem them." But if *Mashiach* will come now, he may still redeem Jews. But if You wait a little longer he will have to redeem gentiles, *goyim*. For the *goyim* are You sending Mashiach?

"Thus said the Shpoler Zeide, and I, too," continued the Rizhiner, "agree with him that Israel will not return in repentance before the Redemption, but when *Mashiach* comes, they will certainly repent. Just as we cry in our prayers, וּמִפְּנֵי חֲטָאֵינוּ גָּלִינוּ מֵאַרְצֵנוּ, 'And for our sins we have been exiled from our land' — (מִפְּנֵי — *before*), that is, even before we sinned, exile from our land had been decreed upon us, as Hashem informed Avrohom in the Covenant between the Parts, *For your descendants will be strangers in a land that is not theirs* (*Bereishis* 15:13) — consequently, Hashem, You are responsible now to redeem them from the bitter exile *before* they repent and return to You, just as You decreed the Exile upon them before they sinned."

On Rosh Hashanah in Kamenitz, the Rizhiner came to the table with great trepidation and said, "When it is written in the High

Holidays liturgy, 'If we are like children … or if we are like servants,' Hashem, Blessed is He, is saying, 'If you will act like servants, true to My service, then I will be to you as a father to his children.' And the Jews answer, 'If You will be to us as a father, we will serve You like servants.' " He was silent for some time. Then he cried, "Master of the World, I have known You these thirty years, that You run the world with strict justice, but have You been able to accomplish anything in the world?! I say, instead, that it would be better for You to run this world with mercy and loving kindness and bless them with all good things and then the Jews will be able to serve You from a vantage point of plenty. And if You refuse to hearken to me, what am I doing in this world?"

"DO YOU SEE, HASHEM,…?"

THE RIZHINER WAS A TRUE DISCIPLE OF THE BERDITCHEVER RAV WHEN IT came to finding a *limud z'chus* to contend with Hashem in defense of the Jewish people. He said that when the Berditchever would see a Jew walking to the synagogue with his *tallis* and *tefillin* under his arm, he would immediately turn heavenward and argue before Hashem, "Do You, Hashem, see a Jew leaving his home and business and going to *daven* to You, and You, Master of the World, still come stealthily upon Israel?!"

The Rizhiner added, "How much more so would the Berditchever see today a Jew going to pray and not leaving in his house even a penny with which to buy a cookie for his children, leaving them unprotected against the kidnappers who might come and take his children from him. What would R' Levi Yitzchok then argue before Hashem? Indeed, in these times, when a Jew takes his *tallis* and *tefillin* and goes to pray, he is considered like the Baal Shem Tov and my grandfather, the Maggid, in their days."

THE RAMBAM CRITIQUED

THE RIZHINER'S INTELLECT WAS BROAD AND ENCOMPASSED MANY AREAS. He involved himself in the study of Kabbalah and the *Sefiros*, yet he was also familiar with Rambam's *Guide to the*

Perplexed. Once, in discussion with some of his chassidiim, including rabbis and scholars, there arose the subject of the Rambam, and the opposition to his views stated by several of his famed contemporaries. The Rizhiner asked why there was such opposition to the Rambam. One of those present answered that it was because he maintained that Aristotle was able to divine more of the heavenly spheres, reaching up to the eighth sphere, higher even than the level of the prophet Yechezkel. The Rebbe said: "The Rambam is right. It reminds me of two men who came to the king's castle. One concentrated solely on the king, whom he had come to see, and paid no attention to his chambers, furniture or riches. The second man, when he entered the castle, began to wander, dazzled by the abundance of the king's wealth, his glorious chambers and furniture. He is so preoccupied with external matters that he is oblivious even to the presence of the king. Thus Yechezkel concerned himself with Divine matters and paid less attention to the sparkle of the spheres. Aristotle however concerned himself only with the external spheres and never reached the Divine chambers. The Rambam was a saint without an equal. In one respect, however, his detractors are correct, for many times the 'Guide' quotes the views of Aristotle and other philosophers. Though he later disputes and contradicts these views, a Jew who reads the book and grows drowsy might fall asleep after reading the views of Aristotle and before reaching the later refutations brought by the Rambam. The result will be that he will fall asleep while not under the *ol Malchus Shamayim* (the yoke of Heaven)."

EVEN IN THE MIDST OF HIS MASSES OF FOLLOWERS AND ADMIRERS, THE Rizhiner considered himself alone in his generation. When he was

AMBIVALENCE confronted by the ignorance of the common folk, he bitterly denounced them as a lowly generation and admonished them. At those times he would bear bitter resentment toward his ancestors and cry, "I have a strong grievance against my ancestors who brought me into such a dismal generation." But, he also felt gratitude toward them, for he felt that he was in the right place and that he was needed by the generation, and that the generation was necessary to him if he were to fulfill his own potential. His special mission on this earth was one which could only be fulfilled in a lowly generation. If he could not fully meet his obligations, this was the fault of the generation, but whatever he could accomplish would certainly be beneficial. This idea was clear to him from his first moments as a leader. On the first Yom Kippur Eve after his inauguration as Rebbe, prior to the *Kol Nidrei* prayer, he told of the Rebbe, R' Baruch of Mezhibozh, who used to explain the passage of Yom Kippur thus, *And you shall afflict* (וְעִנִּיתֶם), *your souls* (*Vayikra* 16:31) — the word "afflict" comes from the root meaning "claim, defense, self-protection." That is, "You shall argue and defend yourselves before Hashem." With what means will you defend yourselves? You will say to Hashem, "These are the souls which we have accepted, but which cannot be elevated any higher." But I, a lofty soul, how shall I save myself? The answer is again, *And you shall afflict your souls.* When I am taken with these humble souls, I am regarded as good — just as I am now."

CHAPTER XVII

THE RIZHINER SYNTHESIS

HE RIZHINER'S GRANDSON, R' YISROEL OF CHORTKOV, WROTE THAT IT was the intention of his grandfather that all of his activities be on behalf of the people of Israel, and so he conducted himself

A KING MAY NOT FORGO...
with regal honor, acquired beautiful houses and exquisite furniture in order to ensure that he would have some contact with material life and thereby a relationship with the populace, so that he could *daven* and intercede for them. This was what he meant when he said, *And I shall remember My covenant with Yaakov* — this refers to my father, R' Sholom Shachna, may his memory be a blessing. *My covenant with Yitzchok* refers to my grandfather, R' Avrohom the Malach, and *My covenant with Avrohom* refers to my great-grandfather, R' Dov Ber, the Maggid of Mezritch. *And the land I will remember* (*Vayikra* 26:42) — this is myself, so I must maintain a connection with the material existence of my generation.

He used to say that there were those who questioned his fitness for the title of *tzaddik*. "Actually, I am not a *tzaddik*. I am nothing. I know my own value, and I tell only the truth. But those who persecute me, it is as if they hurl words at the face of Heaven."

R' SHOLOM SHACHNA CLAIMED THE RIGHT TO SERVE AS THE LEADER OF the generation by virtue of the power he inherited as grandson of the

LINEAGE —
THE TREE OF LIFE

Maggid, whose lineage is traced to King Dovid. His son, the Rizhiner, also believed in this destiny. He remembered that his great-grandfather, the Maggid, was the incarnation of the crown of Torah and the crown of royalty, and that his descendants were inheritors of these crowns. If the students of the Maggid took for themselves the crown of Torah, at least the crown of royalty remained with his descendants alone. He viewed and identified his father, R' Sholom Shachna, with King Dovid; and himself, with King Shlomo.

FROM HIS GREAT-GRANDFATHER, THE MAGGID OF MEZRITCH, HE LEARNED that although the quality of modesty is excellent, much praised by

A HUMBLE AND
A KINGLY SUIT

the Torah when embodied in the person of Moshe, still there are times when modesty is not appropriate. The Maggid of Mezritch used to say, "Whoever engages in Torah study for its own sake merits many things, 'And it clothes him in modesty' (*Avos* 6:1), which can be taken to mean that modesty should be like a garment which is sometimes worn and sometimes cast off."

AS SOON AS R' YISROEL BECAME REBBE, AT THE AGE OF 16, FOLLOWING THE passing of his brother, he moved from Prohobisht to Skver. He did not

THE HOUSE
OF RIZHIN

remain there long, since his followers had, in the meantime, bought him a home and property in Rizhin, in the province of Kiev. Rizhin became the great center of Chassidus for Russian Jewry. There were other *tzaddikim* living there, especially the house of Chernobyl, which was close to the house of Rizhin and linked to it by marriage. Still, the house of Rizhin dominated the community, due to the authoritative influence of the *tzaddik*. Everything there was invested with his aura of royalty; the furniture and vessels of the household, his wardrobe, the very beams of the roof and bricks of the walls, all evoked his presence. The children of the *tzaddik*, too, in countenance and dress seemed no less than the highest nobility; their coaches, their liveried servants, the ostentation of their wealth, entranced the masses. Even his neighbors, landowners of the Russian upper classes, admired the Rebbe. More than once, they turned to him for advice, and he served as a go-between for them in their affairs, helping to settle their quarrels. Rich Jews among the privileged classes were also his followers, often bringing him expensive gifts and money for *tikkun* (redemption of the soul).

R' YISROEL POSSESSED A SENSE OF HUMOR THAT MADE HIM APPEALING TO his listeners. A man once came over to him and said, "Rebbe, I so

A LIGHTER TOUCH

wish to repent, but I don't know what to do."

"And to sin you knew what to do?" retorted the Rizhiner.

"Yes, but that was easy. First I sinned and then I realized that I had erred," said the man.

"Exactly! Now do the same the other way around. Start by repenting, you will know later," said the Rebbe.

Another example of his wit occurred when R' Meir'l of Premishlan once sent him a letter with this question: A person is required to eat *kreplach* on Shavuos. There is no source to tell us how much. One would not be enough, and two is an inauspicious number coming from unholy spheres. So R' Meir asked what should be done. The Rizhiner replied, "Eat one the size of two!"

ONCE THE REBBE VISITED A CERTAIN TOWN AND STAYED AT THE HOME OF one of its wealthy men. The people who came to the Rebbe brought

THE MUD OF A JEW

in a good deal of mud on their shoes and dirtied the floor, which made the wealthy man very angry at them. The Rebbe told him the following story:

"A poor man lived in a certain village. He had a wife, six children and his parents eating at his table. All winter long, he could not earn a living and, when Pesach came, he did not have the wherewithal to prepare for the holiday. He traveled to the city in order to find some income for the holiday. Hashem helped him and he earned 6 gold pieces, enough to bake matzah for the holiday, so he returned to his family. On the way back, the wagon got stuck in the mud, and the poor horse could not extricate it. At that instant, a rich Jew passed by in his coach. When he heard the poor Jew crying, he alighted from his coach, pulled the poor Jew out of the mud, took him in his coach and conveyed him back to his home in the village. When he saw the impoverished dwelling, he gave him 600 golden coins to enable him to buy a decent house and to prepare properly for Pesach. Then, the rich man went home. Soon afterwards he passed away.

"When he reached the heavenly court they asked him, "Did you deal faithfully in business?" The prosecuting angels came from all sides to recount the various sins he had committed throughout his life. Just as the court was about to sentence him to Gehinnom, one angel came and shouted, "How can you send him to Gehinnom? Is it not true that one who sustains one life in Israel is considered to have saved an entire world? (*Sanhedrin* 37a). This man saved ten people from poverty and want." The court commanded that the value of these mitzvos be weighed on one side of the scale and the sins on the other. When they weighed the good, they found that the evil side outweighed it. What did the angelic defense attorney do? He brought the poor Jew who had been saved from the mud and from poverty and desolation and placed him, his wife, his six children and his parents on the side of the scale containing the good deeds. Still the other side weighed more. Then the angel went and brought the mud and mire into which the poor man had fallen and this was enough to tip the scales.

"So you see," concluded the Rizhiner, "sometimes even the mire and the mud of a Jew can save one from Gehinnom. Do not scorn, therefore, the mud of a Jew!"

HE UNDERSTOOD THAT MAN WILL NEVER BE STRONG ENOUGH TO BRING

WISDOM AND PROPHECY

about universal change. Like the Shpoler Zeide and R' Levi Yitzchok of Berditchev, he turned to Hashem and took part in his quarrels with man, and like his predecessors pleaded the cause of man. His exceptional intuition helped him to foresee what was to come; that the world was doomed, the earth rushing to its downfall. With the dawning of the end of time, good and evil will go hand in hand and become one. Light will become indistinguishable from darkness, daybreak from dusk, silence from words, words from truth, truth from fear, and fear from death. He continued, "A day will come when ignorance will reign. The most pious Jew will be incapable of reciting a verse from *Tehillim*. I tell you this so you will know that how it will be. That is how it will be."

THE RIZHINER'S PHILOSOPHY WAS QUITE DIFFERENT THAN THAT OF MOST other chassidim. Once upon a time Chassidus meant emphasis on

A BREAK WITH THE PAST

inner truth and fervor, a return to the contemplative life, to genuine beauty, to closeness with nature. There was no need for castles and servants in order to feel at home amid Hashem's creation. To *possess* meant nothing, to *be* meant everything. In Mezhibozh and Mezritch, in Chernobyl and Berditchev, the chassid tried to overcome poverty by means other than money, to defeat sadness by means other than ostentation. Chassidus in those days mocked appearance and scorned comfort. They advocated joy within melancholy. But in Rizhin it was aristocracy that set the tone. Greatness had to be displayed to be recognized.

The pomp and pageantry of the Rizhiner's court was a way of consolidating and comforting his chassidim, to show that the dream was still there, that they could see if they tried, and that the reality of exile does not preclude the royal vision of redemption. Perhaps this was the way of reminding them that *malchus*, royalty, is also an attribute of Hashem, and that Hashem of Israel is also the King of Israel, a King Whose oft-destroyed and oft-dispersed kingdom remains, nevertheless, indestructible. Perhaps he wanted to add emphasis to R' Shlomo Karliner's declaration that we are all princes, and that to forget that is the greatest sin of all.

CHAPTER XVIII

THE RIZHINER AND ERETZ YISROEL

T HE RELATIONSHIP BETWEEN THE CHASSIDIC MOVEMENT AND ERETZ Yisroel in general, and the settling of the land in our time, in particular, was not only positive but also full of enthusiasm and longing for the Holy Land. The immigration of chassidim from among the disciples of the Maggid of Mezritch, many years before, had laid the foundation for new settlements in the Land.

IN ADDITION TO HIS PREOCCUPATION WITH THE WELFARE OF THE JEWISH communities of Eastern Europe, the Rizhiner was deeply concerned **CONNECTION** with the welfare of the small Jewish community in Eretz Yisroel. "The soul is what gives life to everything," he remarked. "The soul of the world is Eretz Yisroel, the soul of Eretz Yisroel is the *Beis HaMikdash*, the soul of the *Beis HaMikdash* is the Holy of Holies, the soul of the year is

Yom Kippur and the soul of the people of Israel is the *Kohen Gadol*."
The Rebbe saw himself, a descendant of King Dovid, as having a
particular responsibility to those Diaspora Jews who would commit
themselves to the rebuilding of Eretz Yisroel.

MORE THAN ANY OTHER CHASSIDIC TEACHING, RIZHINER DISCOURSES ARE
often *Mashiach*-oriented. Even as the Rebbe speculated on the nature

IN THE FOOTSTEPS OF MASHIACH

of the redemption of the Jews by
Mashiach, he was keenly aware of their
suffering. Indeed, the suffering of Russian
Jewry in his days was an indication that
the redemption was near. The Czar issued
edicts forcing Jews to convert to Christianity. Jewish children were
forcibly conscripted into the Russian army, and many died *al kiddush
Hashem* (in the sanctification of Hashem's Name), rather than sub-
mit. Heavy, humiliating taxes were imposed on Jews' property and
clothing, even their beards.

*Memorial honoring the martyrs of Iassy, with
the Apter Rav's synagogue in the background*

The troubles and oppression
of Russian Jewry did not let the
Rizhiner rest. Then came the
terrible pogroms, when
Ukrainian Jews were attacked
by roving hordes of anti-
Semitic Cossacks, who ravaged
town after town, killing their
defenseless victims by the thousands. The Rizhiner not only
prayed for their safety but actually ordered the young men to
organize themselves into self-
defense units.

The Rizhiner considered those
days to be harbingers of redemption. "*Mashiach* will come first to
Russia," he would say, and he
tried to bring relief, encourage-

ment and redemptive hope to the Jews of the *cherta,* or Russian ghetto. In the depths of his heart, he felt the spark of *Mashiach,* and though he did not say it publicly, in private he would quite often mention that he was a descendant of the royal House of Dovid. He once explained to his close friends that while all of the other *tzaddikim* spoke of the coming of *Mashiach,* he would not. "It is comparable," he would say, "to the in-laws who meet and excitedly discuss an engagement, but the bridegroom himself sits impassive

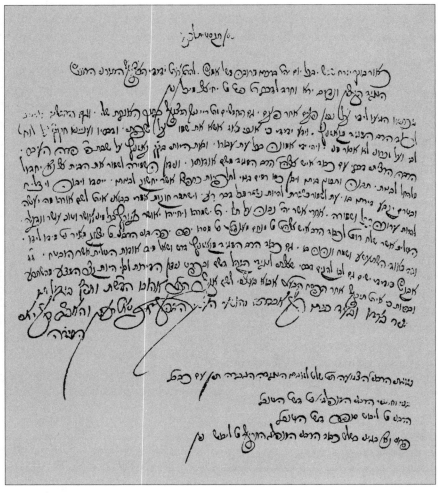

Letter written and signed by the Apter Rav

and quiet." He felt, in this respect, as if somehow he himself were the groom, and was therefore silent.

THE SENIOR LEADER OF THE GENERATION, R' AVROHOM YEHOSHUA HESCHEL of Apt, would collect money for the needy of Eretz Yisroel, and would

EMISSARIES   then give it to those *shadarim* (emissaries) who arrived from the Holy Land, for distribution there. He would greatly honor such messengers. When he learned that one was coming, he and all the elders of his town would go out to greet the individual and escort him into the town, all the while praising his virtues. When the emissary left the town, he would again be escorted by all the elders, and the musicians would play.

ONCE THE APTER RAV FOUND OUT THAT SEVERAL OF THE EMISSARIES WERE dishonest and were pocketing some of the money for themselves.

PERFIDY   He nevertheless changed nothing in the reception he offered them. He came out with all the elders to greet them, and when they left the town, escorted them personally. The only difference was that he ordered his people to let these emissaries be escorted out of town by himself alone, without the elders. As he did so, he told them, "Do not think for an instant that you are fooling me. I know that you are keeping some of the money donated for yourselves. Why, then, do I honor you so in my town? For the small amount of money that does find its way to the poor of Eretz Yisroel. Even if a person does little for Eretz Yisroel, he deserves to be honored. The reason I alone escorted you was so that no one else might know what is afoot, lest the people start contributing less to Eretz Yisroel."

The Apter Rav appointed the Rizhiner to be the *nasi*, or president, of all chassidic *kollel* communities in Eretz Yisroel. At this time, the Land was extremely desolate under the dominion of the Turks, who limited Jewish immigration. Of those Jews who had settled in Eretz Yisroel, the majority subsisted on the *chalukah*, the charitable donations which were apportioned to each *kollel* by the representatives of every European Jewish community in the Holy Land. The Rizhiner, in his capacity as the president of the Kollel Vohlin of Russia, was in constant contact with his *gabbaim*, who monitored the activity of the *kollel*, and so he knew of everything that transpired in Israel. Anyone who wanted to go to Israel had to receive the consent and a hand-written letter signed by the Rebbe, in order to be eligible for the benefits of the *kollel* and the *chalukah*.

AT THIS TIME, THERE WERE APPROXIMATELY FOUR THOUSAND JEWS IN THE Holy Land, most of whom were concentrated in the four "holy cities": Safed, Tiberias, Hebron and Jerusalem. In one incident which is particularly indicative of the Rebbe's involvement with the community, he authorized special aid to the victims of the Safed earthquake in 1837, shortly before his imprisonment. Many of those living in the Holy Land had fled there to escape financial deprivation in Russia.

מְתֵי מִסְפָּר
— FEW IN NUMBER

Because of the troubles and hardships which fell to the lot of Russian Jewry, many were seeking refuge in the Holy Land, and they arrived there empty-handed, and became a burden on the *kollel*, which was unable to support them.

IN ORDER TO REDUCE THE BURDEN IMPOSED BY THE NEW IMMIGRANTS, THE Rebbe wanted to allow them to go to Eretz Yisroel only on condition that they had the resources to support themselves for the first three years after their arrival. He wrote to the administrators and members of the Kollel Vohlin in Jerusalem:

HARD REALITIES

> I find myself duty bound to strengthen the foundation of returning to Eretz Yisroel. And, behold, today, I decree upon our brothers, the Children of Israel in the Diaspora, that it is forbidden for any man to travel to Eretz Yisroel unless he can support himself and his family for three years, in addition to the cost of transport to the Land. Those who do not possess the aforementioned means of support are prohibited from going to the Holy Land, lest

they become a burden upon the whole community of Eretz Yisroel. Therefore, after much deliberation, I decree and order to those in charge, that from today onward, not a kopek (penny) from the *chalukah* fund be given to any new settler for three years, if he does not travel with my written consent …

And it is forbidden for anyone to leave Israel without a written permit by those appointed as administrators of the *chalukah* (from the Friedman Collection; see *Ner Israel* II, p. 120).

This letter was intended only for a transitional period. As soon as the famine and distress were eased, the Rizhiner again began to encourage everyone to immigrate.

On another occasion in that same year, a chassid came to the Rebbe to ask permission to emigrate to the Holy Land. The Rebbe said, "One can go to the Holy Land only if he feels the taste of it, like the *tzaddik*, R' Velvel. But any Jew who wants to worship Hashem may also go if he cannot do so here" (*Beis Yisroel*, p. 28).

THE HEAVENLY PARADIGM

R' YISROEL OF CHORTKOV RELATES THAT IN THE DAYS OF HIS GRANDFATHER, the Rizhiner, there was a chassid who used to involve himself with secular studies. People in the community were surprised at this and told the Rizhiner about it. The Rizhiner asked the man why he studied these things. The chassid answered that his entire intention was for the sake of Heaven. The Rizhiner asked him, "Are you an expert in these matters?" He answered, "I have a great deal of knowledge concerning them." The Rizhiner continued, "Are all the experts in these matters in agreement?" The chassid answered him, "No, many people have different ideas. Each person tries to prove that he is correct." The Rizhiner asked, "Is it possible for them all to be right? The truth is that everything is dependent upon the way a *tzaddik* acts. He is a paradigm for all of Heaven."

When these sayings were repeated to the Rizhiner's son, he explained that in the *Zohar*, the *tzaddik* is compared to the heavens.

UDEL, THE DAUGHTER OF R' BORUCH OF MEZHIBOZH, TOLD THE RIZHINER that she had once come to her father's house and found him walk-

HASHEM DECREES, THE TZADDIK ...

ing back and forth in his room, saying, "Hashem, how fortunate for the world that You are its Master." When the Rizhiner heard these words, he became visibly upset and remained deep in meditation for one hour. Later, he said, "How correct R' Boruch was in his comment, for our Sages have told us, 'Hashem decrees things and the *tzaddik* is able to nullify them.' This is true when there is a *tzaddik* in the world to nullify them. However, when there is no *tzaddik*, Hashem is left by Himself. Therefore, how fortunate it is for the world that You are ruling it by Yourself. Isn't Hashem Himself the most righteous being in the world? Therefore, when there is a *tzaddik*, the only reason Hashem makes the decree is that the *tzaddik* should nullify it. When there is no *tzaddik*, He will nullify it Himself."

From other sources we learn about the love of Eretz Yisroel that pervaded the royal house of Rizhin. A special choir accompanying the *chazzan* would sing liturgical and national songs expressing yearning and deep nostalgia for the Holy Land. Especially popular was the Rizhiner song, "Your Hand will lead me to the Holy Land."

THE GAON, R' SHLOMO KLUGER, IN HIS RESPONSUM *HaELEPH LECHA Shlomo*, ruled, "In our days we do not force the woman to follow her

IN FORCE, OR NOT IN FORCE...

husband and go to Eretz Yisroel, because nowadays there is no commandment to settle there." He supported this view by adding, "Why don't the chassidic rebbes go to the Land of Israel, for it is surely in their power to go there? Why did not the famous Rabbi Yisroel of Rizhin and his blessed sons go to Eretz Yisroel? Therefore, the general view supports the rabbis who say that there is currently no mitzvah to go to Eretz Yisroel."

In truth, R' Shlomo Kluger was mistaken in his assumption, for the Rebbe believed that it was, indeed, a mitzvah to live in Eretz Yisroel and that a woman should be required by the rabbinic court to follow

Niggun "Adir Hu" of Rabbi Boruch of Mezhibozh

her husband there. In 1835, while he was in the city of Lemberg, for medical reasons, the Rizhiner was asked to determine the case of a woman who refused to follow her husband to Eretz Yisroel. He sent his final decision to R' Shimon Preutz.[1]

> Since we learn in the Mishnah at the end of *Kesubos* that from all countries, excepting Babylonia, a woman must leave to go to Israel, I therefore order her, by the authority vested in me, to go immediately with her husband and not to delay any longer so that she may not regret it or be put to shame ... I ask that you persuade her to do what I have said to do for my sake, and do not change my words.

The Rizhiner was in this way faithful to the spirit of the Baal Shem Tov, who explained the Biblical verse *To these the Land shall be divided* (*Bamidbar* 26:52), as "the Holy Land can bring a separation between a woman and her husband when he wants to go to Eretz Yisroel and she wants to remain in exile."

IT WAS KNOWN THAT THE RIZHINER HIMSELF WANTED VERY MUCH TO immigrate to Eretz Yisroel but was prevented from carrying out his

THWARTED intent for various reasons. He was heard to say that it would be impossible to leave his fellow Jews behind him, suffering under their persecutions. He said, "If I would go to Eretz Yisroel, they would ask me, 'Why have you come here without your Jews?,' and what would I then answer them?" This leader of Israel, who was the father and patron of thousands of Jews and connected to them by all the cords of his holy soul, could not allow himself to go to Eretz Yisroel with his family and leave the rest of his people in exile. A mass *aliyah* in those years was also impossible for many reasons, nor could the land at that time support them all.

Concerning the trip of R' Mendel of Vitebsk (1748-1781) to the Holy Land, he said, "His trip served the same function as that of Avrohom our father, to blaze the trail before Hashem and Israel."

---

1. This letter is preserved in the archives of the Rebbe of Sadagora, ibid., p. 121.

Chassidim tell that once an emissary arrived from Eretz Yisroel and the Rebbe received him very cordially. He explained to his as-

AND NOT THROUGH AN EMISSARY...

sociates the great mitzvah of the settling of Eretz Yisroel in this way: "We can work in two ways to bring the Redemption closer. The first way is to immigrate to Eretz Yisroel. The second way is monetarily to support the people of the *Yishuv* (Settlement). The Mishnah alludes to this in the tractate *Kiddushin* (41a): 'A man can betroth a woman either by himself or through an emissary,' i.e. helping emissaries from the Land in their mission. The Gemara there asks, 'If I know that he can betroth through his messenger, do I need to be told that he can do it himself?' That is to say, 'now,' at this time we are forced to fulfill our obligation through emissaries ... but in the same Gemara Rav Yosef says that even in this time, it is a greater mitzvah for him to do it by himself than through an emissary."

On another occasion, R' Hershele of Tiberias, a grandson of the Baal Shem Tov, visited the Rizhiner. The Rizhiner questioned him in the most minute detail regarding all the news from Tiberias, until finally R' Hershele was reduced to telling him about a quarrel in a certain synagogue between two tailors. The Rizhiner then responded that this was the news he needed to know, adding, "You should know that I am interested in this kind of news, too, for a quarrel in the Holy Land, even between two simple people, makes a greater impression in the world above than a quarrel between two very great people in the Diaspora." Every visitor from Eretz Yisroel was accorded the highest of honors when he was a guest of the Rizhiner.

On the last day of Pesach, 5607 (1847), the Rebbe's wife, Sarah, passed away. On the day of the funeral, he wept profusely the

MY BETTER HALF

whole day long. When the chassidim asked him about this, he replied, "The Baal Shem Tov, after the passing of his wife, decided to immigrate to Eretz Yisroel, but on the way a great storm arose and he was detained by Heaven. When he finally reached the port of Constantinople, he saw other heavenly signs indicating that he should return, at which point he said, 'All my life I yearned to come to Eretz Yisroel, and now I am being prevented. Since half of me is remaining in the Diaspora, it is decreed that I, too, shall remain.' And I, too," concluded the Rebbe, "yearned and hoped for the day that I would go to Eretz Yisroel, and now that half of me remains here, I am afraid that I will remain here, and for this I weep."

AFTER A FEW YEARS PASSED, THE SITUATION IN RUSSIA IMPROVED SOMEWHAT and the Rizhiner gave his consent to his chassidim who requested

THE GLORY OF ISRAEL permission to immigrate to Eretz Yisroel. He involved himself with them and cared for them, never losing interest in their welfare and in the most mundane details of happenings in Israel. One of his major accomplishments in the Holy Land was the building of a synagogue in Jerusalem which was named after him, *Tiferes Yisroel*, the Glory of Israel.

IN THE YEAR 1843, R' NISSAN BECK OF JERUSALEM CAME TO VISIT THE Rebbe in Sadagora. Along with the news he brought from the

TO FOIL THE CZAR Holy Land was that he had heard from officers of the Turkish government that Nicholas, the Czar of Russia, was planning to buy a plot of land next to the Western Wall, in order to build a large church and a monastery. When he heard this, the Rebbe became very agitated and said, "*Ponye* (used here as a euphemism for Russia) wants to block the way to the Western Wall with his impurity. He shall not be able to do it; we shall not allow him!"

R' Nissan hurried to comply with the Rebbe's command. As soon as he returned to Jerusalem he spoke to the Arab owners of the land. With great difficulty, after interminable debates and arguments, he was able to buy the land for a huge sum. A few days after the purchase had been completed, an order came from Czar Nicholas to the

Russian consul in Jerusalem urging him to conclude the purchase. But it was too late.

It is told that after the Czar was informed that the plot of land had been "snatched away," by his enemy, the *tzaddik* of Rizhin, he became extremely angry and cried out, "He always stands in my way!" By then, nothing could be done, for the Rebbe had already received Turkish citizenship papers and had been registered as a citizen of Jerusalem, so that the Czar had no alternative but to buy a different plot of land outside the walls of Jerusalem for a church. The area is known today as the "Russian Quarter."

According to the directions of the Rebbe, R' Nissan immediately hired workers to clear the property he had purchased for the building. R' Nissan, himself, was the architect and the contractor. Even at the outset, however, many obstacles presented themselves. It transpired, for example, that the burial place of a sheik was beneath the plot of land; it was therefore necessary to move the grave elsewhere. Permission was obtained from the Moslem *kadi* (religious judge), but it was necessary to do it quietly, so as not to arouse the attention of the Moslem masses. Unfortunately, a too curious Arab saw what was happening and demanded a bribe not to reveal the secret. R' Nissan refused to pay the bribe. On Friday, when the Moslems gathered in the Mosque of Omar to pray, the Arab revealed to them that the sheik had appeared to him in a dream, complaining that his pious brothers had allowed his grave to be desecrated and removed. He succeeded in inflaming all present, and they decided to visit the *kadi*, to ask him to halt further construction. The *kadi*, intimidated by the mob, promised that he would, and work on the building came to a halt.

R' Nissan, however, understood the psychology of his Arab neighbors. He waited until the community's anger dissipated. Then he went to the the Grand Sheik of the Mosque of Omar and the *kadi* and persuaded them to rescind their prohibition, as well as to pacify the masses sufficiently to ensure that they not interfere with the construction of the synagogue. On the following Friday, when the worshipers came to pray at the Mosque, the Grand Sheik told them in his discourse that the dead sheik had appeared to him in a dream, saying, "What do you have against me? For preventing the Jews from building their house of prayer I was called to our Patriarch, Ibrahim (beloved of All-ah), in the Garden of Eden, and he berated me, saying, 'Why do the children of your nation prevent the children of my nation from building a house of prayer in Jerusalem, the Holy City? Watch yourself, lest you be punished! Now, instead of deterring them, you will assist the sons of Avrohom, Yitzchok and Yaakov to build their house of prayer at my former place of burial. This will give me in my grave great satisfaction and peace.' " The Grand Sheik concluded, "So harshly did he speak to me that I have promised him that I will command you to do his will. Now I command you to do my bidding!"

At once, all the gathered worshipers became excited and went to the *kadi* to ask him to rescind his prohibition. Many of them came to help in the laying of the foundation. This was also difficult, as there was no rock on the site with which to build the foundation. Further delays ensued.

It is told that during the laying of the foundation, the Rizhiner saw in a dream the Biblical verse addressed to King Dovid, when he wanted to build the Temple. *You, however, shall not build the Temple. Rather your son shall build the Temple for My Name* (I Kings 8:19). The Rebbe then sent a letter to his followers in Jerusalem, directing them to stop the construction. It stopped until his demise in 1850, was renewed by his son, R' Avrohom Yaakov of Sadagora, and continued, with sporadic interruptions, until 1872.

IN 1869, WHEN KAISER FRANZ JOSEF VISITED JERUSALEM ON HIS WAY TO inaugurate the Suez Canal, he found the beautiful building of the

A VISIT FROM THE KAISER

synagogue standing without its roof. He asked the reason for this and R' Nissan Beck, who was accompanying the Kaiser's touring party in the walled city, replied, "Why, the synagogue took off its hat in honor of Your Majesty." The Kaiser smiled and added, "I hope that the roof will be built soon." He left the Austrian consul a huge sum towards the completion of the synagogue, the roof of which was called from then on, "Franz Josef's cap."

R' AVROHOM YAAKOV SENT ONE OF HIS CHASSIDIM TO SEE TO THE
completion of the building, which was duly completed in the

IN MEMORY OF THE
RIZHINER TZADDIK

month of Av 1872, and inaugurated on the fifteenth of that
month, at which time the Kollel
Vohlin distributed four hundred meals to needy Jews of the community. The festivity was great as the masses, including gentiles,
came to witness the bringing of the Torah Scrolls into the synagogue. All the chassidim of Rizhin-Sadagora journeyed from
throughout the country to participate in the dedication of the
Tiferes Yisroel synagogue, in memory of the Rizhiner *tzaddik*.
Some called it the Shul of Nissan Beck, and it was considered one
of the richest and most beautiful synagogues of Jerusalem, until
its destruction by the Jordanians in 1948.[1] The Temple Mount
was visible through its windows, and superb decorations and silver objects were donated by various chassidim. The descendants
of the Rebbe bought themselves seats in this great synagogue,
and all chassidim of Rizhin especially Boyan would walk

The Tiferes Yisroel Synagogue

1. See *Lunz, Guide*, pp. 154-155, *HaMaggid*, 1864, *Halevanon* 21 Shevat 1864-65 vol. II,
No. 4, ibid. Gat, pp. 198-199, *Havazeles* 19 Av 1872, Vol. II pp.333-335.

on Shabbos to pray there, at this unifying "small Temple" of their great Rebbes. At the time of this writing, despite the present reconstruction of the Old City of Jerusalem, its ruins still await rebuilding.

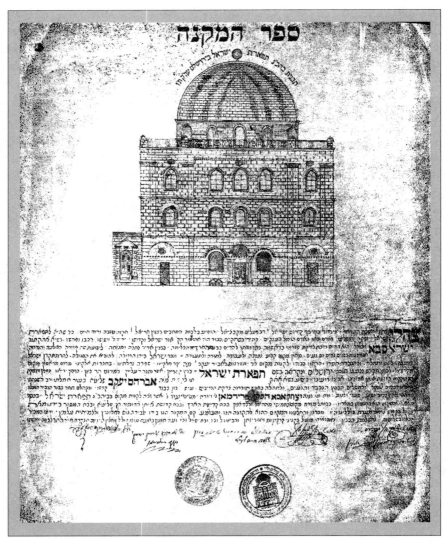

Document conveying the ownership of the Tiferes Yisroel shul to the Rizhiner's son, the Rebbe of Sadagora

AT HIS LAST PESACH SEDER, SURROUNDED BY HIS CHILDREN, THE RIZHINER conducted the Seder with unusual ecstatic fervor. When he reached

FOR THIS HE LIVED the prayer, וְהִיא שֶׁעָמְדָה, that Hashem's promise to Avrohom has protected the Jewish people from centuries of oppression, he repeated these words over and over, sixty times, his face changing with every repetition until he stopped. All participants realized that he was completely abstracted from this world and absorbed in the upper spheres. All were quiet, and waited. Suddenly he aroused himself, a puzzled expression on his face, and began to read with ecstatic intensity. Then he stopped, turned to his sons, and said, "There will come a time when the nations will be replenished with hatred against the Jews, but when they realize that they cannot destroy us, they will chase us out of their lands to our Holy land. It will be an insult to us, that our redemption should begin in this way, but, be that as it may, as long as we escape together from their clutches, the other nations will come to us anyway, just as they did at our Exodus from Egypt, whence we were also expelled by force. I say redemption through natural means is greater than redemption through miracles and wonders. I see in the Torah that for seven days Moshe was reluctant to take up the Divine mission of redeeming our forefathers from Egypt. Do you know why he refused? He saw that the redemption from Egypt would be through miracles, while he wanted it to be through natural means. If it occurs through miracles, it is subtracted from our merits, and thus the forces of Satan become active. The proof is that immediately after the liberation from Egypt, the strength of Amalek, the classic enemy of Israel, was increased. Had the redemption occurred in a natural way, Amalek would not have had the power to fight us... Happy is the one who will at least be worthy of that ..."

THESE PROPHETIC WORDS APPEAR TO PREFIGURE, NEARLY A CENTURY AFTER he spoke them, the Holocaust and the establishment of a Jewish

THESE PROPHETIC WORDS homeland in Eretz Yisroel. The hope for Jewish redemption from the *galus* was the main motive of his existence. He always spoke about it and always waited for it. In all his personal trials and suffering of his people he saw signs of *Mashiach's* approach. He would say, "When a woman is overtaken by labor pains during her eighth month, one tries to assuage the pains with medication. But when this happens in the ninth month, one tries to *increase* those same pains with medication, in order to accelerate the delivery. So it is with our people. If the earlier *tzaddikim* had prayed to Hashem to remove the suffering of the Jewish people, they would have been answered, for the time of redemption was not yet ripe. But now, since the redemption is near, prayer does not help to remove the suffering of the Jews. On the contrary, the pain must increase, so that the redemption will come sooner."

THE FAMILY OF THE HOUSE OF RIZHIN ALWAYS STOOD IN THE VANGUARD of those heralding the Jewish Redemption. R' Yisroel did not cease

ETERNAL TRIANGLE to be a "citizen of Jerusalem" even when he was in Rizhin and later in Sadagora. The love of Hashem and His Torah, the love of Israel and the love of Eretz Yisroel — "the eternal triangle" of Chassidus — accompanied him always. This capacity for love he implanted in the hearts of his sons and in the hearts of the tens of thousands whom he guided and inspired.

THE RIZHINER TRULY BELIEVED THAT EVERY JEW, ON HIS OWN LEVEL must redeem himself, from the personal *galus.* Every person is a

PREPARING THE GROUND microcosm and is included in the supreme elevation of *Klal Yisroel.* If everyone would cast off the yoke of Satan, and restore his own structure and set his eyes and heart on personal redemption, this would necessarily bring about the collective redemption.

The Rizhiner's position, as well as that of his sons and of the following generations was one of constant anticipation of the redemption by direct action and by deeds for the sake of immigration to, and the rebuilding of, Eretz Yisroel. His sons continued in this path, until their offspring reached Eretz Yisroel in our time and participated actively in the upbuilding of the Land.

Faithful to the Rizhiner's example, his descendants considered themselves citizens of Jerusalem and always desired to acquire land in Israel. It all began when the Rizhiner set into motion plans to build the famous Tiferes Yisroel synagogue in Jerusalem, near the Temple Mount. The synagogue was the point of assembly for all Rizhiner Rebbes who would celebrate the anniversary of the third of Cheshvan — the *yahrzeit* of the Rizhiner. This great edifice was the last redoubt of the Irgun in 1948 before it was destroyed by the Arab Legion. The chassidim of the Rizhiner dynasty were devastated by the destruction of their spiritual center in the Old City.

When the Boyaner Rebbe, R' Mordechai Shlomo of New York (my revered father-in-law, *zt"l*), visited Jerusalem in 1953, he instructed the chassidim to erect a new Tiferes Yisroel edifice in Jerusalem — the Mesivta Tifereth Israel of Rizhin which soon became and has remained the spiritual center of Rizhiner chassidim all over the world.

CHAPTER XIX

THE SUNSET OF
THE RIZHINER

THE RIZHINER'S STRENGTH HAD BEEN SEVERELY UNDERMINED. HIS terms of imprisonment, the need to be constantly on the move as a result of persecution by the Russian government, separation from his family, the lifelong burden of leadership and his total identification with *Yiddishe tzores* (Jewish suffering) — all had taken their toll upon his health. Moreover, frequent fasts had left their mark, and even the regal lifestyle at Sadagora was insufficient to restore his health and strength.

SHORTLY AFTER THE PASSING OF HIS WIFE, REBBETZIN SARAH, IN 1847, TWO of his chassidim suggested that he marry the widow of the *tzaddik*, R'

**MARRIAGE OF
WINTER AND SPRING**

Tzvi Hirsch of Rimanov. He agreed to this, and sent a proposal to her. She consented and they married shortly before the Days of Awe of that same year. His second wife brought two small children — a girl of 7, and a boy of 3 with her — from her previous marriage. The Rizhiner grew as close to the children as a natural father, loving and caring for them as if they were his own.

At the Rebbe's request, there were few people at the ceremony, which was conducted by the Gaon of Skolya, the author of the *Beis Shlomo*. There were no children from the union, however, and they were together for only two years.

The Rebbe seemed aware that his days were soon to end. During the last year of his life, he requested that his sons and sons-in-law come to him, and he spoke privately with each one of them.

ON THE EVE OF PESACH, BEFORE THE SEARCHING FOR THE *CHAMETZ* (leaven), he opened the cabinet containing his silver and said:

THE JEWEL IN THE CROWN

My grandfather, the Maggid of Mezritch, was the head of *Mashiach*. His student, R' Ara'le of Tetiev, was the right hand of *Mashiach*. R' Boruch of Mezhibozh was the left hand of *Mashiach*. The Rav of Berditchev was the heart of *Mashiach*... and what am I? The jewel, the jewel in the crown. Pains of persecution were felt by Yaakov our father and also by King Dovid. In terms of suffering, I have borne no less, neither am I embarrassed at my sufferings, in comparison to the Patriarchs ... When *Mashiach* will come, I will prepare a feast for all the Jews and especially for our people. I will then display all of these silver vessels on the table. I will have *nachas* (gratification) from them and they will have *nachas* from me, and Hashem will delight in us all.

IT HAPPENED IN THE LAST YEAR OF THE RIZHINER'S LIFE (1850), THAT A chassid came to R' Meir of Premishlan and handed him a *kvitel*. R' Meir

THE EXTINGUISHED CANDLE

took the *kvitel* and lay his head on his arms in deep meditation. Then he said: "Do know that a serious danger is hovering over you and that you need Divine mercy?

However, there is a way of salvation. Every year I send to the needy Jews of the Holy land 702 gold rubles, which is the numerical value of the Hebrew word Shabbos. Half of this sum I send before Pesach, and half before Rosh Hashanah. Now, Pesach is almost here and I haven't a single kopek. Supply me with the 351 gold rubles that I need now and no evil will befall you." The fearful chassid replied that he was willing to do so, but that he did not have the money with him. "Let me go to Lvov to borrow the sum and I shall bring it to you," he said. "If this is the case," said R' Meir, "you can be redeemed through another way. Here is a message for you to take to the Rizhiner instead of the money." Delighted, the chassid agreed to the mission, excited to visit the Rizhiner and to personally deliver his Rebbe's message.

R' Meir then said: "Travel directly to Sadagora, the moment you arrive there go straight to the Rizhiner's *hoif* and tell his *gabbaim* that you have a personal message from me for the Rebbe. You will arrive there Friday morning and when you enter the Rebbe's study you will address him in these exact words: 'Meir has given you the following order. Our passports have already been approved by the higher government, giving us free passage through all the borders. Indeed, 80,000 souls are waiting to welcome you. For Meir, also souls are waiting — but Meir's passport is stamped with an earlier date, and he must therefore soon depart.' "

Feeling faint, the shocked chassid implored his Rebbe to absolve him from such a mission, offering instead to get the 351 gold rubles for his Rebbe's charity, but R' Meir insisted and ordered him to carry out his mission in full.

Left with no alternative, the chassid journeyed to Sadagora. He arrived on Friday morning and went straight to the Rebbe, but the *gabbai* refused him entry since the Rizhiner had special hours for visitors. But when the chassid mentioned R' Meir's name, the *gabbai* admitted him at once. The chassid approached the *tzaddik* with a *kvitel*, as was the custom, but the Rizhiner refused to read it, stating that this was no time for accepting the *kvitel*. He eagerly asked the purpose of this hasty visit.

With awe and trepidation the chassid said, "Before I respond, I would like to receive the tzaddik's *berachah*, for my holy Rebbe of Premishlan has warned me that he sees ominous decrees hovering over me. I therefore beg first for the *tzaddik's berachah*."

The Rizhiner gave him his blessing, and the chassid faithfully delivered R' Meir's message, word for word. The Rizhiner was seated at his table with his sons when the message arrived. He turned to them and asked, "What is he telling us here? He thinks he has brought news, but it is really a simple matter. Bear this in mind, my children. Anyone who is indispensable to his generation cannot be affected by a supreme decree. But once his relationship to the generation comes to an end, or some other worthy person assumes the responsibility to the generation, he may leave."

Some months later, on a Thursday, R' Meir said to those of his chassidim who were then present: "Whoever does not want a disturbed Shabbos should go home." All of them left, except for the pious R' Yisroel of Kalisch, who asked permission to remain. "If you wish to stay," said R' Meir, "remember that Shabbos is Shabbos."

On that Shabbos, the eve of the month of Sivan, R' Meir passed away.

On *Motzaei Shabbos,* while the Rizhiner was sitting at his table on which stood two lighted candles, one candle suddenly went out. When it was re-lit, the other candle went out. "There is a great darkness in the world," said the *tzaddik.* The next day, the news from Premishlan reached him. He sighed and said, "We did not realize his greatness while he was alive." A few months later the Rizhiner, too, passed away.

THE *TZADDIK* R' MOSHE OF LELOV WANTED TO SETTLE IN ERETZ YISROEL that same year. He decided, before he left, to bid farewell to the

I CAN WAIT NO LONGER

three *tzaddikim* of his time, R' Meir'l of Premishlan, R' Sholom of Belz and R' Yisroel of Rizhin. By the time he arrived in Premishlan, R' Meir'l had passed away. He traveled to Belz, and finally to Sadagora. The Rizhiner pleaded with him, "Please wait with me here, and we will travel together." R' Moshe of Lelov tugged at his white beard, stared at the Rizhiner and said, "I can wait no longer." He was at that time seventy-four years old. He lived in the Holy Land for 74 days after his arrival there, and passed away on the twenty-fourth of Teves, 1851.

THE RIZHINER'S FRIEND, R' MOSHE OF KOBRIN (D. 1857), VISITED HIM FOR
the last time about a month before his death. The Rebbe was then at

THE FRUIT HAS RIPENED ON THE TREE

his summer home in the town of Zlati Potik, near Sadagora. It was Shabbos, near the time of *ra'ava d'raavin* (רַעֲוָא דְרַעֲוִין — favor of Divine favors) at the *shalosh seudos* (the third meal). The Rebbe received the Kobriner in his garden, the trees of which were heavy with ripe fruit. In the midst of their discussion the Rizhiner suddenly remarked, "Indeed, it is true that we can fulfill the obligation of the third meal on the Shabbos with fruits." Both were still for a few moments. The Rebbe arose, pulled R' Moshe's *gartel* (prayer belt), and motioned to him to take a walk in the garden. When they returned, the Rebbe asked, "R' Moshe, you are surely learned. Is it not true that one can fulfill the obligation of the third Shabbos meal by eating fruit?" R' Moshe realized that the Rebbe was intimating that his own days were limited, and the world would have to "fulfill its obligation" with his fruits, his offspring. R' Moshe began to wail, "But Rebbe, the world still needs you!"

"The fruit has ripened on the tree," said the Rebbe conclusively.

THAT YEAR, IN THE WEEK OF THE PORTION *KI SAVO*, THE REBBE WENT WITH
his sons and his son-in-law, R' Mendel of Vishnitz, for his daily car-

AN ESTATE FOR THE HOLIDAYS!

riage ride. On the way, when they stopped for a rest, a Jew approached and gave the Rebbe a *kvitel*, in the hope that the Rebbe would pray for his wife, who was having difficulty in childbirth. The Rebbe took the *kvitel* and said, "Are the Satanic separating curtains intervening so that no one reveals to me from Heaven that there is a woman in labor pains?" He turned to his sons and said, "My sons, I have but one request: that total redemption should come soon. If, Heaven forbid, the redemption should not come quickly, I ask that the Baal Shem Tov return again to the decadent world and set the generation right... My sons, do not think that I bought the estate in Zlati Potik for myself. I have already purchased for myself an even more beautiful estate for after the holidays..."

That same Shabbos, at the time of *Kiddush,* he said, "וְהָיָה כִּי תָבוֹא, *And when you shall come...* (*Devarim* 26:1). It has been noted that the word וְהָיָה connotes joy, to teach that one cannot rejoice until he is settled in Eretz Yisroel. And I say that even in this world, every man can reach spiritual perfection and wholeness of soul, according to his own capabilities. And he should rejoice, for he who prepares on the day before Shabbos, eats on Shabbos (*Avodah Zarah* 3a)."

AMONG THE CHASSIDIM WHO WOULD COME TO HIM ON THE DAYS OF AWE was one by the name of R' Asher. The *tzaddik* honored him greatly,

A SOUL FOR A SOUL!

commenting that he surely possessed an exalted soul. R' Asher was a man dogged by grave illness. The Rebbe commanded him to eat on Yom Kippur, for it was dangerous for him to fast the full day. Accordingly, at midday, before Mussaf, the Rebbe would bring R' Asher into his chamber and command him to eat something. R' Asher would do so in obedience to his Rebbe. On his last Yom Kippur, the Rizhiner was so deeply absorbed in his prayers that he did not leave the synagogue to rest, as was his wont. He therefore did not command R' Asher to eat — with the result that R' Asher collapsed and died during the midday service. When news of his death was brought to the Rebbe he cried out, "A soul for a soul!" and all knew that he meant himself.

AT THE END OF THE WEEK OF SUCCOS, HE SAID UPON LEAVING THE SUCCAH, "We pray to be worthy to sit in the succah made of the skin of the

THE SWEET LIGHT OF FORGETTING

Leviasan. We also pray, on each day of the holiday, that *He Who is merciful will rebuild the fallen succah of Dovid*" (cf. *Amos* 9:11). He sighed deeply and cried, "Woe to us! Who will stand for us? What should be done that we should not forget the Diaspora when we are in the next world?"

The Apter Rav, at the time of his own death, cried and wept over the withdrawal of the *Shechinah* (Holy Spirit) and the exile of Israel. He would say that the greatest tragedy was that the *Shechinah* too was in exile, therefore *How can we sing the songs of Hashem on alien soil? (Psalms* 137:4). How can we be happy when Hashem is in an alien place, for He is with us in our suffering? Prior to his death, the Apter Rav apologized and said, "How can I help here in exile when my hands are bound together with the hands of all the congregation of Israel. A prisoner cannot free himself by his own effort

The tomb of the Rizhiner in Sadagora

Names of righteous descendants of the Rizhiner engraved on his tomb

alone. But there, in the true world, all of the *tzaddikim* are free men. Yet why do they keep quiet? The Berditchever Rav promised us that he would not rest or keep still until he had brought the redemption…. What did they do in Heaven? They elevated him to high places, and the sweet light made him forget this decadent world. But I," said the Apter Rav, "I will not let them fool me, I will make a lot of noise in the world…."

"And indeed, he makes a lot of noise," added the Rizhiner, "but he is all alone in his work and what can one do alone? We must help him." He finished speaking and was still, and all understood that he was preparing to leave this world. After the Holy Days, he took sick and became bedridden. He developed a serious coronary condition from which he would not recover. A former follower of the Apter Rav came to visit him and the Rebbe requested that the man recount to him some of the Apter Rav's words that had not been recorded in the latter's book, *Oheiv Yisroel.* The man repeated the Apter Rav's explanation of the *Talmud Yerushalmi, Berachos* 85a: "A man should not rise to pray, unless it is done in the spirit of *halachah.* The halachic ruling is that we follow the majority against the minority. And now the Holy One, Blessed is He, says to us, *Return to Me and I will return to you (Malachi* 3:7). Thus we challenge Hashem, for He is the law — 'He is one' and we are many, and the law follows the majority. So Hashem must begin first by inspiring our hearts with the thought of penitence so that we will return in full penitence before him." When the man finished, the Rizhiner said, "In truth I wanted to hear these words before the coming of *Mashiach.*"

ON ROSH HASHANAH 1850, THE RIZHINER LET IT BE KNOWN THAT DURING the shofar blowing the echo of *Mashiach's* shofar had reached his ears — a hint that his departure was imminent.

I AM THE KAPPARAH

When he entered into the synagogue on the night of *Kol Nidrei* he laid his hand on the *mezuzah* and was heard saying, "I am the atonement for the entire body of Israel." During the Yom Kippur service, the Rizhiner was overcome by intense craving for a drink of water. He sent for the local rav and asked him if it was permissible for him to have a sip of water. The rav however failed to comprehend the urgency of the matter and forbade the Rizhiner to drink. Despite his intense craving, the Rizhiner obeyed the ruling of the rav and somehow completed the fast without a drink. As a result however he fell ill straight after Yom Kippur.

The third day of Cheshvan he passed away as a result of extreme exhaustion caused — according to the testimony of the famous physician of Lvov, Dr. Jacob Rappaport — by the effort to conquer his intense desire for a little water, thus completing his fast without a drop passing his lips. The body of the *tzaddik,* drained of energy, despite the subordination of his physical to his spiritual powers, was nevertheless subject to the everyday laws of nature. He did not recover.

NO PLEASURE FROM THIS WORLD

IN HIS LAST DAYS THE RIZHINER REMAINED COMPLETELY COHERENT AND alert, receiving the stream of chassidim and relatives who came to visit him. When his disciple, R' Shneur Zalman of Fastan, stood beside him, he was lying with his face to the wall. As the man approached, the Rebbe turned his head toward him and said, "Is that you, Shneur? There will come a time before *Mashiach* that even men like you and I will have to go into a corner and be tested in their full faith in the Creator. My advice to you is that you announce that I said this ahead of time." A few moments later he said, "The holy master, R' Yehudah HaNasi, Rabbeinu HaKadosh, testified about himself that he did not take pleasure from this world, even as much as a small finger. I bear self-witness, Heaven and Earth, that I did not take enjoyment from this world even as much as a slender thread. As for my behaving with overt leadership and pomp, this was all done to honor the Holy One, Blessed is He."

With these words his pure and holy soul returned to heaven. It was the third of Cheshvan, 1850. He was only 54.

His life on earth, as was the case with his father and grandfather, was intense and short. Of his grandfather he said, "My grandfather, the Malach, came down to this world, did what he had to do and went back." The Rizhiner, too, passed through this world like a comet, illumining brightly the deep human darkness of the earth and then disappearing into the celestial abode.

CHAPTER XX

DIVREI TORAH, ANECDOTES, PARABLES

D O YOU WANT TO KNOW WHAT CHASSIDUS IS? DO YOU KNOW the story of the blacksmith who wanted to become independent of his master and make it on his own? So he

INTRODUCTION bought an anvil, a hammer and bellows and went to work. Nothing happened — the forge would not start and remained inoperative. So he went for advice to a veteran blacksmith who told him: "My son, you have everything you need, except the spark!" That is what Chassidus is: the spark.

Chassidus stresses *ahavas Hashem* (love of Hashem) and *ahavas Yisroel* (love of fellow Jews). But as a prerequisite to these, man must first and foremost remain faithful to his most intimate, his truest self — for he cannot help others if he negates himself. Furthermore, one cannot claim to love Hashem if one does not first love Hashem's creatures. *Ahavas Hashem* has a precondition: *Ahavas Yisroel*. Conversely, lack of belief in Hashem tends to diminish one's regard for other people. "Beware," said the Baal Shem Tov to his disciples, "your coachman is dangerous and wicked. I saw him walk by the church without crossing himself. If he does not love his religion, why, then, would he love you?!"

Said R' Mechel of Zlotchov, "I have but one request. May I never use my reason against truth."

Therefore, hearing and telling stories of the holy ways of the *tzaddikim*, whose way of life is a manifestation of truth, is a great spiritual practice and is itself a great service of Hashem. R' Yisroel of Rizhin said that praising *tzaddikim* is equivalent to praising Hashem Himself. The Baal Shem Tov said: When one tells stories in praise of the *tzaddikim*, it is as though he were engaged in the mystical study of the Divine Chariot [for the *tzaddikim* are the Divine Chariot] (*Shivchei HaBaal Shem Tov*, #194).

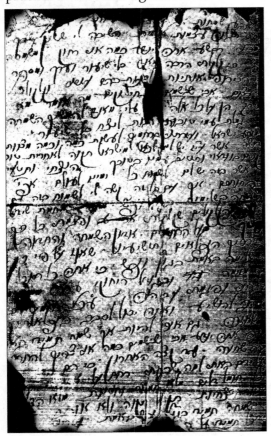

A letter from R' Nosson, the foremost disciple of R' Nachman of Breslov

It is a common practice among chassidim to sit together in a group to sing *niggunim* and tell stories of the *tzaddikim*. R' Menachem Nochum of Shtefanesht (a son of R' Yisroel of Rizhin) would say: Do you think that a person has to tell a story or a teaching of a *tzaddik* to someone else? It is not so at all. Just as when you recite the *Shema* it is between you and Hashem, in the same way, when you tell a story about a *tzaddik* it can be between you and yourself alone (*Beis Rizhin*, p. 328). R' Menachem Nochum particularly recommended telling such stories to oneself (and before Hashem) upon waking, or right before sleep.

A ritual of cardinal importance in chassidic tradition is the fastidiously faithful retelling of stories and tales of *tzaddikim*. Chassidim believe that such tales — *sippurei tzaddikim* — have the innate ability and force to bring about *yeshuah* (Divine help).

R' Nachman of Breslov is said to have uttered on one occasion, "I see that my words of Torah are not affecting you. I shall start to tell you stories." Chassidic tales appeal to the Jewish heart with an uplifting power exemplifying the *zechus* (special merit) of the *tzaddikim,* and the power of faith in their ability to help the needy. The Rizhiner related the following story:

> Once, when the holy Baal Shem Tov wanted to save the life of a sick boy with whom he had a very deep attachment, he ordered a candle to be made of pure wax, carried it into the woods, fastened it to a tree and lit it. Then he recited a long *tefillah*. The candle burned all night. When morning came, the boy was well.
>
> When my grandfather, the Great Maggid, who was the holy Baal Shem's disciple, wanted to effect a similar cure, he no longer knew the secret meaning of the words on which he had to concentrate, but he remembered the tree in the forest. He did as his master had done. He went to the tree and called on His Name. And his efforts met with success.
>
> When R' Moshe Leib of Sassov, the disciple of the disciple of the Great Maggid, wanted to achieve a cure of this kind, he said: "We no longer have the power to do what was done then. We don't know the Baal Shem's *tefillah*, we don't even know the tree at which he prayed, but I remember the story. I shall relate the story of how it was done and Hashem will help." And his efforts, too, met with success. Let us remember the story, let us hold on to the spark!

WHEN THE CHILDREN OF THE RIZHINER AND OF R' YAAKOV YOSEF HALPERN of Berditchev became engaged, R' Yaakov Yosef spoke proudly of

PEDIGREES his family tree, to which the Rizhiner replied, "My dear future *mechutan*, in our family the matter of *yichus* (lineage) is treated differently. While others like to boast of their famous lineage, we take pride in our sons, our descendants. My great-grandfather, the Maggid of Mezritch, used to take pride in his son, my grandfather, the Malach. The Malach, in turn, took pride in the virtues of his son, R' Sholom Shachna, my father. Similarly, I take pride in my son the *chassan*. This is in accord with the verse in *Tehillim* (45:17): *Your sons shall take the place of your forefathers.* And when R' Yisroel led his son, R' Avrohom Yaakov (Sadagora), to the *chuppah* he said, "My father used to say, 'People will know from my sons who I am.' But I say differently: 'People will know from my sons Who Hashem is.' "

Silence, reserve and laconic speech were the hallmark of the House of Rizhin, as he once remarked: "How is one to distinguish the silent sage from the silent fool? The sage does not mind being silent."

A MAN ONCE CAME TO R' MEIR OF PREMISHLAN SEEKING HELP. R' MEIR sent him to the Rizhiner saying: "You need intercession in

MUSIC HELPS Heaven; his is more acceptable than mine. But do what Meir'l tells you. When you arrive in Sadagora, go to the Rebbe's palace and ask to be admitted into his study. When you enter, start singing a special Shabbos song. Sing it even if it is not Shabbos. You will see that you will be helped."

The man obeyed and went to Sadagora. He rushed to the palace and asked to see the Rebbe, explaining that R' Meir had sent him. The Rizhiner *gabbaim* felt that any message from R' Meir would brighten the Rizhiner's mood. When the man entered the Rebbe's palace he started to sing a very long Shabbos song with passion and fervor as though he were singing it on Shabbos and not on an ordinary Wednesday. The Rizhiner's mood changed and he started to laugh. The Rebbe remarked, "I don't know what R' Meir wants of me and why he sent you to me, but you have helped *me,* and therefore you have already been helped."

ANOTHER TIME, R' MEIR SENT ONE OF HIS CHASSIDIM WITH A MESSAGE TO the Rizhiner: "You have taken the high road and Meir is taking the

THE DIFFERENT ROADS

low road; but we shall both arrive at the same place, together." Opposite in their approach and lifestyle, R' Meir and R' Yisroel nevertheless represented the roads leading to the actualization of the Baal Shem Tov's teachings. Indeed, so claims the chassidic dictum, "If you walk the right road, your paths cross."

THE RIZHINER ONCE ASKED THE CHASSID, R' YAAKOV OF YARISHOV: "DID you know R' Boruch of Mezhibozh?"

THEY BELIEVED IN HASHEM

"I did not really know him, but I believed in his holiness," replied the chassid.

Pleased by his answer, the Rizhiner said, "That is, indeed, as it should be," and he elaborated: "When the Israelites went out of Egypt, they reached the heights of human understanding of Hashem. The maidservant who witnessed the miraculous crossing of the Sea of Reeds saw that which the prophet Yechezkel did not see in his vision (*Mechilta, Beshalach,* 3). It was then that the *yetzer hara* came upon them and tried to lead them into sin. 'You have already seen everything,' he said. 'You have reached the limits of understanding.' But they were not led astray. They knew that much more was to be seen, they just needed pure faith. That is why the Torah tells us that, just at that point in time, *They believed in Hashem (Shemos* 14:31) — and the verse continues, *and in His servant Moshe.* For just as man must understand that no matter how much he recognizes the greatness and loftiness of the Creator, he has not reached even an infinitesimal degree of understanding, so he must know that he cannot comprehend the exalted loftiness of the *tzaddik*. He must believe that the *tzaddik's* greatness immeasurably surpasses our comprehension."

SAID THE RIZHINER: "WE READ IN THE TORAH (*BEREISHIS* 49:1): *AND Yaakov called to his sons and said: Gather yourselves together, that I may tell*

THE SHECHINAH'S FLIGHT

you that which shall befall you in the End of Days. Rashi comments there: 'Yaakov desired to reveal the time of the advent of *Mashiach*, but the *Shechinah* departed from him and he was unable to do so.' If we search for a reason we can answer as follows: The Sages teach us that if Yisroel merits it, the end of our *galus* (exile) will be hastened. If not, it will come at its proper time (*Sanhedrin* 98a). Now, Yaakov could reveal the proper, predestined time. But that would indicate that he lacked the belief that Israel merited the advent of the redemption *before* this appointed time, and such an uncharitable view caused the *Shechinah* to depart."

THE RIZHINER ONCE ENTERED HIS *BEIS MIDRASH* AND SAID TO HIS CHASSIDIM, "I will tell you a story:

THE CRY OF THE VILLAGER

An ignorant villager came to the city for Rosh Hashanah. Like many villagers, he did not know the back of the *siddur* from the front of the *siddur*. He walked into the synagogue during the morning prayers and looked around, not uttering a sound. When the worshipers started to say *Shemoneh Esrei*, he noticed that some of them were crying. He thought this very strange. There hadn't been any fighting going on, so why were they crying? He thought and thought and finally came to the conclusion that they were crying because they were hungry and had to stay in shul so long. Since he too was hungry, he also started to cry.

After *Shemoneh Esrei*, he noticed that they were no longer crying. He then recalled that earlier that morning his hostess had put a hard piece of meat into the soup, with the idea that the longer it would cook the softer it would become. Therefore he concluded that going home late from shul was really no cause for tears. But when they started to blow the shofar, his original question repeated itself anew, for by now everyone was crying again. Finally, he found the answer, reasoning that: True it is that the broth will be richer and tastier after cooking so long. But we don't have the strength to wait so long. And with this pitiful and heartfelt intuition, he too began to cry with the whole congregation."

The Rebbe left the room. The chassidim interpreted the story as a Rizhiner parable about the long Jewish exile.

TOWARD THE END OF HIS LIFE, R' MOSHE OF KOBRIN (1784-1858), A Rebbe himself, would travel to the Rizhiner just like a chassid making the pilgrimage to his Rebbe. When R' Moshe of Kobrin paid a visit to R' Yisroel of Rizhin, the latter came out to meet him while he was still a good distance from the town. Greeting him, he said, "I felt your approach of truth while you were still several miles away" (*Ohr Yesharim*, Petrikov, 1924).

CHASSIDIC ESP[1]

R' YISROEL OF RIZHIN ONCE SAID: "R' AHARON THE GREAT OF KARLIN (d. 1765) was the truth of the world. His son, R' Asher (1763-1827), walked all his life in the path of truth, and as for his grandson, R' Aharon (1826-1872), if he knew that a crumb of truth was hidden under the floor, he would pull up the floorboards with his fingernails."

SEARCHING THE TRUTH

R' LEVI YITZCHOK OF BERDITCHEV USED TO VISIT EVERY SICK PERSON IN town. Once, he visited a very sick man and found him in the grip of anxiety. Asked R' Levi Yitzchok, "Why are you

FEELING JEWISH PAIN

1. Extrasensory perception

worried?" Answered the man in a depressed tone, "Rebbe, I feel my hours are numbered and my heart is sorrowful and worried as I face the heavenly court and contemplate my poor prospects of getting a portion in the World to Come." The Rebbe stood up and said, "I hereby give you as a final gift my own portion of *Olam Haba*."

On the spot R' Levi Yitzchok drew up a contract. The face of the sick man lit up with happiness, but a few minutes later he passed away. In amazement, one of the bystanders, a friend of the Rebbe, asked him, "Rebbe, for sure your intention was to raise the spirits of the sick man, to give him support and thereby keep him alive a while longer. But you realized also that these were his last moments and that your encouragement would no longer help him, why then all this unique effort on your part?"

"Listen, my son," replied the Rebbe, "I prefer to give away my entire *Olam Haba* if by that I can spare a terminally sick Jew even one minute of pain."

THE RIZHINER ONCE SAID: "DO YOU THINK THAT THE *REISH BIRYONI* (THE Jewish anti-Roman rebels of Jerusalem) mentioned in the tractate

WHICH FAITH?

Gittin (56a) were simple men? They were great men: the only thing they lacked was faith in the Sages. Who were the *tzaddikim* of that generation? They were the *Tannaim* who tried to pacify the Romans. But the *Reish Biryoni* did not listen to them. The *Reish Biryoni* consisted of two groups. One was a force for bad, for depravity; the other for good, except for the fact that they did not want to listen to the *tzaddikim*. The decision came from Heaven that the souls of these people would have to return to this world at the End of Days (*acharis hayamim*, the pre-Messianic era) in order to mend their ways. These two groups are found in the world today. One group consists of the soldiers taken into the Russian army; the other places its faith in a stick and believes in it..." (see *Shnei HaMeoros* by R' Shmuel of Kaminka).

An honest and pious Jew was trying desperately to achieve Divine Inspiration (*ruach hakodesh*). He carefully refrained from any idle talk

IN SEARCH OF
THE DIVINE SPIRIT

for forty days and nights, since he had read in a *sefer* that through such action a person merits *ruach hakodesh*. The prescribed period passed — not a word or sign of the Divine Inspiration. In deep consternation and disappointment, he decided to present his problem to the Rizhiner. The Rizhiner's court was known for its royal style. When this Jew saw all this luxury, he was bewildered that this should be the *tzaddik's* lifestyle. Was this the *derech haTorah?!* (the way of the Torah). After a while, he decided that he would not be able to discuss this matter of *ruach hakodesh* with the Rebbe, after all. On the very day that he was leaving Rizhin without calling on the Rebbe, he saw the Rizhiner preparing to be conveyed in his royal carriage with the four white stallions. Before alighting, the Rebbe approached one of the horses and patted his back three times. Dumbstruck, the visitor could not hold himself back. Plucking up his courage, he approached the Rebbe and asked, "What kind of *avodah* (Divine Service) is this for a *tzaddik* to pat his horse?"

"I want you to know," explained the Rizhiner, "not a single word of idle talk has passed the lips of this horse for forty whole days."

The story is told of a young Ukrainian chassid who had money and merchandise aplenty. Only one thing he lacked — children; and

WHOSE OATH GIVES
WAY TO WHOSE?

he tirelessly importuned his Rebbe with his request for this blessing. Every time he asked, though, his entreaty was deferred by the Rebbe, R' Aryeh Leib of Shpole, who was known as the Shpoler Zeide, until one day the chassid decided that he would give him no rest, and plead with him with such clamorous urgency that the *tzaddik* would be forced to grant him his request. However, when he opened with his barrage of pleas, the *tzaddik*, who was contemplating secrets of the higher spheres, said to him: "Please leave me for the moment, for I am now involved In a matter concerning the House of Israel at large; this is not a propitious time for me to undertake the request of an individual." "Ah!" thought the chassid, "If this is indeed a propitious hour, and that is why he is occupied with the needs of all of Israel, then I am not going to budge from here until he grants me my request." And he continued to pester the *tzaddik* relentlessly, so much so that he was utterly unable to concentrate. The Shpoler Zeide first implored him to give him some peace, and later warned him that he would live to regret his insistence, but to no avail, until, in a moment of anger, he said: "I swear that you will never have children!"

The chassid was terror stricken. "My soul-root does not belong here," he concluded, and taking his leave from the Rebbe, he left Shpole with a heavy heart.

Some time later his business interests brought him to Koritz. One day, his transactions completed, he retired to the *beis midrash* in which R' Pinchos of Koritz used to study and pray. Now, although R' Pinchos was as yet unknown as a *tzaddik,* this chassid had an eye for these things; he perceived that this man had a lofty soul, and surmised that he was probably inspired as well by *ruach hakodesh.* He interested himself in his material situation, and was told by neighbors that R' Pinchos was penniless. To make matters worse, the month of Nissan was already underway and the festival of Pesach, with its extra household expenses, was just around the corner. On top of that, as the guest heard from some of the townsmen, what bothered R' Pinchos the most was that he would be losing precious time from his learning Torah on account of the preparations that had to be made at home for the approaching festival. "This could be my lucky hour," thought the visiting chassid.

He went straight to the home of R' Pinchos and asked his wife whether she had whatever she needed for Pesach. When she told him that she did not have so much as a single copper coin, he took out his wallet and gave her money enough to enable her to buy the flour which was scrupulously guarded against contact with moisture, to pay the baker who made the matzos, and to buy fish and meat and all manner of dishes in honor of the forthcoming Yom Tov. He then went out himself and bought a table and benches and a bed as well, and asked her to arrange everything in the most generous style possible, for he wanted to be their guest for Pesach. He asked her to keep these preparations a secret from her husband until Pesach eve. To this she agreed and day by day he would call at her home to see whether there was anything lacking.

R' Pinchos was somewhat surprised that his wife was not bothering him with requests for money to cover the expenses of the festival. He did not raise the subject, however, and continued with his studies in the *beis midrash* as before, night and day.

Before sunset on the eve of Pesach, when the *tzaddik* was already at prayers, the chassid paid one last visit to his house to ensure that everything was as it should be. When the *tzaddik* came home and opened the door to his humble dwelling, he was greeted by a table decked with all manner of dishes and delicacies and a room lit up on all sides by tall white candles. He was overjoyed, and asked his wife where all this festive cheer had come from. "Our guest, who stands here before you, he provided it all," she said. The *tzaddik* greeted his guest warmly, but did not ask him any questions, and they sat down at once to the Seder service, which R' Pinchos conducted with joy and with fervor. Later on in the evening, in the course of the meal, he turned to his guest and asked: "What brings you here? Do you have a request?"

The chassid explained that he was childless and he had come to request that R' Pinchos promise him a child. The chassid did not let on that the Shpoler Zeide had already sworn that he would not have children. R' Pinchos thereupon said: "If any good deed I have ever done carries any weight in heaven, I swear to you that this year your wife will bear a son." And his blessing was fulfilled within the year.

When R' Yisroel of Rizhin recounted this story he added: "At the moment when R' Pinchos of Koritz made his oath, the entire heavenly court was thrown into confusion: Whose oath would give way to whose? And the verdict was that the oath of him who had never made an oath in his life before, even a truthful one, was to prevail. The records were searched, and the heavenly court accordingly honored the oath of R' Pinchos."

But the *tzaddik* of Rizhin had one further comment: "From this episode we see how one should not be obstinate in the face of a *tzaddik's* decree. For the grandson of that chassid, who came into the world through the oath of R' Pinchos, grew up to be a treacherous enemy of Israel who slandered Pinchos's own grandchildren, the saintly brothers of Slavita, the publishers of the Talmud, to the barbarous authorities, causing them to be beaten mercilessly and imprisoned by the cruel Cossacks."

THE SERAPH OF STRELISK WAS ONCE TOLD OF THE APPARENT EXULTATION of the Rizhiner as he listened to the orchestra that he kept in his court.

BODILY TRANSFORMATION The Strelisker wanted to know what the Rizhiner looked like when he was listening to his musicians. He was painted a picture of inspired ecstasy. The Strelisker commented: "Concerning the Prophet Eliyahu we are told that 'the girdle of his loins was a girdle of leather.' This really means that in his case, his very loins, his very body, was like a leather girdle that he could put on and take off at will. And so it is with the *tzaddik* of Rizhin. When he so wishes, he can divest himself of his body, and when he wills otherwise, he can clothe himself in his body."

THE RIZHINER ONCE COMMENTED ON *TEHILLIM* 137:4: *"HOW CAN WE*

HOW CAN WE SING? *sing the song of Hashem in a strange exile land.* How can we sing songs when the *Shechinah* is in exile?"[1]

THE RIZHINER WOULD TAKE A LONG TIME OVER HIS *TEFILLOS*; R' SHOLOM OF Belz would recite his *tefillos* very quickly. On this phenomenon one of

TWO TYPES OF PRAYER the rabbis commented that both of them cherished every word of the *tefillos*: the Rizhiner loved them so much that he could not bring himself to part with them, while the Belzer, for the same reason, could not restrain his eagerness to make them his, by reciting them all.

---

1. For the *Shechinah*, too, is in exile (see *Megillah* 29a).

ONCE HE WAS HEARD TO SAY, "IF PEOPLE KNEW THE BENEFIT THAT THEIR children would have from coming to me, they would force them to

PURPOSEFUL VISITS

come; and if the only benefit they received was that I taught them to speak without coarseness or crudity, this would be enough." For indeed it was not merely this or that aspect that he stressed — he held, as others had before him, in different times and different climes, that *"Derech eretz* make the man."

The author of *Megaleh Amukos HaChadash* states in the name of the Rizhiner that a person should not go to sleep at night until after three hours devoted to the study of Torah. The Rizhiner was asked: "Is it better that a person should sleep earlier and get up earlier; or should a person go to sleep late and learn and wake up later?" His answer was: "It would be better for a person to go to sleep early and get up early, but only if he is sure that he will indeed get up early."

IN DUBENKA THERE WAS A TIMBER MERCHANT WITH BUSINESS IN DANZIG who was a follower of the Rizhiner. Once, the Rizhiner asked him

IN SCARCITY THERE IS VALUE

where his thoughts were more pure — at home or in Danzig? His thoughts were much clearer, he answered, in Danzig, even though in that place the fear of Hashem was almost non-existent. The Rizhiner explained this by saying that in Danzig sacredness is foreign to people and therefore stands out in relief so much more than when he is at home. So when sacredness meets a Jew there it holds on to him with greater tenacity.

SAID R' YISROEL: "THERE ARE TWO WAYS TO INFLUENCE MEN TO DO GOOD. One is by sermons of a serious and profound character — when the

ON TELLING STORIES

audience is highly intelligent. The other is by sermons of a light, popular nature, interpolated with stories and parables — when the audience consists of ordinary men and women of little education. And this is the meaning of the verse: *We have a little sister, her time of spiritual maturity has not come. What shall we do for our sister in the day when she shall be spoken for (Song of Songs 8:8)?* We have a little sister: namely, an audience of but little education; she is as yet undeveloped and immature. What shall we do for our sister? How shall we influence such an assembly? 'In the day' — on the Shabbos or Holy Day she shall he spoken to — namely, told stories."

IT ONCE HAPPENED THAT THE CHASSIDIM WERE SITTING TOGETHER WHEN the *tzaddik* of Rizhin came by with his pipe in his hand. The chassidim called out to him, "Master! Please inform us of the way to serve Hashem honestly, without deceiving oneself." The Rebbe replied, "How should I know?" But he did tell them the following story: "A king sentenced two dear friends to death. The king really wished to pardon them, but could not do so because he was obliged to uphold the laws of his realm and they were indeed guilty. The sentence was, therefore, that a long, taut rope be thrown across a fierce river and if the men were able to cross the river on the rope their lives would be spared. The first man succeeded in the crossing whereupon his friend called out to him, 'Dear friend! Please tell me how you managed to achieve such a hazardous crossing on the tightrope so that I, too, may do likewise.' The friend replied, 'I really do not know. I know only that as I was crossing on the rope, whenever I felt myself going over to one side I leaned in the opposite direction.'" The Rebbe meant that one must avoid extremes, and always hew to the middle road, the "golden path."

MAINTAINING EQUILIBRIUM

ONE OF THE RIZHINER'S CHASSIDIM, A MERCHANT BY TRADE, TOOK GREAT pride in his humility. Suddenly, he began to suffer significant reverses in his business and complained to the Rizhiner. The Rebbe warned him to abandon his habit of openly displaying his humility, but the merchant soon forgot the Rebbe's warning and in his pride, refused

TRUE HUMILITY

to ask his friends for temporary loans to carry him over the crisis. This false meekness forced him to liquidate his business. Still, he failed to change his character and soon after his house was burned to the ground. Instead of appealing to his friends for help, however, he left town and began wandering from town to town. He was arrested on suspicion of vagrancy and put in jail. Sunk in thought, the depressed prisoner allowed the cigarette he was smoking to fall upon his cloak and he was severely burned. In the hospital a relative visited him and, for the first time, the destitute merchant broke through his pride and, weeping, described his miserable lot. The relative promised to help him and the unfortunate man was gradually able to overcome his troubles. In the end, his fortunes were restored. When he next visited the Rizhiner, the Rebbe said: "Be sure now to maintain the spirit of sincere humility and your success will endure."

R' DOVID MOSHE OF CHORTKOV ONCE QUOTED HIS FATHER, SAYING: "My father, the Rizhiner, used to say that because people did not

THE BROKEN WATCH

give credence to the greatness of holy men in the time of the Baal Shem Tov, it was decreed that they should be forced to believe in 'staffs' (unworthy Rebbes). For faith is a precious gift. A parable explains it. A man owned an expensive gold watch that suddenly ceased to keep time. Since he could not take the watch to a watchmaker for repairs, he began to shake the mechanism, although he knew it wouldn't help, just to prevent corrosion. The shaking is not a cure for the malady, but it helps until we are able to find something that is truly effective. Like this man, we give our allegiance to a minor *tzaddik* until we discover a major *tzaddik*. We must not become unaccustomed to reverence for the *tzaddik,* for the main issue is to get the tools of faith. Without it, all knowledge is superfluous. And this was the contribution made by earlier *tzaddikim* — to instill *emunah* (faith) in people's hearts. And when they are worthy to achieve knowledge of Hashem, they will then use it for faith in Hashem and in the true *tzaddikim"* (*Divrei Dovid*).

R' Moshe, the Rebbe of Kobrin, once visited the Rizhiner on the eve of Shabbos, and found the Rebbe standing in the middle of the

THE SMOKE OF EREV SHABBOS room smoking furiously, his pipe in his hand and clouds of smoke filling up the room. Upon seeing his visitor, the Rizhiner narrated the following story: "There was once a man who lost his way in the forest at twilight on the eve of Shabbos. Suddenly, he saw a house in the distance and began walking toward it. When he entered the house he found himself facing a fierce-looking bandit, and on the table in front of him lay a loaded gun. The bandit jumped up from his seat, but before he could get hold of the gun the man had seized it. Quick as lightning he thought: 'If I shoot him, I save myself. Even if I miss, the room will still be full of smoke and I will be able to escape.' " The Rizhiner put down his pipe and said: "It is Shabbos now!" He then concluded: "In order to purify my mind for Shabbos, I think holy thoughts and smoke my pipe. If my thoughts fail me, the tobacco fumes may at least dull my mind so that I do not think unholy thoughts."

The Rizhiner once told the following parable: "There was a man who had decided to dedicate his son to Hashem. When the youngster reached maturity, full of Torah learning and worthy deeds, his

ON THE DAY OF JUDGMENT father planned to marry him to the daughter of the holiest man of the generation. He went into the woods and fervently prayed to Hashem to send him wealth so that the holy man might agree to become his son's father-in-law. With this wealth he would find renown as a philanthropist. Hashem listened to his prayers and sent him bountiful blessings in all his endeavors. A neighbor of his became puzzled at the man's sudden wealth and succeeded in finding the reason. He, too, entreated Hashem for bountiful blessings, claiming also learning and holy deeds for his son. But the heavenly tribunal recognized the hypocrisy of his behavior and riches were not bestowed upon him. On the Day of Judgment," continued the Rizhiner, "the nations will see bountiful rewards granted to Israel and will claim them the same for themselves. But the heavenly tribunal will speedily see through their pretensions."

ON HOW TO ATTRACT CHASSIDIM

R' NAFTOLI OF ROPSHITZ, WHO WAS KNOWN FOR HIS SHARP WIT, ONCE visited the Rizhiner. The Rizhiner asked him: "Do you know that flies are drawn to fire?"

"Yes," retorted the Ropshitzer, "and cream draws flies, too."

CREATION

COMMENTING ON THE PROPHETIC VERSE, *FOR INSTRUCTION SHALL GO forth from Me* (*Yeshayah* 51:4), R' Yisroel said: "The Torah's teachings will never be changed. The first Book of Moshe will forever be the Book of *Bereishis* which informs us what befell our forefathers from the day that Hashem created the world. However, there is something which is hidden from us; what Hashem wrought before He created the world. And this is the meaning of the words: *Now it is said of Yaakov and of Yisroel, what has Hashem wrought* (*Bamidbar* 23:23), and the same is the meaning of the verse: *For instruction shall go forth from Me* — telling what I wrought before I created the world."

AN ALTAR OF SILENCE

QUOTING THE VERSES IN *SHEMOS* (20:21-22), *AN ALTAR OF EARTH YOU shall make for Me... and if you will make for Me an Altar of stones you shall not build it out of hewn stones; for if you will have wrought it with your sword, you will have desecrated it.* The *Altar of earth* the Rizhiner interpreted as the altar of silence (אֲדָמָה, "earth"/דְּמָמָה, "silence"), which is more pleasing to Hashem than anything else; but if the Altar were to be constructed of words, they must not be hewn (not prepared homiletics), for such artifice would desecrate it.

A RICH FUR MERCHANT MARRIED HIS SON AND DAUGHTER INTO WEALTHY families and continued to rejoice in his successful life. But the wheel

CHILDREN'S OPPORTUNISM

of fortune turned; his wife died, and his business floundered. Neither his son nor his daughter came to his assistance. In consternation and dismay he complained to the Rizhiner. The Rebbe wrote letters to his chassidim enjoining them to help the poor man. The chassidim contributed handsomely and with the money thus collected, the man reestablished himself in business and his efforts were attended with success. Soon after, he married a widow and lived very happily.

Hearing of his renewed prosperity, both the son and daughter began urging their father to live with them and to divorce their new stepmother. On his way to the Leipzig Fair, the merchant stopped over to visit the Rizhiner, and told him of his children's grievances. The Rebbe said: "On your way back, stop here again and I will advise you what to do." Upon his return the Rebbe said:

"Write three letters: one to your wife, another to your son and a third to your daughter. Each letter should read as follows: 'A great tragedy has befallen me. My fur became moth eaten and worthless. I sold some of my own clothes in order to enable me to leave Leipzig, and I had just enough money to reach the home of the Rizhiner. I beg of you to send me sufficient money to return home.' Then," continued the Rebbe, "show me the replies you receive."

The merchant followed the Rizhiner's advice. Both the son and daughter sent their excuses for failing to send him any money and advised him to stay with the Rebbe. His wife, however, sent him sufficient money, consoled him, and promised to join him and together rebuild his business. When he returned home, no one but his wife welcomed him. He then told her that he was richer than ever and wrote a will leaving her his entire property. When his children found out about their father's decision, they protested, but he showed them the three replies to his letters, and ordered them from his home.

SPEAKING OF REPENTANCE, THE RIZHINER SAID: "IT IS REQUIRED OF US that we repent and atone before redemption, but we have lost the means

REDEMPTION FIRST

to do so, for we are staggering under the burden of our tribulations, like drunken men who cannot walk a straight path. When our Sages said that overwhelming poverty makes men turn away from knowledge of the Creator (*Eruvin* 41b), they implied that Hashem should provide redemption before we repent."

R' NECHEMIA'LE, SON OF THE "HOLY YUD" (THE HOLY JEW, R' YITZCHOK Rabinowitz), said: "I heard from the Rizhiner an explanation of the Talmudic dictum that "when one runs away from fame, honors pur-

HUMILITY BEARS HONORS

sue him" (*Eruvin* 13a). It would then seem more just that Hashem should fulfill the will of those who fear Him (*Tehillim* 145:19), and not cause unwanted honors to pursue the G-d-fearing man. The Rizhiner's answer is that if a man still feels the necessity of running away from honors, that shows us that he is conceited, fearful that honors will really make him arrogant and proud, and he is, therefore, not truly a G-d-fearing man. Honors pursue him for the sake of disciplining his character, so that no amount of honor can weaken his humility. For then, he will no longer need to run away from it."

WHEN THE RIZHINER WAS STILL A CHILD, HE WAS ONCE WALKING UP AND down in the courtyard on a Friday during twilight when every-

THE HEAVEN OF SHABBOS

body had already gone to the *kloiz* to *daven*. A chassid saw him and asked: "Why don't you go *daven*? Shabbos has already begun."

"Shabbos hasn't begun yet," the child replied.

"But how do you know that?" asked the chassid.

"On Shabbos," the child answered, "there always appears a new Heaven and so far I can't see any sign of it."

ONCE, IN THE PRESENCE OF THE RIZHINER, CHASSIDIM DISCUSSED THE many miracles performed by the *tzaddikim*. The Rizhiner stated, "The

PRAYER NOT SUPERSTITION more miracles are attributed to the *tzaddikim*, the more the ground is prepared for imposture by visionaries, soothsayers and medical charlatans. A *tzaddik* should merely offer prayer to the Almighty and if he is a real *tzaddik*, his prayer will be heard."

THE RIZHINER WAS ONCE ASKED TO INTERPRET THE *PASSUK* REFERRING to the Israelites standing at the foot of Mount Sinai (*Shemos* 20:15):

AT MOUNT SINAI *And the people saw [the revelation of Hashem] and trembled and stood from afar.* What is meant by this? Is not the entire universe filled with the Divine glory? How then is it possible to "stand afar from Hashem"?

The Rizhiner explained: "Miracles are for those who have little faith. Basically when Israel saw that Hashem was performing miracles for them, they knew that they still had to stand far off; but at the same time, however, they yearned for perfect faith in Hashem with all the strength of their passionate hearts."

THE STORY IS TOLD OF A CHASSID OF THE RIZHINER WHOSE DAUGHTER was afflicted with deteriorating vision, a condition for which

STRANGE ADVICE there was no known medical cure. Time and again he implored the *tzaddik* to heal her, but no help was granted him. Finally, when the girl became blind, the Rizhiner said to him, unbidden: "Take your daughter to Lemberg, and when you get there, search for the vendors who go about the streets and advertise their goods, each with his own singsong or jingle — for instance: 'Fine pretzels, fresh pretzels!' He whose cry you like best is the one who can cure your daughter."

The chassid followed the Rebbe's instructions and soon came upon the man whose jingle was most to his liking. He bought a pretzel from him and asked him to bring some to the inn where he lodged the next day. When the vendor entered his room, the chassid locked the door and repeated the words of the Rizhiner. The vendor's eyes flashed and he yelled: "Let me out of here, or I'll make a heap of bones of you along with your Rebbe." The chassid opened the door in panic. The vendor disappeared, but the chassid's daughter was cured.

AT ONE OF HIS SHABBOS MEALS, R' YISROEL TURNED TO HIS CHASSIDIM AND said: "The days are approaching when all will be well with the non-

THE LAST THREE HOURS religious man both in body and in soul, but all will not be well with the religious man, not in body and not in soul, and he will not even be able to recite one chapter of *Tehillim*. Why do I tell you this? So that your hearts shall not be distressed; it ought to be so, it must be so." On another occasion, he said: "In the last three hours before the *geulah* (redemption) it will be as difficult to cling to Judaism as to climb a smooth wall of ice. That is why, in the *Hoshanos* prayer, on Succos, we say, 'Hoshana, please save,' over the course of three hours." Those are meant to be the last hours before the coming of *Mashiach*.

SAID THE PORISSOVER RAV: "SOME CHASSIDIM ARE SO ARROGANT ON

SUFFERING FROM LOVE account of their piety that they cannot believe Hashem sends them afflictions in order to awaken in them *teshuvah* for their sins. They

claim, 'I am a perfect Jew, and I will accept these problems, these afflictions, from love.' But *yissurim shel ahavah* (afflictions from love), are not sent without reason: They are intended as a means to arouse one to do *teshuvah*. When the Rizhiner was imprisoned, he cried. He was asked: 'Why do you not accept this affliction as imposed out of love?' He answered: 'When Hashem sends pain, we are supposed to feel it.' "

ONCE, ON *SHABBOS SHUVAH* (THE SHABBOS OF RETURN, OR REPENTANCE, occurring between Rosh Hashanah and Yom Kippur), the Rizhiner

THE SHABBOS OF REPENTANCE expounded: "Hoshea says: *Return, O Israel, to Hashem your G-d* (14:2). That message was addressed to the whole world and to all the creatures of heaven and earth. For everything that has been created, below and above, all the servants of the Most High, the angels, the *seraphim*, the heavenly creatures, the holy *Merkavah* (celestial chariot) as far as the throne of Hashem Himself, must actualize this 'turning.' And that is what the words *to Hashem your G-d* mean: All creatures of all rungs, up to the highest — up to the throne of Hashem — must achieve this 'turning.' " Saying this, the Rizhiner addressed himself: "O Yisroel — return to Hashem your G-d."

THE FOLLOWING IS THE RIZHINER'S EXPLANATION OF THE PASSUK, *But all the Children of Israel had light in their dwelling* (Shemos 10:23).

LUSTER OF THE DIAMOND "Each one of us possesses a holy spark, but not everyone displays its light to the best advantage. It is similar to a diamond which cannot cast its brilliance if it is still buried in the ground. But when polished and given a proper setting, it sparkles with a shining light."

THE RIZHINER ELABORATED ON THE TEXT, *AND YOU SHALL NOT ASCEND BY steps to my Altar, that your nakedness be not exposed on* it (*Shemos* 20:23).

THE PROPER WAY TO PRAY "The *beis midrash*," he said, "represents the Altar. The prime requirement when bringing an offering upon the Altar or when *davening* is contrition, humility and remorse at one's shortcomings. We are forbidden to go up to pray in a light-headed mood, lest our evil thoughts confuse our words of *tefillah*. Symbolically, this is hinted in the small letter *aleph* in the word וַיִּקְרָא, *and He [Hashem] called to Moshe* (*Vayikra* 1:1), as if to say that Hashem called out to Moshe because he was humble."

THE RIZHINER ONCE REMARKED: "WHEN TWO CHASSIDIM SEE RABBIS engaged in a disagreement they, too, begin to argue with one another.

HONEST ARGUMENT In reality, however, only the *tzaddikim* are permitted to carry on a dispute for it is a dispute for the sake of heaven לְשֵׁם שָׁמַיִם. That is why it says in the Mishnah: 'What sort of controversy is for the sake of Heaven? That of Hillel and Shammai' (*Avos* 5:20). It does not say of the School of Shammai and the School of Hillel, for a dispute for the sake of Heaven can be waged only by the masters, not by their disciples."

SAID THE RIZHINER: "OUR SAGES EMPLOYED VARIOUS TECHNIQUES IN order to prompt the people to devote a part of their time to earnest spiritual meditation. At first, the Torah

THE EFFECTIVE DISCOURSE ordained that offerings were ordered to be brought before Hashem. In time, however, many people lacked the pure feeling of faith. The Temple was destroyed and prayer took the place of offerings. But these also failed oftentimes to hold the full *kavannah* (concentration) of the worshipers. It became necessary, therefore, to add sermons by the rabbi. It is incumbent upon the preacher to deliver his message in simple terms, interpolated with parables and stories, expressions, epigrams and so forth. Every listener seems to possess an antagonistic inclination which bids him to turn away his thoughts from interest in faith and worship. The same spirit of mischief tries to counteract the effect of a sermon, but if the speaker is skilled at holding the attention of his audience, the yetzer hara will not be able to succeed in distracting the listener until it is too late; the religious teaching has already been absorbed in his mind and retained by his memory."

R' DOVID MOSHE OF CHORTKOV ATTESTED TO THE FOLLOWING STORY: "Before he died, my father could no longer go to pray at the *kloiz*

THE SOUND OF MASHIACH'S SHOFAR on Rosh Hashanah so I prayed with him in his room. His *davening* and *avodah* (service) were more magnificent and intense than ever before. When he had concluded his prayers he said to me: 'Today I heard *Mashiach* blow the shofar.' "

Later, the Chortkover said: "The shofar my father used was big and strange. Its sound was powerful, and the blasts were wondrously clear, but right after Rosh Hashanah the shofar disappeared and was seen no more."

IT HAPPENED ON THE EVE OF PESACH WHEN THE RIZHINER EXPLAINED the rules of *bedikas chametz* (the search for leaven) in the following

THE CHAMETZ OF THE HEART way: "Tonight we search for *chametz*, but we do not burn it before tomorrow morning. The search and the burning are symbolic of things to come. *Galus* (exile) is the night during which we allow the *chametz*, the meaner qualities of our people, to remain in the house. But when the morning of our *geulah* (redemption) comes, they are cast into the fire of our return, and altogether consumed. Then the words of *Yeshayah* (25:8) will be fulfilled to the fullest: *He will swallow up death forever and Hashem will wipe away tears from all faces.*

WHEN ASKED WHY HE INDULGED IN LAVISHNESS AND LUXURY, IN OPULENT and palatial surroundings, the Rizhiner explained as follows:

ON LIVING IN REGAL SPLENDOR AND LUXURY

"When a *tzaddik* lives in poverty, he has only limited conceptions of people's needs, and therefore only prays for them in terms of the basic necessities. However, when he enjoys comfort, he feels bold enough to pray that his chassidim too may have a life of comfort."

R' MOTTEL, THE REBBE OF CHERNOBYL, AND R' YISROEL, THE REBBE OF Rizhin chose to live majestically in magnificent and exquisite splendor, at the opposite extreme from the frugal lifestyle of their parents.

REASON FOR A MAJESTIC DIGNITY

When asked, the Rizhiner gave the following explanation. "Chassidus was burning like live coals and, therefore, was in danger of becoming rapidly extinct. Nowadays, however, we have spread ashes upon these coals, and so it is our hope that they will endure for many, many generations, meaning that the surface opulence concealed and tempered the inner fire."

THE RIZHINER DECLARED: "JUST AS THE HOLY LETTERS OF THE *ALEPH-beis* (Hebrew alphabet) are voiceless without the *nekudos* (vowel signs), and the vowel signs are

THE SYMBIOSIS OF TZADDIKIM AND CHASSIDIM

meaningless without the letters, so *tzaddikim* and chassidim are bound up with one another. The *tzaddikim* are the letters of the alphabet and the chassidim who journey to them are the vowel signs. The chassidim need the *tzaddik* and he needs them. Through the chassidim the *tzaddik* can be uplifted, or because of them he can sink, Hashem forbid! They carry his voice, spread his teachings in the world. Suppose that one of my chassidim is on the road and meets a carriage full of *maskilim* ('enlightened' ones). The chassid persuades the coachmen to let him ride next to him. Then, when the time comes to recite Minchah (the afternoon prayer), he gets down from his seat ready for *tefillah*, and *davens* while the carriage waits, and the waiting passengers are much annoyed and shout at the coachman and heap abuse on him. In the midst of all this, perhaps through all this, they experience a change of heart — and repent."

CONCERNING THE PASSUK IN THE TORAH, *WHEN ANY MAN FROM AMONG*

A REAL MAN *you would bring an offering to the Lord Hashem* (*Vayikra* 1:2), the Rizhiner said: "Only he who brings *himself* to Hashem as an offering may be called אָדָם, man."

THE RIZHINER COMMENTED: WE READ IN *YESHAYAH*: *LET FAVOR BE shown to the wicked, yet will he not learn righteousness* (26:10)? This teaches us

INTENDED that it is better not to learn the duties

TRANSGRESSION of piety if one does not intend to observe them. One who transgresses consciously cannot hope for mercy without *teshuvah* (repentance).

EXPLAINED THE RIZHINER: WE READ IN *TEHILLIM*: *AND HE FORSOOK THE Tabernacle of Shiloh, the tent which He had made to dwell among men*

THE HOLY (78:60). When Hashem gave Israel the Torah He

TEMPLE intended to dwell in the hearts of men; He did not want a dwelling place built for Him. But when Israel transgressed, He ordered a Holy Place to be built for the *Shechinah* to dwell. The prophet Yechezkel bears this out when he says: *Now, son of man, show the house to the House of Israel, that* *they may be ashamed of their iniquities. They should feel shame because their transgressions have made it necessary to build a Holy Temple* (43:10).

HASTEN AND GO UP TO MY FATHER AND TELL HIM, "THUS SAYS YOUR SON *Joseph: Hashem has made me lord of all Egypt"* (*Bereishis* 45:9). Asked

FOR HEAVEN'S SAKE
the Rizhiner: Why should that have been such good news for Yaakov? The answer is that the word שָׂמַנִי, "has made/set me," may be rendered as אֲנִי שָׂם , "I have put/set." Thus, the message which Joseph actually sought to convey to his aged father was not that he, Joseph, had come to great power but that "I established Hashem over all of Egypt"; that he, Joseph, had become the instrument to spread the ways of Hashem so that Hashem would become master of Egypt and all the world.

LET EVERY MAN ABIDE IN HIS PLACE; LET NO MAN GO OUT OF HIS PLACE שְׁבוּ אִישׁ תַּחְתָּיו אַל יֵצֵא אִישׁ מִמְּקֹמוֹ (*Shemos* 16:29). This can also be

THE RIGHT SEAT
rendered, said the Rizhiner, "... let every man abide *below* his place ..." (תַּחְתָּיו, "in his place," literally means "under him"). This means that it behooves every man to seat himself in a place lower than that due him according to his station. "And let no man go out of his place: Under no circumstance may he seat himself in a place higher than the one rightfully due him."

AND I TOOK HOLD OF THE TWO TABLETS, AND CAST THEM OUT OF MY TWO *hands, and broke them before your eyes* (*Devarim* 9:17).

THE FLYING LETTERS
Only the stone tablets that were "before your eyes" were broken. The letters which had been engraved upon them flew away and remained

---

1. *Pseudo Jonathan* ad loc.; *Pesachim* 87b.

whole[1] [cf. Rashi: *And (Joseph) bound (Shimon) before their eyes (Bereishis 42:24)*: This means that he bound Shimon only while his brothers were watching, but later freed him and gave him food and drink.]

UNDERSTANDING

A CHASSID ONCE COMPLAINED TO R' YISROEL THAT HE LACKED ALL THREE things which help bring mental comfort to a man: "a beautiful dwelling, a beautiful wife and beautiful clothes," as taught by the Sages (*Berachos* 57b). R' Yisroel answered him: "These three things make it possible only to broaden a man's understanding and mental tranquillity, but not to create them within him: Therefore, what good will they do for you?"

ON SERVING THE CREATOR

THE RIZHINER ONCE REMARKED: "THIS IS THE SERVICE MAN MUST ENGAGE in all of his lifetime; to transform matter into form (*gashmius* into *ruchniyus*), to purify the flesh and to let the light penetrate the darkness until the darkness itself shines and there is no longer any separation between the two. As it is written: *And there was evening and there was morning — one day*" (*Bereishis* 1:5). On another occasion, he said: "One should not make a big performance about serving Hashem. Does the hand brag when it carries out the will of the heart?"

THE PHANTOM INTRUDER

THE STORY IS TOLD THAT THE RIZHINER WOULD CLIMB TO THE ATTIC AND stay there for about two hours. During that time his *gabbai*, Shmulik, who accompanied him, waited sitting on the stairs. Once, the Rebbe's daughter wanted to fetch something from a cupboard in the attic and found Shmulik sitting on the stairs weeping. She asked him why he was crying. "Someone," he said, "slipped me a lot of money so that I should let him go in to the Rebbe, and now he is inside." He opened his hand and showed her the money. Just then the Rizhiner opened up the door. There was no one in the room. Shmulik looked at his palm and there lay only a few shards of clay.

THEY ASKED THE RIZHINER: "WHAT DOES IT MEAN WHEN IT IS SAID OF someone that he possesses *ruach hakodesh* (Divine Inspiration)?"

POSSESSING RUACH HAKODESH
The *tzaddik* answered, "If a man really has spirit and he does not allow it to become impure, that is called *ruach hakodesh*."

THE RIZHINER EXPOUNDED ON THE VERSE: *He took note of their distress when he heard* רִנָּתָם *(their outcry)* (Tehillim 106:44). But the

TYPES OF JOY
word רִנָּתָם is usually rendered as "their glad cry," or joy. How did such an outcry betoken distress? Often, one can ascertain a person's anguish by what makes him happy. If he rejoices because he has earned a single coin, we may deduce from it how poor he really is. If he is happy because his punishment has been suspended, we may realize thereby how greatly he feared that punishment.

ONCE, ON A ROSH HASHANAH THAT OCCURRED ON A SHABBOS, THE Rizhiner commented: "On such a day the shofar that heralds the

THE SHABBOS ROSH HASHANAH
New Year is not blown (*Rosh Hashanah* 29b). The reason is that on this day Hashem Himself blows the shofar. He surely knows how to blow the shofar! For this reason, on this day our hope is so enlivened because the Source of Divine mercy Himself has given it life."

REMARKED THE RIZHINER: "I DISLIKE THE MAN WHO IS LIKE SNOW, AT

WHITE AS SNOW first white and pure, but later, muddy and dirty."

"WHAT MAKES A REAL *TZADDIK*?" ASKED THE RIZHINER. "THE TRUE *TZADDIK* should be like quicksilver, which instantly indicates any change of

THE TRUE   temperature. A true *tzaddik* must, likewise, instantly register the lack of calm and peace of

TZADDIK   mind among his chassidim."

JUST LIKE SOMEONE WHO, PREPARING TO SPLIT A TREE WITH AN AX, TAKES a powerful swing at it and misses, the ax instead falling into the

    earth, so it is when the *tzaddik* speaks to

ON DEAF EARS   people in order to stimulate their hearts

    to the service of Hashem, but they do not heed his words. They admire only the sagacity and masterful rhetoric of his words: *And they shall hear my words that are sweet, as when one cleaves and breaks up the earth (Tehillim* 41:7). The Kotzker is quoted saying, "All that is thought should not be said. All that is said should not be written. All that is written should not be printed."

THE RIZHINER AS WELL AS HIS SUCCESSORS ALWAYS SPOKE ABOUT *Mashiach* and redemption from the *galus* (diaspora). Once he

BACK TO THE   prophesied that the time would come

    when every country would be ruled by

HOLY LAND   the enemies of Israel, who would force us (Jews) to return to the Holy Land. "It will be a disgrace," he said, "if after so long an exile, we return for this reason. But be this as it may, rewards will attend us in Zion if, for once, we can escape from our enemies."

SAID THE RIZHINER, "I WILL ILLUSTRATE FOR YOU THE NECESSITY OF WARMTH in the service of Hashem. The Torah commands one who is unclean

A FROZEN HEART to make an ablution in water (*mikveh*) and thereby be cleansed (*Vayikra* 14:9), but if the water is frozen, how can we immerse ourselves in it? So, too, a frozen heart cannot purify an unclean life."

ONCE A MAN CAME TO THE RIZHINER AND COMPLAINED ABOUT HIS horrible disease, stating that his affliction interfered with learning

LEARNING AND SUFFERING and praying.
The Rebbe put his hand on the sick man's shoulder and said: "How do you know, my friend, what is more pleasing to Hashem, your studying or your suffering?"

ONCE THE RIZHINER URGED A MERCHANT TO INCREASE HIS DONATION TO A certain charity. "Rebbe," the man objected, "I don't mix in your

NO ONE'S BUSINESS business, please don't mix in mine."
"*Nu, nu* (well, well)," replied the Rebbe. "We will see." Some time passed and the man went bankrupt.

ONE PESACH NIGHT WHEN THE RIZHINER WAS CONDUCTING HIS SEDER and he was at the concluding statement, he stopped and exclaimed:

REAL EMBAR- RASSMENT "G-d of the Universe! Each year I repeat *l'shanah habaah b'Yerushalayim,* praying that next year we will be in Yerushalayim, and yet we are still in exile. I am really embarrassed in front of my gentile servant."

R' Yisroel of Rizhin would say: "A popular proverb says that a fool gives while a wise man takes. This refers to those who give

GIVING AND TAKING *tzedakah.* A fool who gives *tzedakah* thinks he is giving, while a wise man who gives *tzedakah* knows that by his giving he is in reality taking."

The Rizhiner would say: "If a man gives up hope of recovering what he has lost and another subsequently finds the object, it be-

NEVER GIVE UP HOPE longs to the finder. That rule was intended as a penalty to the one who gives up hope. This teaches us that a Jew may never give up hope."

A classic example of the Rizhiner's views on *yichus* (lineage), in a humorous sense, is the following parable:

A PARABLE ON YICHUS A nobleman had a faithful dog who followed him everywhere and guarded his mansion. The dog grew older and could no longer perform his duty but the nobleman did not have the heart to have him killed, so he had the dog wrapped in the skins of a lion, a leopard, a bear and a wolf and sent him into the forest to the other animals.

At that time, the lion, the king of the forest, was holding court, when he noticed that the other animals were deserting him. "What's happening?" he asked the fox.

"A new king of the beasts has come to the forest, a combination of a lion, a leopard, a bear and a wolf." Frightened, the lion asked the fox to investigate. The fox went and bowed down to the new king and humbly asked, "Who are you, sir?"

My great-great-grandfather was a lion," he answered proudly.

The fox bowed again and asked, "Who are you, sir?"

"My great-grandfather was a leopard."

The fox asked again, "But who are you?"

"My grandfather was a bear."

"And who are you, sir?"

"My father was a wolf."

"And who are *you*, sir?"

"I? I am a dog."

The fox bowed and ran back to report to the lion.

Famed ancestors are like a string of zeros. If any number stands at the head of the row, the zeros multiply it, each one by tenfold more than the previous zero. But if a descendant is himself a zero, the string of zeros which stands beside him is of no value.

SAID THE RIZHINER: "*YICHUS* IS LIKE AN UMBRELLA. IT IS USED ONLY when there is a man under it."

R' YISROEL OF RUZHIN ONCE WENT FOR A STROLL WITH ONE OF HIS ELDER chassidim who was a grandson of R' Yechezkel Landau, author of

THE ANTAGONISTIC SOUL

the *Noda B'Yehudah*, and an opponent of Chassidus.

R' Yisroel: "Since you are the grandson of the Rav of Prague, let me tell you what I heard from R' Avrohom Yehoshua Heschel of Apt, who in turn heard it from R' Yechiel Michel of Zlotchov, at the time that the *tzaddik* of Zlotchov was suffering from the antagonism of your grandfather. R' Yechiel Michel said: 'Harbor him no grudge, for Hashem commanded him to oppose the chassidim. You see, when the heavenly court decided that it was time for the soul of the Baal Shem Tov to descend to this world, all kinds of prosecuting angels spoke up, arguing that if this were to be allowed, the *geulah* (Messianic redemption) would be brought about before its time. But at that moment whole choirs of kindlier voices made themselves heard, so it was decided that the soul of the Baal Shem Tov would indeed be sent down to this world, but at the same time another lofty soul would be dispatched down there, to dwell in a man who would also be a leader of his generation, but an antagonist to the teachings of the Baal Shem Tov and his disciples. That men was your grandfather, the sage of Prague. Thus it was R' Yechezkel Landau who caused the soul of the Baal Shem Tov to come down here; without him this would not have taken place. For as our Sages say: Merits are brought about through the meritorious (*Shabbos* 32a).' "

THE COMING OF *MASHIACH* IS DISCUSSED IN MANY OF OUR HOLY BOOKS. There were various indications given as to when he would come,

CONCERNING MASHIACH all based on Biblical verses. That being the case, why did he not come at the time foretold? It is impossible to say that those people really did not grasp the truth. But, actually, as our Sages said, "The coming of *Mashiach* is totally dependent upon repentance" (*Zohar* 3, 122). They have asked: "When will *Mashiach* come?" and have answered, "Today, if we will listen to the voice of Hashem." The earlier Sages, who predicted the advent of *Mashiach,* were not wrong, because he could have come on that day, if only there had been repentance on the part of the people.

THE RIZHINER ONCE SAID: "A *TZADDIK* IS LIKE THE ROOT OF A TREE AND his chassidim are like branches. If one branch is lost it causes great

LIKE A TREE pain to the root. Similarly, if a chassid goes from one *tzaddik* to another, it causes great strife. However, they may all come to me because my name represents the Name of Hashem in its twelve combinations of the Tetragrammaton in correct order."

IN THE BOOK *BEIS AHARON* BY THE RABBI OF OCHAKOV, ON *PIRKEI AVOS,*

IN THE END he writes that he heard from the Rizhiner that — in the end — it will become known that everything comes from Hashem. And all souls will become pure, because none will be driven away. Therefore the prophets said that in the future, *And your people are all righteous* (*Yeshayah* 60:21).

THERE IS A POPULAR SAYING: MAN IS LIKENED TO A CLOCK. THE RIZHINER said that a man should conduct himself like a pendulum that hangs on

THE PENDULUM the wall and swings back and forth. When the house starts to burn, it does not affect the clock at all until the fire reaches it. So a man should be: As long as affliction does not affect him physically he should be willing to accept it with love. In case he is physically afflicted he should then pray to Hashem to save him (*Michtav MiEliyahu*).

ONCE, THE RIZHINER WAS IN THE TOWN OF RADAUTZ, BUKOVINA. ALL THE people gathered to greet him. Among them there was one whom the

SINNER OR HERETIC chassidim felt did not have complete faith in Hashem. On Shabbos, at the *tisch*, the Rizhiner said that many kinds of sinners come to him, but they do not disturb him. However, if a heretic comes, this does upset him and he cannot tolerate it.

SAID THE RIZHINER: "PEOPLE SAY THAT WHEN ONE SPEAKS ABOUT THE BAAL Shem Tov after Shabbos it is a good omen for making a living.

SPEAKING OF TZADDIKIM When one speaks about R' Zusya of Anipoli or his brother, R' Elimelech of Lizhensk, it helps further fear of Hashem and enhances fertility. But I think that it was not necessarily on account of these *tzaddikim*, not necessarily after Shabbos, nor for these specific things. Rather the meaning is that, regarding every *tzaddik*, every time we speak about him it is helpful in every possible way."

"IF ONE GOES BUT DOES NOT ACCOMPLISH, HE GETS A REWARD FOR going" (*Avos* 5:17). The Rizhiner explained this to mean that if a

THE REWARD person goes to a *tzaddik* and the *tzaddik* is unable to do anything for him, he still gets a reward. What is the reward? It is the fact that he went. This means that when he finally comes before Hashem above, he will be able to ask permission that he be taken to *the tzaddik* that he went to during his lifetime.

⚜

A CHASSID OF THE RIZHINER ONCE SUCCUMBED TO TEMPTATION AND sinned. Afterwards, he was very remorseful, but could not bring

THE RIGHT VERSE himself to show his face at the Rebbe's *hoif* (court), and so he stayed away.

A long time passed and one day the man asked himself, "How much longer must I punish myself and stay away? Why should I keep myself from visiting my Rebbe and teacher? Whatever may happen, I must go back to my Rebbe." Weighed down by his conscience, the chassid forced himself to go back to Rizhin. When he came before the Rebbe, he said, full of shame, "I haven't come to the Rebbe for some time because I have sinned." The Rizhiner merely commented, "Go and look up what the Targum says on the verse: *If the spirit that dominates rises upon you, do not abandon your place* (*Koheles* 10:4)." The chassid left the room and hurried to open the Book of *Koheles*, and this is what he read:

"If the spirit of the *yetzer hara* dominates you and seeks to overcome you, do not abandon that best refuge that you have always had, for the words of the Torah were created to bring healing to this world and to cause great sins to be forgotten before Hashem."

The man read these words and understood. Comforted and as a sincere penitent, he resumed his pilgrimage to his Rebbe.

⚜

THE RIZHINER COMMENTED: "IT IS STATED: *WHEN EISAV MY BROTHER should meet you and ask you, saying, 'Whose are you? Where are you go-*

GIFT TO EISAV

ing? For whom are these before you?' Then you shall say: 'They are your servant Yaakov's, it is a present sent to my lord' (Bereishis 32:18). This can be interpreted as fol-lows: When Eisav should meet you — Eisav is the *yetzer hara* (evil inclination) — and sometimes it is he who asks you to give a dis-course on religious subjects before the Children of Israel. You should ask yourself: *Whose are you; and where are you going?* —mean-ing: take a close look at who is anxious to hear Torah subjects taught to them; and what trend will your teaching take: whether it will take a holy turn or be diverted to Satan's camp. Also, make it your busi-ness to inquire *for whom are these before you?* — implying: Find out if these people are in need of learning new interpretations of the Law to satisfy the yearning of their souls. And when you are convinced that all is in good order, you shall say to your servant Yaakov — that is, even after your careful reflection, you still cannot be sure that your Torah lessons are directed absolutely to Yaakov, that is, to the *yetzer tov* (the good inclination), or they are in the category of a gift to send to Eisav, meaning that your urge to good may be due to an ulterior motive fabricated by the *yetzer hara.*"

ONE OF THE RIZHINER'S CHASSIDIM USUALLY VISITED HIM ON A REGULAR basis. He then stopped for his time was taken up with his business.

THE BETTER CHOICE

Then, all of a sudden, his business began to dwindle day by day. Finally he decided to visit the Rizhiner again, to have him *daven* for him that his business fortunes should improve. The Rizhiner told him the story of two brothers who lived in the same house, in a small village. After some time they became angry with each other and did-n't speak to one another. One of the brothers made a wedding, but although the other brother attended, he refused to join in the cele-bration. So angry was he that when he heard the music and dancing he stopped up his ears. One of the musicians went over to the other brother, the *baal hasimchah*, and told him that if he gave him a bottle of liquor, the musician could then get the recalcitrant brother to dance. The brother agreed. The musician played a very beautiful melody and he got the angry brother to come and dance in a very undignified manner. The musician then called out to the dancing brother and said: "Your dancing was so undignified that you looked ridiculous." The dancer answered, "It is better that I should look ridiculous rather than that I should remain angry with my brother."

Indeed, it would have been better if the businessman had looked ridiculous by taking "precious" time from his business to maintain closeness to his Rebbe.

A *BAAL TESHUVAH* WITH A MOST SINFUL PAST ONCE HANDED R' MOTTEL OF Chernobyl a *kvitel* on which he had listed all his grave sins, and

THE WAY TO REPENT

asked the Rebbe to guide him as to how to do complete *teshuvah* and correct his behavior.

"I am an old man," said the Rebbe, "and I no longer have the strength to undertake the difficult task of rehabilitating you. I suggest you go to the Rizhiner. He is still a young man, he will surely help you." The man traveled to the Rizhiner who attentively read his list of sins and prescribed for him a *derech hatikkun* (a course of repentance). First, he was to be fastidious about not saying any prayer or even the simplest blessing by heart, but by reading every word carefully from a *siddur*. Secondly, whenever the Rebbe conducted a *tisch*, the *baal teshuvah* was to look at him attentively during the entire time.

The Rizhiner's son, R' Dovid Moshe of Chortkov, later attested that he knew the penitent who in the course of time developed to be a respectable and pious man.

"But you should not be surprised," the Chortkover went on, "at the seemingly easy regimen for *teshuvah* that my father prescribed for him. Once he fulfilled his guidelines faithfully, from that point on he knew exactly how to behave. In fact, he did continue to repent sincerely and purposefully, rectifying his conduct step by step."

THE RIZHINER WAS ONCE APPROACHED BY A HEARTBROKEN PENITENT (named Meir, a grandson of R' Yaakov Emden), who complained

THE ETERNAL FORGIVER that, as many times as he did penance with good intentions to remain righteous and do good, just as many times he fell back and reverted to his sinful ways. The Rebbe consoled him and explained: "There are different noun forms found in the Yom Kippur *Amidah*, in reference to Hashem the Forgiver. Sometimes he is called *Mochel veSole'ach* (מוֹחֵל וְסוֹלֵחַ — He Who pardons and forgives), at other times He is referred to as *Solchon u'Mocholon* (סָלְחָן וּמָחֳלָן — Forgiver and Pardoner)." The Rizhiner explained: "The word *Sole'ach* refers to one who forgives because he is in a forgiving mood for some other, external reasons — sometimes he forgives and sometimes not; whereas *Solchon* refers to one who is accustomed to forgive time after time." The Rizhiner continued, "We deduce this from the distinction the Talmud (*Bava Metzia* 33a) makes between *rovetz* (רוֹבֵץ — an animal lying under the burden), and *ravtzon* (רַבְצָן — an animal that habitually lies down every time a burden is placed on its back).

"Therefore, even if after Hashem has forgiven you and you repeat the same sin, He will forgive you again and again, as long as you do *teshuvah* sincerely. This is the reason we call Him *Solchon* — the Forgiver."

IT WAS SHABBOS *PARASHAS YISRO*, THE SHABBOS ON WHICH R' MOSHE of Savrani passed away. The Rizhiner was seated at his *seudah*

LAST FAREWELL *shlishis tisch* surrounded by chassidim. He was expounding the Biblical verse "And Moshe went up to Hashem ..." (*Shemos* 19:3). At its conclusion, he said:

"There were once two friends who were watchmen in a forest, and when one of them would call to his friend, the other would call out loudly in return. One day the second watchman left the forest. When the first watchman called out and heard no voice in return, he knew that his friend had gone far away, and was no longer with him in the forest."

On *Shabbos Shirah*, the Shabbos of Song, when the song of Moshe and Israel at the Sea of Reeds is read from the Torah, the

ON SHABBOS SHIRAH

Sadagorer commented, "It is not written that the lsraelites sang the song *immediately* after they crossed the Reed Sea. First they had to reach the rung of absolute faith, as it is written: *and they believed in the Hashem, and in Moshe his servant* (*Shemos* 14:31). Only then come the words: *Then Moshe and the Children of Israel sang this song to Hashem* (ibid. 15:1). Only he who truly believes can sing the song."

Said the Rebbe of Sadagora: "Every nation has its own melody, and none sings the melody of another. But Israel sings all of them, in order

THE SONG OF ISRAEL

to elevate them to Hashem. Thus in the *perek of Shirah* (chapter of Song), every creature on earth and every bird voices his own song, but Israel composes a song out of all their songs in order to elevate them to Hashem."

Once on *Shabbos Shirah* when the *shirah* is read from the Torah, the Sadagorer was asked: "Why is it customary to spread *kasha* (buck-

ON FEEDING THE BIRDS

wheat) and bread crumbs for the birds outside the house today?" The Rebbe replied: "A king had a small pavilion built outside his palace where he could enjoy a little solitude. Nobody was allowed to enter it but the king, not even his servants. Only a songbird shared that space with the king, and he listened to its song, which was more precious to him than all the music of his singers. In the hour when the waters of the sea were split, all the angels and *seraphim* sang praise to Hashem. But He was listening only to the song of his little bird, Israel. That is why we feed the birds on this day."

ONCE A JEW FROM ERETZ YISROEL LEFT THE COUNTRY IN ORDER TO COLLECT money so that he could marry off his daughter. He approached R'

THE AIR OF ERETZ YISRAEL

Yisroel of Rizhin. The Rebbe, seeing that he was an honest man who did not want to remain outside the Holy Land for any length of time, told him to go to R' Meir of Premishlan and that he would help him.

The man arrived in Premishlan and sought lodging for the night. At that exact time, R' Meir sent messengers looking for a guest from Eretz Yisroel, for he felt the presence of the air of Eretz Yisroel. They found the man and brought him to R' Meir, and he explained that he had been sent by the Rizhiner. Upon hearing this, R' Meir immediately took out a bag of coins that he kept under his bed and gave him all its contents, provided that he immediately return to the Holy Land. The puzzled man asked the Rebbe, "Why such a rush?" R' Meir explained: "While Meir'l loves the air of Eretz Yisroel, that air is better when it remains in its own home."

IT IS TOLD THAT THE RIZHINER WAS BOTHERED BY A QUESTION: WHY WAS it that the chassidim who moved to Eretz Yisroel settled primarily in

WHY NOT JERUSALEM?

the Galilee and not Jerusalem? None of the conventional answers satisfied him, so he finally asked R' Moshe of Kobrin, "Why is it that R' Menachem Mendel of Vitebsk did not settle in Jerusalem, site of the *Beis HaMikdash,* and instead established the chassidic movement in Safed and Tiberias?"

R' Moshe replied simply, "R' Menachem Mendel feared the sanctity of Jerusalem."

A CHASSID WISHED TO SETTLE IN ERETZ YISROEL, SO HE CAME TO THE Rizhiner for a blessing. " Know that Eretz Yisroel is like a feather

THE DOWN QUILT

bed, a down quilt," said the Rebbe. "In the winter, a man

crawls under the quilt. At first it is very cold, but as it gathers up the warmth of the man's body, in turn it warms him. So it is with the Holy Land. If a man of fire comes to live in her, she adds the heat of holiness to him in his devotion. But to a cold soul, she remains as cold as she was before. If a stone crawls under the quilt, the stone does not warm the quilt, and neither does the quilt warm the stone."

THE RIZHINER ENDEAVORED TO RETURN THE JEWISH PEOPLE TO ITS HONOR and glory. He demanded of them that they be well mannered, well **STANDARDS** dressed, well spoken and polite and pleasant to all their neighbors, both Jew and gentile. All this in order that the Name of Heaven should become loved through their behavior as our Sages demanded (*Yoma* 86a).

R' YISROEL OF RIZHIN RECOUNTED THAT R' ZUSYA OF ANIPOLI WAS once present in the home of his Rebbe, the Maggid of Mezritch, **R' ZUSYA'S** when a man entered and proceeded to recite his list of requests. With the penetrating per- **LESSON** ception which accompanies the Divine gift of *ruach hakodesh*, R' Zusya saw that this man's sins were grave indeed. He was indignant. How dare the man stand so fearlessly and impertinently before the holy R' Dov Ber of Mezritch! "A man who has done such things!" he exclaimed, "Is such a man not ashamed to stand there before the *tzaddik* without at least a glimmer of *teshuvah*?!"

After the man left, R' Zusya expressed his profound regret at having spoken thus in the presence of his Rebbe, whereupon the Maggid gave him blessing that from that day on he would never see evil in a fellow Jew, only good.

WHEN THE ROPSHITZER WAS VISITING THE RIZHINER, THE RIZHINER SAID, "You are considered a sage, so please tell us a story." R' Naftoli com-

TRICK FOR A MISER plied and told an astounding story about how he had once deceived a notorious village miser so that he would have the merit of charity in the World to Come. R' Naftoli impersonated the son-in-law of the famous wonder-worker of the second century, R' Meir Baal Haness. He asked for a *nedavah* (donation) and, surprisingly, the miser gave him some money. The Ropshitzer and his friends sat down to drink *l'chaim*. The Rizhiner commented, "I knew that you were a sage, but not like this."

After the Ropshitzer left, the Rizhiner remarked, "R' Naftoli possesses the wisdom of King Shlomo."

R' AARON MARCUS WRITES IN HIS BOOK, *HACHASSIDUS*: "I HEARD FROM R' Avrohom Twerski, the Maggid of Trisk, that when he was vis-

INNER FLAME iting a Ukrainian town, the room in which he stayed had a large iron stove that radiated great heat, but when the fire was almost out, the room was as cold as ice. One local man mentioned it and the Rebbe answered, 'That oven epitomizes the nature of a young chassid. One minute he is inflamed like a torch of fire and shortly afterwards he is as cold as ice.' "

The Rizhiner said, "When the Holy *Chozeh* (Seer) of Lublin lived, Chassidus was like a torch of fire rising up, and when he passed away, it cooled off. My uncle, R' Mottel of Chernobyl, and I cover the coal and embers with ashes. To the naked eye it seems that there is no flame, but in spite of this the fire is alive within."

THE RIZHINER PRAYED IN A SPECIAL SIDE ROOM OF HIS *BEIS midrash*, as do all his descendants. When he would finish his *daven-*

TURNING THE PAGE *ing*, he would move the doorknob as a sign that the *chazzan*, the *shliach tzibbur*, should continue the *davening*. One Yom Kippur during *Ne'ilah*, the Rebbe gave no sign that he had completed his *davening*, although the hour was late. They waited for two hours, still fasting and in fear. Finally, R' Sholom Yosef, his eldest son, took courage and entered his father's room. He approached the *shtender* (lectern) where the Rebbe's *machzor* lay and turned the page. Moments later the Rebbe signaled that he had completed his prayers.

When R' Sholom Yosef was asked what had happened, he answered, "I realized that my father stood before Hashem in such fear that he did not dare lift his hand to turn the page of the *machzor*. Since he did not wish to *daven* from memory, he could not continue, but stood in silence, trembling. I turned the page and he was able to complete the *tefillos*."

THE RIZHINER ASKED R' GERSHON OF KOLOMAYA IF HE HAD EVER BEEN in the presence of *tzaddikim*. R' Gershon said that he often traveled to

THE CREDIT DUE R' Uri, the Seraph (fiery angel) of Strelisk. The Rebbe asked R' Gershon to tell him something of the Strelisker.

"Once," said R' Gershon, "the Seraph asked me to write the title page of a manuscript. I told him that great patience was required, and that it would be preferable to do it after *davening*. He told me that it was not his manuscript and that, being ready to die *al kiddush Hashem* at any moment, he might not return home after *davening* and therefore people will attribute the manuscript to him, with all the *divrei Torah* in it. This was the reason he asked me to write the author's name immediately."

THE RIZHINER'S MOTHER RECEIVED A MESSAGE FROM HIM WHILE HE WAS IN prison saying that she was responsible for his being interned.

A HEAVY PRICE She explained that once her son had told her that Heaven had informed him that it was in his power to bring an elevated soul into the world, a soul so sublime that it appears only once in a thousand years. But he would have to accept suffering to do so. He had asked her if he should agree to the condition. She had answered, "What does a father not do for his children?"

He had agreed to accept the suffering and his youngest son, R' Shraga Feivish of Husyatin, was born. Now that he was imprisoned, he wished to remind his mother of her advice, so that she need not feel distressed over him.

A WEALTHY MAN, WHO HAD JUST RETURNED FROM ERETZ YISROEL CAME TO visit the Rizhiner. "How was your trip?" asked the Rebbe. The man

THE BEHOLDER replied, without enthusiasm, "It had been disappointing." Deeply disturbed, the Rebbe replied: "Let me tell you a story: There was once a rich man who had several daughters for whom he made very fine matches with *talmidei chachamim* (Torah scholars), except for his youngest daughter. There had been no one suitable and he had had to settle for a simple tailor. As was the custom, the father would buy beautiful jewelry for the bride as part of the dowry, but this bride refused to accept any. She said angrily, 'What for? When my sisters married brilliant scholars and received jewelry, that was befitting, because they deserved it. But my *chassan*, a simple tailor, wouldn't even know how to appreciate such jewelry. So why bother?' The same applies to Eretz Yisroel," concluded the Rizhiner. "It is a land of much bounty and spiritual beauty. But that depends on the eye of the beholder. Some will see the sublime beauty of Eretz Yisroel while others unfortunately will be blind to it."

A LOVER OF NATURE AND A CONNOISSEUR OF AESTHETICS AND TRUE beauty, the Rizhiner once exclaimed, "Look around you; works of

THE REAL MASTERPIECE art are cherished, esteemed and protected, while man, Hashem's masterpiece, lies in the dust!"

ON THE DYNASTY OF R' BORUCH OF MEZHIBOZH, THE RIZHINER SAID: "In his presence the wise man is able to acquire bucketsful of *yiras*

PERSONALITY OF OTHER TZADDIKIM

Shamayim (fear of Heaven) but the foolish man, by the same token, only increases his folly there."

"A GENUINE *TZADDIK* IS GREATER THAN AN ANGEL. AN ANGEL CANNOT ascend to a higher level but the *tzaddik* can do so. My grandfather

THE TZADDIK IS GREATER THAN AN ANGEL

Avrohom was an angel in his body, but a *tzaddik* in his soul."

"HE WHO WISHES FOR HAPPINESS MUST BEAR WITH PATIENCE A MEASURE OF unhappiness. Light can enter only where darkness has been."

A RABBI POURED OUT HIS HEART TO THE RIZHINER, SAYING, "WHEN I study a subject of the Torah, I feel encompassed by holy light, but

THE ORIGINAL LIGHT

when I halt my studies, I feel chilled and surrounded by darkness." The Rizhiner commented: "Whenever you are not oc-

cupied with the study of Torah, occupy yourself with practice of a mitzvah, and then the light will not fail you." He continued: "The light which you feel around you during your studies is the light borrowed from the souls of the ages. However, a light derived from your performance of mitzvos is your own light."

IN THE DAYS OF THE BAAL SHEM TOV, THERE WAS A MAN WHO GLEANED from the holy books that the Divine Spirit (*ruach hakodesh*) would

IDLE TALK

rest upon man if he refrained from idle talk for forty consecutive days. He did so. However, at the end of the fortieth day he felt no sense of the Divine Spirit. He went to the Baal Shem Tov to ask him the reason.

"Were you careful about every word that passed your lips?" asked the Rebbe.

"Yes, Rebbe," said the man. "I didn't say a word."

"Did you say *Tehillim*?"

"That, yes. With great ease."

"Well, then," said the Baal Shem Tov, "now we've found the answer. If it was with great ease, that was your idle talk."

ONE OF THE CHASSIDIM OF THE RIZHINER WAS AN EXTREMELY WEALTHY MAN. He had a fabulously beautiful cup of Eliyahu. Every year he would

THE STRANGER

embellish it with more rare and precious gems. In the course of time he lost his fortune and became so poor that that year he was not even going to be able to buy food for Pesach. No one was yet aware of his poverty, and since he would never accept charity, he suggested to his wife that they should sell the cup of Eliyahu. His wife said that it would be better to starve than to sell the cup that they had so beautified to honor Eliyahu HaNavi, may he be remembered for good.

It was the eve of Pesach and the man went early to the *beis midrash*. In his absence, a distinguished-looking individual came to his house and asked if he could be their guest for the Seder, since he was a stranger in town. The woman, not without embarrassment, told him of their misfortune, and that there was no food for Pesach. He responded by giving her money to buy all the necessary provisions. The husband remained in the shul until all the congregants had left, not wanting anyone to sense his dejection. As he approached his house, he was surprised to see light through the windows. When he opened the door he saw a perfectly set Seder table. His wife told him of all that had happened.

They waited for the stranger. When he entered, he blessed them with a blessing for wealth and *hatzlachah* (success). After the blessing, he immediately disappeared. They realized that this was not an ordinary event.

The following Yom Tov, they traveled to the Rizhiner and told him what had happened. The Rebbe told them that they had been visited by Eliyahu HaNavi. Because they had so greatly valued his cup, they had been found worthy of a visitation. He had appeared to the woman twice, because it was she who refused to sell the cup.

ONE OF THE RIZHINER'S CHASSIDIM, A *SHOCHET*, WAS KNOWN FOR HIS hospitality. After the death of his wife he remarried, but his new wife

THE BITTER WATERS would not receive a single guest into her house. When the Rebbe found out about this behavior, he summoned the chassid to Rizhin and asked him why he had ceased his tradition of hospitality. The *shochet* replied that it was his wife's fault but that surely he did not have to divorce her for her attitude. The Rizhiner reacted by quoting the verse: *And when they came to Marah, they could not drink of the waters of Marah for they were bitter, therefore they called her name Marah* (*Shemos* 15:23). In the original context, "they" refers to the waters of Marah, and "her name" refers to the name of the place, Marah, which means bitter. The *shochet* understood the Rebbe's reference to himself and to his inhospitable wife: *For they were bitter, therefore they called her name Marah.*

A CHASSID ONCE CAME TO THE RIZHINER AND COMPLAINED, "REBBE, I AM suffering tremendous pain and I cannot bear it."

SUFFERING REWARDED "Let me tell you a story," said the *tzaddik*. "A man died and came before the heavenly tribunal to be judged. They placed all his mitzvos on one balance pan and all his *aveiros* in the other, and the *aveiros* outweighed the mitzvos. One of the angels stood up for him and said, 'This man has had many troubles in his life, it is only right that his suffering should be counted with his mitzvos.' Then they placed all his suffering on the pan of his mitzvos and they did not outweigh the *aveiros*, and the man was sentenced to *Gehinnom*. As he was being led away he cried out,

'G-d of the Universe, You have the power to do anything. Couldn't You have made me suffer a little more?' "

A YOUNG CHASSID FROM THE TOWN OF KORITZ TOLD THE REBBE OF HIS plans to move to another town to become a *melamed* (teacher) be-

PRIZE FOR FAITH

cause he could not find *parnassah* in Koritz.
    "What?" exclaimed the Rizhiner. "Another teacher!? No! I want you to become rich!" And so great was the chassid's faith in his Rebbe that he went into business and soon after became very rich.

ONCE A CHASSID ASKED THE RIZHINER TO SHOW HIM THE RIGHT WAY OF religious conduct in daily life. The answer was short: "Whatever is for-

DELIBERATION

bidden is forbidden, and even that which is permitted, do it without undue haste."

SAID THE RIZHINER: "JUST AS THE HEART DECIDES WHEN IT IS TIME TO eat or drink, so should the heart require prayer when it is time to

THE REMINDING SIGNAL

pray, or to do the other mitzvos." Once the Rizhiner raised his hand and said: "My hand is requesting me to don *tefillin*."

THE RIZHINER COMMENTED ON THE WORDS (*VAYIKRA* 11:19), "וְאֶת הַחֲסִידָה.
The stork is listed among the contaminated birds. Rashi asks, 'Why

FALSE CHESSED

is it called *chassidah*? Because it displays kindness (*chessed*) toward others of its species, sharing food with them' (*Rashi, Chullin* 63a). The question is then: If she is so compassionate, why is she 'stigmatized' as a nonkosher bird? The answer is because it directs its kindness exclusively toward its fellows, but will not help other species. To Jews this is not an admirable characteristic."

A YOUNG MAN ONCE CAME TO THE RIZHINER AND IMPLORED HIM TO HELP him find a method to break his *yetzer hara.* The Rizhiner told him:

BREAKING THE INSTINCTUAL DRIVE

"You can break your back or your leg and even then you will not break your *yetzer hara.* But if you *daven,* learn and perform mitzvos with the right *kavannah,* the *yetzer hara* will disappear by itself."

AFTER THE PASSING OF REB URI OF STRELISK, HIS SON, R' SHLOMO, JOURNEYED to visit the Rizhiner. On his arrival, the Rizhiner asked him to repeat

PIETY AND HONESTY

some quotable saying or to tell of some noteworthy practice of his father, who was called the Seraph (fiery angel) on account of the ecstatic nature of his *davening.* R' Shlomo thereupon told him two things: First, every morning before Reb Uri went off to *daven,* he would go to the kitchen to exchange farewells with his *rebbetzin* and his children, being fearful lest his soul break loose from his body in the ecstatic *d'veikus* of his *davening.* Secondly, on each such occasion he used to say: "Keep in mind that the manuscripts in the chest were authored by my teacher, Reb Shlomo of Karlin, and not by me. And the Talmudic novellae appearing there should not be attributed to me."

The Rizhiner was very pleased and said that he valued the second statement even more than the first.

THE PSALMIST EXCLAIMS (62:13): "TO YOU, HASHEM, BELONGS

THE POWER OF L'CHAIM

lovingkindness because You repay man according to his deeds." This is difficult to understand because if Hashem pays man according to his deeds, why should this be a special kindness or *chessed*? The Rizhiner explained this by telling the following story.

A rich business man once bought a very expensive chandelier which he duly hung from the ceiling in his living room. However, he did not want to use it all the time. He arranged to have someone attach a cord to the chandelier, so that he could lower it when he wanted to use it and hoist it up when he did not. Once a poor man came to this rich man, hoping for a donation. On being shown into the room, he saw no one was around, but noticed the rope attached to the chandelier. He knew the value of the rope but he did not bother looking at the chandelier, for he had no appreciation for it. Accordingly, he cut the rope and the chandelier came crashing down.

The owner and his entire household ran into the living room and when they saw the precious chandelier was broken they got very upset. The master of the house took away the cap of the poor man who had cut the cord. His family looked at him in surprise . How was it possible that an almost worthless cap could pay for the expensive chandelier!? The rich man explained that his poor man had not intended to damage the valuable chandelier whose value he did not even appreciate. He had just wanted to take the cord. For this he would pay and not for something he had no intention of damaging. We find a similar thing, concluded the Rebbe, with Hashem. He makes us pay only for those things which we had the intention to transgress and possibly enjoy. But He does not make us pay for the repercussions that these sins may have in heaven, though the damage up there may have been very extensive.

THE FIRST TIME R' DOVID (DUDYE) ORTENBERG (THE *DAYAN* OF Berditchev) came to see the Rizhiner he came with his father. After

BRING THE CHILDREN

they left he told his father that he would like to visit the Rebbe again. His father told him: "Stay home and study Torah in the house rather than go to the Rebbe." They finally agreed to visit the Rebbe so that he should decide between them. The Rebbe said: "If they would all have real understanding they would all bring their children to the Rebbe."

WE READ IN THE TORAH, *HASHEM IS A WARRIOR; HASHEM IS HIS NAME* (*Shemos* 15:3). The *Midrash HaGadol* (ad loc.) states: "Hashem appeared at the sea as a mighty warrior; He

DIVINE GOODNESS appeared at Sinai as an old man full of compassion." Our Sages tell us (*Nedarim* 40a) that when old and wise people destroy something it is for a constructive purpose. One may not question Hashem's deeds even if they appear to be destructive for they are surely constructive. We must thank Him for the bad as well as for the good.

NO MAN SHALL GO UP WITH YOU [TO MOUNT SINAI] (*SHEMOS* 34:3). Said the Rizhiner: "Anyone who considers himself 'a man,' someone

ASCENSION important,'will not come up with you.' Such a man will not ascend the rungs of Torah study and fear of Hashem."

"IN RECOUNTING THE PROFESSIONS OF KAYIN AND HEVEL, THE TORAH states of Hevel, וַיְהִי, *he was a shepherd*, and of Kayin it says וְהָיָה, *he was a worker of the ground* (*Bereishis* 4:2). When

DIVINE FAVORITISM used in Scripture, the Hebrew word הָיָה denotes happiness. Kayin was happy that he was involved in material pursuits, and was not concerned about the spiritual. That is why Hashem paid heed to Hevel's sacrifice and not to Kayin's."

WHEN A PERSON REPENTS AND DIRECTS HIS LOVE TOWARDS HASHEM, HE thinks, "Why did I expend my love for physical things? Isn't it bet-

ON REPENTANCE ter for me to love the root of all roots?" His love is then rectified and he draws the sparks of holiness out of the husks (*klippos*).

ONE CANNOT CONSTANTLY BE IN A STATE OF AWE BEFORE HASHEM. BUT whenever anything holy is removed, it leaves a mark. The mark left

ON HUMILITY by such awe and reverence is humility.

WHEN R' LEVI YITZCHOK READ THE *TANYA* FOR THE FIRST TIME HE exclaimed ecstatically, "It is truly amazing that R' Shneur Zalman

SMALL BOOK was able to contain an infinite G-d in such a small book."

PART III:
THE RIZHINER'S CHILDREN

CHAPTER XXI

THE RIZHINER'S CHILDREN

THE RIZHINER SAID, "MY FATHER THE *TZADDIK* USED TO SAY, 'FROM my sons it will become known who I am,' and I say, 'From my sons it will become known who Hashem is.' "

He had ten children, six sons and four daughters, in the following order:

1. R' Sholom Yosef of Sadagora (1813-1851).

2. Chaya Malka (1814), married to R' Yitzchok of Skver (1812-1885), son of R' Mottel of Chernobyl.

3. R' Avrohom Yaakov of Sadagora (1819-1883).

4. Gittel Tova (1822), married to R' Yosef, son of R' Dovid Manzon, a renowned banker of Berditchev. Their son, R' Levi Yitzchok of Ozierni, was the author of *Becha Yevarech Yisroel*.

5. R' Menachem Nochum of Shtefanesht (1823-1868).

6. Miriam (1826-1882), married to R' Menachem Mendel Hager of Vizhnitz, son of R' Chaim of Kossov.

7. R' Dov Ber of Leova (1827-1875).

8. R' Dovid Moshe of Chortkov (1828-1903).

9. Leah (1830), married to R' Dovid, son of R' Yaakov Yosef of Halperin, of Berditchev. Their daughter Faige married her first cousin, R' Shlomo, son of R' Avrohom Yaakov of Sadagora. Their son R' Sholom married Chanah Sarah, daughter of R' Yitzchok of Buhush, and established the House of Vasloi.

10. R' Mordechai Shraga of Husyatin (1834-1894).

The Rizhiner thought highly of his children and lavished praise on them.

When the Rizhiner escaped from Russia, throngs of people came to greet him. A group from the nearby city of Kossov also gathered to journey to visit the Rizhiner. A young lad saw them leave and asked what was the purpose of the visit. He was told that a great Rebbe had come, an angel of Hashem; these people were going to visit him. The young boy thought that he would also like to see this. He did not tell his father and paid his own passage with the

R' Sholom Halperin, Admor of Vasloi

group and entered with them to greet the Rebbe. When they left, he remained behind. He looked all around. The Rebbe's *gabbai* asked him from where he came and he answered that he was from the city of Kossov.

"What are you doing here?" asked the *gabbai*. He answered that he had heard that an angel of Hashem had come.

"I remembered that I had learned with my teacher, before Shavuos, that an angel of Hashem has six wings. I would like to see the wings of the angel." The Rizhiner overheard what he said and told the *gabbai* to bring the boy to his six sons, who were his six wings.

R' Raphael of Bershad once asked the Rizhiner why his children, who were then very small, wore suspenders. He answered, "What else should they do if they do not have a body upon which their pants can hang?"

Rav Gutman, the Rabbi of Iassy, mentioned the words of the Rizhiner that "just as in the time of the Temple they would inquire of the *Urim* and *Tumim*, so they will inquire of my sons."

The Rizhiner once said that he heard from his great-grandfather, the Great Maggid, a promise from heaven, that his greatness

Three descendants of the Rizhiner. From l-r: The Gvodzitzer, the Buhusher and the Kossover Rebbes

would continue for one hundred and fifty years. The Rizhiner *davened* that it should not stop after that time, and they called down from heaven that it was Hashem's promise that from then until the days of *Mashiach*, *tzaddikim* would always issue from the Rizhiner's descendants.

Once the Rizhiner heard that there was discord among his children. He summoned them and called the matter to their attention. "Isn't it enough that the Children of Israel should suffer because of the sale of Yosef. Know that disharmony among you could cause damage to all of Israel."

The Rizhiner made a *shidduch* (match) with R' Yaakov Yosef Halperin of Berditchev. The custom at the time was to reveal the ancestral records of the respective families, which the two fathers duly did.

The Rizhiner then said, "The word יִחוּס, *yichus*, lineage, comes from the root word meaning barrier (as in מַחְסֶה, *barrier*). It serves as a protection against all harm. Our grandfather, the Maggid, was protected by his son the Malach, and the Malach was protected by his son R' Sholom; my father was protected by me and I am protected by my holy sons." One Shavuos morning he confided that the Maggid's father had in his possession ancestral records dating back to King Chizkiyah. However, they told him from heaven that with him a new lineage would begin. He hid the book of lineage under a stone whose location he alone knew, so confident was he that his sons would have no need of it.

Since the Rizhiner passed away at a young age, relatively few of his grandchildren merited the good fortune to know and learn from their illustrious ancestor. One of those fortunate few was R' Levi Yitzchok Manzon (1843-1916), who later became renowned as the Rebbe of Ozierni and author of *Becha Yevarech Yisroel*. His mother, Gittel Tova, was a daughter of the Rizhiner, and she married R' Yosef Manzon from Berditchev. The Rizhiner held her in high esteem and proclaimed that if only she had been a boy, "she would have been distinguished, even among my sons."

In his book R' Levi Yitzchok recalls an incident from his childhood. "I remember that when I was 7 years old, I had the merit to travel together with my holy grandfather, the Rizhiner, in his wagon. On the way we stopped to recite Minchah. My father later told me that my grandfather observed how I davened. When we arrived home, my grandfather told me that he enjoyed seeing how meticulously I had pounded my chest upon saying, 'Forgive us, O Father — *Selach lonu Ovinu*.' If only I was as pure now — as I was then..."

The town of Ozierni in Eastern Ukraine was fortunate that R' Levi Yitzchok settled there. Under his influence, Ozierni became a well-known chassidic center. Many came to discuss their problems with R' Levi Yitzchok for he was known to have an astute mind and a healthy acumen. He was acclaimed for his expertise in Torah, so much so that the famous community of Berditchev sought to have him appointed as a senior *dayan* in their *beis din*. R' Levi Yitzchok, who remained faithful to the Rizhiner discipline not to display one's Torah knowledge in public, turned down the offer. His only surviving son, R' Moshe, assumed his position as Rebbe in Vienna, where he passed away on Yom Kippur.

R' Levi Yitzchok had a younger brother, R' Chaim Dov, the Rebbe of Brod (1849-1932). He moved to Brod in 1878 and remained there until his death. His chassidim provided him with a large Beis Hamedrash and court from where he commanded a respectable following. His son R' Yisroel (1876-1957) immigrated to America in 1939, where he was regarded as one of the senior Rebbes of New York. The Manzon family descendants include R' Chaim Dov's grandchildren, the families of R' Yisroel Weinstock and R' Eliezer Grahame (died Kislev 2002). R' Eliezer Grahame was a philanthropist of note and he regarded himself as a true friend and supporter of Rizhin. The Rizhiner Yeshivah in Jerusalem was especially close to his heart. Other descendants of the Manzon family are the Rapotchinsky (Raviv) Family of Chernovitz and later of Eretz Yisroel, and the Shorr family from Berditchev.

The Rizhiner's youngest daughter, Leah, married R' Dovid Halpern of Berditchev. From them descended the Rebbes of the

The home of the Rebbe in Vasloi

dynasty of Vasloi. Their son, R' Sholom Halpern (1856-1939), was the founder of the House of Vasloi. R' Sholom was regarded by all as a saintly and holy man. Upon the instruction of his father-in-law, R' Yitzchok of Buhush, R' Sholom began to lead his own chassidim when he turned forty years of age.

In Vasloi a large court and *Beis Hamidrash* were built. Every Friday night the entire town would assemble around Reb Sholom's *tish* to watch him as he recited *Kiddush*, his soul-piercing voice causing many a heart to miss a beat.

Among the constant stream of chassidim who came to Vasloi were quite a number of great *talmidei chachamim*, who would come to speak in learning with R' Sholom. One of the greatest rabbinical authorities in Romania, R' Chaim Mordechai Roller, author of the classic responsa *Be'er Chaim Mordechai*, had become close with R' Sholom from his days in Buhush.

R' Roller would come to Vasloi once a month to visit R' Sholom. Each time he came, they would seclude themselves in a room for hours on end, engaging in deep Talmudic discussion. R' Roller did not cease praising R' Sholom and would say that he is one of the major *talmidei chachamim* of the generation, someone who is truly familiar with any subject about which he is asked.

R' Sholom also excelled in Kabbalah. One of the famous *mekubalim* of Yerushalayim, R' Asher Zelig Margolios, lived for a short time in Romania. During his stay there he was a frequent visitor in Vasloi. Even many years later R' Asher Zelig would say that although one cannot compare living in Eretz Yisroel to living in *chutz la'aretz* (the diaspora), he does miss not hearing R' Sholom's Kabbalistic insights.

In R' Sholom's later years, his chassidim decided that it was necessary to build an extension to his court. After the extension was completed the chassidim wanted him to go and look the new quarters that had been built. R' Sholom, however, refused their request. The inspection could wait until *Erev* Pesach when he would have an opportunity to view the new rooms while he conducted *bedikas chametz*. To go in the middle of the year would be a waste of precious time which could be better spent learning.

Indeed, those who still remember R' Sholom recount that even more impressive than all the miracles that he performed was his unbelievable diligence in learning. Every spare second was utilized for learning. He would forgo buttering his bread during meals. Time was simply too precious to be wasted on such trivial pursuits.

Despite his fierceness against anything that was deemed a threat to Torah-true *Yiddishkeit,* he led his chassidim like a true shepherd, caring for all their problems and worries. Every broken heart was sure to be warmly received and R' Sholom would comfort and console all who came to him. Even those who had strayed from the path of Judaism would be given his undivided care and attention until their problems had been solved. At the same time R' Sholom would try to convince them to better their ways.

He would often say that it is forbidden to give up hope on any Jew, however low he has fallen, for every Jew has within him a spark which, when ignited, will bring him back to Torah and mitzvos. In this way he explained the words of the Talmud in *Masechta Berachos,* that a person must always ensure that his *yetzer hatov* controls his *yetzer hara* and not vice versa. If the person feels that his *yetzer hara* is gaining control, then he should learn Torah in order to defeat it. If the *yetzer hara* is not subdued through his learning, he should recite *Shema.* If this also does not help, he should remind himself that a person does not live forever and one day he will have to account for his actions.

R' Sholom would say that these three different methods mentioned in the *Gemara* allude to the three different categories in *Klal Yisroel.* The first category is that of *talmidei chachamim* — those who learn Torah. Afterwards come those who, even if they cannot learn, are nevertheless G-d-fearing people who place their trust in Hashem and *daven* three times daily to Hashem. The last category is the Jew who has fallen by the wayside, and although he does not keep the Torah and mitzvos, he still remembers to come to shul once a year on his parents' *yahrtzeit* to recite *Kaddish* for them. Even such a person should not be given up on and is still capable of defeating and conquering his *yetzer hara* if he has the will to do so. In keeping with his words, Reb Sholom sought to help and encourage every *Yid* who knocked on his door, no matter how far he had strayed.

Just days after his demise on the 24th of Av 5699 (1939), the Second World War broke out in all its fury, destroying the court of Vasloi with all its chassidim. Reb Sholom's only son, R' Chaim Dov, assumed his father's position and after many miracles left Romania in 1950 for Eretz Yisroel where he was *niftar* in Sivan 5717 (1957).

Reb Chaim Dov was succeeded by his son Reb Yaakov Yosef Shlomo. He moved to Tel Aviv where he opened his *Beis Hamidrash*, a beacon of light in a secular city. His son, Reb Avrohom Shimshon Sholom, the present Rebbe of Vasloi, continues to ensure that the beacon of light burns brightly, succeeded him.

Other members of the Vasloier family include the late R' Shaul Eidelstein of Tel Aviv. His son-in-law, Dayan Riger, also resides in Tel Aviv. Another descendant, R' Chaim Dov Halpern is a rav in Pennsylvania, in the United States.

CHAPTER XXII

R' SHOLOM YOSEF
OF SADAGORA
(1813-1851)

R' SHOLOM YOSEF WAS THE FIRSTBORN OF THE RIZHINER, AND the very image of his father. The Rizhiner died when R' Sholom Yosef was 37 and grief stricken, he survived his father by less than a year. Chassidim claimed that he began his work where his father had left off — namely, to bring *Mashiach* — and for this reason did not outlive him (since the attempt on the part of a *tzaddik* to "force the hand" of Hashem on this issue usually brings about his own premature demise). His spirit left him on his way from Karlsbad to Leipzig (his burial place) on 11th Elul, 1851, the result of a heart attack brought on by unendurable yearning. So potent was his own charisma that the chassidim who had rested their hopes upon him mourned his death more bitterly than that of his father before him. In his brothers' eyes his death crystallized the extent of his resemblance to his father — from his looks to his exquisite manners, to the modesty of his ways in work and prayer.

R' Pinchos of Dubenka repeated what he had heard from a man who witnessed R' Sholom Yosef's *davening*. This man had not budged but all that he had heard over the course of many hours was the sound of R' Sholom Yosef, walking to and fro, to and fro. His prayer finished, the *gabbai* entered, and than exited from the chamber with a sopping garment, which he wrung out and hung up to dry. He said that this happened every day. At the completion of his prayer, the wet garment would be exchanged for a dry one. The same man, very often a guest of R' Letishy of Tomashov, told him of this extraordinary thing. This was of the same order, he commented, as we find in the Rosh Hashanah liturgy: זֵעוֹת בְּלִי לֵעוֹת, "perspiration without fatigue."

It was R' Sholom Yosef's custom very often to go without any or with very little food for days. On one occasion his daughter, Rachel Leah, entered his room several times when they brought him his food. She saw that the food lay before him but that he ate very little, and she began to cry. He said to her, "Why are you crying, my daughter? You think that because I eat very little my strength will diminish?" He walked over to the very large and heavy chair standing there and picked it up with two fingers. He walked with it to and fro and said, "You should know, my daughter, that if one nourishes the soul, one can be strong without food." His daughter also related that once she happened upon her father at an unscheduled hour. He was very upset at the interruption since he had been discussing with his father, the Rizhiner, things that happen in the World of Truth. "I was beginning to talk about my weakness when you came in with your mother, and I was unable to continue."

The Rizhiner said of his son, R' Sholom Yosef, that he was strong, rich and wise. "He was worthy that Hashem's Presence should hover over him, but the generation did not merit it." R' Aharon of Ochakov, in his book *Beis Aharon* (on Tractate *Avos, Perek* 6), states in R' Sholom Yosef's name: "A man does not become a leader on earth until he has been adjudged an evil person from above. A person should walk humbly with Hashem (וְהַצְנֵעַ לֶכֶת עִם אֱלֹקֶיךָ, *Michah* 6:8) — but when he is shown honor and respect and is promoted to leadership, he begins to think that he is as humble as Hashem Himself. This makes him an evil person in the eyes of Heaven" (*Beis Yisroel*, p. 3a).

R' Sholom Yosef was still very young when his parents finalized the agreement for his marriage to the daughter of R' Dov, the son of R' Yitzchok of Radzivil. The young *chassan* was wearing expensive clothes after the fashion of noblemen, and the Rizhiner put him on his lap. R' Yitzchok was taken aback and asked if their fathers had pampered their children in a similar fashion. The Rizhiner answered him that since they had no money they did not act this way. R' Yitzchok again asked him, "What about וּבְחֻקֹּתֵיהֶם לֹא תֵלֵכוּ (*Vayikra* 18:3), that we should not follow the ways of the gentiles?" The Rizhiner answered, "Before I thought you were only being frivolous, but now, since I see that you are serious, I will tell you that *Tishbi yetaretz* (תִּשְׁבִּי יְתָרֵץ), Eliyahu HaNavi will answer all unsolved questions when he comes." Then the Apter Rav said, "Yes, yes, all the customs of our Rebbe, Eliyahu HaNavi will explain." When the Rizhiner kissed his son on his head the Radziviler asked, "How is it possible that you kissed flesh?" and he answered, "To me, he is the source of my strength" (see *Bereishis* 49:3).

Once, R' Sholom Yosef had to go to Lvov to visit a doctor. He attempted to conceal his identity, saying he was a Jew from Leipzig, but when he arrived in Lvov the people recognized him and came to him for blessings, which he gave, but he refused to accept money. He explained that once he went traveling with his father, the Rizhiner. Suddenly, his father told the wagon driver to go off the main road on to a side route. When they came to a certain place, he told the attendant to throw a *kerbel* (ruble) on the ground. Then he ordered the wagon driver to whip the horses in order to speed them from the place to their destination. Toward evening they came to an inn and began to recite Minchah. The Rizhiner extended his Minchah prayer until midnight. After he finished his prayer, he asked his son if he knew what had happened on the way. R' Sholom replied that he had seen nothing. The Rizhiner explained that there had been a very wretched soul lying there. "When he came to the World of Truth," continued the Rizhiner, "he had no merits, save that he had given money to a number of *tzaddikim*, including myself. He was placed into the charge of two angels, who brought him to various *tzaddikim* to see if they could help him." Explained the Rizhiner, "As long as he had not yet visited all the *tzaddikim*, nothing bad could happen to

L-R R' Yehudah Leib of Pishkan R' Avrohom Yehoshua Heschel of Adjud, grandchildren of R' Sholom Yosef

him. He went to all the *tzaddikim*, but they were not able to help him because he was so wretched. I was the only one left to whom he could come. The angels decided not to bring him to me as I probably would not be able to help, which would bring strict judgment on him. Better that he should remain with one *tzaddik* left to visit so the harsh judgment would be delayed. He had remained at the place for two years. When I passed by, it occurred to me that I should help him since he had given me money — a ruble. I saw that he was very wretched and I wanted to leave as soon as possible. Therefore, we had compassion on him and threw him something and left immediately. They began in Heaven to administer the strict judgment upon him. I ordered that we travel very quickly so that I might be able to help him with the *tefillah* of Minchah. When I said *Shemoneh Esrei*, I was forced to descend to a very low place. With Hashem's help, I was able to help him." R' Sholom Yosef concluded: "Is it so easy to take a *kerbel* (ruble) from a Jew?" (*Beis Yisroel*, p. 40).

The Rizhiner said about R' Sholom Yosef, "He is my firstborn, he is me, and I am him." R' Sholom was considered the mediator

MUTUAL IDENTITY between his father and the elder chassidim. When the Rizhiner first saw his baby boy he exclaimed, "This is a priceless piece of silk from Leipzig."

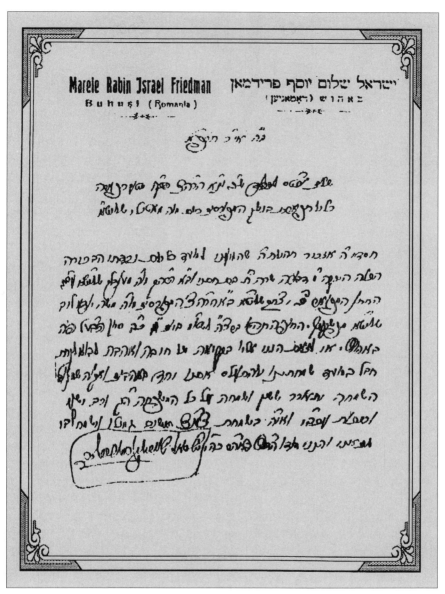

Invitation from R' Yisrael Sholom Yosef of Buhush

R' Yitzchok Friedman of Buhush-Bnei Brak

The chassidim had no idea what their Rebbe meant. Years later the Rizhiner's remark became meaningful. R' Dovid Halperin, son-in-law of the Rizhiner, related that his father R' Yaakov Yosef, a wealthy merchant who did business in Leipzig, was once summoned by the Rizhiner who gave him a large sum of money and told him to deliver the money to the leaders of the Leipzig community to purchase land to be set aside for a Jewish cemetery. Years later when R' Sholom Yosef died in Leipzig and was buried there the chassidim understood their Rebbe's reason.

THE AUTHOR HEARD THE FOLLOWING FROM HIS FATHER-IN-LAW, THE LATE Boyaner Rebbe of New York. "When I last visited my brother, the

STRANGE HABITAT
Boyaner-Leipziger Rebbe, R' Yisroel, in Tel Aviv, he told me, 'I was always puzzled why my destiny was to reside in Leipzig, far from my family and the chassidic world. When the German authorities in Leipzig decided to move the old Jewish cemetery to another location, I was directly involved in the ritual process of transferring the remains of our great-uncle, R' Sholom Yosef. And, lo and behold, the body was intact as if he had just been buried. So I realized that my mission to deal with the *tzaddik's* transfer was enough cause, and it was my *zechus* to live in Leipzig.' "

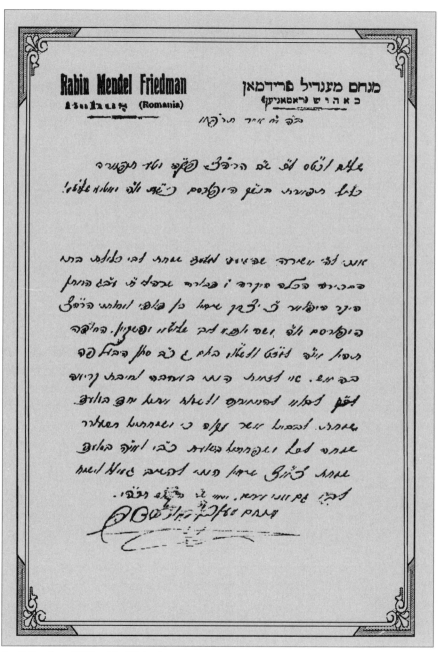

Invitation from R' Mendel of Buhush

Chapter XXII: R' Sholom Yosef of Sadagora / 347

R' Sholom Yosef said: "There are three comparisons that imply rebuke for one and commendation for someone else. In all three, the

THREE THINGS one being criticized is better then the one being praised. These are: That which is reprehensible in Torah and worship is better than someone praised for his 'brains' (but who lacks Torah and worship). The lowest in prayer for himself is better than the praised in prayer before the *amud* (who will be led to pride) and the worst while sitting at home is better than the praised one while on the road."

R' Sholom Yosef left a 16-year-old son who in the course of time became famous as R' Yitzchok, the Rebbe of Buhush, Romania. The eldest grandchild of the Rizhiner, R' Yitzchok (1835-1896) was cared for and educated by the Rizhiner himself. Only a year younger than the Rizhiner's youngest son, the Buhusher was regarded as one of the Rizhiner's children more than as his grandchild.

From a letter written by the Sanzer Rav, R' Chaim Halberstam it is apparent that R' Yitzchok was no ordinary child. In the letter, written many decades later to a community in Romania, the Sanzer Rav wrote, "And why don't you settle your problem through the help of the Rebbe of Buhush? I remember that when I visited his grandfather, the holy Rizhiner, I saw him when he was still a child, and already then his face shone like that of a heavenly angel."

R' Yitzchok's arrival in Buhush transformed the town into a vibrant center for all Romanian Jewry. Thousands of chassidim flocked to Buhush to bask in his holiness and to receive his blessings

He was very active in helping the *Yishuv* in Eretz Yisroel to stand on its own feet. Under his guidance and help, the town of Rosh Pinah was founded in the north of Eretz Yisroel. R' Yitzchok was once approached by a group of secular Zionists who wanted to enlist him in their group. They explained that the Jews needed their own homeland where they would be safe from outside disturbances. "But why have you selected Eretz Yisroel as your land?" the Rebbe asked them. The group was rather surprised by his question and they answered, "Eretz Yisroel is our land; it belongs to the Jewish people."

"Do you have any documents proving that it is your land?" the Rebbe asked them. The bewildered group did not know what to answer. They did not have any documents whatsoever. "I'll show you the document," R' Yitzchok told them, and with that he opened a *Chumash* to *Parashas Ki Savo*. "This is our document," the Rebbe explained to them. "Here it is written that Hashem has given Eretz Yisroel to the Jews. But, there were conditions under which the deal was made. It says here that the Jews have to keep the Torah and mitzvos and abide by Hashem's commandments. If you keep these conditions then you have a rightful claim to the land and I will help you to achieve your goal."

Among the masses who came knocking on the Rebbe's door were many who were far removed from Torah observance. They came because they had heard of the Rebbe's reputation as a miracle worker, and they wanted the Rebbe to give them his blessings. One such person came to the Rebbe and asked him for a *berachah* that he should not have to serve in the army.

"Do you put on *tefillin* every day?" the Rebbe asked. Stuttering with shame, the young man admitted that he did not. "Do you keep the laws of Shabbos?" the Rebbe asked further. Again the man answered in the negative. "How can I help you?" the Rebbe told him, "You haven't any merits for which I can bless you. All I can wish you is that the army be as disappointed in you as I am!" When the young man, who was strong and healthy, went for his medical examination, the officer in charge took one look at him and screamed at him to leave at once, and he added, "How dare such a misfit step foot inside my office!" In due course the young man repented his ways.

R' Yitzchok's sons were also recognized as great leaders of Romanian Jewry. The oldest son, R' Yisroel Sholom Yosef (1857-1923), assumed his father's position in Buhush while his younger brothers moved further afield. R' Avrohom Yehoshua (1858-1940) moved to the town of Adjud and R' Moshe Yehudah Leib (1865-1947) moved to the town of Pashkan from where he exercised great influence on all aspects of life affecting Romanian Jewry. The

Engelstein family of Antwerp, Belgium, and the Milgrom, Bornstein and Shperber in Eretz Yisroel are descendants of the Pashkaner Rebbe. In recent times the Buhusher dynasty was continued by R' Yitzchok of Buhush (1903-1992) who was a grandson of R' Dovid of Buhush (who passed away during the life of his father, the first R' Yitzchok of Buhush). A legendary figure, he was greatly venerated by the masses who regarded him as a last remnant of a glorious past. He is

Pishkaner Rebbe, Reb Moshe Yehudah Leib succeeded by his grandson, R' Yaakov Mendel, the present Rebbe of Buhush who resides in Bnei Brak, from where he presides over the blossoming Buhusher institutions. Other descendants of Buhush include R' Dovid Levanon, who is a well-known dayan in Yerushalayim.

The Trisker Rebbe R' Yaakov Aryeh Twersky (1885-1979), was an active and senior figure in pre-war London. He opened the first chassidic shul in the Stamford Hill area of the city. He too was descended from Buhush. His father, R' Mordechai Zusya of Trisk-Yas, was a son-in-law of R' Yitzchok of Buhush.

Another offshoot of R' Sholom Yosef are the descendants of his son-in-law, R' Avrohom Yehoshua Heschel (1832-1881), author of *Ohr Yehoshua*. R' Avrohom Yehoshua had the privilege of being titled Rebbe of Mezhibozh, the hometown of the Baal Shem Tov, a great distinction indeed. His position was later assumed by his son R' Yisroel Sholom Yosef (1853-1911), a man of rare nobility and extreme humility. He continued the path of his namesake, the Rav of Apt, who is popularly known by the title of his book, *Oheiv Yisroel*. It was his custom to deliver free bundles of wood to the poor. This he would do late at night, when the streets were empty. Disguising himself in a long simple cloak that concealed most of

הרב"ב"הצ"ר'
שראל שלום יוסף
מעזיבי"ש

R' Yisroel Sholom Yosef of Mezhibozh, father-in-law of the Boyaner Rebbe — R' Mordechai Shlomo

his face, he would discreetly drop off the bundles at the homes of those who needed it most. The previous Boyaner Rebbe, R' Mordechai Shlomo, was his son-in-law, as was the Sadagora Rebbe, R' Mordechai Sholom Yosef.

Much of R' Yisroel Sholom Yosef's family was destroyed in the Second World War. His oldest son, the *tzaddik* R' Avrohom Yehoshua Heschel of Tarnapol, met a martyr's death together with his mother, brothers and sisters. A second son, R' Yitchok Meir, survived and opened his *Beis Hamidrash* in Haifa. The Marcus, Glickman and Shefer families in Eretz Yisroel are his descendants. A grandson, R' Yisroel Sholom Yosef Glickman serves as a *dayan* in Haifa. In America, the Assaf family of Lakewood, New Jersey also are among the descendants of R' Yisroel Sholom Yosef.

CHAPTER XXIII

R' AVROHOM YAAKOV
OF SADAGORA
(1819-1883)

THE SECOND SON, R' AVROHOM YAAKOV, RESEMBLED HIS FATHER intellectually and in the self-confidence evident in his behavior and grace. However, he did not indulge in storytelling and in proverbs. If a son's strength is not equal to his father's, then he becomes estranged and he is apt to belittle himself in the father's presence. He will speak in a muted, not a full-throated fashion, in order once again to be close to him. He shrinks into himself and diminishes in stature. So it is that his sayings carry a touch of alienation. This is the "punishment" of honoring a great father, for the privilege of having such fathers is also a responsibility; "noblesse oblige," which is not only a gift but a challenge. The countenance of R' Avrohom Yaakov, as if of marble carved, was never marred by chagrin or the ripples of unseemly laughter. An

R' Avrohom Yaakov of Sadagora

unnecessary or improper word never passed his lips. Fleeting impressions of awe and repentance touched all who visited Sadagora. R' Avrohom Yaakov declared that whoever would so much as touch the doorknob of his chamber would surely walk away with a *hirhur teshuvah*, a thought of repentance. Such impressions float before us — when we reach for them there is only empty space. Imagination cannot conjure nor memory form but a quintessential glow. Who tries for more nets only the emptiest form. R' Avrohom Yaakov's erudition was universally recognized, although he did not wish to parade it.

R' Pinchos Burstein, the Rabbi of Seret, who reached the venerable age of 95, an avowed *misnaged*, testified to his conviction that R' Avrohom Yaakov knew by heart the responsa of R' Samuel de Modena, a book of great import, and a rarity in the responsa literature.

R' Avrohom Yaakov's speech is spiced with intellectual riddles and wit. It is told of him that once, when he came to his brother's house in Chortkov, he demanded a lighted candle and then walked in all of the rooms and searched the way one searches for *chametz* (leavened bread). When asked what he was looking for, he answered: "It is said, 'Do not judge your fellow until you have reached his place' (*Avos* 2:5). I have just come to my brother's home and I smell a spirit of *yiras Shamayim* (fear of Hashem) emanating from every nook and cranny of the house. I asked myself where is this hidden fragrance that gives off the smell of fear of Hashem, and I went to search for the fragrance. They truthfully say that there is no Jew as holy as he."

Gruss aus der Bukowina
Palais des Wunderrabbi in Sadagora

The Rebbe's palatial home in Sadagora

It is told that in the town a large synagogue was being built to accommodate a thousand congregants. R' Dovid Moshe and R' Avrohom Yaakov sat together at the time of the consecration and were talking. R' Avrohom Yaakov asked: "Where does one get a big enough olive harvest to *heat* such a large house?" R' Dovid Moshe answered: "How do you *light* such a large house?"

These were two brothers from the house of Rizhin with identical styles, even though they were different in their manner of speaking and their mannerisms. In the matter of Kabbalah, they presented a new plan, in the form of a declaration included in the preamble of the book *Chessed L'Avrohom* written by the Malach: "In the spirit of this holy book which has come down to us from our parents." Quietly, like a still small voice that silenced the storm in Eliyahu's presence, the trembling of the earth, and the outbursts of the volcano, he brushed aside the tenets of the various Kabbalah systems and their special symbolic names which have entrenched themselves among us. Before his spiritual eyes there hovered the sphere of concepts of the earlier schools of prophecy from whose source he drew, striving as he did to perpetuate, without a flaw, the tradition which proceeds from Moshe to the Rambam, which was epitomized in the thirteen principles of faith. In this way, he made an effort to raise the Divine wisdom of Kabbalah, as he called it, out of the exiled darkness and to return it to its original luster.

He held that the true leader of the generation (*nasi hador*), who knows both how to guide the masses and how to attract the individual to him with the charm of his personality, must be aware that he must remain at his exalted spiritual level in order to elevate his followers. He should not also take upon himself the role of the teacher if that would entail a descent from the heights of his sphere of vision to the mental and spiritual level of his followers, lest they succeed in pulling him down before he can raise them up.

R' Sholom Rokeach of Belz, though he did not know R' Avrohom Yaakov personally, graced him with the title *komah shleimah* (קוֹמָה שְׁלֵימָה), "perfect stature," implying that he was a man free of defect or deficiency. He compared him to R' Levi Yitzchok of Berditchev.

Once the governor of the district invited the venerable R' Sholom Rokeach to his office and said to him: "Do you know that I am the second Haman?" R' Sholom's reply was: "Luck was not on the side of the first one, either." The Rebbe's firm stand made a strong impression on the governor; he thereupon promised the Rebbe to put an end to the persecutions of the Jews.

R' Avrohom Yaakov II of Sadagora with R' Yaakov of Husyatin-Tel Aviv, author of Oholei Yaakov

To the extent that the *maskilim* dreamed day and night of ways to steer the Jewish masses away from the religious path of the forefathers, to the same extent the chassidim directed all their energy and activity to the dissemination of Torah. The provincially minded villagers, whose only objective in life was business, were crushed between these two grindstones.

After R' Sholom's demise the best of his young followers, among them hundreds of recognized *talmidei chachamim*, flocked to R' Avrohom Yaakov of Sadagora. They came also from Congress Poland where the greatest Rebbes were in the camp of his father's admirers: such men as R' Yitzchok of Vorki (a descendant of R' Avrohom Galanti of Safed). Even R' Yitzchok Meir of Warsaw, the first Rebbe of Gur, did not hesitate to set out on a long trip to the Rizhiner after he had seen — from close quarters as a friend and disciple of the Kotzker Rebbe — the results of this philosophic system (*derech*). The children and grandchildren of the great *tzaddikim*, as well as the disciples of the Chozeh of Lublin, almost all flocked to R' Avrohom Yaakov to demonstrate their admiration for him. In Russia, where the mode of life of R' Mottel of Chernobyl was transmitted to his eight sons, the Twerski family, the superb nobility and wisdom of the Rebbe of Sadagora was also recognized. (Some of them attached themselves to his family in marriage.) Thus, the plan of the Sadagora's grandfather, R' Sholom Shachna of Prohobisht, for the revival of the lofty position of Exilarch was realized. The sudden independent upsurge of the religious-national life of the people took form in the demeanor of the royal court, magnificent synagogues, communal prayers permeated with spiritual splendor, a great re-birth and flowering in a setting of Polish

R' Avrohom Yaakov of Sadagora-Tel Aviv

slovenliness. All these were thorns in the eyes of the enemies of chassidism. They plotted against Sadagora and reported the Rebbe to the authorities on a trumped-up charge, and R' Avrohom Yaakov was jailed for the offense of counterfeiting. His father-in-law, the famous R' Aharon of Karlin, author of *Beis Aharon,* son of R' Asher, and grandson of the first Rebbe of Karlin, R' Aharon, succeeded in getting a permit to visit him in prison. He asked him: "How far have you gone?" The Sadagorer Rebbe replied: "I have not yet reached שִׁוִּיתִי ה' לְנֶגְדִּי תָמִיד, *I keep Hashem before me always (Tehillim* 16:8)."

Finally, after the falseness of the charge had been proven, the Sadagorer was freed on the 23rd of Tammuz, in 1857. He hesitated for a long while before he left the seclusion of his prison cell to re-enter the turmoil of secular life.

Upon his return home, the Sadagorer became so weak that the doctors feared his end was near. The deterioration of his health was the result of the confinement in prison.

At the same time, his brother, R' Dovid Moshe of Chortkov, came out to address the people gathered around the house of the gravely sick Rebbe, saying: "Chassidim, is there anyone among you ready to take upon himself the verdict that has been handed down against my brother?" (This view, prevalent in chassidic circles, derives from the frequent assertions made by the author of *Maggid Mesharim,* the famous codifier R' Yosef Karo, who, in a moment of mortal danger, had his life spared by means of a reversal of the sentence on High and its imposition upon another volunteering in his place.) A young chassid, Mordechai Michael of Liska, promptly stepped forward and declared that he was ready to forfeit his life for the Rebbe. It is possible that someone will explain this as an effect of autosuggestion, or the like, but the fact remains that the selfsame volunteer fell sick on the next day, summoned the burial society, took leave of his friends in a happy mood and departed this world. The Rebbe himself regained his health, and before long, celebrated the marriage of his son, R' Shlomo, to the daughter of R' Tzvi Hirsch of Rimanov. The affair became the focus of a national celebration, the participants numbering in the tens of thousands.

When R' Avrohom Yaakov died after the shock of losing two illustrious members of his family — his son R' Shlomo (1843-1881), and his son-in-law, R' Nochum Ber (1843-1883) — Prof. Ludvig Franesky of the University of Cracow, who had been called to treat the patient, declared that the *tzaddik* had succumbed to hunger, since no other symptom was present. The body, long habituated to a frugal diet, refused in the subsiding of his spirits to take in any more of the meager fare. He thus died on 11 Elul, 1883 after thirty-two years of an exemplary life as the Rebbe of Sadagora. The date coincided with the *yahrzeit* (remembrance day) of his older brother, R' Sholom Yosef. He was buried next to his father in Sadagora.

Following the unique *"nusach* Rizhin," the House of Sadagora excelled in its aristocratic conduct of princely splendor, tasteful standards and aesthetic mannerism, coupled with *ahavas Yisrael* (love and concern for Israel) and the pursuit of peace. The *tzaddik's* solemn appearance inspired awe and dignity, just as his speech was lyrical, witty, sharp and metaphoric. He was acknowledged by all other *tzaddikim* as the true leader and *tzaddik hador*.

R' Avrohom Yaakov emphasized the importance of the *tzaddik*, who together with *Klal Yisrael* is considered one. "All of the souls are bound up in the soul of the *tzaddik*. Through faith in the *tzaddik* one can reach faith in Hashem; from faith in Hashem one reaches fear and supreme love of Hashem."

The Rebbe's role as the supreme leader of Israel was recognized even by the most secular of Jews. "Over there (in Eretz Yisrael) we will build a more beautiful Sadagora for the Wonder Rebbe." These are the entry words written by Theodor Herzl in his diary (June 16, 1896). Herzl actually visited Sadagora and wanted "the Wonder Rebbe of Sadagora to be brought [to Israel]" and installed as the spiritual leader. He envisioned the Jewish State as "a destination for the civilized world which will come to visit as it now visits ... Sadagora" (Herzl's diary of June 6, 1895). The Rebbe however rejected the man and his plans.

A pilgrimage to Sadagora was considered *aliyah l'regel* — similar to the pilgrimage to the Jerusalem Temple. Here, chassidim by the thousands drew courage, joy and exultation in the worship of Hashem. Indeed, Sadagora *niggunim* became a prototype in the *nusach hatefillah*, or the melody of prayer, known world over as the "Sadagora *Nusach*."

The Sadagorer believed in the mission of heralding divinity to worship Hashem in a garb of beauty, splendor and with shining countenance befitting only someone who always stands in front of the King of kings. The spirit of gladness, mobility and honor hovered over the court of Sadagora. This spirit of happiness and blessing inspired all the chassidim and suffering Jews of Galicia, Romania and the Ukraine as they visited their Rebbe.

R' Avrohom Yaakov's influence in Romania was great. Like his father he was arrested, in 1857, because of a slander and spent fifteen months in the Czernovitz prison. An inspiring personality, he was widely admired for his wisdom and keen intellect. Part of his teachings are collected in *Irin Kadishin, Knesses Yisrael, Beis Yisrael, Binyan Shlomo,* and *Emes L'Yaakov.*

He was able to complete the construction, initiated by his father, of the famous and largest synagogue Tiferes Yisrael, in Jerusalem, facing the Temple Mount and destroyed by the Jordanians in 1948. Generous contributors to the *Yishuv* in Israel, Sadagora-Boyan *tzaddikim* actually settled in Israel just as their chassidim were among the early builders of the *Yishuv.*

Upon the death of R' Avrohom Yaakov his position in Sadagora was assumed by his younger son R' Yisroel, while the older son, R' Yitzchok, settled in Boyan. The oldest son, R' Shlomo, had died suddenly some two years earlier. He had been widely regarded as a holy and saintly man and his premature death cast a veritable cloud over Sadagora. His younger brother R' Yisroel was also acknowledged as one of the great *tzaddikim* of his time and under his rule the House of Sadagora continued to flourish and prosper. According to the testimony of his son R' Aharon of Sadagora, R' Yisroel was able "to guide every single person on his own wavelength and level. He was able to arouse and implant a deep belief of Hashem into the hearts of even the most simple, even into the hearts of those who had distanced themselves from Judaism." He longed for the coming of the *Mashiach.* He was wont to gaze out of the window while he uttered a heartfelt wish: "Let's see if the *Mashiach* is here already!"

The esteemed Rabbi Binyomin Weiss of Chernovitz once proclaimed: "R' Yisroel has a head similar to that of the Rashba!" Further testimony to his standing can be gleaned from the words of R' Aharon Cohen, the Chief Rabbi of Cairo, Egypt. After R' Yisroel's demise on the 13th Tishrei 5667 (1907) R' Cohen printed a eulogy on the Rebbe titled *Oveil Mitzrayim*. It appears that the Rebbe's influence had spread even to that distant land. In his eulogy R' Cohen wrote:

"We have much to weep about, the loss of the great *tzaddik*, the Sadagora Rebbe, is an irreplaceable blow. During his lifetime, we all believed that his merit was protecting us. Who else is there like him? Many thousands saw for themselves his greatness in Torah, his amazing fluency in *Shas* and *poskim*. All who knew him, myself included, can testify to his greatness, all the *seforim* of the Zohar and the Arizal he knew by heart.

"This holy one of Israel left behind him sons who are also great in Torah and great in their fear of Heaven. It is our hope that these sons will now rise up and bring salvation to *Klal Yisroel* in the way their father did."

R' Yisroel left five sons who all donned the mantle of the rabbinate. The phenomenon of Sadagora being split into five branches did not cause this illustrious House to become fragmented. At first, the five brothers continued to live together in Sadagora. Due to his status, the oldest son, R' Aharon (1876-1912), conducted his tisch in the main *Beis Hamidrash* while the younger broth-

R' Mordechai Sholom Yosef of Sadagora

ers were each allotted a side room. In hindsight, a second reason for R' Aharon's favored position also emerged. The Divine providence has decreed that the continuation of the Sadagora dynasty should issue forth only from the oldest son. R' Aharon's position was assumed by his son R' Mordechai Sholom Yosef (1896-1979). An active and pragmatic personality, he was well known in Agudah circles where he played an important role. His son, R' Avrohom Yaakov, the present Sadagora Rebbe, is also a leading member of Agudath Yisroel and presides over the various flourishing Sadagora institutions and *mosdos* which he has painstakingly built up over the years. His son R' Yisroel Moshe Friedman is Rav of the Sadagora *Kloiz* in London. Another grandson of R' Mordechai Sholom Yosef, R' Daniel Friedman and his family reside in Yerushalayim.

The second son of R' Yisroel was R' Sholom Yosef (1879-1935). He continued in Sadagora for only a short while; later on he moved to Chernovitz where he opened his own court. Noble and modest, he was admired and beloved by all. He was survived by his late son R' Boruch Friedman of Haifa.

The third son, R' Yitzchok (1886-1924), became known as the "Rimanover" after he moved to that town in 1912. He commanded a large following and was greatly respected by the wider populace. In 1924 he finally gave in to the many pleas of his American Rizhiner chassidim, to visit New York and instill in them much needed inspiration. His visit, one of the first by a chassidic Rebbe, attracted widespread attention and thousands flocked to him to receive his blessings and advice. While in New York he suddenly fell ill and died on the 11th of Kislev. His grave in a Brooklyn cemetery is until today a popular place of prayer. His grandchildren, Mr. Yitzchok Friedman and Mr. Menachem Hirsh, and with their families, continue to

l-r: R' Eliezer of Vizhnitz, R' Avrohom Yaakov of Sadagora-Tel Aviv, R' Avrohom Yehoshua Heschel of Kopitchinitz reside in America. R' Yisroel Hirsh serves as a rav in Flatbush, New York.

R' Avrohom Yaakov (1884-1960) was the fourth son. During the First World War he moved to Vienna and in 1938 to Eretz Yisroel. There he became acclaimed as one of the great leaders who were instrumental in rebuilding *Klal Yisroel* from the ashes of the Holocaust. His home became a center for many *Yidden* from all sections of the community. His opinion was sought by leading rebbes and *roshei yeshivah* who considered him their final address. His discourses are printed in *Abir Yaakov*. He died without children. After his demise on the 5th of Teves 1960, his place was assumed by his younger brother R' Shlomo Chaim (1887-1972).

Although R' Shlomo Chaim assumed his brother's place he refused to be officially installed as Rebbe, and did not allow people to call him by the title "Sadagora Rebbe." Despite the chassidim's vigorous protests, he refused to retract his decision; he wanted to serve Hashem in the way that suited him. In a letter to one of the chassidim, R' Shlomo Chaim wrote, "I never accepted to be a Rebbe in the usual sense, I wish to go in my own way, the way of life that I have chosen for myself over many years. My *derech* is the *derech* of many of the *talmidim* of the Baal Shem Tov.

The Sadagorer Rebbe, R' Avrohom Yaakov, speaking at a meeting of the Rebbes of Rizhin on behalf of Chinuch Atzmai. From right to left: Reb Yitzchok of Buhush, Reb Yaakov Dovid of Pishkan, Reb Mordechai Sholom Yosef of Sadagor, Reb Tzvi Aryeh Twersky of Zlatipol and Reb Shlomo of Chortkov

R' Shlomo Chaim of Sadagora

Praise to Hashem I have succeeded in my path and Hashem should help me succeed further."

In another letter, he wrote, "My position as a Rebbe is not confined to a particular spot. It is a moving position, each time it finds itself in a different place. Sometimes it is in a cellar or in a shack which serves as a house for a poor family. Other times it is in a rich man's office where I remind him of his duty to his less fortunate brothers. Or it is in the council offices where I draw their attention to some important matter."

R' Avrohom Yaakov of Sadagora had a son-in-law by the name of R' Nochum Ber. From his youngest years he was treasured by all for his holy ways and his encyclopedic knowledge of *seforim*. He amassed a vast library of rare books and manuscripts, in which sphere he was acknowledged as a world authority. He was the delight of the chassidim who mourned his premature death bitterly. His eldest son, R' Sholom Yosef (died 1927), was known as the Melinitzer after the town Melinitz, where he was Rebbe. His son R' Aharon Moshe assumed his position. He met a martyr's death at the hands of the Nazis. Mr. Sholom Yosef Friedman (grandson of the Melinitzer) lives in Flatbush, New York.

R' Yitzchok Mordechai of Gvodzitz

The dynasty of Gvodzitz also traces its roots to the house of Sadagora. R' Yitzchok Mordechai Shapiro (1867-1930), who was Rebbe in Gvodzitz, was a son-in-law of R' Yisroel of Sadagora. His father, R' Zelig Shapiro, was a son-in-law of the Rizhiner's son R' Avrohom Yaakov. R' Yitzchok Mordechai's son, R'

R' Chaim Meir Yechiel of Drohibisht

Dovid Moshe (1904-1988), moved to New York in 1941 where he opened his *Beis Hamidrash*. Today the *Beis Hamidrash* is in the capable hands of his only son, R' Yitzchok Mordechai.

R' Yitzchok Mordechai's brother, R' Chaim Meir Yechiel (1864-1924), was known as the Drohibishter Rebbe. Two years before his death he moved to Jerusalem where he was greatly respected. He was succeeded by his son R' Avrohom Yaakov (1883-1964) who was a founding member of the town Kfar Chassidim. R' Aviezer Shapiro, Rav of the Drohibishter shul in Geula, Jerusalem, is a descendant of R' Yitzchok Mordechai and R' Chaim Meir Yechiel.

CHAPTER XXIV

THOUGHTS OF R' AVROHOM YAAKOV

THE FOLLOWING IS A SELECTION OF THE THOUGHTS OF R' AVROHOM Yaakov of Sadagora:

You shall rise and have mercy upon Zion because the time to favor her [עֵת לְחֶנְנָהּ], *for the appointed time will have come* (*Tehillim* 102:14). The

GIFT OR BELIEF word *chaninah* (חֲנִינָה), *favor,* applies when a man simply gives a friend a present,

but when a man has to repay a debt to his friend according to law, that is not *chaninah.* This is the meaning of the aforementioned verse, *You shall rise and have mercy upon Zion,* because it is the time of *chaninah* — at this time You still have a chance to do this in terms of *chessed,* because the appointed time has not yet come. Later, when the appointed time will have come, You will be required to bring the *Geulah,* and it will be like one who has to pay a debt (*Nachalas Yisroel,* pp. 30-31).

R' Avrohom Yaakov of Sadagora carried on the traditions of the Rizhiner dynasty. He demonstrated to his followers great religious

ON BEING A TZADDIK

tranquility, and pointed out to them how to reach the level of a *tzaddik*. The tranquillity of the *tzaddik*, called *menuchah*, stems from his being untroubled by any worldly inclinations. The *tzaddik*, therefore, worships Hashem without thought of reward, *b'chinam*. These concepts (through re-arrangement of letters) are stated in the verse, *"These are the generations of Noach. Noach was a tzaddik… Noach walked with G-d" (Bereishis* 6:9). Noach was a *tzaddik menuchah*, Noach walked with G-d, Noach-*chinam*.

MENTAL HYGIENE

The way a man acts will have a certain effect on his state of mind. Chassidus always tried to emphasize man's humility, for this would have an assuredly positive effect on his religious state of mind. *Parashas Emor* begins with the words, …*Say to the Kohanim the children of Aaron* (*Vayikra* 21:1). R' Avrohom Yaakov stressed the chassidic ideal of humility with much cogency, claiming that the *tzaddikim*, who are called the children of Aaron, should not have even a spark of boastfulness in them. This is what is meant in Rashi, "To warn the great ones about the little things; the 'little things' allude to humility."

THE FORGETTING OF THE REQUEST

A chassid came from afar to get advice on a complicated matter, and when he reached the Rebbe to receive his blessings, he became absent minded, forgetting the entire matter and all his problems. He left the Rebbe without so much as discussing it. On the following day he returned and, to his amazement, forgot his problem again. It was also this way the third time. Finally, he asked the Rebbe the reason for the forgetfulness. R' Avrohom Yaakov answered: It is written in Mishnah *Yoma* concerning the *Kohen Gadol* who entered the Holy of Holies on Yom Kippur and upon leaving would offer a short prayer on the needs of the people of Israel. Initially it seems difficult: The *Kohen Gadol* was sanctified with many preparations (*kedushos*) prior to Yom Kippur — but when the Holy Day came and he was privileged to enter the Holy of Holies (קֹדֶשׁ הַקֳּדָשִׁים, *Kodesh Hakodashim*), he did not pour out his plea on behalf of the needs of Israel. Rather, he was satisfied with uttering a short prayer only when leaving. Why? The explanation is that when he stood inside and gazed on the splendor of the *Shechinah* he forgot all the material matters of the lowly world; only when he had departed from holiness did he remember something of the needs of Israel. Since the entire material world appeared to him as unimportant, he would recite a short prayer and depart.

Chassidim found an allusion in what is written about Esther: *When she came before the king she did not ask for a thing* (*Esther* 2:15).

In *Bereishis*, Rashi explained that the first word of the Torah, בְּרֵאשִׁית, usually translated "In the beginning," actually carries a different message. The word alludes to the Torah, which is called *reishis* (first), and Israel, which is called *reishis*, first of his crop (*Bereishis* 1:1). Thus, Rashi explains, we are told that the universe was created for the sake of Torah and Israel. R' Avrohom Yaakov explained, "This text tells the expounder to expound the honor of Torah and Israel. When someone understands this primary obligation, mundane matters become insignificant."

IN THE MAJESTIC FAREWELL SONG OF MOSHE RABBEINU, HE APPEALED first to the heavens to hear him, only then did he say, *Let the earth*

LISTEN O HEAVENS — (HAAZINU HA'SHAMAYIM)

hear the words of my mouth (*Devarim* 32:1). Torah without fear of Heaven does not flutter upward. Only he who has *yiras Shamayim* can expect to be listened to by people. Therefore Moshe spoke first to the heavens, as if to say, only He Who is in the heavens has His words listened to; then, even on the earth His words are heeded.

EVERY NATION HAS ITS OWN *NIGGUN* (MELODY); ONE NATION DOES NOT sing the melody of another. Israel knows all the melodies and

A NATION AND ITS MELODIES plays all types of instruments at once, to elevate them all before Hashem. The animals and birds sing (only) stanzas of their song, but Israel sings the songs of all [similar to the seventy offerings on the Festival of Succos, on behalf of the nations of the world].

THE TALMUD STATES: BEIS SHAMMAI SAY: "BETTER FOR MAN NOT TO BE created than to be created." And Beis Hillel say: "Better to be cre-

ON THE SOUL ated than not to be created" (*Eruvin* 13b). The Sadagorer explained the basis of the dispute between them as follows. There are two kinds of souls: a new soul and a soul that comes into existence through the process of *gilgul* (metempsychosis or reincarnation) of the soul. Beis Shammai say: "A new soul that had not previously been created is better than a soul that comes in *gilgul.*" Beis Hillel say: "A soul that is already created is better than a totally new soul." And the Rabbis decided: "Better not to be created than to be created." In our times, new souls do not go down to the world; only those souls that were already created and were here in the world return to it.

THE *YETZER HARA* CREATES NEW SINS AND IMPERFECTIONS IN THE BODY. Therefore, in every generation there are new diseases that did not ex-

NEW DISEASES AND NEW CURES ist previously. Yet, the *yetzer hatov* adds new mitzvos and new cures for the new diseases that have developed. And this is what is meant by: בּוֹרֵא רְפוּאוֹת, "Creator of Cures," in the morning prayers.

THE SADAGORER ONCE REPRIMANDED A MERCHANT WHO DEALT VERY harshly with his debtors. "Rebbe," said the man with *chutzpah,*

CHANGING PLACES "you should have followed the ways of the Baal Shem Tov who dwelled in the forests, rather than living in the city and admonishing businessmen like me." Retorted the Sadagorer, "On the contrary, the Baal Shem Tov lived in the forests because in his times there were brigands in the forests, so he wished to protect innocent people from them. Nowadays, the brigands live in the cities, so I, too, need to be there, to try and help those who are defenseless. In earlier times," he continued, "when the Jews in all lands were *shomrei Shabbos,* the gentiles did not compete with them economically. But, once the Jews began to compete with the gentiles by desecrating the Shabbos, then the gentiles came and competed with them and became a hindrance to their *parnassah* in the villages."

THERE ARE *TZADDIKIM* WHO TEACH TORAH, BUT ARE REMOVED FROM the spirit of the traits and sayings that they preach to others. How

UTTERANCES OF THE HEART can they influence their listeners if they themselves do not fulfill the essence of their words? And this is the intent of the saying, "Words that come from the heart enter the heart." Thus, words that have now flown from the heart of the *tzaddik,* that are sincere and consistent, enter the heart of the people.

THE SADAGORER WAS ONCE ACCUSED BY A NEWCOMER OF FAVORING HIS wealthy chassidim. "When a poor man walks into your *hoif,* he is in

FAVORING THE WEALTHY and out in a short time, while the rich have an opportunity to spend more time with you." The Sadagorer responded, "You are totally mistaken as to the reason why the rich stay longer. When a poor man comes to visit me, he knows exactly what he is

R' Shlomo Chayim of Sadagora in London

lacking and what he wants from me. A rich man thinks that he has made it and lacks nothing, not the physical and not the spiritual. Thus it takes me longer to penetrate him, that he should realize that he is also lacking and is not perfect."

ONCE, ON THE EVENING OF SIMCHAS TORAH, HE SAID, "IT IS NECESSARY to give Israel the benefit of the doubt. For what shall they do dur-

THE BENEFIT OF THE DOUBT TO TODAY'S EXILER

ing this lengthy exile when Hashem conceals Himself for so long? Behold, in the exile of Babylonia there were only seventy years, and

there were many great pious men then; nevertheless there were some of them who married gentile women. Even the angels were sent to the lowly world, *And they took as wives whomsoever they chose* (*Bereishis* 6:2). And man — what shall he do during the lengthy exile, and the present concealment of Hashem? Nonetheless, there is faith in Hashem, which is the epitome of the entire Torah, as the Sages have said: 'Chabakkuk came and based it on one principle, which is faith' (*Makkos* 24a). It is evident, then, that faith is the epitome of the observance of the Torah. And the virtue of faith somehow is nevertheless found in these generations and they are worthy of redemption."

Our Rabbis say in *Avos* (4:3): "There is nothing that does not have its place" — man also is included in this category. Why, then,

MAN AND SPACE when many people gather, is space limited? Does not each one have his own place? Congestion — overcrowding — is due to the fact that when people assemble together everyone wants to grab the place of his friend. The Sages have said, "Who is a wise man? He who recognizes his place." Thus, *Chazal* said that the air of Eretz Yisroel makes a man wise (*Bava Basra* 158b). When Israel was established on its land and every man was perceptive and wise, no one ever said of his place in the *Beis HaMikdash* that it was too crowded for him (*Avos* 5:7).

Scripture promises Israel that the soul will not abhor the body, that the speech that issues from it will be sifted and purified by the

MY SOUL SHOULD NOT ABHOR YOU soul. And this is the intention of the text: *The Torah of Hashem restores the soul* (*Tehillim* 19:8), because the Torah returns the soul to the body, that it should not become disgusted with it and flee from it.

"*Ribbono Shel Olam*, forever you have a generation that is completely righteous and worthy of redemption" (*Sanhedrin* 98a).

A GENERATION THAT IS COMPLETELY RIGHTEOUS It is accepted that *tzaddikim* upon death are called living (*Berachos* 18a). And how many *tzaddikim* remain living before You from the Creation of the world until our time? The existence of the wicked is no obstacle, because when the wicked are alive they are called dead (ibid.), and therefore it is as if they do not exist. And if so You always have a generation that is completely righteous."

It was the regular practice of the Rizhiner every year on the night of Yom Kippur to invoke the name of R' Levi Yitzchok of **A MAN FOR** Berditchev. One did not have to seek far to **THE SEASON** understand his reasoning, as he made clear: Since that *tzaddik* was defense counsel *par excellence* for the people of Israel before the heavenly tribunal, the very mention of his name also served to sweeten the verdict on the Day of Judgment.

R' Avrohom Yaakov went further, stating that, "Merely the mention of the town of Berditchev was sufficient to bring the merits of R' Levi Yitzchok into play in defense of Israel. We have a proof by analogy for this in Tractate *Yoma* (Chaps. 3,5 ,7), where the order of events in the Temple on the morning of the Yom Kippur is described. When the sentry standing on lookout in the *Beis HaMikdash* was asked at sunrise, *barkai*, whether or not there was light enough to begin the day's offerings, the question was put to him indirectly. What they asked him was: "Have the rays of the sun already reached Chevron?" Rashi brings the *Talmud Yerushalmi* by way of explanation, namely, that the burial place of the *Avos* was in this way recalled, in order to allude to the merit of the *Avos*.

It once fell to the lot of R' Avrohom Yaakov of Sadagora — and no less than him — to sit in his succah to partake of the meal **UNWITTING** and to have forgotten to pronounce **TRANSGRESSION** the blessing in praise of Him "Who commanded us to dwell in the succah!" He realized his omission when the morsel over which he had recited the blessing of *hamotzi* (Who brings forth bread from the earth) was already moist in his mouth. His thought, in response, was to recite the blessing over the next morsel, which he would take from the other challah on the table. Unaccountably, he again forgot, realizing only when the fish course was on the table. At this point he confided his pain to those sitting at his table.

To that same company of chassidim seated at his table he recounted the story of R' Avrohom Yehoshua Heschel of Apt, who once

The tombstone of R' Levi Yitzchok of Berditchev

on the Seder night forgot to recite the blessing עַל אֲכִילַת מַצָּה, "concerning the eating of matzos." When he realized his mistake, he cited the Mishnah that, taken in its plain sense, teaches that an unwitting error in observance caused by lack of proper study is accounted as if it was a wanton transgression (*Avos* 4:13). The Apter Rav, however, taking the phrase "is accounted" [מַעֲלֶה עָלָיו הַכָּתוּב] on the non-literal level of *drush* (homiletical exposition), used its alternative meaning "is elevated." Accordingly, the unwitting error of a *tzaddik* occurs for the good of others, that through it he should be enabled to repair and, as it were, convert the transgressions of his fellows. This can be achieved only through his first being under the obligation to do it for himself, in conformity with the rule, "Whoever is not himself obligated to perform a certain mitzvah is unqualified to fulfill it on behalf of others" (*Kiddushin* 31a). Therein lies the reason why the Almighty causes the *tzaddik* to stumble by way of a *shgagah* (unwitting transgression) — to empower him to elevate himself in its wake, and thereby to transform the transgressions of his fellow Jews.

EACH YEAR, ON THE EVENING WHEN *BEDIKAS CHAMETZ* (SEARCH FOR leaven) is made the night before Pesach, R' Avrohom Yaakov of

THE REDEMPTION OF ISRAEL

Sadagora told the following story: In a village, not far from the city of Kolbasov, lived a Jew who rented the tavern from the *poritz*, the local lord in whose estate the village lay. His affairs did not prosper and he was unable to pay the rent. The landlord warned him once, then again. And on the morning of *Shabbas HaGadol* (Shabbos before Pesach), he sent his servants to vandalize the tavern-keeper's home, as a warning. They spilled the pail of slops on the ground, overturned the pot of cholent, broke the table and smashed the dishes. They left confusion and destruction behind them, and a family shocked and weeping. The Jew thought to soften his suffering and went to the city to listen to the sermon of the Oheiv Yisroel of Apt, who served, at the time, as the Rav of Kolbasov. When he came to the *Beis Hakenesses,* the Rav was in the midst of his talk and he heard him say, "There are two blessings: one with a concluding phrase in the past tense — גָּאַל יִשְׂרָאֵל, 'He Who redeemed Israel' — which we say in the Haggadah on the evening of the Seder, and also prior to the *Shemoneh Esrei* in Shacharis, and Maariv. The other, which ends in the present tense — גּוֹאֵל יִשְׂרָאֵל, 'He Who redeems Israel' — is the seventh blessing of the *Shemoneh Esrei,* the blessing which begins 'Look upon our afflictions.' The first speaks of the redemption that was in the past, the deliverance from the exile of Egypt and the receiving of the Torah at Sinai. The second refers to the redemption that occurs at all times, so that, even if there is a Jew in some village who cannot manage to pay the rent on time and the landlord sends his Cossacks to overturn his house, even for such a Jew, the Holy One brings forth redemption and rescues him from his suffering."

The tavern-keeper heard this and was filled with joy. He returned home happily and sang, "The Rebbe said, 'He Who redeems Israel!' " While he was in this mood, the landlord's servants arrived. Their master wished to see if the Jew had learned his lesson. The servants came back with a bizarre tale. The Jew was singing and dancing!

The landlord summoned the Jew who appeared before him with a shining countenance, certain that the words of the Rebbe would come true. The landlord was convinced that the Jew had become insane from his sufferings. He felt compassion and said, "Moshke, why are you such an unfortunate? You are a pauper. You cannot pay your debts and you do not even have money to buy spirits on which you might make a profit."

"What shall I do, then?" asked the tavern-keeper.

"I'll tell you what to do. I'll give you a letter for the distillery, telling them to sell you spirits on credit. You'll sell at a profit, save money — and bit by bit pay me your debt."

The tavern-keeper did exactly as the *poritz* had suggested and after making a nice profit paid off the debt to the landlord and had enough money left over to prepare for Pesach. *Erev* Pesach he went to the Rabbi of Kolbasov, gave him a sum of money and said, "I have brought the Rabbi money for *'Goel Yisroel' (Goel Yisroel Gelt)*

R' MOSHE DOVID GUTMAN, THE PERSONAL *SHAMMAS* (ATTENDANT) OF R' Avrohom Yaakov of Sadagora, would stand at his post each

CAUSE FOR INSOMNIA

evening until the Rebbe would bid him "good night," and go to bed. At times, when the Rebbe was absorbed in his thoughts and the hour was late, R' Moshe Dovid would cause a slight noise, by moving a table or chair, to remind the Rebbe that he should take a brief rest. One night, many hours had passed; the Rebbe paced back and forth, caught up in his thoughts. The attendant moved the chairs and tapped on the windows, without success. Finally, not long before dawn, he gathered his courage, approached the Rebbe and said, "Will the Rebbe please excuse me, but the sun will soon be up and you have not yet rested."

"For you it is easy," said the Rebbe. "You can sleep in peace. But what am I to do? I had a visitor today for whom my soul finds no solution. Should I include him as part of Israel? I find that bitter as gall; he is frightfully polluted. Shall I excommunicate him? I find that very difficult; after all, he is a Jew!" (*Eser Oros* 9).

SEVERAL FREE-THINKING "ENLIGHTENED" JEWS (*MASKILIM*) HAD ARRANGED among themselves to be present at the *tisch* of R' Avrohom Yaakov

RELEVANT TESTIMONY of Sadagora to scoff and mock him when he recited *Kiddush* over the wine. When they arrived, the Rebbe's face lit up with pleasure. "How fitting it is to say *Kiddush* now," he said. "When we pronounce the passage of וַיְכֻלּוּ, we bear witness to the creation of the heaven and earth and the dominion of the Holy One over His world. Testimony is only relevant when doubts are cast and protest is raised. Let us stand before those who protest, and bear witness out loud." And with that he began the *Kiddush* (*Imrei Tzaddikim*, 4).

ONCE THE SADAGORER SAT DOWN TO HIS MIDDAY MEAL, HEAVED A SIGH and left his meal untouched. His sister, Gittele, asked him what was

PREMATURE SIGHS wrong, but her questions fell on deaf ears. At last he answered her with a question of his own. "Have you not heard the reports of the plight of our brethren in Russia?" "It seems to me," she replied, "that these sufferings might be the birth pangs that herald the coming of *Mashiach*." The *tzaddik* brooded a while. "Perhaps, perhaps," he finally said, "but when suffering is about to reach its climax the *Yidden* cry out to Hashem, complaining that they cannot bear the pain, and Hashem hears them and takes mercy on them — He relieves the suffering and postpones redemption."

A DESCENDANT OF *TZADDIKIM* WAS ONCE THE GUEST OF R' AVROHOM Yaakov of Sadagora. In the course of the conversation they dis-

THE PRICE OF A CRITIC cussed the man's home town. He described his neighbors in the most unflattering terms.

The Rebbe stopped him with a sharp retort and ignored him completely afterwards. The chassidim who were present were puzzled. The Rebbe was known to be very courteous, and especially respectful to the many distinguished guests.

The Rebbe noticed their startled looks and explained, "The generation of the desert, who were highly intelligent and honorable, referred to the manna as לֶחֶם הַקְּלֹקֵל, 'inferior bread.' How could they have inferred that manna was inferior bread? The answer is given in the Gemara (*Yoma* 76a). The Torah describes the manna as similar to coriander seed (זֶרַע גַד), and the Gemara expounds the word גַד to mean 'telling' (from the root הַגֵּד). The manna was able to 'tell' and reveal who was righteous and who was not. It fell at the doorsteps of the *tzaddikim* and the others had to walk some distance to gather their daily portion (ibid.). Since the manna unpleasantly revealed the frailties and sins of the people, the Jews felt justified in calling it inferior bread. This teaches us that anyone who points out the faults of his fellow Jews can rightfully be called an inferior person."

IT IS TOLD OF THE TWO BROTHERS, R' ELIMELECH OF LIZHENSK AND R' Zusya of Anipoli, who were wandering in *galus* (self-imposed exile),

FIXING THE FUR COAT sharing the fate of the *Shechinah* in order to restore the spiritual harmony in this world. They lodged at a tailor's home. At midnight, while still awake, they saw the tailor get up, light a candle and start to mend a ripped fur coat. Suddenly, they heard the tailor's wife calling him and saying: "Hurry up and fix the fur coat while the candle is still burning." Said R' Elimelech to his brother: "Do you hear what the *balaboste* is saying to her husband? This is an important lesson for us. You have to fix yourself and repent while the flame of your souls still burns within you" (*Siach Sarfei Kodesh*, 2, Lodz, 1928).

THE SADAGORER WAS ONCE ASKED: "HOW CAN WE EXPLAIN THAT A number of *tzaddikim* who lived before our time alluded to a date

THE WANDERING LIGHT on which *Mashiach* will come? The era they indicated has come and gone, but *Mashiach* has failed to appear." The Rebbe replied: "My father said as follows: 'In the

Talmud (*Rosh Hashanah* 31a), we find that all the calculated dates of redemption have passed. But just as the *Shechinah* left the Sanctuary and underwent a course of ten journeys into the exile, so the light of redemption lingers between Heaven and earth and cannot come to earth all at once. And every date the *Shechinah* is descending one rung. Now, the light of *Mashiach* is dwelling in the lowest sphere called וילון, *Curtain.*' This is what my father said. But I say: The light of redemption is spread about us at the level of our heads. We do not notice it because our heads are bowed beneath the burden of exile. May Hashem delay no more and lift our heads."

EATING SHOULD BE A DEVOTIONAL ACT. ON THE HIGHER LEVELS OF SPIRITUAL attainment, the motive of eating should not be to satisfy our personal

ON EATING need or pleasure, but should be connected to Hashem, and be a service of Hashem.

SAID THE SADAGORER: WE MAY LEARN SOME GOOD OF EVERYTHING. THE punctuality of the train teaches us that every minute counts. A

LESSONS FROM EVERYDAY THINGS moment's delay in coming to someone's aid might jeopardize everything. The telegraph teaches us that every word must be accounted for. The telephone teaches us that a word spoken here is heard elsewhere.

WHEN MOSHE *DAVENED* THAT THE JEWISH PEOPLE BE SPARED AFTER THE sin of the Golden Calf, he said, *And now if You forgive their sin — and*

THE BAAL SHEM TOV'S MIRACLE *if not, erase my name* (*Shemos* 32:32). The Sadagorer Rebbe once told the following story: Whenever the Baal Shem Tov paid his annual visit to a certain township, he always stayed at the home of the same householder, who was one of the more prosperous of the local townspeople. One Friday he arrived in town during a season when he was least expected, and settled in for Shabbos in the synagogue. His usual host asked him to be his guest as always, but the *tzaddik* declined to join him. All the townsmen were soon assembled in shul, and after evening prayers the Baal Shem Tov instructed them to stay on and recite *Tehillim* together. As midnight approached he asked to have the Shabbos meal brought to him and told the worshippers to join their families for the mitzvah of eating the Shabbos meal, and then to return. And so the whole congregation continued reciting *Tehillim* in unison all the way through the night. After they had completed Shacharis the *tzaddik* told his former host that he would now be pleased to accept his invitation for the midday meal.

After *Kiddush*, when all those around the long table were feeling refreshed by the joyous spirit of Shabbos, a gentile suddenly entered the room and asked for a drink of vodka. The Baal Shem Tov requested the host to oblige, and asked the gentile to tell him what he knew.

"Yesterday," said the *goy*, "just before evening, the squire who owns this estate summoned all the gentiles from the surrounding villages, gave them armfuls of weapons and ammunition and told them to go out and wipe out all the Jews of this township. All night long they waited impatiently for the order to go ahead. But just before dawn, along rolled a carriage and out came some important government official and entered the home of the *poritz*. They spent a long time talking. After this the *poritz* ordered us to disperse without giving any reason why he had changed his mind."

Said the Baal Shem Tov, "I will tell you what happened. The *poritz* was a very wealthy man who had more money than he could spend, but he couldn't sell his crop because he demanded an exorbitant price. Therefore, his crops were rotting in the barn. The local anti-Semites tried to convince the *poritz* that the Jews were responsible for this state of affairs. I had to bring the *poritz's* friend who had been dead for forty years to visit him (the *poritz*). The *poritz* didn't know that he was dead. The *poritz* told his guest that he had ordered the extermination of all the Jews under his jurisdiction. The guest told him that he was doing the wrong thing because he himself had become rich through doing business with the Jews, who were his best customers. He therefore advised the *poritz* to cancel his decree. The Cossacks and the villagers were ordered to return home and the Jews were saved."

THE SADAGORER ONCE QUOTED HIS FATHER, THE RIZHINER, CONCERNING the railroad which had come into use in his time. He said it could

THE TRAIN AND THE REDEMPTION

be considered similar to the Biblical verse, *And I shall carry you on the wings of eagles* (*Shemos* 19:4). Then R' Avrohom Yaakov added, "It is as if, G-d forbid, Israel should not merit a complete supernatural redemption, but one that would first have to come through natural means. Only afterwards would the supernatural aspect reveal itself. Since by natural means it is impossible to bring all of Israel simultaneously into the Land of Israel, therefore it is absolutely necessary that the beginning of the ingathering be through the help of the train. The invention of the railroad was completed during my father's time, for that very purpose." So concluded the Sadagorer.

THE SADAGORER WAS VERY ACTIVE IN SUPPORTING THE OLD *YISHUV* (settlement) in the Land of Israel. Generously, he sent substantial

THE SADAGORER REBBE AND MOSES MONTEFIORE

sums of money, in his capacity as the president of the Kollel Vohlin, an honorary title inherited from his father, the Rizhiner. In 1854, the Sadagorer wrote to Sir Moses Montefiore, who at that time was visiting St. Petersburg in order to intercede on behalf of the Jews in Russia. In his letter, the Sadagorer asked Montefiore to "try and use his good offices to secure permission for the Jews living in Russia to donate their 'shekels' to the Holy Land — as they do in other lands." This historic document reflects the status of the Jews under the Czar Nicholas I, since 1827, particularly with regard to the cruel decree of the Cantonists. Montefiore responded, and successfully interceded on behalf of his oppressed co-religionists.

HE ONCE EXPLAINED THE PRAYER בָּרוּךְ שֶׁאָמַר וְהָיָה הָעוֹלָם, "BLESSED IS He Who decrees and the world came into being": If a nobleman or

THE AFFLICTION OF ABOVE

a judge decrees a particular edict upon someone and afflicts him with severe punishments, it is possible that the man will be unable to endure the suffering and die. But if the Holy One, Blessed is He, decrees that a man shall be afflicted, then G-d Himself, in His own glory, sustains him to enable him to endure the decree. This is the meaning of "בָּרוּךְ גוֹזֵר וּמְקַיֵּים."

The Rimanover Rebbe, R' Yitzchok Friedman

CHAPTER XXV

R' MENACHEM NOCHUM OF SHTEFANESHT

(1823-1869)

FTER THE DEMISE OF THEIR FATHER, THE RIZHINER, AND THEIR oldest brother, R' Sholom Yosef, the brothers dispersed and settled in various places. Rabbi Dov Ber and Rabbi Menachem Nochum took up residence in Moldavia. The former found a strong base of admirers in Leova, while the latter settled in Stefanesht, Romania. The venerable *tzaddik,* R' Sholom Rokeach of Belz, expressed his wonder that the two distinguished brothers had settled in an uneducated region of Romania. However, they would surely raise the spiritual level of their brethren and connect them to their Father in Heaven.

The Rizhiner's third son was R' Menachem Nochum of Shtefanesht, who died in 1869 in Iassy. R' Nochum was one of a kind. He said of himself that all the other character traits that his brothers had not taken he inherited from their father: first and foremost, majesty. The

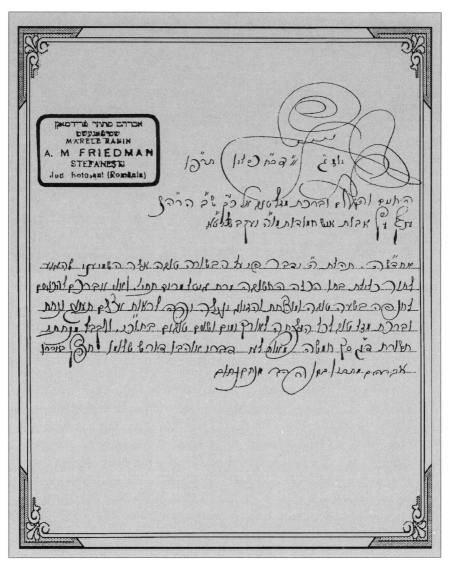

Letter written by R' Avrohom Mattisyahu of Shtefanesht to R' Yaakov of Husyatin

light jest, the smile, the delicacy, the good cheer, the ability to penetrate without piercing and the ability to touch one point without touching the boundary. Like his father before him, he liked to tell stories of action, but did not have his father's gift for symbolic abstraction.

The tablet on the wall of the mausoleum of R' Menachem Nochum of Shtefanesht in Iassy. It includes a list of the rabbis and tzaddikim of Iassy.

R' Nochum built himself a magnificent palace in Shtefanesht as his father did in Zlati Potik; he planted a large garden, placed streams in the garden and rode on horses. His affable disposition and deep sensitivity in dealing with people became proverbial. The writer of these lines still remembers from his youth the majestic architecture of the Rebbe's palace and the lofty surroundings in Shtefanesht. Two hours before R' Nochum passed away, he asked for water, washed his face, fixed his *peyos* and combed his beard. Following that he asked that he be dressed in his Shabbos clothing and began singing a *niggun* of the House of Rizhin. He continued singing until his soul was transported to Heaven.

R' NOCHUM WAS ONCE ASKED TO *DAVEN* FOR A PARTICULAR INDIVIDUAL. The Rebbe was told that this person was very *frum* and merited the

DEVOUTNESS IN FEAR

Rebbe's help. The Rebbe said: "Personally I do not know at all what is the meaning of the word *frum* also my father did not mention such a word to me. But it appears to me that it is a type of

An invitation for the Chevra Mishnayos from R' Avrohom Mattisyahu of Shtefanesht

garment whose outward cover is pride, whose lining is anger and which is sewn with the black of depression."

HE FOUND A GROUP OF CHASSIDIM SITTING AND PLAYING CHESS. WHEN they saw their Rebbe, they quaked in his presence and stopped their

THE GAME OF CHESS

game. The Rebbe said to them: "Continue, continue. But I will tell you what the game of chess teaches us. We learn the following rules: 1. You give up one piece to save two. 2. You cannot make two moves at once. 3. You are not allowed to have regrets. 4. You only go ahead, you do not retreat. 5. Once you go up, the way is open on all sides."

A STORY IS TOLD THAT R' NOCHUM, WHILE RECITING *KIDDUSH*, STUMBLED over the words, owing to his great devotion. He came to a stop and

A DEAR PARTNER

said with bitterness: "I forgot the order of *Kiddush*." One chassid said to him: "Apparently the Rebbe forgot himself." R' Nochum said: "It is the way of chassidim to exaggerate about the Rebbe. When you do not know how to say *Kiddush* you enter into the matter of *ka-*

vannah (intention)." He was quiet, and then concluded: "The truth is that *Kiddush* is not an easy matter. And the Rabbis said long ago: 'Whoever says וַיְכֻלּוּ in *Kiddush* is as if he becomes a partner to *HaKadosh Boruch Hu* in the creation of the World.' And when you enter into partnership with *Hashem Yisborach,* you must consider very well with what a dear Partner you enter this enterprise."

THE GEMARA (*SANHEDRIN* 98A) STATES: "*MASHIACH* WILL COME ONLY IN A generation which is totally sinful." R' Nochum explained as follows: "When a Jew is affluent and his life is good in conventional terms,

JEWISH RATIONALIZATION

and when he meets a friend of his, he says, 'You don't know how thankful I am to the Almighty.' And when life is not good to him, he says to his friend, 'I don't understand why the Almighty is giving me such a hard time.' In his own eyes he is not guilty at all. This is the meaning of the Gemara's statement, 'a generation which considers the Almighty the guilty one.' "

Rabbi Yosef Brayer, who was born in Rizhin and was the last Rav of Shtefanesht. (Father of the author)

R' Avrohom Yehoshua Heschel, the last Rebbe of Shtefanesht. Due to his mother's illness, he joined her in Tarnapol where he was killed in the Holocaust.

As an example of Rizhiner Chassidus, and its views about the proper performance of rituals, we will relate a story dealing with

COALS AND ASHES

the form of worship Rizhin promoted. It was after the death of R' Uri of Strelisk, known as the *Seraph,* whose chassidim were known to be highly vociferous and ecstatic during the services, worshipping with verve and total abandon. After their Rebbe's death, many of them traveled to Sadagora to the Rizhiner, and also to his sons. One Strelisker chassid arrived in Shtefanesht-Moldavia where R' Nochum was Rebbe. The chassid prayed loudly and in a high-pitched tone of voice, just as he was accustomed to do in Strelisk. The local chassidim could neither tolerate nor get used to such loud prayers. They spoke to him and asked him to consider the feelings of the others, to pray quietly and with a little restraint; but to no avail. Having no choice, they complained to R' Nochum and asked

The golden triple crown used at the Seder by R' Avrohom Mattisyahu of Shtefanesht — now in a London museum

him to intervene and put the young newcomer in his place.

It was a cold winter night. The Rebbe called in the young chassid, who entered the Rebbe's hall trembling with fear, expecting the Rebbe to admonish him. R' Nochum was sitting in his armchair next to the fireplace holding a poker in his hand and alternately placing the burning coals on the ashes and turning the ashes over the coals. Time passed by — the chassid waiting anxiously and impatiently for the Rebbe to say something while the Rebbe calmly played with the ashes and the cinders. Then, R' Nochum turned to him and said, "Young man, you see coals over ashes, ashes over coals, but deep in the heart there burns a fire. This is the meaning of our morning prayer where we say, וּמַשְׁמִיעִים בְּיִרְאָה יַחַד בְּקוֹל, '[the

R' Avrohom Mattisyahu of Shtefanesht

ministering angels] proclaim with awe, together, loudly [the words of the living G-d].' This means that awe and fear must go together and be equal to one another. A Jew should see to it that his voice is on the same level with his awe (of Hashem) and should not let his voice dominate."

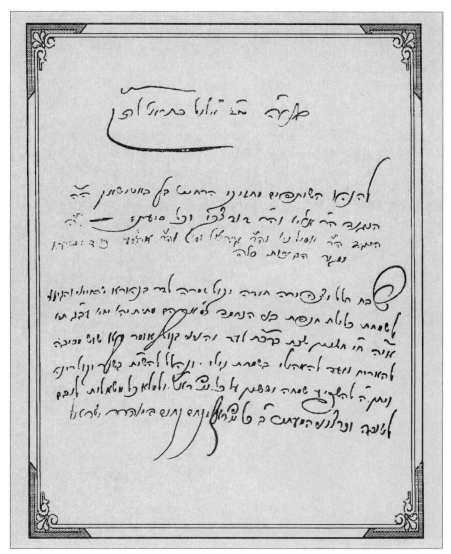

R' Nochum of Shtefanesht's invitation to his son R' Avrohom Mattisyahu's wedding.

R' NOCHUM OF SHTEFANESHT ONCE SAID TO THE CHASSIDIM GATHERED about him: "If we could hang all our sorrows on pegs and we were

THE RIGHT CHOICE allowed to choose those we liked best, every one of us would take back his own, for all the rest would seem even more difficult to bear."

THE ONLY SON OF RABBI NOCHUM, R' AVROHOM MATTISYAHU WAS BORN in Sadagora on *Zos Chanukah* 1847. At his *bris*, his grandfather, the

RABBI AVRAHAM MATTISYAHU OF SHTEFANESHT Rizhiner, gave him a second name of Mattisyahu after the *Kohen Gadol* Mattisyahu, stating "he is really the hero of Chanukah." R' Avrohom recalled when his grandfather the

Rizhiner taught him the *aleph beis*. When they got to the letter Yud, he exclaimed, *"Itst bistu a Yid,"* ("Now you are a *Yid*"). He was raised in the *hoif*, surrounded by the old chassidim, constantly listening to their conversations, absorbed in their customs and emulating their chassidic behavior. He excelled in Torah and

Talmud. And, as he reached the age of 13, his father said, "My son Mattisyahu is like a fruitless tree," hinting that his son would not have progeny.

He married the daughter of R' Yitzchak Reich from Reisha, but divorced her after eleven years and then married Sarah Tzipporah, the daughter of R' Yosef Manzon. She brought along to Shtefanesht her three children from her previous marriage and R' Mattisyahu adopted them as his own children.

R' Avrohom Mattisyahu of Shtefanesht, with his two attendants

The Rebbe's devotion and saintly behavior was exemplary.

He excelled in silence, and at his *tisch* he never spoke. His very presence created an atmosphere of profound meditation and awe (as witnessed by the writer of these lines). At the age of 21, he assumed his father's rabbinic position and led his people for sixty-five years. He enjoyed the love and respect of Romanian Jews who considered him their father, their protector, and their Rebbe. He had thousands of followers who came seeking the Rebbe's *berachah* as if he were a *Kohen Gadol*. The author of these lines recalls vividly the Rebbe's long *na-anu'im* of Succos and the exuberant dancing on Simchas Torah.

He died on the 21st of Tammuz, 1933, and was buried in Shtefanesht. In 1969 he was re-interred at Nachalat Yitzchok in Tel Aviv. His grave is frequently visited by thousands of worshippers.

CHAPTER XXVI

R' DOV BER
OF LEOVA
(1827-1875)

R'DOV BER, THE FOURTH SON OF THE RIZHINER, FOLLOWED THE example of his father and brothers in expounding the philosophy of Chassidus. He also inherited his father's humility. Among his sayings are the following:

CHAZAL TEACH US THAT WHEN A MAN SEES TROUBLES BEARING DOWN upon him he should look into his deeds for the cause. If he finds that

SAVED FROM AFFLICTION he is blameless, he should attribute the cause to *bitul Torah* (the unjustified neglect of Torah study).

But we have a difficulty here. If in fact no man is perfect, how then should he fail to discover some plausible cause for his troubles? Further, is not *bitul Torah* in itself a sin? However, the answer is that it is his good deeds into which a man must look, for these will save him from affliction. And if he cannot find any good deeds, then let him put it down to *bitul Torah;* that is, let him pray to Hashem to remove these afflictions from him, enabling him to learn and to avoid *bitul Torah.*

IT IS AMAZING BUT TRUE THAT WHEN ONE DAY OF POSSIBLE TORAH-LEARNING is wasted, one is depressed and feels as if he knows nothing.

MEDICINE FOR THE SOUL

When, by contrast, he learns a page of *Gemara,* his mind regains its vigor and he feels himself a man of consequence. And yet logic should dictate the opposite: His memory of past neglect and the shame he felt should make him immune to pride during his studies.

However, we should regard this phenomenon in the way that we do a man who has contracted a skin ailment and goes for help to his doctor. If this doctor is mediocre, he applies a poultice and that cures the sore in a superficial way. When the bandage is removed, in a matter of days the spot festers and the disease return.

He then goes to a specialist, but achieves only a longer remission, not a complete cure. Finally, he goes to a top specialist, who gives him a strong medicine, something to be swallowed, something which penetrates all the organs, with the shocking result that immediately the disease intensifies and spreads to all the extremities of the body. He returns to the specialist, anguished and confused, and howls: "What have you done to me! If you could not cure me, did you have to make me a thousand times worse!" Quietly the specialist replies: "Trust me. I do not come like the others to effect a surface cure. My course was to broaden the sickness so as to uproot it from within and bring it to the surface. Now I will give you a salve and all will be well with you."

When a man exempts himself from Torah study, even though initially he is remorseful and dejected, it is possible that this is only a transient state, a thing of outer appearances. But if he toils in Torah, the Torah flushes and draws to the outside all the concealed haughtiness, with the result that he sees he was not cured and understands that he must rid himself of the last vestiges of the illness.

THE ANGER OF MOSHE

HOW ARE WE TO EXPLAIN THE ANGER OF MOSHE WHEN HE DESCENDED from the mountain only to discover the people worshipping the Golden Calf? (*Shemos* 19:14). Have not *Chazal* said: "He who breaks dishes in his anger, it is as if he were involved in idol-worship" (*Zohar* 1:27)? If so, how do we justify Moshe's anger that was so intense that he broke the Tablets of the Law? But the point is that the *tzaddik* who seeks to elevate the souls of Israel must himself go down to the nation, lower himself to the level of sinners, in order to raise up the sparks of holiness that are concealed in their impurity. And we do not have to fear that perhaps his soul will fall from its level, because a *tzaddik* falls only to rise again. In the episode of the Golden Calf, Israel sinned grossly, their idolatry causing them to fall to such depths that Moshe could not rescue them without descending there himself, since descent in his case is followed by ascent. For this reason, Moshe broke the Tablets and exposed himself to the sin of idolatry. (This thought is also attributed to the Rizhiner himself.)

ENJOYING GOOD ADVICE

"OFFER NO ADVICE WHICH YOUR OWN EXPERIENCE HAS NOT PROVED TO be beneficial. If the advice is good, you should be the first to enjoy the benefits it confers."

ASPIRATION — SPIRITUAL WEALTH

"MAN'S WANTS ARE MANY BECAUSE HIS UNDERSTANDING IS NARROW. Man feels that he should aspire to something. If he seeks to achieve riches and honors, rather than wealth of the spirit, he aspires wrongly."

THERE IS A SIMILARITY BETWEEN THE SAYING OF THE BRESLOVER AND the Leover. Said the Breslover: "Give me bricks and mortar

BUILDING — and with them I will build wonderful mansions." Said

MANSIONS AND MEN the Leover: "Give me men endowed with suitable traits and habits and with them I will build the ideal Chassidus."

"IF SOMEONE COMES TO YOU FOR ASSISTANCE AND YOU SAY TO HIM: 'Hashem will help you,' you become a

CHARITY — disloyal servant of Hashem. You must

PROVIDING AID understand that Hashem has sent *you*

YOURSELF to aid the petitioner, and not to refer him back to Hashem."

"IN *EICHAH* 1:8, WE READ, *JERUSALEM SINNED GRIEVOUSLY; THEREFORE* she *has become a wanderer.* This verse applies to the Babylonian Exile. The transgressors were aware

THE TWO EXILES of their sins, repented of them and after a lapse of seventy years were returned to holiness. *Eichah* 1:9 reads: *Her impurity is on her hems; she was heedless of her end.* This verse applies to the present exile. The latter exile had been decreed by Hashem as the penalty for our hatred of one another, a sin that we scarcely recognize as an offense. Therefore we do not repent of it, and the termination of our exile remains, therefore, unknown."

"WE READ IN THE TALMUD (*SOTAH* 50A): 'NO ONE COMMITS A SIN UNTIL THE spirit of folly has entered into him.' If we ask: 'How can the spirit of folly enter into a man

FOLLY AND FOOLS — who is sinless?' the an-

WITHOUT MODERATION swer is: even a good deed done without moderation

brings on the spirit of folly which causes sin."

הַמִּתְפַּלֵּל בְּעַד חֲבֵרוֹ הוּא נַעֲנֶה תְּחִלָּה. "THERE ARE TWO TYPES OF Rebbes. There are those who *daven* on behalf of their chassidim, for

FRIEND NOT MASTER that is their task in life, to help others. Some *tzaddikim*, however, *daven* on behalf of their chassidim because they are genuinely upset by the person's problems. The *tzaddik* who fills the role of a friend in his *tefillah* for another receives a readier response to his own petitions than one who *davens* in the role of a master."

"AN AMULET CONFERS A BENEFIT ONLY UPON HIM WHOSE SPIRIT IS submissive to the will of Hashem. But such a man has no need of an

MAGIC — AN AMULET AND ITS EFFICACY amulet." "Why do you come to me? You seek light from me, when I am myself in darkness. You look to me for the secret of happiness, when I myself am unhappy."

SAID THE LEOVER: "HE WHO INSISTS THAT OTHERS OBEY EVERY STATUTE

MERCY — MILDNESS IN CENSURE strictly will be judged strictly in Heaven. But he who is merciful in judgment will be judged with mercy in Heaven."

"THE TORAH COMMENCES WITH THE WORDS 'IN THE BEGINNING.' THIS hints to us that a man should always regard himself as being

MODESTY — SELF-INCRIMINATION merely at the commencement of the performance of his moral and religious duties. He who has the feeling that he has advanced far in his service to Hashem is, on the contrary, very remote from Hashem."

"BEFORE THE HEAVENLY COURT A SOUL IS ASKED: 'WHAT IS THE CORRECT

PUNISHMENT — HIS OWN JUDGE penalty for this or that sin?' The soul prescribes the penalty, and is then informed that it has committed that very offense." "We read in *Avos* 4:1: *Who is mighty? He who subdues his passions.* I declare this to mean that a man should subdue both his passions: his passion to do good, as well as his passion to do evil. Both should be done secretly, not publicly."

IN ACCORDANCE WITH THEIR CUSTOM, THE DISCIPLES OF R' DOV BER of Leova came to the Rebbe's synagogue after they finished the
TIKKUN SHAVUOS
Shavuos evening *seudah* (meal), in order to recite the compilation known as the *Tikkun Leil Shavuos.*
The Rebbe, however, spent the entire night speaking of other matters. When daylight arrived, the Rebbe remarked: "There is a better *tikkun* than the printed book. Search your souls thoroughly to discover whether since last Shavuos you have performed that which Hashem has commanded you. And resolve to perform that which you have omitted to do. To this we also give the name *tikkun,* for *tikkun,* as you know, means improvement — improvement of your character."

"IF TRIBULATION OVERTAKES YOU, EXAMINE THE RECORD OF YOUR LIFE, TO discover, if you can, some meritorious deed you may have per-
TRIBULATIONS — FOR THE SAKE OF TORAH
formed. For the sake of this good deed, you may petition Hashem for clemency. If, however, you cannot discover any conspicuous good deed in your past, then you may invite
Hashem's compassion for the sake of Torah, since your suffering makes you unable to learn."

THE LEOVER ONCE EXCLAIMED: "HOW CAN ANYONE SAY THAT THERE IS
UNBELIEVERS
wisdom in the words of unbelievers? Do not their efforts tend to lower man to the
status of animals?"

IT IS GOOD THAT IN THESE DAYS MEN ARE ACTING WITH MORE GREATNESS than in the past. *Chazal* tell us that the pre-Messianic era will be a

BEHAVIOR IN GREATNESS

time of great turmoil and upheaval. If we respond to it with narrow-mindedness and fear, rather than with magnanimity and openness, we would not be acting in a fitting manner, but, since in fact we do see acts of greatness and expansiveness, even the unavoidable worry and fear is on an altogether different scale, and is worthy of the time.

RAV DOV BER OF LEOVA NEVER WANTED TO ACT AS A CHASSIDIC REBBE similar to other Rebbes, so he stepped down from the position. Pressured by his childless *Rebbetzin* and his *gabbaim*, he tacitly left Leova and returned to Sadagora where he kept a low profile until he died. He was buried in Sadagora. His Torah is printed in *sefer Dover Meisharim*.

CHAPTER XXVII

R' DOVID MOSHE OF CHORTKOV

(1828-1903)

R'DOVID MOSHE, THE FIFTH SON OF THE RIZHINER, BECAME active as a Rebbe after his father's death and resided first in Zlati Potik, then settled in Chortkov-Galicia, a town that became a center for a multitude of chassidim from Russia, Poland and the Ukraine. His novellae on Torah appeared in *Beis Yisroel, Knesses Yisroel, Divrei Dovid* and *Toras HaAdom.* Like his brother, R' Mordechai Shraga, the Rebbe of Husyatin, he was known as a silent *tzaddik.* He passed away on Hoshana Rabbah, 1903.

R' Dovid Moshe was strong willed, humble and very patient. There was never a smile on his lips and he never jested. On the night of Hoshana Rabbah, at 8 o'clock, he put on his new white *chalat* (robe), blessed his son Yisroel, and said to him: "You should be privileged, my son, to go with *Klal Yisroel* to Eretz Yisroel." Thereafter, he began to recite with deep fervor the Shabbos prayer, נִשְׁמַת כָּל חַי תְּבָרֵךְ אֶת שִׁמְךָ ה' אֱלֹקֵינוּ. Those present heard him conclude with the words, לְדָוִד בָּרְכִי נַפְשִׁי אֶת ה׳, and then his soul departed Heavenwards.

THE TZADDIK OF EVERY GENERATION

IN EVERY GENERATION THERE ARE MANY *TZADDIKIM*, BUT THERE IS ALWAYS one *tzaddik* who on investigation is found to possess the characteristic of royalty. Therefore, all of the other *tzaddikim* are required to be subordinate to him.

While R' Menachem Nochum of Shtefanesht was having a discussion with his brother, R' Dovid Moshe, he pointed out that R' Dovid Moshe's inheritance from his father was in the sphere of awe of Hashem — *yiras Shamayim*. R' Dovid Moshe separated himself from all worldly pleasures. He ate little and he scarcely slept. He would say, "I have agreed with my body that it must not demand anything. Whether it eats or not, whether it sleeps or not, it is all the same." Although many believed that he was the crown of the House of Rizhin, he altered some of what was customary to Rizhin, and he paved a new path. R' Dovid Moshe returned the crown to the former, austere way, which was in contrast to the spirit of Rizhin, which delighted in riddles, faith and a smiling, happy spirit.

BIRTH OF A NIGGUN

AT TIMES, TWO KINGDOMS ENGAGE IN A WAR AND THE WAR CONTINUES FOR many years. From the voices of rejoicing of the fallen in the war and the shout *heidad*, signifying victory, a *niggun* is born.

DOS PINTELE YID

THE HOLY ONE, BLESSED IS HE, TESTS ISRAEL, NOW IN THIS GARB, NOW in that; but the *pintele Yid*, the inner essence of the Jew, is indestructible: This is symbolized by the smallest letter in the Hebrew alphabet (*yid*) and the unalterable core of a Jewish heart. Whereas other letters can be misformed and become unrecognizable where they are too small or out of proportion, the *Yid* always remains a *Yid* regardless.

The magnificent shul of the Rebbes in Chortkov

"OF YEHOSHUA, IT SAYS (*BAMIDBAR* 27:23), *HE [MOSHE] PLACED HIS HANDS on him,* and Rashi explains that Moshe Rabbeinu made

A PRECIOUS VESSEL

Yehoshua like an overflowing vessel, meaning that Moshe infused Yehoshua so generously with wisdom that Yehoshua was like a vessel overflowing with precious contents. The contents of a vessel are hidden and only what flows over its sides indicate what it contains. So too, the inwardness of a *tzaddik* is in hiding and only what he reveals gives an inkling of what is within him. In this overflowing holiness we see the greatness of the *tzaddik* — it 'brims over'; it cannot be contained."

Once at the *Simchas Beis Hasho'eivah* R' Dovid Moshe was very happy and he danced with great fervor and from the midst of his dancing and devotion his voice was heard saying: "But what will the *tzaddikim* who came to them without containers do?" One chassid said to him: "Rebbe, there is a solution. It is possible to borrow a vessel from the master of the well." The

Chortkover replied: "But there is no one who can lend him one," meaning that one must be personally worthy to draw from the source of holiness.

ON THE NIGHT OF ROSH HASHANAH IN THE YEAR OF HIS PASSING, HE said: "*Hashem Yisborach* is able to do all and His salvation is instant.

ON THE EXPANSION OF KNOWLEDGE

He sits on the throne of mercy and is full of limitless mercy. What is man and what are his sins compared to Hashem's great mercy? Behold You, the Blessed Creator, have no end and everything in the universe is nullified by Your infinite greatness. Perhaps a Jew is faulty, G-d forbid, in something, but this is like a drop in the ocean. Jews are born to grow in knowledge, to grow without limit. When a Jew has acquired such growth, he prays with satisfaction, out of a sense of plenitude. But when, G-d forbid, they load onto his back trouble and pain and anxiety, what is he to do? They tighten the screw until life itself becomes unbearable. But a Jew who has grown, whose wings have spread and borne him aloft — such a one is capable of repairing his ways, of directing himself to the path of truth. Jews are princes — they must have this growth and expansion, for out of this comes their tranquillity and rest.

SPEAK TO THE KOHANIM ... AND SAY (VAYIKRA 21:1) — THE ADULTS ARE obliged to instruct the young (Rashi).

THE TZITZIS-JEW

The custom in the household of the Rizhiner was to clothe each male child in a *tallis katan* fringed with *tzitzis*, from the age of 30 days. It happened that one of his infant sons — destined for fame decades later as R' Dovid Moshe of Chortkov — caused his mother considerable anxiety by crying endlessly, refusing to nurse and failing to fall asleep, despite all her motherly efforts to soothe him with fondling and caresses. She was reluctant to call a doctor without first informing her husband, but the Rizhiner was not the least bit perturbed: "Someone must have forgotten to put on the baby's *tzitzis*," he said. The Rebbetzin ran to check and saw that it was so. She clothed him in his little garment, and the crying stopped — and from then on his brothers nicknamed him "the *tzitzis*-Jew."

A CHASSID CAME TO THE RIZHINER FOR ADVICE. AS HE WAS AWAITING HIS turn to see the Rebbe, Dovid Moshe of Chortkov, then 3 years old,

BEFORE REDEMPTION

came up to him and asked him what he wanted. "I need a *yeshuah*," said the man. Young Dovid Moshe replied, "I'll wait here for you. I'd like to know what my father told you." A few minutes later, the man emerged and reported, "The Rebbe assured me that Hashem would help."

"And what will be until He helps?" asked the boy. "I really don't know," said the man helplessly.

"Go back and ask my father," instructed little Dovid Moshe. The man reentered and repeated the boy's question. Said the Rebbe, "Hashem will also help until He helps! And there is proof for it.

R' Dovid Moshe of Chortkov

R' Yisroel of Chortkov

Hashem promised Yaakov not to abandon him *until I have done what I have spoken to you* (*Genesis* 28:15). This actually means that even before the ultimate help comes, Hashem will also stand by and assist in the meantime."

AT THE DEDICATION OF A NEW *SEFER TORAH* IN THE SYNAGOGUE, THE Chortkover would hold the heavy Torah in his arms and dance with

THE TORAH IS NOT HEAVY
it. One chassid asked him: "Rebbe, perhaps the *Sefer Torah* is heavy?" R' Dovid Moshe answered: "No, the Torah is not heavy once you hold it tightly."

THIS GENERATION, IN WHICH THE HOLY ONE BLESSED IS HE DEALS WITH us with great secrecy, is nicer and more pleasant than the genera-

OUR GENERATION
tion of the desert. And what if that generation *was* superior to ours — is it not surprising that that generation of the desert were masters of high achievement and men and women of wisdom, after they had such a great revelation, when the maidservant saw at the Sea [of Reeds] what Ezekiel the prophet did not see, and they had great minds and spiritual powers and their teacher was Moshe Rabbeinu? Nowadays, with great and small minds, but without such figures as Moshe and Aaron — when Israel is granted the *least* revelation — they are elated and happy, and this is worthy in the eyes of Hashem. Indeed, this generation is much worthier than the generation of the desert.

WE SAY IN THE *HAVDALAH* AT THE END OF SHABBOS, לַיְּהוּדִים הָיְתָה אוֹרָה וְשִׂמְחָה וְשָׂשׂוֹן וִיקָר, *For the Jews there was light, gladness, joy and honor*

THE PRECIOUS TEFILLIN
(*Esther* 8:16). The Sages teach that the term *and honor* [וִיקָר] alludes to the mitzvah of *tefillin* (*Megillah* 16b). Some two years after the demise of the Rizhiner, his son R' Avrohom Yaakov of Sadagora, having kindled the Chanukah lights, was sitting among his followers and delivering chassidic insights to them.

There escaped from him a remark, as if he were confiding to himself, "How I envy my brother R' Dovid Moshe, who wears the *tefillin* of our great-great-grandfather, the Maggid of Mezritch." When they heard this, two of the young men seated there blanched instantly. Finally, one of them gathered sufficient courage to say: "Rebbe! It is time to confess my misdeed. It seems but yesterday — although it is two years — when my friend that you see beside me and myself saw how the Rebbe yearned to wear those *tefillin*, we pledged to take the parchment scrolls from his *tefillin* and place them in the Rebbe's *tefillin*. We carried out our plan. We extracted the *parshios* from your brother's *tefillin* and replaced them with other scrolls. Ever since we have been looking for a chance to inform the Rebbe of what we did, but we were full of misgivings and doubts about the correctness of our act, and that held us back. Now that the Rebbe has again spoken of the *tefillin*, we felt obliged to reveal our secret; and now we will bring you the *parshios*."

With difficulty the little crowd of listeners curbed its sense of shock and disbelief. To begin with, it was more than they could comprehend, that the two young men had dared even to conceive of such an adventure. On top of this, was it not strange that R' Dovid Moshe had not had some inkling that all was not right with his *tefillin*?

Whatever the case, as soon as the *parshios* came into his possession, the Sadagorer asked that the episode not be allowed to go beyond the four walls of the room. In addition, they were all to ready themselves for a journey to Zlati Potik immediately after Chanukah.

The day following their arrival in Zlati Potik, R' Avrohom Yaakov entered the room where his younger brother, R' Dovid Moshe, *davened*. There on the table his eyes lit upon two pairs of *tefillin* — the priceless heirloom of the Maggid, and another pair. R' Dovid Moshe entered and, as if by habit, picked up the Maggid's *tefillin*, gazed upon them with a sigh, and returned them to the table. It was the other pair that he then proceeded to unwind and place in the customary way, on the biceps and above the forehead. "My brother," exclaimed R' Avrohom Yaakov, "why do you not use the *tefillin* that by lottery fell to you?"

"The truth is," his brother replied, "for two years now those holy *tefillin* have lain unused. For when I come to pick them up, I am seized with the sense of my own unworthiness. So, with a heart brought low, I leave them where they lie and use these others."

R' Avraham Yaakov was impelled to speak: "No, no, my dear brother! You are far from being unworthy of the Maggid's *tefillin*. The reason lies elsewhere — their special sanctity has been absent from them, that is why you have not felt it. Look, here are the missing *parshios!* Replace them! Use them! You are worthy!"

THE CHORTKOVER SAID: "IN *PIRKEI AVOS* WE READ: 'SILENCE IS A FENCE around wisdom.' The question then is, 'What then is wisdom itself?'

WHAT IS WISDOM?

It is the ability to engage in a dispute without allowing oneself to be bothered by the opponent's insults and to accept everything calmly without reacting."

THE CHORTKOVER REBBE REPORTED THAT AS EARLY AS HIS SEVENTH birthday he had made a vow never to harm any living creature. A

NONVIOLENCE

chassid objected: "Suppose a wicked gentile attacks an innocent Jew, what would the reaction of the Rebbe be?" Replied the Rebbe: " I would *daven* with all my strength that the Jew be preserved from all harm, and I have faith that my *tefillah* would not be unanswered. As for the assailant, he would not be my concern."

THE CHORTKOVER SAID: "AS YOU, O G-D, ARE ENDLESS, SO ARE YOUR mercies without limit. Of what account, therefore, can the offenses

ARGUMENTS WITH HASHEM

of Israel, Your people, be in Your eyes? The Children of Israel have royal blood — ease, tranquillity and joy should be their portion, for they cannot bring forth goodness in poverty. I implore You for their sake to ease their condition, to lift from them their dire need, and then they will turn to the life of the spirit and serve You well."

THE RAMBAM CONCEIVED OF TRUE *TESHUVAH* AS SUCH SINCERE remorse for one's past deeds that Hashem Himself can bear witness

TESHUVAH — RETURN, O ISRAEL

that they will not be repeated. And his source for this thought? Perhaps from this very verse: *Return, O Israel* (*Hoshea* 14:2). It contains the prophet's exhortation that Israel should repent and return עַד, "unto," Hashem. The word עַד can be vowelized עֵד, "witness," a reading which would mean that the repentance should be so complete that Hashem Himself bears witness to its sincerity.

"IN EVERYTHING," OPINED THE CHORTKOVER, "THERE IS SOME GOOD." In the craving for tobacco there are surely no redeeming features,

TOBACCO

and yet it is often the medium through which acts of kindness are performed. This means that there is perhaps a germ of holiness to be found in it. What then are these acts of kindness? Be he rich or poor, a man will liberally offer his cigarettes to others; rich or poor, he will not blush to ask for one!

THE CHORTKOVER EXPLAINED WHY CHASSIDIM CELEBRATE THE *YAHRTZEIT*, or anniversary of a *tzaddik's* death, with rich fare and festivities.

THE YAHRZEIT SIMCHAH

"The loftiness of the soul of a *tzaddik* is innate and does not depend upon residence in this world — the world of corporeality — for its exaltation. Rather it is sent from on High to perform the task of elevating other souls that lack such perfection. Nonetheless, as long as the *tzaddik's* soul is in his body, there is a constant threat that it will fall from its high state. Therefore, when its mission is accomplished and the soul takes wing, it is filled with joy because it returns to Heaven pure and unsullied. That joy is our joy also, as we celebrate the *yahrtzeit* of a *tzaddik's* death."

A GRANDSON OF THE RIMANOVER TOLD THE CHORTKOVER THAT HIS

HUMAN ICEBERGS

grandfather regularly spoke of the uncommitted as icebergs. To which the Chortkover replied: "If they are indeed so, then there is a way to remake them. It is by fiery reproof, for even an iceberg will melt when the surrounding air is sufficiently heated."

SHEMINI ATZERES — A GENERATION TO RECKON WITH

ON SHEMINI ATZERES, THE CHASSIDIM IN THE CHORTKOVER'S synagogue were jubilant. The Rebbe exclaimed: "This generation surpasses in merit the generation of the Exodus! At that time Moshe Rabbeinu presided as the Holy Leader — prophecy and miracles were everyday occurrences. Yet, for all this, the Almighty had to show his loving care constantly in order to arouse the people to faith and trust in Him. But what have we today? No revelation, no preeminent leader, no instant response to our cries. Yet the Holy Day itself raises Israel to the Source of Holiness on High, and brings joy to the hearts of the people. Yes, I say it again: This is a generation to reckon with!"

ON SILENCE

CHASSIDIM LOYAL TO THE CHORTKOVER REBBE VEHEMENTLY URGED HIM to respond to the criticisms of the chassidim of Sanz. The Chortkover answered: "Silence is so restful, one cannot get too much of it. From silence you do not become weary."

THE TRUTH IN REFLECTION

A VISITOR TO THE CHORTKOVER TZADDIK WAS STRUCK BY THE PRESENCE OF a large and ornate mirror in the reception room. He mused, "Can it be that the tzaddik is so taken with his looks?" The Rebbe realized what he was thinking and remarked, "The mirror was a present to my father, the Rizhiner. The giver had been overheard by my father, saying: 'The tzaddik, too, wishes to gaze upon the face of the tzaddik.' My father replied to this, 'That is not the case, indeed not. But I desire my visitors to see in this mirror the visage and the joy that accompany them when they come to me.' "

R' DOVID MOSHE SAID: "HASHEM SAYS TO MOSHE: *BEHOLD, I COME to you in the thickness of the cloud so that people will hear as I speak*

CLOUDS THAT REVERBERATE

with you (*Shemos* 19:9). There is always the danger that the spirit of the *tzaddik* may rise too high and lose touch with the spirit of his generation. For this reason Hashem heaps heavy and opaque clouds of sorrow over the *tzaddik* and confines his soul within a measure, so that the word he receives can indeed reach the ears of the people. But when sorrow descends upon the *tzaddik* he finds Hashem even in the sorrow, as it is written, *and Moshe approached the thick cloud where Hashem was* (ibid. 20:18)."

R' Dovid Moshe of Chortkov used to recount the following story: "When R' Aharon of Titiev, grandson of the Baal Shem Tov, was a young man and not yet Rebbe, he lived in the most abject poverty. It came to the point that one Shabbos there was not a crumb in the house to eat. That Shabbos, unable to endure it anymore, R' Aharon expressed his pain before his fellow worshippers in the synagogue. "Is it not a scandal that a grandson of the Baal Shem Tov should he so utterly neglected by his townsmen that he should lack the means to keep body and soul together?" This stung their consciences and the worshippers duly undertook to provide a weekly stipend for R' Aharon. They decided to meet after Shabbos in order to concretize their plans, with the appointment of collectors and so forth.

But at the departure of Shabbos, R' Aharon was stricken with remorse. What had he done! Had he not, in one moment of weakness, gone back on his commitment never to depend on the favors of his fellowman but to place all his trust in the Almighty? And, even worse, had he not sought these very favors by exploiting the name of his saintly grandfather, the Baal Shem Tov? Tormented, he finally entreated Hashem that it should be as if he had never said a thing, and that his townsmen should continue as before, indifferent to his welfare. This prayer was acceded to, and all was as it had been.

R' Dovid Moshe liked to use this story to illuminate the meaning of the Midrash which speaks of Yosef and Pharaoh's butler in prison. The Midrash speaks of Yosef in terms of the verse: *Blessed is the man who makes Hashem his trust, and turns not to the arrogant ones.* (*Tehillim* 40:5) This presents difficulties, for instead of trusting in Hashem, Yosef did in fact ask the butler to mention him to Pharaoh. However, in presenting the result of this request, the Biblical narrative uses a curious, apparently tautological, form: *And the butler did not remember Yosef, and he forgot him* (*Bereishis* 40:23). The explanation is that Yosef repented of his having sought help from mortal man and, accordingly, *davened* that the butler would forget him.

"FRATERNITY AMONG FRIENDS IS ONE OF THE MOST NOBLE TRAITS. BY radiating true fellowship, friends can have a great impact on one

THE TETHERED SHIPS

another, but superficial friendship leads nowhere. One can metaphorically find this idea expressed in the Mishnah: 'If two ships owned by different people are tied together, one may carry an object from one ship to another on Shabbos' (*Shabbos* 100b). However, if they are not tied up to each other, even though they are moored alongside each other, you may not carry from one ship to the other on Shabbos (because they may drift apart and are not considered one domain). Man, said the Chortkover, may be compared to a ship sailing on the stormy sea of life. The soul is like a ship that is sent from Above to this world to perform a certain mission, and then it must return to its celestial source. The Mishnah states: If two ships (i.e. people) are closely connected, you may transfer things from one to the other, because they are 'influenced' by each other's good qualities. But if they are not tied to each other you may not carry from one to the other — people who are only casual friends cannot influence each other to perform good deeds."

AFTER KORACH'S REBELLION AGAINST MOSHE, TWELVE STAFFS WERE TAKEN from the leaders of the tribes to see whose staff would blossom,

THE TEST OF THE STAFFS that of Aharon or any other tribal leader. The next day, Aharon HaKohen's staff blossomed. Then Moshe brought out the staffs and *each man saw and took his staff* (*Bamidbar* 17:24). Said R' Dovid Moshe: "This passage is puzzling. Obviously, Aharon would take his staff, since it had blossomed and produced almonds in a miraculous vindication of his claim to the *Kehunah* (priesthood). But why did the leaders of the tribes take their staffs and show them to the entire congregation? Weren't these staffs a sign of Divine rejection and humiliation for them? Why does the Torah stress this point? This teaches us a very important lesson. The leaders of the tribes deliberately took their staffs to show that they had not blossomed. The Torah emphasizes that 'they saw it and each man took his own staff' — a tribute to the leaders' bold strength of character. They had the bravery and strength to stand up and declare publicly that Aharon was the chosen one and not they."

"IT IS QUITE INEXPLICABLE. JOY IS BESTOWED UPON US FROM HEAVEN, AND similarly, pain and suffering are also decreed from Heaven. Why

THE SOURCE OF JOY then is there such a large disparity in the ways we accept these emotions? Why do we eagerly accept joy, and yet it is so difficult for us to accept pain? But let us reflect. Every Jewish soul is carved out from beneath the Divine Throne, a heavenly site which is called *Strength and joy are in His place* (*I Chronicles* 16:27). Thus, the soul had been accustomed to happiness and joy throughout its timeless existence in the heavenly abode. For this reason, in this world, too, the soul is eager to enjoy happiness and joy, just as it had done in Heaven, before it was sent down to earth."

Upon the death of R' Dovid Moshe his position was assumed by his son, R' Yisroel. Renowned as a genius and outstanding scholar, he brought new prestige and honor to the Chortkov dynasty. Besides his role as a powerful chassidic Rebbe, he was also internationally recognized as one of the foremost leaders and spokesmen that world Jewry possessed.

In the years before the Second World War he emerged as one of the foremost leaders and pathfinders of world Jewry. The Rebbe's legacy can be felt to this day especially in the field of *chinuch*. He constantly stressed that yeshivos and schools must be housed in premises that will portray the importance of the study that takes place in their walls.

The famous and grand Yeshivas Chachmei Lublin, which was founded and headed by the Rav of Lublin, R' Meir Shapiro, had its origins firmly rooted in R' Meir Shapiro's inner spiritual bond to the Rebbe and the majestic *derech* of Chortkov. In his biography (*Harav Hagadol*, Jerusalem 1990) about R' Meir Shapiro, his close talmid R' Yehoshua Baumel wrote: "There was one path of Chassidus to which R' Meir felt drawn from his earliest years, the way that was derived from the kabbalistic concept of *"Hod She'be'Tiferes* — Glory in Majesty."

R' Meir felt attached to the revered Rebbe of Chortkov who followed this path, and under his Rebbe's influence, R' Meir's inner ideas and visions of majesty began to take shape. In R' Meir's later years the *derech* of Chortkov was evident in him for all to see, glowing brightly inside him. These feelings gathered force inside his mind and being, until they finally emerged in the guise of Yeshivas Chachmei Lublin, a true Torah "palace of majesty."

In the Warsaw daily newspaper *Dos Yiddishe Togblatt (published by Agudath Israel)*, a second Rav, R' Tzvi Hirschorn, also stressed this inner connection between the Rebbe and R' Meir's yeshivah. "He who has a deep understanding in the holy path of the Chassidus of Chortkov, where the Torah is housed in halls of luxury in royal palaces, and felt the sudden fear of Heaven that aroused all who entered its confines, he can attempt to appreciate the meaning of a *'mikdash me'at'* and try to imagine the beauty of our destroyed *Beis HaMikdash*.

"He who once went in the Rebbe's glorious garden in the shadow of hundreds of tall erect trees and beautiful flowers and saw the fish swimming in the pond. And at the same time watched the Chortkover Rebbe walking in the garden, almost bent over to the ground under the weight of the daily sorrows of *Yidden*. He who saw the Rebbe with his *Tehillim* in his hand, and there between the trees saw him pouring out his heart over the long *galus* and the sorrows of *Yidden*. Or those who saw his actions as he learned a paragraph from the holy *Zohar* — they knew that in this wonderful garden broken hearts of stone and even restricted souls were instilled with a fear and love of Hashem.

"He who saw the holy Torah weeping in its royal palace, he was the one who could understand the inner connection that bonded the Rebbe's magnificent court in Chortkov with the palatial mansion of Torah and *yirah* (awe) that is the yeshivah of Lublin. He could appreciate why, despite his failing health and the long journey involved, the Chortkover Rebbe made such an effort to attend the laying of the cornerstone and opening ceremony of the yeshivah."

Upon the death of R' Yisroel in Vienna (13 Kislev 5694, 1933), his two sons R' Nochum Mordechai and R' Dov Ber filled his place. Both of them were well known to the chassidim and were

held in high esteem. R' Nochum Mordechai, the older brother, was born in 1874. During his 60 years he had succeeded in perfecting himself until all who came into contact with him could testify that he was a holy person. He married his first cousin, daughter of his uncle R' Shlomo of Sadagora.

The younger son, R' Dov Ber, born in 1882, was greatly respected for his vast Torah knowledge and his deep and penetrating views and knowledge on any topic that he was

The Chortkover Rebbe, Reb Yisroel zt"l

asked. He also married his first cousin, daughter of the Boyaner Rebbe, the Pachad Yitzchok.

Only two years after assuming the mantle of Chortkov the younger brother fell ill and died on the 24th of Elul (5696, 1936).

Dos Yiddishe Togblatt printed the following obituary: "From Vienna has come the news that the *tzaddik* R' Dov Ber Friedman was *niftar*. Harav HaTzaddik R' Dov Ber is no longer! The legendary Agudah leader whose whole being belonged to the Agudah, who constantly worried and thought about the movement is no more! This is a difficult and major loss for all *chareidim*.

"We have lost that legendary figure that bestowed on us his light at every Agudah conclave. Everybody was always overawed by his noble and royal conduct, which was steeped in the wondrous path of Rizhin. Always we waited to hear from him something new, some novel idea which would ignite everyone's heart and instill in our minds the obligation to strive ever higher.

"In the Agudah world where R' Dov Ber was recognized as a deep thinker and a man responsible for his actions, great hopes

were pinned on him. Everyone was convinced that from this man would emerge strong words that would shake *frum Yidden* across the world to the core. In his few years he had dedicated himself to *Klal Yisroel* and it had been hoped that *Klal Yisroel* would still benefit from his service many long years to come.

"Throughout the wider community and especially in the Chortkover community his passing has brought a deep mourning. People are undertaking an accounting of their actions, that a great prince has been taken from

R' Nochum Mordechai of Chortkov-Tel Aviv

our midst. Great and deep is the pain that this tragedy has caused us. We can only try to emulate his special ways and wondrous personality. He will always remain an example to us all. May his memory be blessed!"

R' Nochum Mordechai was left to shoulder the yoke by himself, and in ever more difficult times he rose to the challenge. When the Nazis marched into Vienna in 1938, R' Nochum Mordechai comforted and aided his stricken brethren. He ultimately escaped the Germans' clutches, arriving in the Holy Land for Pesach 5699 (1939).

The Rebbe arrived in Eretz Yisroel a broken and sick man. The suffering of his fellow Jews lay heavily on his heart. Yet although R' Nochum Mordechai had succeeded in escaping from Europe he was not yet safe from Nazi hands. In 1941 the situation in Eretz Yisroel was critical. The Germans had already conquered most of Europe, Egypt was under German control and they were threatening to invade Eretz Yisroel any day. When the situation deteriorated even further the Chortkover chassidim in Eretz Yisroel came to plead with the Rebbe to *daven* for them. They explained the situation, adding that short of a miracle nothing could save them.

In his short biography (*Doresh Tov*, Jerusalem 1964), R' Dovid Moshe Spiegel described the event, "I remember that serious and emotional meeting. The Rebbe sat, his holy heart overflowing with mercy, his eyes aglow, listening to the words of his chassidim as they entreated him to save them. He sat deep in thought and then he said, 'It is well known that in order to perform a miracle which does not infringe on the boundaries of nature, it is enough if one has just a few *zechusim* (merits). It seems, however, that the strength of the enemy is very great. He has destroyed many strong and powerful nations with the greatest of ease. Normal warfare against him is useless. Therefore we need a supernatural miracle to annul the evil decrees against us, to silence the enemy. To perform such a miracle is however very difficult, and so we have to find a method of defeating the enemy through natural means. We must *daven* that they should make a mistake, for anybody is capable of miscalculating and making a mistake. Let us *daven* that the enemy makes a fatal mistake that will cost them the war and bring about their defeat.'

"And so it was; the Germans made a fatal mistake by attacking Russia. The British Prime Minister, Winston Churchill, wrote in his book *The Second World War*: 'The German invasion of Russia changed the course of the war and its outcome. The Russians were far stronger than the Germans had thought and this caused their downfall.'"

In his last years, R' Nochum Mordechai became weaker and weaker. When the terrible news arrived in Eretz Yisroel of the true extent of the Holocaust, his soft heart broke totally. He took to his bed and his health deteriorated. During his *tischen* when he spoke about the state of European Jewry, deep sighs and sobs often accompanied his words. His face a ghostly white, his body racked with an inner emotional pain over the loss of his fellow *Yidden*, R' Nochum Mordechai could not hold himself back from mentioning the terrible loss at every speech and occasion. As a result of this mental agony, the Rebbe's temperature often rose and spiraled out of control when he mentioned the suffering of *Klal Yisrael* during the Holocaust, and by the end of a *tisch*, a doctor had to be summoned.

On the eighteenth of Adar 1946, R' Nochum Mordechai's soul ascended upwards. He was only 72 years old. After the funeral, the chassidim crowned the Rebbe's only son R' Shlomo as the Chortkover Rebbe. R' Nochum Mordechai's daughter was mar-

R' Nochum Mordechai of Chortkov-Tel Aviv

ried to R' Yaakov Heschel who was a distinguished rav in Edgeware, London.

R' Shlomo assumed the mantle of leadership in a difficult period for Chortkov. This once great Chassidus which had boasted masses of chassidim, including many *gedolim,* was no longer. Its numerous *kehillos* and shuls lay destroyed across Europe. Wherever one turned, all one found was despair and anguish. In these trying times R' Shlomo ascended to the challenge.

Supporting the growth of Torah and *chinuch* was a major goal in the Rebbe's itinerary. He did not limit himself just to helping those in his own camp or Chassidus. Wherever and whenever some new plan or idea was broached, the Rebbe was invariably involved.

Despite all of R' Shlomo's efforts to rebuild the shattered Chassidus and restore it to its former glory, Heaven had decreed otherwise. Only a few years after R' Shlomo became Rebbe, he fell ill with a life-threatening disease. Frequently he was forced to take to his bed and cancel his daily schedule. He passed away on the 15th of Cheshvan 5719 (1958).

R' Shlomo did not leave any sons or grandsons. His only daughter also had one daughter (the Katz family of Efrat, Eretz Yisroel), and with his death the orphaned chassidim turned to R' Hershele Twersky, the son-in-law of R' Yisroel of Chortkov, to lead them.

Already as a young man R' Hershele had earned the highest praises from his father-in-law. When someone once commented to R' Yisroel that the young Hershele was not very tall, the Rebbe remarked. "He might be physically short but spiritually he is very tall. He possesses a high and lofty *neshamah!*"

For almost a decade R' Hershele guided the Chortkover chassidim until his demise in his 78th year. On his last day, (18th Av 5728, 1968), he said, with tears in his eyes, to those next to him: "Only a thin curtain still separates us from the coming of *Mashiach*. How upsetting it is to have to depart this world just now, on the eve of his arrival..." R' Hershele's grandson, R' Chaim Michoel Biberfeld, serves as a rav in London.

After R' Hershele's demise the chassidim set their eyes on R' Dovid Moshe Friedman who lived in London, the only son of R' Dov Ber, and the only surviving grandson of R' Yisroel of Chortkov.

Three weeks after R' Hershele's demise, Chortkover chassidim gathered together and unanimously agreed to appoint R' Dovid Moshe as the new Chortkover Rebbe. A specially drafted letter was sent to R' Dovid Moshe signed by all the chassidim accepting him as their Rebbe. In it, they wrote:

"We have come to a unanimous decision with one voice, to appoint his holy honor as the new Rebbe for the chassidim of the House of Chortkov and to bind ourselves to him with all the fibers in our bodies. The Rebbe will lead his flock in the way he has been guided by his holy and pure forefathers, in the path of purity, truth, faith and love.

"We attach our signatures as testimony that we hereby obligate ourselves to accept his rule and to listen and obey him as we did to his ancestors without any prior conditions."

R' Dovid Moshe, however, refused to hear of the idea and adamantly rejected the notion of being Rebbe. Nevertheless the chassidim also remained steadfast in their desire that R' Dovid Moshe become their Rebbe and decided to treat him as their leader regardless whether he consented or not. Over the years they constantly begged him and sent many delegations and distinguished *rabbanim* to try and make him change his mind. But it was all to no avail. This tug of war continued for many years until eventually the chassidim realized with a heavy heart that they would just have to accept and respect R' Dovid Moshe's decision.

Nevertheless, although R' Dovid Moshe was unwilling to act as the official Rebbe of Chortkov he was willing to act and guide the chassidim in an unofficial capacity. Thus from then on, until his death on the 27th of Shevat 5748 (1988), R' Dovid Moshe was regarded as the uncrowned Rebbe of Chortkov.

R' Dovid Moshe is survived by his wife, three children and grandchildren. His oldest son, R' Dov Ber, is one of the leading figures in the Chortkover *kloiz* in Antwerp. The second son, R' Yisroel, heads the Chortkover *kloiz* in Manchester and authored *The Golden Dynasty* (Jerusalem 1997), the first book to be published in English about the Rizhiner Dynasty. His daughter, Miriam, is married to R' Yitzchok Halpern, son of R' Shimshon Halpern, the Rebbe of Vasloi in Bnei Brak.

CHAPTER XXVIII

R' MORDECHAI SHRAGA OF HUSYATIN
(1834-1894)

EGARDING THE YOUNGEST OF HIS SONS, MORDECHAI SHRAGA, the Rizhiner once said: "In one way he surpasses me, for he is capable of concentrating on one subject for forty-eight hours, while I am capable of doing so for only twenty-eight hours." Only one who had the opportunity personally to observe R' Mordechai Shraga and probe into the influence that the thinking apparatus had over the nervous system, only such a person could grasp the meaning of such total concentration. (One can thus understand R' Uri of Strelisker's idea of holding on to one thought for a period of a thousand days.) R' Mordechai Shraga of Husyatin was a very retiring *tzaddik*. He did not say Torah and did not tell stories. He was a "loner," and was known for his followers, including many famous rabbis. His taciturnity was proverbial. His brother, R' Menachem Nochum, said of him that his role was one of silence and withdrawal from society. Nevertheless, R' Mordechai Shraga was the first *shliach tzibbur* in the House of Rizhin for the closing prayer of *Ne'ilah*, on Yom Kippur.

After the passing of the Rizhiner, R' Mordechai Shraga left Sadagora and settled with his family in Mikulintza-Strusov in Galicia. At his departure, his brother, R' Menachem Nochum of Shtefanesht, remarked: "If I had the money, I would acquire the entire town of Mikulintza and the environs and take my brother as a *maggid* for myself."

R' Mordechai Shraga was born in Rizhin in 1834. He married Brachah Dinah, his cousin, the daughter of R' Dovid Tzvi Kablansky. After his father's passing, he became Rebbe, first in Mikulintza-Strusov and then, in 1865, in Husyatin, where he resided until his death in 1894. The chassidic historian Aaron Marcus, who visited the Rebbe four times and was present at his *tisch*, speaks of the awe and fear that the Rebbe's mystic powers inspired in him. The Rebbe would sit erect like a marble pole, immobile, ignoring the fly biting his eye, fully absorbed in elevated concentration of the mind (*aliyas machshavah*), totally removed from this world — then, gradually returning back to this material milieu as if a celestial being had just descended.

R' Yisroel of Husyatin-Tel Aviv

Unlike his brothers who engaged in chassidic discourse and exposition, he never said Torah at the *tish*. Quietude was his specialty. He represented an ancient type of nobility and charismatic charm, holiness and majesty combined. His *tisch* left an indelible impression and an inner call for *teshuvah*. It was reminiscent of the saying of his father, the Rizhiner: "If after my *tisch* one can return to a materialistic being — *gashmius* — what then is the wonder that, after experiencing the Covenant of Sinai, came the sin of the Golden Calf?"

His ardent chassidim included great rabbinic authorities, such as R' Yaakov Weidenfeld, the Harimolover Rav, who declared that his Rebbe surprised him with his knowledge of the subject of *mikvaos*.

ON THE TOLDOS

ONCE THE HUSYATINER WAS SHOWN THE *SEMICHAH* OF THE TOLDOS, R' Yaakov Yosef of Polonoye, who was ordained by the *Noda B'Yehudah*, R' Yechezkel Landau of Prague. It contained a clause that the Toldos should not issue *gittin* (divorces). Commented the Husyatiner: "The Toldos was an accomplished man all round. He was also a gaon in the laws of divorce. However, since he used to make *yichudim* to his words — i.e., expressions showing the spiritual unity of all aspects of Creation — it was difficult for him to answer the examiner's questions dealing with *gittin*, which connote separation. He therefore answered the rest of the questions dealing with other laws where it was easier for him to make a *yichud*."

TOTAL ABSORPTION

THE UNIQUE MANNER IN WHICH HE CONDUCTED HIS *TISCH* WAS PROVERBIAL. His ritual *tisch* represented a combination of supreme devotion and a royal aura. Absorbed in deep meditation, his face changed colors as he sat silently erect without the slightest motion. Usually, the chassidim present at his *tisch* displayed a fearful and awestruck attitude. You could have heard a needle drop. Silent and awestruck, all watched the Rebbe in holy reverence, while he never uttered a word, and never said Torah.

I heard from my revered father, R' Yosef Brayer, *zt"l*, a chassid of Husyatin, that once, while the Rebbe was sitting at his *tisch*, a mosquito bit him on his forehead, which began to bleed. The Rebbe remained calm, not reacting, immobile in his chair, still in deep meditation.

He once said: "Whoever fulfills the 613 mitzvos is considered a Jew. If one also discards his bad manners, he is considered a pious

A GOOD JEW Jew. But a *gitter Yid* (a good Jew — a *'gitter Yid'* in this connotation refers to a Rebbe), this is entirely a different story."

Once, chassidim traveled to the old Rebbe, R' Mordechai Shraga of Husyatin, by sled. The sled held six seats, three of them facing forward and three with their backs to the horses.

THE REBBE'S MEDICINE While galloping on the road, one of the horses raised its foot and hit one of the chassidim in the neck. As they watched their friend bleeding profusely, the chassidim could not decide whether they should continue their journey to Husyatin or not. They finally continued and reached their Rebbe's *hoif*. The Rebbe told them to call a doctor. The doctor arrived, checked the wound and said: "The patient can survive for only one more day." The Rebbe reacted, "Why should a Jew who travels to me be condemned to die?" He then told the victim to return home and apply cold bandages to the wound. The chassid followed the Rebbe's advice and fully recovered.

R' Yisroel of Husyatin-Tel Aviv

He once explained why the *Shiras HaYam* (the Song of the Sea) is

THE EMPTY SPACE written in the Torah in symmetrically arranged "half a brick above a whole brick" (*Sofrim* 12:10). "It is to teach us that the empty space in the Torah parchment between the lines supersedes the written text, because the ideas contained in them are inexpressible." Such a statement befits the behavior of the Rebbe whose taciturnity was unique.

Nevertheless, the Rebbe's conduct attracted such Torah giants as R' Meir Arak, R' Avrohom Steinberg of Brody, R' Yaakov Weidenfeld and his three sons, of Harimolov, Dombrova and Tchebin, and many others who all became his devoted chassidim.

REB YISROEL OF HUSYATIN

THE IDENTICAL TRAIT OF HUMILITY AND PIOUS MODESTY WAS VISIBLE in the quiet demeanor and invariable composure of R' Mordechai Shraga's son, R' Yisroel of Husyatin, who was a classic example of princely elegance. His love for Eretz Yisroel prompted him to ascend there in 1937. His thorough knowledge of rabbinic literature was attested to by great rabbinic authorities who revered him, such as the Rebbe of Belz, R' Aharon Rokeach, and R' Yitzchak Isaac Herzog who, upon the Rebbe's arrival in Eretz Yisroel, kissed his hand. His statements were considered prophetic. His *p'nimius* (devout inwardness), coupled with his absolute integrity, was admired by all, both the secular and the religious. He was known for his paternal warmth, which drew thousands of admirers who loved him dearly. After his death, a note written in his handwriting was found under his pillow, stating: "If I knew that 2,000 miles away from my town there

R' Yisroel of Husyatin on a visit to Eretz Yisroel

lived the *tzaddik* of the generation, I would go to him on foot. When I say this (at the conclusion of the *Shemoneh Esrei*), I say it in all truth."

S. Y. AGNON'S PUZZLE

S. Y. AGNON, THE NOBEL LAUREATE, HIMSELF A SON OF CHORTKOVER chassidim, visited R' Yisroel on Succos during the *naanuim* service (shaking the *lulav* and *esrog*). He watched the Rebbe, his long *tallis* over his head, covering his face and reaching his chest, and in his hands the *lulav* and *esrog*. The famous Hebrew writer looked at his watch and realized, to his surprise, that each section of the *naanuim* in *Hallel* had taken up exactly the same amount of time, without the Rebbe looking at the clock.

FRONT AND BACK

HIS CHARISMATIC APPEARANCE EXPRESSED LOVE AND KINDNESS TO ALL. His immaculate attire and his composure and quest for esthetics gave the external appearance elevated meaning to integrate with his *p'nimius*. To the Rebbe, outwardness and inwardness were one and the same thing, not exclusive of each other. The following anecdote exemplifies his honesty and moral integrity.

He once summoned an upholsterer in Tel Aviv and gave him the necessary material to cover a sofa. At the conclusion of the job, the upholsterer brought him the newly covered sofa with a big piece of the material left over. The Rebbe was puzzled and asked the man: "Didn't we measure exactly

R' Yitzchok of Husyatin

how much material was necessary to cover the sofa? Why is some unused?" The man replied that he did not cover the backside of the sofa facing the wall since no one can see it anyway. The Rebbe immediately retorted: "To us, that what is visible and that which is hidden from view are identical."

HE WAS ONCE TOLD BY HIS CHASSIDIM THAT A *BAAL AVEIRAH* (SINNER) WAS frequenting the Rebbe's *beis midrash* and that he should be expelled. The Rebbe ignored them and asked if this Jew has *parnassah* (a livelihood). Sometime later, the chassidim once again asked the Rebbe to have the man banished, and again the Rebbe asked if he was making a living. Then the Rebbe intervened and found him a job. The Jew succeeded financially and eventually emigrated overseas, where he became a *baal teshuvah* and frequently wrote the Rebbe letters with spiritual content. The Rebbe showed these letters to his congregants and said: "They worried over his spiritual state, while I worried over his material state. See now what became of him in the end."

KIRUV — A REAL CONCERN

IN HER PRAYER, CHANNAH EXCLAIMS, *HE WILL GUARD THE FOOTSTEPS OF HIS* devout ones (*I Samuel* 2:9). The following episode illustrates her statement: R' Yisroel of Husyatin once arrived by train in a Galician town. As the steps down from the wagon ended some distance above the ground, a valise was placed on the ground for the Rebbe to step on. As his foot touched the valise, he shuddered and refused to step down on it. When the valise was opened later, they found a holy book in it.

DEVOUT STEPS

IT WAS THE YEAR 1942. THE GERMAN MARSHAL ERWIN ROMMEL REACHED Al Alamein, Egypt, coming close to the Palestinian border. The entire *Yishuv* was gripped by terror, fearing his inevitable invasion of

A TRUE PROPHECY

Eretz Yisroel and the threat to the Jewish population. At that time, the Husyatiner was visiting Yerushalayim. On the *yahrzeit* of R' Chaim ibn Attar, the *Ohr HaChaim HaKadosh* (d. Tammuz 1743), the Rebbe, followed by his chassidim, visited his grave on the Mount of Olives. To the surprise of the chassidim, the Rebbe spent much time there in prayer. Upon his return, his face radiant, he told them that Rommel would not advance any further, for "I have seen the Holy Tetragrammaton hovering over the grave in the perfect sequence of its letters" (signifying absolute *rachamim,* Divine mercy). Such openly prophetic statements were extremely rare in the House of Rizhin. This story became the sensational topic of the day. The "prophecy" was fulfilled, for Rommel's advance was stalled at Al Alamein.

R' Yisroel of Husyatin left no sons and his post was assumed by his son-in-law R' Yaakov Friedman (1878-1957), the youngest son of R' Yitzchok of Buhush. Famed as an outstanding scholar, his caliber was the envy of many famous rabbinical authorities. He authored the work *Oholei Yaakov* in which his brilliance is plainly evident. Most of his time was taken up in his studies; he could often be seen pacing up and down for hours in a stretch as his brain grappled with some intricate Talmudical dispute. He was in turn succeeded by his son R' Yitzchok (1900-1968), the last Rebbe of the Husyatiner dynasty. He authored the work *Siach Yitzchok,* an extremely well-received *sefer* among Rizhiner chassidim. R' Yaakov had one daughter. The Bauminger family of Eretz Yisroel are her descendants. The Husyatiner *kloiz* in Bialik Street, Tel Aviv still functions to this day, a silent reminder of the great *tzaddikim* who once served Hashem from within its confines.

The Kopitchinitzer dynasty also has its roots firmly imbedded in the House of Husyatin. The first Rebbe of Kopitchinitz, R' Yitzchok Meir Heschel (1861-1935), was a son-in-law of R' Mordechai Shraga of Husyatin. Beloved for his kind heart and generosity he attracted a large following of devoted chassidim. His son and successor R' Avrohom Yehoshua Heschel (1888-1967) was similarly endowed. R' Aharon Kotler was wont to say: "The Kopitchinitzer Rebbe is the *gadol hador* in *tzedakah,* (charity) and *chessed,* (lovingkindness)." By personal example, he showed the way for many in America who regarded him as a father figure. The grief of his fellow Jews tormented him much more than his own afflictions, and indeed the Rebbe often put his name and honor at risk in an attempt to help others.

A man once came to the Rebbe crying hysterically. He had just arrived from Europe and was hoping to settle in America. His wife, however, had been refused entry due to her ill health and was in Ellis Island awaiting deportation. "Don't worry," R' Avrohom Yehoshua Heschel consoled him, "I promise you that by next week your wife will be here together with you." Hearing the Rebbe's words the man calmed down and departed, his hope restored.

One of the chassidim who had witnessed the scene plucked up his courage and asked the Rebbe how he was able to make such a promise with such ease. "You saw how hysterical that man was," the Rebbe replied. "My first concern was to calm him down and thanks to Hashem I succeeded. At least for the next week he will feel better. If after a week he sees that I was wrong and his wife was deported, he will say, 'Avrohom Yehoshua Heschel is not a real Rebbe, Avrohom Yehoshua Heschel is a liar.' But at least for a week I succeeded in helping him." With that the Rebbe took out a *Tehillim* and started to cry: "Please, Hashem, see to it that Avrohom Yehoshua Heschel didn't say a lie, please don't make me a liar!" Hashem heard his prayers and within a week the woman was granted permission to stay in America, and was reunited with her husband.

He visited Eretz Yisroel ten times during which he invested much strength and energy involving himself in a broad spectrum of issues and concerns. He helped to shoulder the heavy burden of Chinuch Atzmai ensuring that thousands of children receive a Torah-true education.

R' Avrohom Yehoshua Heschel left three sons and seven daughters. The oldest son R' Yisroel, who did not have children, refused to become Rebbe despite the widely held belief that he was worthy of the task. The second son R' Moshe Mordechai (1927-1975) rose to the challenge and assumed the mantle of greatness. Like his father, he too was acclaimed for his goodness of heart and extreme kindness. In a short span of time he succeeded in gaining the respect and admiration of many who perceived him to be a mirror image of his father in *middos* (character) and *maasim tovim* (good deeds). However, Providence had decreed otherwise and only a short seven years after becoming Rebbe he succumbed to illness on the 17th of Nissan and is buried in Teverya next to his father. He is survived by three sons, R' Yitzchok Meir, R' Yekusiel Zusya and R' Avrohom Yehoshua Heschel and a daughter who reside in America where they continue the Kopitchinitzer tradition.

The third son of R' Avrohom Yehoshua Heschel is R' Sysche (Zisha) who is well known and appreciated as a pillar of the New York community. He is highly regarded by many who have benefited from his knowledge and personality over the decades. In particular he had a profound influence on thousands of young people as the spiritual dynamo of Camp Agudah for over two decades. He is also the father-in-law of the present Boyaner Rebbe *shlita* who resides in Yerushalayim. Another grandson of R' Avrohom Yehoshua Heschel who resides in Eretz Yisroel is R' Yitzchok Meir Flintenstein. He presides over the Oheiv Yisroel institutions and is founder of the well-known publishing house, Machon Sifsei Tzaddikim.

The Kopitchinitzer Rebbe, R' Avrohom Yehoshua Heschel, during a tisch

The renowned halachic authority, R' Shlomo Zalman Auerbach, was a *mechutan* with the Kopitchinitzer Rebbe, R' Avrohom Yehoshua Heschel. His son R' Mordechai married a granddaughter of the Rebbe. R' Mordechai lives in Tel Aviv where he is Rav of the Abir Yaakov Shul, where he leads a flourishing community and highly active outreach and *kiruv* program.

Among the other descendants of Kopitchinitz was the grandson of R' Yitzchok Meir Heschel, the late R' Eliezer Heschel of Antwerp. He is survived by his widow, his son R' Moshe Heschel of Yerushalayim, and a daughter who is married to R' Betzalel Halpern of Manchester, England.

CHAPTER XXIX

THE HOUSE OF BOYAN

R' YITZCHOK OF BOYAN

HE SON OF R' AVROHOM YAAKOV OF SADAGORA AND GRANDSON OF the Rizhiner, R' Yitzchok Friedman of Boyan (1849-1917), known as the Pachad Yitzchak, was the founder of the Boyan dynasty. He settled as *admor* in Boyan near Sadagora, an area which was part of Austria from 1774-1918. The town became a chassidic center which flourished around the Boyaner *hoif* and the grandiose court of the Rebbe. In 1914, with the invasion of the Bolsheviks, the *hoif* was destroyed and the Rebbe, like his relatives of the House of Rizhin, left for Vienna, where he settled.

A son-in-law of R' Yochanan of Rachmastrivka, who was the youngest son of R' Mottel of Chernobyl, the Boyaner was renowned for his matchless piety and modesty. He incorporated the princely mode of *Malchus Rizhin* with all its regal elegance, combined with a genuine sense of humility, spiritual modesty and purity of a lofty and saintly character. Torah scholarship and deep concern for *Klal Yisroel*, emanating from profound *ahavas Yisroel*, became the leitmotif of Boyan. The Boyaner Rebbes were known for their active leadership role within the Jewish community, lending the chassidic tone to all meaningful endeavors, and being staunch supporters of the *Yishuv* in Eretz Yisroel.

The Pachad Yitzchak enhanced his worship and prayer by having a classic *chazzan*, the well-known musician and composer, R' Pinye Spector, who composed dozens of *niggunim*, which he sang with his choir during the Rebbe's *tisch* and at other occasions.

The Boyaner chassidim came from various countries: Russia, Romania, Galicia, Poland, Bessarabia and Eretz Yisroel. Many of them would cross the Russian border under perilous conditions to come to Boyan and receive the Rebbe's *berachah*. R' Yitzchok inherited from his father the keen exegetic approach to Torah exposition. His sayings (still in manuscript) represent a homiletic style in which, after the manner of the kabbalists, symbolic *remez* (allusion) and *sod* (the hidden dimensions of knowledge) are entwined. Throughout his Torah discourses, there is always the transcending leitmotif of

R' Yochanon of Rachmastrivka — youngest son of R' Mottel of Chernobyl amd father-in-law of R' Yitzchok of Boyan

Shechinta begalusa — the *Shechinah* in exile — the fervent prayer for the redemption of the Divine Presence concurrent with that of His nation Israel, through repentance and national unity, echoed by the deep yearning for the coming of *Mashiach*. This hopeful theme can be found in all of his sons' Torah as the classic finale of their discourses. Humility was considered the hallmark of the Boyaner Rebbe. His modesty concealed the full extent of his greatness. As the Rabbis state (*Pesikta Zutresa, Bamidbar*, 17), "Tzaddikim humble themselves in proportion to their greatness." This is basically the meaning of וְהָלַכְתָּ בִּדְרָכָיו (*Devarim* 28:9), the commandment of following in Hashem's ways, manifested in the Divine attribute of humility.

NO DISPUTE IN THE WORLD OF DIVINE EMANATION, THERE IS NO DIFFERENCE OF OPINION. Generally the halachah does not follow R' Shimon bar Yochai, since he received his teaching from the world of emanation, where there is total clarity, without difference of opinion. When there is no difference of opinion, there is no halachah, because disputation defines the distinctions that are the essence of halachah.

THE REBBE'S ADVICE IT IS TOLD OF RABBI YITZCHOK OF BOYAN THAT A CHASSID ONCE CAME TO him for advice. "Rebbe, should I settle in Eretz Yisroel?"

"And your children," the Rebbe asked, "will they go along with you?"

The chassid replied, "My sons, their money is invested in property, they cannot join me."

"If so," the Rebbe returned, "stay here — not going is preferable, for your sons need you and your guidance in the path of the just. You should know that the Holy One, Blessed is He, loves Zion and relishes Jerusalem; nevertheless, as long as His children — Israel — dwell in exile, the Holy One, Blessed is He, is with them, and the Divine Presence is in exile."

The palace of the Rebbe of Sadagora

Concerning the Biblical verse, *You shall be wholehearted with Hashem, Your G-d* (*Devarim* 18:13), Rashi comments, "Walk before Him wholeheartedly, put your hope in Him and do not attempt to investigate the future, and then you shall be with Him and become His portion." Said the Pachad Yitzchak: "When man is one with G-d Almighty, for Whom past and present are equal, for He is above time, there is no more need to search the mysteries of the future, for then the light of redemption is seen in the here and now" (see *Ohr HaChaim* ad loc.).

JEWISH DIVISIVENESS

THE REBBE CONSTANTLY PREACHED UNITY AND PEACE, BEING A *MELAMED zechus* (advocate) for *Klal Yisroel*. He once commented, "The Sages say, קָשֶׁה עָלַי פְּרִידַתְכֶם, 'Your departure is hard for Me' (*Succah* 55b). All the things which the Rabbis classify as difficult for the Holy One, Blessed is He, so to speak, are as difficult as the splitting of the Sea of Reeds (*Pesachim* 18a, *Bereishis Rabbah* 20:9). The matchmaking of man is difficult (*Vayikra Rabbah* 8); the sustenance of man is difficult (*Pesachim* ibid.). But how can we say that something is difficult for the Master of the World?! Rather the word פירוד connotes schism, separation, meaning that it is displeasing for

R' N0chum Dov Brayer of Boyan lighting the hadlakah on Lag BaOmer in Meron

Hashem when there is divisiveness among the Children of Israel. But when there is true unity among them, nothing is too difficult."

THE REBBE'S PLEA

PLEADING THE CAUSE OF THE JEWISH PEOPLE, HE ONCE CRIED OUT TO Heaven: "O Lord, *You have separated man in the beginning,* אַתָּה הִבְדַּלְתָּ אֱנוֹשׁ מֵרֹאשׁ (from the *Ne'ilah* prayer). You have separated the head — the mind — from man. Because of economic concerns and stress, man does not have a head, or the time, to meditate upon the meaning of life and 'You recognized him to stand before You.' Nevertheless, You wish him to repent. O G-d, grant man the time and space to meditate his head — his mind — too, and he will certainly repent."

Tomb of R' Yitzchok of Boyan in Vienna

The Boyaner dynasty also inherited the honorable tradition and privilege to be the first to light the torch — the *hadlakah* on Lag BaOmer — at the grave of R' Shimon bar Yochai in Meron. The right and the *z'chus* to perform this ritual was bought by the Rizhiner from the Sephardic guardians of Meron and Tzefas. It is carried out nowadays by the present Boyaner Rebbe, R' Nochum Dov Brayer of Jerusalem. This yearly ritual is attended by thousands of pilgrims (estimated at 300,000 in 2001) as a religious festivity celebrated with song and dance.

R' Yitzchok also inherited from his father the title *Nassi* of the Kolel Vohlin in the Holy Land, coordinating all welfare funds for the support of the Orthodox community in Israel. His son, R' Yisroel of Leipzig, who settled in Eretz Yisroel, and all Boyaner Rebbes who visited Eretz Yisroel, supported the chassidim there and encouraged their chassidim in the Diaspora to settle in Eretz Yisroel. The four sons of R' Yitzchok each developed an independent branch of Boyan, with his own style, in various countries of Eastern Europe.

BOYANER SONS R' YITZCHOK HAD FOUR SONS, EACH OF whom served as leaders of Chassidic sects.

R' Menachem Nochum of Boyan-Chernovitz

1. R' Menachem Nochum of Boyan-Chernovitz (1868-1936), the oldest son, became *admor* in 1917, in Chernovitz. He married the daughter of R' Mordechai Shraga of Husyatin. A man of splendid stature and appearance, with a large following of chassidim, he passed away in Vienna and was interred in his father's mausoleum. His orations are edited in *Tiferes Menachem,* and his biography in *Mishkenos HaRoyim.* His son, R' Aharon, son-in-law of R' Chaim of Atinia, perished in 1942 in

Transnistria, a victim of the Nazis. His second son, R' Mordechai Shraga, son-in-law of R' Yisroel of Vizhnitz, perished at the same time as his brother.

R' Yisroel of Boyan-Leipzig

2. R' Yisroel of Boyan-Leipzig (1879-1951). Son-in-law of R' Shlomo of Sadagora, he served as *admor* in Leipzig from 1917 on, then settled in Tel Aviv in 1939. Quiet by nature, he was known for his tolerance and impartiality. He was survived by two daughters: Gittel, married to R' Avrohom Yaakov Shapira of Drohobitch, and Chava, married R' Mordechai Shraga Heschel of Kopitchenitz.

R' Avrohom Yaakov of Boyan-Lemberg

3. R' Avrohom Yaakov of Boyan-Lemberg (1886-1942), son-in-law of R' Mordechai Twerski of Loyev. He was renowned for his erudition and broad charity and hospitality, opening his doors to many rabbis and rebbeim, refugees of the Nazi regime, who found a haven in his home. He chose to share the tragic lot of his community and refused to be saved without them. He was murdered in Strij in 1942. His edited discourses were published in *Nachalas Yaakov*, Jerusalem, 1973.

4. R' Mordechai Shlomo of Boyan-New York (1890-1971), was the youngest of R' Yitzchok's sons. He married Chavah Sarah Heschel, daughter of R' Yisroel Sholom Yosef of Mezhibozh, great-grandson of the Apter Rebbe. He settled as a young *admor* in New York in 1925, on the Lower East Side, where his *beis medrash* became the center for Rizhiner chassidim in America. He served in the Presidium of Agudas Yisroel and was the lifetime president of Agudas HaAdmorim. Beloved and revered by thousands of chassidim and adherents, he founded and built the Mesivta Tiferes Yisroel of

R' Mordechai Shlomo of Boyan

Rizhin in Jerusalem. This was the first yeshivah built and dedicated in the name of the Rizhiner, as a living testimony after the destruction of the famous Rizhiner Synagogue in the Old City by the Arab Legion during the War of Independence in 1948. He visited Eretz Yisroel four times and was actively involved in the religious life in Eretz Yisroel. He died on the fifth day of Adar 1971 and was buried on the Mount of Olives in Jerusalem. The present author's prepared his orations for publication under the title *Ateres Mordechai.*

SON OF R' SHOLOM YOSEF OF HUSYATIN AND SON-IN-LAW OF R' MENACHEM Nochum of Boyan-Chernovitz, R' Moshe gained worldwide renown

R' MOSHE OF BOYAN-CRACOW (1881-1943)

for his vast erudition and for his Responsa, which were published as *Daas Moshe* (Jerusalem 1948). He served as the head of Yeshivas Chachmei Lublin from 1934 after the

demise of R' Meir Shapiro. R' Moshe died in the gas chambers of Belzec in 1943. His tragic death and martyrdom were described in a document miraculously unearthed from the ashes of Auschwitz, and published in Hebrew translation under the name *Megillas*

Auschwitz, written by Ber Mark, the former director of the Jewish Historical Institute in Communist Poland (*Sifrias Hapoalim, Hashomer Hatzair*, Israel). The book contains three original documents recorded by the Jewish Historical Institute of Poland. These documents are extremely revealing and important for the researcher of the *Churban* or "*Shoah*" [large-scale destruction; term commonly used in place of the "Holocaust"] literature. The treacherous tendency of the Nazis to deny their barbaric atrocities in the death camps, particularly the Auschwitz camp, erected specifically for the purpose of exterminating European Jews, was a cynical historical distortion. This diabolical act was fully revealed in a small booklet named "Report of the Research Committee of the Soviet Government, officially published in May 1975, in Russian, in Moscow, and later also in Polish translation.

This report states that in January 1945, the Soviet army occupied the Auschwitz camp and found there several thousand survivors, a minute remnant of the camp population. Some of them, exactly 2819, were repeatedly interrogated at length by the investigation committee which included medical doctors specializing in different diseases.

How in fact was the gruesome reality of the Auschwitz atrocities distorted by the Russians? The official Soviet report totally ignored the fundamental fact that the victims were overwhelmingly Jews from all occupied lands of Eastern Europe. The above Soviet report reads as follows: "In the Auschwitz camp the Germans killed by shooting, gassing, and through the use of excruciating torture, over four million citizens of Russia and other Eastern European countries."

R' Moshe of Boyan-Cracow

At Auschwitz there were found gas chambers, crematoria, departments of surgery and "research labs" — all for the purpose of exterminating people en masse. After tedious research and painstaking labor by a team of scholars at the Jewish Historical Institute in Poland, they were able to decipher the names of the authors of the recording notes: Zalman Gradovsky, Leib Langfiiss and Zalman Leventhal. From the depositions we learn firsthand of the true *kiddush Hashem* shown by the inmates of the death camps. One of the documents entitled "Horrors of Murder" begins with the following heartrending lines: "Among the transports arriving from Bendin and Sosnovitz there was an old rabbi. Since they were inhabitants of the locality (Auschwitz being near the Zaglembi sector), the prisoners of the transport knew quite well that they were being led to be shot. But the rabbi entered the undressing room while singing," and indeed this episode is entitled in the original document — *"Al kiddush Hashem."* A most revealing fragment of the document relates to the appearance of the Boyaner Rebbe, R' Mosheniu Friedman of Cracow, leader of the Council of Torah Sages of the Agudath Israel and spiritual leader of the famous Yeshivas Chachmei Lublin. Besides being a chassidic rebbe, R' Mosheniu was also known as a gaon and *poseik*. The following is the fragment found on the grounds of the Auschwitz camp.

It happened *erev* Pesach in the year 1943 … a transport arrived. In the transport there were some very important Jewish personalities, one of them — the Boyaner Rebbe — R' Moshe Friedman, who was known as one of the leading rabbinic luminaries in Poland. A very patriarchal personality. He undressed together with the others. But then he turned to the SS Oberscherfuehrer, and grabbing him by the lapels of his uniform, he proclaimed in (perfect) German: "You cruel murderers! You, the scum of the earth! Do not think that you will be able to exterminate the Jewish people. The Jewish people will survive forever and will not disappear from the stage of history. But you, abominable murderers, you will be paid (punished) as you deserve. The pure blood which you shed will be demanded of you. Our blood will not be appeased until the flaming anger will destroy the animal blood within you!" The Boyaner Rebbe

spoke with extraordinary excitement and with great force. Then, as he finished talking, he covered his head and pronounced with enormous enthusiasm, "*Shema Yisroel.*" And together with him, the entire crowd exploded with powerful devotion, "*Shema Yisroel!*"

From l. to r: R' Yisroel of Husyatin with R' Moshe of Boyan-Cracow

This was a moment of spiritual elevation which is unsurpassed in human life, a mode of exaltation that proves the eternity of the spiritual value of Judaism. As an addendum to the above authentic document from the underground notes recorded by an eyewitness, it is important to add the following: The name of the Oberscherfuehrer who led the Boyaner Rebbe to martyrdom in Auschwitz was Eric Musfeld. He was caught after the war and brought to trial for his atrocities, and was hanged on December 22, 1947.

CHAPTER XXX

R' Mordechai Shlomo of Boyan-New York

(1890-1971)

R'Mordechai Shlomo was born in 1890 in Boyan-Bukovina, and raised and educated under the tutelage of his great and awesome father in the Boyaner Court surrounded by sagacious mentors, in a princely lifestyle and in an atmosphere of genuine piety. He was the object of special fondness and attention, being his father's *mezinik* (youngest child). At his birth, his father called him a *chiddush* — something unusually new — meaning a pure and new *neshamah*.

The custom in Boyan was that the four brothers visited their father once weekly by rotation. Once Malka, the Rebbetzin of Boyan, found her youngest child, Mordechai Shlomo, crying bitterly. When asked for the cause of his crying, the child answered, "I want to see my father." The concerned mother entered the Rebbe's chamber and conveyed the child's wish to her husband. The Rebbe responded: "I allow myself the pleasure of seeing him only on Shabbos and Yom Tov." A sensitive and refined child, the young Mottele became the darling of the chassidim, in whose company he spent much time, listening to their stories and showing concern, at a young age, for their problems. Diligent and studious, he grew up to be a devout *oved Hashem* (servant of G-d), upright and serious. When World War I broke out in 1914, R' Yitzchok and his entire family escaped to Vienna, leaving behind the splendid court with all their belongings to become the booty of the rampaging Bolsheviks. Vienna became a haven for Jewish refugees, among them all rebbes of the Rizhin dynasty, as well as for many famous Torah luminaries of that era.

R' Yitzchok of Boyan died on 17 Adar, 1917, and was buried in Vienna. Thereafter the four sons continued as Boyaner Rebbes, each one in a different country. The oldest son, R' Menachem Nochum, settled in Chernovitz, near Boyan; his brother, R' Yisroel, in Leipzig; R' Avrohom Yaakov in Lemberg; while R' Mordechai Shlomo remained with his mother for another five years in Vienna. He then received an invitation from the Rizhiner chassidim in America and another invitation from the chassidim of Drohobitch. R' Mordechai Shlomo hesitated to accept their offer; he worried that in the spiritual wastelands of America he would not be able to educate his children as he would like. His uncle R' Yisroel of Chortkov allayed his fears and advised him to move.

The passage of time has proved the Rebbe of Chortkov was right. R' Mordechai Shlomo's three children are well-known pillars of the community. His oldest son, R' Yisroel, who is president of the American office of the Rizhiner Yeshivah, is known for his unstinting work and efforts on behalf of the yeshivah and on behalf of Rizhiner Chassidus in general. The younger son R' Yitzchok is also very active on behalf of Rizhiner institutions. His son-in-law R' Ezra Labaton serves as a rav in Deal, New Jersey. R' Mordechai Shlomo's daughter Malkah, married to the author of this work, is the mother of the present Boyaner Rebbe. Her other children are R' Yisroel Avrohom and Nechama Chaya, wife of R' Gedalyah Block.

The Boyaner Rebbe arrived in the United States on the 21st of Cheshvan 1927 in the port of New York, to the rapturous welcome of many happy chassidim.

America in those years was considered a desert, a *terra incognita* for Orthodox Judaism, even more so for Chassidus. Boyan was the pioneering herald of Chassidus in the United States. The Rebbe, a recent immigrant to the New World, never forgot his princely ancestry and was soon surrounded by chassidim, among them young people thirsty for the word of Hashem, who looked up to him as their newly adopted spiritual father, one who would infuse their souls with fresh hope and faith in the Almighty and His Torah. In a secular environment of Jewish ignorance, total alienation from traditional values and a socialist milieu, the Boyaner *beis midrash* at 247 East Broadway, on the Lower East Side of New York, became the communal address for all, a shelter for Chassidus and a haven for young *baalei teshuvah.*

The Rebbe's charismatic personality, paternal warmth and humane concern for all who crossed his path attracted the younger

The Boyaner Rebbe with the Kollel Boyan in Yerushalayim

generation in particular, who flocked to him in search of a spiritual role model who could show tolerance and understanding for their searching souls. The Rebbe's simplicity, informality and personal interest in his followers' lives and their problems, his tenderness and charm, were admired by all. Everyone who connected with the Rebbe felt his spiritual spark ignited, and experienced a yearning for Divine grace, bestowed by the Rebbe's blessings and fostered by his piety. He was beloved by all segments of the Jewish arena, *misnagdim*, the yeshivah world, *baalebatim*, the modern intelligentsia and, above all, by the other chassidic leaders who arrived later to the American shores, as well as the rabbinic leaders abroad. Such was their admiration and respect for the Boyaner Rebbe who preserved the stock of the Rizhiner *derech* of Eastern Europe and transplanted it in the soil of the New World. Thus were sown in America the early seeds of Chassidus.

Whoever had the *zechus* to attend the Rebbe's *tisch* on Shabbos and Yom Tov or at a chassidic *hilulah* (commemoration of a *yahrzeit*) became deeply impressed by the spiritual decorum and repose — but more so by the majestic stature of the Rebbe who sat absorbed in deep meditation, his eyes closed, as if migrating in higher celestial spheres, sitting erect and immobile, rarely making eye contact with those sitting around the table, all of whom possessed an awesome reverence, their eyes glued to his angelic presence. They tried to swallow every word uttered by their master when saying "Torah," his pale face changing color, his voice a faint tremolo accompanied by painful heartrending sighs for the *Shechinta begalusa* (exiled *Shechinah*).

The Rebbe's worship was always mysteriously contained. Only inner fervor, no vocal outcries, no demonstration of ecstasy or excitement, just a burning inner flame of feeling glowing in the deep recesses of the soul, yearning to make contact with Heaven, inwardly engulfed in emotional passion and devotion to reach the Creator. The Rebbe was always laconic, fastidious of speech, every word carefully measured and logically balanced. His responses were cautiously uttered, directed at the central issue. His tone of voice was always warm and moderate, laced with a keen sense of humor, often seasoned with a parable to clarify his point — in the words of Moshe ibn Ezra, "Words that come from the heart penetrate the heart" (*Shiras Yisroel*, p. 156).

His followers perceived him as a saint of generations past, a father-figure and devoted shepherd. His peaceful and tranquil approach to everyday life, combined with his plain and humble manner, contributed to the Rebbe's being perceived as a mediator between the various currents of the Orthodox community at large. A promoter of peace and unity, his influence extended beyond the chassidic arena, and his spirituality and concern for *ahavas Yisroel* encompassed Jews in all walks of life.

CLASHING POLARITIES

IN THE EARLY PERIOD AFTER HIS ARRIVAL, THE REBBE HAD TO STRUGGLE for a *parnassah*, refusing to be supported by the well-to-do chassidim, so that he would not be obligated to individuals. These were the years of the Depression.

I was told that in those difficult years a Boyaner chassid traveled to Chernovitz for business. Since the Rebbe's oldest brother lived there, the chassid visited the local Boyaner Rebbe and brought regards from the Boyaner Rebbe in New York. The Chernovitzer asked the chassid how his brother's *parnassah* was, to which he replied: "He is going through hard times at present."

The Chernovitzer then remarked: "America is the *mekor hasheker* (source of falsehood), and my brother is the *mekor ha'emes* (source of truth). How can these two opposites be reconciled?"

Humble and modest even with the young, the Rebbe showed genuine humility to all. In his *beis midrash* there would sit a youngster who learned at night. Once, as he sat there, the young man heard the Rebbe walk through the hall upstairs late at night to retire to his room on the first floor. But then, he heard again the Rebbe's footsteps walking down the flight of stairs. Opening the door of the *beis midrash,* the Rebbe said to the astonished youngster: "I am sorry, I walked upstairs without saying good night to you. Have a good night!"

He interpreted the Talmudic dispute (*Shabbos* 86b) as to the exact day when the Ten Commandments were given, as telling us

HUMILITY RESTORED that the holy Torah is above time. Just as the Torah transcends time, so it transcends space, as the Rabbis state (*Berachos* 8a), "The tablets and the broken tablets were placed together in the Ark while its place is not part of the measurable dimensions because it didn't occupy any space."

Mount Sinai is among the smaller mountains — the idea being that it does not occupy any space because of its humility.

He said: Toiling in the Torah is performed by several categories. The Gemara states (*Megillah* 6b), "If a person tells you: 'I toiled and

TOILING IN TORAH I found — believe it,' " meaning that even those who are toiling in Torah must believe that after all the effort and labor it is considered no more than something that is "found," i.e., that Hashem is rewarding them for their toil.

The beis midrash in Boyan

THE REBBE SHOWED CONCERN AND WAS ATTENTIVE TO THE INDIVIDUAL and to *Klal Yisroel* alike. He ardently loved every Jew and found a

BEFORE LEAVING

zechus for everyone, without exception. Once before visiting Eretz Yisroel he was asked what he was thinking before leaving for the Holy Land. Was he thinking of the holy places, or of the sanctity of the Land itself, of the religious institutions or of the chassidim who were waiting for him? The Rebbe replied that he was mainly concerned to bring more charity money with him for the needy. In fact, he borrowed large amounts of money to dispense to the poor in Eretz Yisroel. This trait of *ahavas Yisroel* he inherited from his great-grandfather, the Rizhiner, who exclaimed: "I am a part of the Jewish collective soul. If a Jew at the end of the world hurts his finger, I feel his pain in my own body." When the Rebbe was seriously ill at the Beth Israel hospital in New York, he was visited by one of the Jewish community leaders who wished the Rebbe a *refuah sheleimah.* The Rebbe said to him, "Who am I that I should deserve a *matnas chinam* (free gift)? But the Sages say (*Bava Kamma* 92a), 'One who solicits mercy for his fellow while he himself is in need of the same thing will be answered first.' And indeed, I never stop praying for

Rizhiner descendants at the Rizhiner shul in the Old City of Yerushalayim

others." In all his endeavors, the Boyaner Rebbe's goal was to restore *Nusach Rizhin* and the Jewish crown to their former glory, to elevate the Jewish consciousness and royal honor of days gone by.

SETTLING IN ISRAEL SINCE THE EARLY DAYS OF THE BAAL SHEM TOV AND HIS YEARNING TO settle in the Holy Land (see his classic letter sent to his brother-in-law, R' Gershon of Kitev, who settled in Eretz Yisroel; see end of *Ben Porat Yosef*), the same dream possessed his descendants. The Baal Shem Tov writes, "The Almighty knows that I am not giving up my plan of leaving for Eretz Yisroel if this will be the will of Hashem." Similarly, the disciples of the Maggid of Mezritch, who made *aliyah* as chassidic pioneers, built bridges between Russia and the Holy Land. The Great Maggid of Mezritch used to say: "The entire universe nurses its vitality from Zion, which is the essence of the universe and the vitality of the entire world" (*Ohr Torah*).

The Rizhiner's progeny followed in his footsteps and continued as presidents of the Kollel Vohlin (Association of Ukrainian Jews in

R' Mordechai Shlomo testing the students in the Rizhiner Yeshivah

Palestine), magnanimously providing large sums of money year after year, as well as solid moral support for the old *Yishuv*. This function has been maintained by the Boyaner dynasty down to the present day.

The Rizhiner expressed his longing for the Holy Land also by singing with fervor the liturgical hymn, יָדְךָ תַּנְחֵנוּ אֶל אֶרֶץ הַקְּדוֹשָׁה, "May Your hand lead us to the Holy Land," and another song, חַשׁ תֶּן לָנוּ חֵלֶק בְּדָוִד וְגַם נַחֲלָה בְּבֶן יִשַׁי, "Quickly give us a share in Dovid and an inheritance in the son of Yishai" — both liturgical poems composed by the poet, R' Yisroel Najara (16th c.), a disciple of the *Ari Hakadosh*. The magnum opus of the Rizhiner and his son R' Avrohom Yaakov was indeed the erection of the great synagogue Tiferes Yisroel, called also Nissan Beck's Shul, in the Old City near the Kosel. It constituted the center of the Rizhiner chassidim, where all the Rizhiner Rebbes conducted their *tisch*. This magnificent edifice, the tallest building in Jerusalem, became the last bastion of the Irgun, and was plundered and reduced to rubble by Jordan's Arab Legion in the War of Independence in 1948.

LET YOUR EYES SEE YOUR MASTER

THE BOYANER REBBE WAS THE OBJECT OF THE LOVE AND DEVOTION OF his chassidim, young and old. All were attracted by his charismatic personality as a warm, benevolent father. The Rebbe worked for large goals that transcend self-interest. He counseled and guided his flock with keen understanding and genuine empathy, with an aura of ho-

liness, gaining a new generation of followers. He always stressed the impor- tance of studying Torah, virtuous manners, concern for one's fellow man and, above all, humility. He thus followed the path of his great-grandfather the Rizhiner, who said, "I have gathered souls until the coming of *Mashiach*."

L-R: R' Mordechai Shlomo of Boyan-New York, his son-in- law R' Menachem M. Brayer and R' Avrohom Yehoshua Heschel of Kopitchinitz of N.Y.

LIKE ALL OTHER DESCENDANTS OF RIZHIN, THE REBBE CARRIED A TURKISH passport identifying him as a citizen of Palestine. He showed

LOVE FOR ZION special affection for his chassidim in Eretz Yisroel who came to visit him, and was always inquiring about the economic and educational state of affairs there. The Rebbe visited Eretz Yisroel four times, leaving an indelible impression on his followers and sympathizers. His *tischen* were most impressive, causing in many hearts a spiritual reawakening to Jewish tradition and Torah values.

I KNOW OF A REPUTABLE *SHADAR* (EMISSARY FOR ISRAELI INSTITUTIONS OF learning and charity) of a well-known yeshivah in Israel who vis-

ON GIVING CHARITY ited the Rebbe to collect money. It happened at a time when the Rebbe was in a very precarious financial situation. Nevertheless, he searched all over, found a small sum of money and gave it to the *shadar.* The man remarked that he had come for an important cause and asked for a larger donation. The Rebbe got up quickly from his chair, went out to a neighbor, borrowed a substantial sum and gave it to the *shadar,* adding on blessings and thanking

the *shadar* for enabling him to perform the mitzvah of supporting Torah study in Israel.

I RECALL THAT IN THE LAST YEAR OF his life he was given a small stone

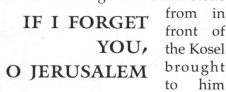

IF I FORGET YOU, O JERUSALEM from in front of the Kosel brought to him

by a chassid from Jerusalem. The Rebbe kept it next to him all the

From right to left: The Sadagorer Rebbe, R' Avrohom Yaakov and the Boyaner Rebbe, R' Mordechai Shlomo time, taking pleasure in it and kissing it often.

CHAPTER XXXI

HIS LOVE FOR ERETZ YISROEL

EVERY SUMMER, BEFORE MY REVERED FATHER-IN-LAW, R' MORDECHAI Shlomo, came to stay with us in Sackett Lake (upstate New York), he would ask me to bring along Tractate

TRACTATE MAKKOS

Makkos to make a *siyum* (completion of the intensive study of a major section of Talmud) in the Nine Days Of Mourning.

When I questioned him as to why he studied the same tractate every summer, he replied that this was the custom of his father in Boyan, because *Mesechta Makkos* concludes with the statement, "Akiva, you have consoled us," which points to the Divine promise of rebuilding the Temple and the consolation of Zion.

LOOKING AT ERETZ ISRAEL

ON HIS FIRST VISIT TO ERETZ YISRAEL, R' MORDECHAI SHLOMO WAS received festively by his devoted chassidim, who had arranged a bus packed with his followers to escort the Rebbe on the way from

R' Mordechai Shlomo of Boyan and R' Avrohom Yehoshua Heschel of Kopitchinitz,
with the author in the center.

Jerusalem to Tzefas. Although the chassidim eagerly awaited the
Rebbe's words, all he did was to look out the window with great con-
centration. One of the chassidim could not contain himself and asked:
"Can the Rebbe tell us what there is to be seen from the window?"
The Rebbe replied: "Of Eretz Yisrael it is said that *the eyes of Hashem,
your G-d, are upon it from the beginning of the year to the end of the year*
(*Devarim* 11:12). Certainly then, if Hashem Almighty looks at it, we
ought to look at it."

ON THE SEDER NIGHT OF PESACH, HE COMMENTED ON THE CUSTOM OF
placing a fifth full cup of wine on the Seder table. The Rebbe ex-

THE FIFTH plained the reason that according to the
Rabbis the four cups of wine represent the
SEDER CUP four expressions of Divine promise of redemption mentioned in the Torah. The fifth Hebrew term is
וְהֵבֵאתִי, "and I shall bring (you)" to the Promised Land. Since
this promise has not yet been fulfilled, we fill up the fifth cup but
we do not drink it, waiting for the Prophet Eliyahu to herald the
future redemption.

THE BOYANER VISITED ISRAEL IN 1958. ON HIS WAY TO TIBERIAS, WITH AN escort of chassidim, the bus broke down in Lod. The Rebbe

IN PRAISE OF THE HOLY LAND

alighted with fifty of his chassidim, to tour Lod while repairs were made. There he met an Oriental Jew from Casablanca, Morocco, and asked him about his origins, about his work and how long he had been in the Land. The Jew replied that he had been living in Israel for the past seven years, and that, thank G-d, he had sufficient income. The Rebbe met a second Jew, this time from Poland, and once again asked the same questions, and once again the Jew responded that, thank G-d, he had adequate *parnassah.* He also received the same answer from one of his followers from Sadagora who had settled in Israel. The Rebbe turned to his chassidim and said: "It was worthwhile to sojourn in Lod, if only to hear three Jews praise the Creator for their sustenance in the Holy Land."

RETURNING TO NEW YORK FROM JERUSALEM IN 1960, HE TOLD HIS chassidim at the airport. "The *Anshei Knesses HaGedolah* did not per-

LIGHT OVER DARKNESS

mit us to distract our mind from Eretz Yisrael even for one moment. They therefore instituted in the *Shemoneh Esrei,* 'And to Jerusalem Your city may You return in compassion ... And may our eyes behold Your return to Zion in compassion.' For when you leave Eretz Yisrael for the Diaspora, the difference is as great as from day to night" — the superiority of light over darkness.

THE REBBE TOLD ME THIS IN THE NAME OF HIS GRANDFATHER, R' Yochanan of Rachmistrivka. R' Yochanan visited his brother, R'

WINE FROM ERETZ YISRAEL

Dovid'l of Tolna, one Shabbos. Honoring his guest, R' Dovid'l ordered his *gabbai* to bring from the cellar special wine imported from the Holy Land for *Kiddush,* but R' Yochanan chose to make *Kiddush* on the local, Ukrainian wine. Puzzled by his action, R' Dovid'l asked, "I especially ordered wine from the Holy Land for you. Have you perhaps, dear brother, any doubt regarding the wine of Eretz Yisrael?" R' Yochanan replied: "G-d forbid, I am far from being a connoisseur of wines. For when do I drink wine? Only for *Kiddush, Havdalah* and the Four Cups of the Pesach Seder. My dear brother, you don't know the tactics of the *yetzer hara.* For if I were to drink the wine from the Holy Land and it did not please me, then I would think and speak ill of the fruit of Eretz Yisrael. Therefore, I preclude the possibility of entertaining such a temptation, and I make *Kiddush* on the local wine."

THE REBBE AGAIN QUOTED TO ME FROM HIS GRANDFATHER, R' YOCHANAN, who stated: "It is required to recite the *berachah* on Succos specifi-

ESROGIM FROM ERETZ YISRAEL

cally on an *esrog* grown in the Holy Land, and not on one from Morocco or from Italy. The reason is simple. The Holy Torah commands us, *and you should take for yourselves the fruit of a beautiful tree* (*Vayikara* 23:40). Is it conceivable that the Torah was referring to the *esrogim* of Corfu or Yanova (Genoa, Italy), and not to the fruit of Eretz Yisrael?" And indeed it is the custom of all *tzaddikim* of the House of Rizhin to recite the *berachah* on an *esrog* specifically over *esrogim* grown in Eretz Yisrael.

FERVENT WAS THE REBBE'S WISH TO SETTLE IN ERETZ YISRAEL AND TO perpetuate Boyaner Chassidus in the Chosen Land. Various plans were formulated in the 60's, but to no practical effect, on account of

LIKE A FEATHER BED

the Rebbe's weak constitution. His strong ties and affinity with his chassidim in Eretz Yisrael drew him there all the time, as he expressed in one of his letters. "It says, *As face answers face reflected in the water, so one man's heart answers another's* (*Mishlei* 27:19), so too, I feel nostalgic for our people in Eretz Yisrael. I know they want me to come there, but how can I, in my poor state of health?" This reminds us of a story about two Jews who came to the Rizhiner to get his blessing for their decision to settle in Eretz Yisrael. The *tzaddik* approved of one but refused to give his blessing to the other. "Why?"

asked the man. The Rizhiner explained: "I shall give you an example. It is similar to a man who wants to warm himself up. He goes and covers himself with a feather bed. He warms the feather bed up with his own body and the feather bed warms him in turn. But if we place a rock under the feather bed, both the rock and the feather bed will remain cold because of the lack of warmth of the rock itself. This parable," continued the Rizhiner, "applies to both of you. The man whose departure I approved of made preparations and got himself ready to go to Eretz Yisrael, therefore the land will absorb him. But as for you, you are not ready to tolerate the land; you are better off remaining here, for the land has nothing to offer you."

THE TOLNER REBBE TOLD ME OF A YERUSHALMI JEW WHO CAME TO THE Boyaner Rebbe on the Lower East Side for charity. It was a time

ON GIVING
TZEDAKAH

when the Rebbe himself was struggling to make ends meet. Nevertheless, the Rebbe searched and found a few dollars and gave them to the man with an affable smile. The Jew hinted uncomfortably that he was collecting for an important institution and that he was expecting a larger contribution. The Rebbe then told him, "Go to the house of Reb Mordechai of Tolna tonight, there you will receive a substantial sum of money." Meanwhile, the Rebbe contacted a few rich Jews and collected a substantial sum of money,

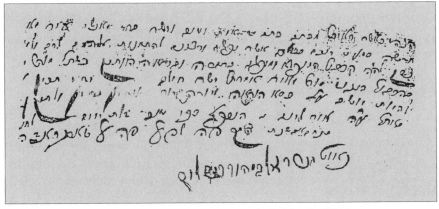

A writ of Semichah (ordination) given by R' Yisroel of Rizhin

and brought it clandestinely to the house of the Tolner Rebbe. In the evening, the man arrived at the Tolner's house and duly received a large sum of money, to his great satisfaction.

THE REBBE TOLD ME THAT WHILE STILL IN VIENNA HE WAS VISITED BY the famous Gaon, R' Meir Arik. "He had not come especially to

HUMILITY see me," said the Rebbe, "however, in the same building where I lived there was also an *esrog* salesman. The Gaon had come to buy an *esrog*, and as it started raining he came up to my apartment ..."

THE REBBE ALSO TOLD ME THAT THE *TZADDIK* OF MOGELNITZA CAME TO THE Rizhiner to receive rabbinic ordination from him. The Rizhiner told

SHARING JEWISH PAIN him, "With us, what counts most is to fully share the pain of a Jew, even before we read his *kvitel*. I mean actually to feel his pain."

IN CONNECTION WITH THE ABOVE, THE REBBE TOLD ME THAT AFTER THE demise of the Lelover Rebbe, his son, R' Dovid'l, refused to become

REAL HONESTY Rebbe. He was finally persuaded to consult R' Avrohom Yaakov of Sadagora and hear his opinion. The Sadagorer asked him, "Why don't you follow your father's path and become Lelover Rebbe?" R' Dovid'l answered him as follows: "How can I consider becoming Rebbe, when I know that if a mother came to me asking me to pray for her sick son; and I know that if my own son were sick, I would feel more pain and pray with more *kavannah* and fervor ... How then can I be a Rebbe?"

A YOUNG MAN CAME ONCE TO THE RIZHINER AND ASKED TO BE

A FIFTH SHULCHAN ARUCH ordained as a rabbi. "Do you know how many sections there are in the *Shulchan Aruch*?" asked the Rizhiner. The young man replied, "Four, of course."

"And the fifth part, do you know of that?" continued the Rizhiner. "I never heard of a fifth part," said the young man, puzzled.

"I will tell you what it is," replied the Rebbe. "לְעוֹלָם יְהֵא אָדָם אָדָם, '[Whatever else he may be] let a person always be a *mentch*.' "

CONCERN FOR ERETZ YISRAEL

IN 1967, JUST BEFORE THE SIX DAY WAR, AN EMERGENCY MEETING WAS called by the Moetzes Gedolei HaTorah in New York to devise a strategy to help our brethren in Eretz Yisrael. The tension was high and the concern very serious. The participants were notified by the Rebbe's family that on doctor's orders the Boyaner Rebbe should not attend the meeting, and therefore the meeting should not take place in his house as planned. How surprised were the participants to see the Boyaner Rebbe appearing at the door of the meeting hall, excusing himself by saying, "It was very hard for me to come here, but it was even harder for me to remain at home a time when our Jewish brothers are in danger. Our brethren in Eretz Yisrael are in need of much *rachamim*. Jews are praying and hoping for a *yeshuah*, how could anyone stay home at a time of such crisis?" The Rebbe sat down and participated throughout the meeting and all deliberations, his body visibly contorted with pain. As he tried to get up from his chair, sighing and trembling with deep physical anguish, a rabbi approached him and reproached him politely: "Why doesn't the Rebbe take care of his health rather than endangering it by forcing himself to attend this meeting?" The Rebbe answered him, "It doesn't matter. Jews are in danger, I am therefore allowed to feel a little pain because of them."

R' Mordechai Shlomo of Boyan

AFTER THE VICTORIOUS OUTCOME OF THE SIX DAY WAR HE TOLD ONE of his chassidim, *"Baruch Hashem,* now *Mashiach* surely has to come. Who could have foretold that the *Kosel*

PRAISE G–D *HaMaaravi* would now be in our hands, or that the Arabs and the Russians would acknowledge their downfall? The Arabs will feel their defeat for a short period, but the Russians... The entire Jewish nation are pleased and joyous. Thank G-d for the victory. The Almighty will guard the Jewish people, His people. They have no place to go. Our land is so small. But we all know that the hand of G-d did it all."

WHEN IN JERUSALEM, HE WAS TREATED WITH GREAT HOSPITALITY AT THE house of his chassid, R' Moshe Ludmir. One morning, R' Moshe saw the Rebbe pacing the floor self-absorbed and

REASON FOR worried, sighing heavily after a sleepless

INSOMNIA night. R' Moshe pleaded with the Rebbe to watch his health and asked why he was so distressed. The Rebbe replied: "What shall I do? Yesterday a Jew gave me a *kvitel,* full of *tzores* and pain. It affected me so badly that I couldn't sleep."

WHILE VISITING TIBERIAS, THE REBBE WAS LODGING AT THE HOUSE OF one of his chassidim. The owner found a rare coin while cleaning the house. He immediately inquired of

TO AVOID BLAME the chassidim and the visitors who had come to see the Rebbe if any of them had lost a coin. Before the Rebbe's departure the owner approached the Rebbe, perhaps it was he who had lost the coin. To the owner's surprise the Rebbe answered in the affirmative. He did indeed have two coins that he had received from one of his chassidim who inherited them from his grandfather, who in turn received them from the Rebbe's grandfather R' Avrohom Yaakov, the Sadagorer Rebbe. The chassid asked again in shock: "And why didn't the Rebbe say so earlier when he actually lost it?" Answered the Rebbe: "I was afraid that the coin would not be found, and that the Jewish maid would be suspected and blamed. I suppressed my frustration not to cause affliction to a Jewish daughter."

ALTHOUGH THE REBBE'S HOUSE WAS OFTEN IN SERIOUS FINANCIAL STRAITS, the Rebbe stretched out his hands to the needy and to all who

A REASON FOR TZEDAKAH knocked at his door. When he was once asked why he was spending more than he had on *tzedakah* and why he did not follow the teaching of the Mishnah (*Yerushalmi Peah* 1:1), that one who spends money for *tzedakah* should not exceed one fifth of what he has, the Rebbe directed the inquirer to quote the conclusion of the Mishnah, namely, "in order that he should not come to depend on other people." "This does not apply to me," the Rebbe said, "since I anyway depend on other people."

THE REBBE TOLD ME THAT A JEW ONCE CAME TO HIS FATHER, THE PACHAD Yitzchak, seeking advice about settling in Israel. Knowing this per-

NOT TO LEAVE ISRAEL son to be the type of man who could not sustain the hardships of the Holy Land and knowing he would return to the Diaspora, the Rebbe told him, "Going to Eretz Yisrael is very good, but to leave the Land is not good at all."

THE RABBIS SAID, "A SAGE IS SUPERIOR TO A PROPHET" (*BAVA BASRA* 12A). The Rebbe foresaw with pain and deep concern that Rizhiner

FROM THE ASHES Chassidus would have to rise from the ashes after World War II. The Rebbe therefore envisioned and planned the building of the Rizhiner Yeshivah, Tiferes Yisrael, in Jerusalem, which was to constitute the main center of Torah and Rizhiner Chassidus. With the full support of all Rebbes of the Rizhin dynasty, the yeshivah was inaugurated in 1957 and soon became a beacon of Torah study. The Rebbe declared, "I am not forgetting the yeshivah, not for one moment." Indeed, this was the first chassidic yeshivah built by a descendant of Rizhin to salvage the future generations of this chassidic branch. For the Rebbe, the immersion in the study of Torah and Chassidus was the only solution with which to combat alienation and assimilation.

GEMILUS CHESSED ALL PROCEEDS THE REBBE RECEIVED FROM THE *KVITLECH* IN ERETZ YISRAEL, he refused to use for himself, instead dedicating them for the *Gemilas Chessed* of Boyan, for the poor in Eretz Yisrael.

Upon his return from his last visit to Israel, I was told by my mother-in-law, Rebbetzin Chava Sarah, *z"l*, that all the proceeds the Rebbe received during his visit to Israel and Europe were distributed by the Rebbe to the needy and to religious institutions, leaving himself penniless and forced to borrow money for a return plane ticket.

A TRUE MODEL NEVER DID THE REBBE ALLOW HIMSELF TO BE SWEPT UP IN POLITICS. Nevertheless he always expressed his views in matters important to the Jewish community here and abroad, with conviction and decisiveness. His calm, quiet voice was attentively listened to, and his advice followed, even within nonchassidic circles. It is inconceivable how a person of such weak physical constitution could immerse himself in the sea of Torah and worship, ignoring his own personal needs, worrying about his fellow Jew in the Rizhiner spirit of *ahavas Yisrael*. Cheerful but compassionate, perceptive and with keen intuition, the Rebbe was always in command of his own thoughts, his speech and his actions. Always humble and sensitive not to offend anyone's feelings, yielding to the needs of others at his own expense, he acted as an ideal role model in showing how one can sanctify the Divine Name in a variety of activities and settings in this materialistic world.

THE MODEST LIFESTYLE AS AN EXAMPLE OF HIS MODEST LIFESTYLE HE NEVER ALLOWED HIS OLD furniture to be replaced, and so it has remained to this day. The Rebbe never bemoaned his lot, and never appealed to his chassidim for support. In his later years his followers wanted him to move to a more comfortable home in Boro Park, but he refused, categorically stating that he did not want to pirate people away from other rebbes or other synagogues.

ENCOUNTERING TREMENDOUS DIFFICULTIES AND WITH NO OUTSIDE HELP he continued to fight ignorance and obscurantism, and with his

PIONEER OF AMERICAN CHASSIDUS

unique affability he excelled in bringing new souls to *Yiddishkeit*. Said R' Yaakov Yosef of Skver, "The Boyaner Rebbe's settling in New York was a Divine miracle and *kiddush Hashem*, in order to pave a new *derech* of Chassidus in America."

AS A *MANHIG YISRAEL* (LEADER OF ISRAEL), HIS NAME WAS ALWAYS pronounced with reverence and deep respect. He was a pillar of

JEWISH LEADERSHIP

Agudas Israel and showed unusual *mesiras nefesh* (self-sacrifice) for this organization. As an active member of the Presidium, and as a member of the Moetzes Gedolei HaTorah, he participated in all deliberations and meetings in New York. His opinion was always appreciated and considered by the leading participants in matters important to the religious, political and social issues vital to the Jewish community. The Rebbe was a lifetime President of Agudas HaAdmorim of America. Together with Agudas HaRabbanim, he helped organize the Vaad Hatzalah during World War II, and helped Torah leaders escape the Nazi inferno in Poland and Eastern Europe.

ONE OF THE CHASSIDIM COMPLAINED TO THE REBBE THAT AT THE beginning of every job he ever attempted he encountered difficul-

ALL BEGINNINGS ARE DIFFICULT

ties and all kinds of obstacles. The Rebbe answered him, "It says, *And though your beginning was small, yet your end shall greatly increase* (Iyov 8:7). The beginnings are indeed difficult, the question is how much time is considered a beginning: hours, days, months? This is the meaning of the verse, 'Hashem will help you' — so that the main difficulty, the beginning of your labor, will be of short duration, but your concluding work will greatly prosper."

THE REBBE ALSO COMMENTED: "THE GREATEST MERIT AND THE PRE-eminent purpose is for one to hold oneself insignificant — as

CLASSIC HUMILITY
Yaakov said, *I am not worthy of all the mercies and of all the truth that You have shown Your servant* (*Bereishis* 32:11). If one holds himself unworthy of Hashem, Hashem elevates him, as the Psalmist declares, *Who raises up the poor from the dust* (*Tehillim* 113:7), or as we say in our morning prayer, "Who lifts the lowly."

HE ALSO COMMENTED ON THE VERSE, *AND HASHEM SAID TO YAAKOV, 'ARISE, go up to Beth El and dwell there, and make there an altar to Hashem Who*

DIVINE REVELATION
appeared to you when you fled from before Esav, your brother (*Bereishis* 35:1), as follows: "Proportionate to one's distancing himself from evil (symbolized by his flight from Esav), Hashem appeared to Yaakov, the ratio of one's turning away from evil coinciding with the Divine revelation to every Jewish person."

SPEAKING ONCE OF HIS FATHER, THE REBBE STATED: "MY HOLY FATHER doesn't belong to this generation." Of his grandfather, the

ON THE ANCESTORS
Sadagorer, he said: "The chassidim who trav-eled to see him, no sooner did they come to the outskirts of the town of Sadagora, from which its rooftops were visible, that they already felt engulfed in a *hirhur teshuvah* (thought of repentance)." Of his great-grandfather, the Rizhiner, he said "He was incomprehensible. At times he spoke of himself 'very high' and at other times he perceived himself as 'very low.' However, never challenged, he enjoyed the approbation and acceptance of the entire world." (See Ch. 10)

WHILE IN PHILADELPHIA, HE RECEIVED VISITORS IN THE EVENINGS AFTER work hours. During the day he spent all the time in the local

HELPING BUILD
yeshivah discussing Torah with the students, reviewing the *shiurim*, and

helping the yeshivah contribute to the city as a *makom* Torah, a place of Torah.

RESPECT FOR THE DIVINE IMAGE

THE REBBE ALWAYS SHOWED GREAT RESPECT FOR OTHERS, REGARDLESS OF status or age. He always tried not to impose upon others, nor to touch upon their sensitivities or their money. A Boyaner chassid told of his experience while entering the Rebbe's *kloiz* on *Erev* Pesach, usually a time when everyone is busy with the many preparations for the holiday. To his astonishment he found the Rebbe dusting the benches of the *kloiz*. The chassid took a dust cloth, intending to do the task in place of the Rebbe, while asking him why he was doing the dusting all by himself. After all, the Rebbe has *gabbaim* who can do such things. In his usual quiet manner the Rebbe answered: "The *gabbaim* surely must be over their heads now with all the strenuous preparations for Yom Tov. How can I leave the benches without cleaning off the dust, when tonight Jews are coming all dressed up in their new clothes for Yom Tov. Why should they get them dirty?"

IDENTIFYING WITH OTHERS

DURING THE BAKING OF MATZOS FOR PESACH, THE REBBE WAS ENGAGED IN pouring the water into the *shmurah* flour with great *kavannah*. Wearing a new white apron, he carried out this holy service like the *Kohen Gadol* in the *Beis HaMikdash*. He refused to sit while supervising the entire baking process with extreme care; he would not sit while the workers were standing.

HOW TO STUDY TORAH

THE REBBE ONCE REMARKED: "THE *TANNA* IN *AVOS* 6:4 STATES: 'THIS IS the way of Torah: Eat bread with salt, drink water in small measure, sleep on the ground, live a life of deprivation — but toil in the Torah.' The Mishnah only suggests this approach to study Torah, but surely it isn't a positive commandment that this is the only way to study the Torah."

CHAPTER XXXII

HIS LOVE
OF TORAH

AFTER INAUGURATING A NEW *MIKVEH* IN TEL AVIV, WHICH THE
Rebbe helped to build by raising funds, the Rebbe accompanied by his chassid, R' Chaim Brim, visited the
renowned Gaon, the Chazon Ish, *zt"l,* in
Bnei Brak, where he was received with
great respect. The Chazon Ish and the
Rebbe indulged in an intense discussion on *mikvaos.* At its conclusion,
the Chazon Ish escorted the Rebbe to his car. Upon his return to his
study he was asked what impression the Rebbe had made on him. The
Gaon answered: "He is יְסוֹד שֶׁבִּיסוֹד, the very foundation of holiness.
He is a Rebbe in the revealed Torah (*nigleh*) and a gaon in mystic learning (*nistar*)." When the Chazon Ish published his volume on *Mikvaos,*
he sent the Rebbe a copy, and addressed him in the dedication:
"לְמַעֲלַת כְּבוֹד הַדְרַת גְּאוֹנוּ שליט"א — To his honor, the esteemed and majestic gaon, may he live long and happily."

**WITH THE
CHAZON ISH**

THE LATE RABBI DOVID PERKOVITZ RELATED TO ME THAT HE ONCE accompanied the Boyaner Rebbe to the airport in London. Arriving

TALMUDIC PROFICIENCY there they were told that the plane was delayed for several hours. So they sat down on a bench and engaged in a discussion related to a *sugya* in Tractate *Bechoros*. The Rabbi was amazed to hear the Boyaner Rebbe quote from memory entire sections of the *Maharit Algazi* in its original.

A BOYANER CHASSID TOLD ME THAT HE RODE THE NEW YORK SUBWAY TO and from work. Once, on his way home, the train stopped, and as

RESPECT FOR THE WORKINGMAN the door opened he saw the Boyaner Rebbe walking into this car packed with tired people going home from work. The chassid immediately got up and, still in shock, offered the Rebbe his seat. But to his surprise the Rebbe vehemently refused to sit down, saying, "You work a whole day and stand on your feet, therefore you have to sit down and rest after a hard day's work. I sit the whole day, standing won't affect me." And so he remained standing throughout the subway ride.

R' MOSHE LUDMIR, A WELL-KNOWN BOYANER CHASSID FROM JERUSALEM, told me that while the Rebbe was lodging in his house in

SELF–SERVING Jerusalem, the members of his family were arguing as to who should have the *zechus* to serve him and set his room in order. But as they entered the Rebbe's room in the morning, they were amazed to find the room clean, the bed made and everything set in order as if the room had never been used.

WHILE THE REBBE WAS WAITING ON MADISON STREET FOR THE BUS TO GO to an important meeting at Agudas Israel in downtown New York,

AN EXPENSIVE FAVOR a young man saw him standing in line. The young man, who was driving his own car to attend his *shiur* at Yeshivah Rabbi Jacob Joseph, approached the Rebbe and offered to drive him to his destination. The Rebbe asked him where he was traveling and the the fellow answered that he was going to his *shiur* at the yeshivah, and that nothing would happen if he were a bit late. "No thank you," said the Rebbe, I don't want you to get to the yeshivah ten minutes late on my account."

ONCE THE REBBE ENTERED HIS *BEIS MIDRASH* AND FOUND TWO YOUNG men studying Tractate *Berachos.* The Rebbe asked them why they

TORAH LISHMAH

had chosen this particular Gemara. The men answered that they had in mind to finish the entire *Shas,* and therefore began at the beginning. The Rebbe remarked: "Know that when one begins studying with the intent to finish, it usually happens that he doesn't finish. We have to study for the sake of study — *lishmah* — and if we finish, all the better. But the initial intent should be to study for the sake of study."

REFERRING TO DREAMS, THE REBBE SAID: "THE GEMARA IN *BERACHOS* 55B states: 'All dreams follow the mouth,' that is, all events and occur-

LIKE A DREAM

rences of this world, which is like a dream, are to be resolved by the mouth that is engaged in the study of Torah. The Torah is compared to water (*Bava Kamma* I7a), and, indeed, Torah is similar to a well: בְּאֵר לַחַי רֹאִי (the well of the living). The natural thing to do when digging a well and trying to unearth fresh and pure water is to dig deep. The earth which we dig out we transfer elsewhere, for the deeper one digs, the better and clearer will be the water that one discovers. The same method should be employed by a person who wants to acquire the knowledge of Torah — *kinyan haTorah*. He should repeatedly say to himself that the more he will dig and search within himself and remove from himself the undesirable material he 'unearths,' the better will he be able to reach the 'form' (*tzurah*), the source of water. A person cannot acquire the Torah with physical pleasures, but must make sure that through

R' Nochum Dov, the present Boyaner Rebbe, with HaGaon R' Chaim Brim (standing) and the Rebbe's father, author of this book

his actions it can be called *his* Torah." All those who were close to the Rebbe knew full well how he embodied the above qualities.

NOT ONLY DID THE REBBE NOT ALLOW OTHERS TO SERVE HIM, BUT HE IN-sisted on serving others, irrespective of their position. One morning

INFORMAL HELPER he was standing in a long line in front of an office building in New York. When asked why he was waiting in line, he answered: "A young man had an important appointment to keep but he was afraid to go alone. So I offered to accompany him, and now I am holding his place in line."

HIS OWN COMFORT NEVER TOOK PRECEDENCE. HE WOULD NEVER USE

A MAN OF PEACE AND TRUTH public funds when traveling for *tzorchei tzibbur* (communal needs). He would travel by subway rather than take a taxi, in order not to use *tzedakah* money. In all his endeavors there would be a transcendent trait of deep humility and genuine humbleness, a pure strain of searching for the truth. The Rebbe would ask charity collectors not to exaggerate or inflate the number of students studying in the yeshivah they represent, but to tell the truth and not commit a *chilul Hashem* (desecration of Hashem's Name).

As much as he was *Ish HaEmes* (man of truth), he was also *Ish HaSholom* (man of peace), striving ceaselessly for unity and peace. He would often say, "It's all right to have *chilukei dayos* (differences of opinion), but never *pirud halevovos* (separation of hearts, enmity)."

SALVATION AND RESCUE

WHEN HE WAS ELECTED PRESIDENT OF VAAD HAEZRA, HE WAS ABLE TO RAISE large sums of money to aid the destitute in post-World War II Europe. This was in addition to Vaad HaHatzalah. Those who survived the Holocaust and were able to get visas to America were personally greeted by the Rebbe on their arrival, helped with the absorption process and, later on, helped to receive rabbinical or educational positions. His deep concern for *klal Yisrael* is expressed in a letter saying, "... The *goyim* here are celebrating

The Boyaner Rebbe, R' Mordechai Shlomo, with the Mezhibozher Rebbe, R' Yitzchok Meir Heschel, at his left

with parades to mark their victory in the war. We Jews, however, have lost the war, we have lost everything."

INTROSPECTION

ON HIS WAY TO ISRAEL IN 1949, THE PLANE FLEW OVER THE SWISS ALPS. The Rebbe's *gabbai* R' Levi Hirsch was spellbound by the view and wanted the Rebbe also to look at the magnificent scenery. The Rebbe however was engrossed in his *seforim* and was quite oblivious to all around him. The *gabbai*, who normally would never have disturbed the Rebbe from his learning, was unable to hold himself back and begged him to look out the window, telling him that it was נִפְלָאוֹת הַבּוֹרֵא, the wondrous creations of Hashem. The Rebbe opened his hand and exclaimed, מִבְּשָׂרִי אֶחֱזֶה אֱלוֹק, and immediately continued his learning.

R' Mordechai Shlomo of Boyan ascends the steps up to the Boyaner shul in Jerusalem

While the Rebbe never sought to display his erudition, the rabbinic scholars who came in contact with him unfailingly acknowledged his scholarship. Although he followed the Maggid's custom to *daven* alone in his *kleizel* (small room) adjacent to the *kloiz* of his chassidim, the Rebbe was very active in communal affairs and in all endeavors related to traditional Judaism.

SELF-RESPECT

WHEN THE BOYANER REBBE WAS HOSPITALIZED, HE WAS VISITED BY R' YOEL Teitelbaum, the Satmar Rebbe, who was accompanied by a large entourage. The *gabbai* of the Boyaner asked the Satmarer to wait in the hall until the Boyaner was ready to receive them. They waited ten minutes, twenty minutes... and still were not allowed into the room. The

Satmarer chassidim were distressed, considering it a disrespect to their Rebbe. Finally, after half an hour, the Satmarer was allowed to enter. The visiting Rebbe found the Boyaner sitting in a chair, fully dressed in his rabbinical garb, hat and tie. "Satmarer Rebbe," the Boyaner addressed him, "excuse me for keeping you waiting. As you know we are descendants of the royal Rebbes of Rizhin. Out of respect to them, I could not allow you to see me in my pajamas."

A TRUE REPRESENTATIVE OF *MALCHUS RIZHIN* (ROYAL HOUSE OF Rizhin), his radiating charisma and grace gave him a special aura

NO DISCRIMINATION of love and respect. Modest and unassuming, the Rebbe combined paternal concern and humane regard for all those who crossed his path. A liberal minister, leader of the American Jewish Congress, met the Boyaner Rebbe on a plane flying from Switzerland to America. Wanting to daven *Shacharis,* but not carrying his *tefillin* with him, he somewhat hesitantly approached the Rebbe and asked him if he could use the Rebbe's *tefillin.* The Rebbe gladly gave him his *tefillin,* without inquiring about his religious affiliation.

Always displaying a patriarchal calm and a benevolent disposition, he embodied genuine goodness and the willingness to enter into friendly involvement, drawing every person he met closer and igniting the inner spark of his soul.

THE BOYANER REBBE WAS A MODEL OF PUNCTUALITY AND WAS ALWAYS reality oriented. He was a source of encouragement to his followers

NOT ENOUGH in their new Torah projects and initiatives, similarly encouraging them to practice in their daily lives lovingkindness and humane concern for fellow men, and not to boast or brag over past achievements. He was fond of quoting the Gemara (*Succah* 1b), " 'You shall make the festival of Succos' — You shall build a succah anew, not use an existing one. A person shouldn't be satisfied with his past accomplishments, but should always strive to achieve more."

AT AN ASSEMBLY OF THE AGUDAS HARABBANIM AND ADMORIM IN NEW York, the issue of building new *mikvaos* was the first item on the **REALISTIC** agenda. One of the participants suggested **ASSESSMENT** launched, and that a campaign to raise $5 million be above purpose be established. The Rebbe asked permission to speak and said: "We find in the *Tosefta,* 'If one jumps into the *mikveh,* his immersion is invalid.' The question arises, why is it invalid? The *Rosh* explains that the person jumping into the *mikveh* considers it a 'cooling agent,' not an instrument of purification. It seems to me," the Rebbe continued, "that if we set goals for ourselves of astronomical sums which are not realistic, we will not reach our goal and we won't achieve anything because people will very quickly get cold feet. Every endeavor has to be considered realistically, performed calmly and planned with clarity and peace of mind."

THE STORY IS TOLD THAT WHILE PARTICIPATING IN ONE OF THE CONFERENCES of Agudas HaRabbanim, two renowned *roshei yeshivah* argued about a Talmudic source, and one **FOR SHALOM BAYIS** of them claimed that the source did not exist. The Rebbe remarked, "Just recently I studied that topic and the source is a *Yerushalmi.*" On the way back from the conference, the Bluzhover Rebbe and the Boyaner Rebbe were in the same car. The Bluzhover Rebbe turned to the Rebbe and said: "Boyaner Rebbe, you cannot give me the same excuse. Tell me, did you indeed *just recently* study the topic with the source in *Yerushalmi?*" In his genuinely modest fashion the Rebbe replied: "For the *roshei yeshivah,* the Talmud is to what they dedicate their lives. How would it look if a chassidic Rebbe would know of that source and they themselves not? So, for reasons of *sholom bayis* one is allowed to change a little."

LIKE A REAL CARING FATHER, THE REBBE SHOWED GREAT INTEREST IN THE personal lives of his chassidim, and in **NOSTALGIA FOR** their day-to-day problems. On numer- **THE REBBE** ous occasions I was present, watching the Rebbe, who was totally absorbed in reading the *kvitel* the chassid handed to him. He would inquire about the health of the family members, their sustenance and the education of the children. He would make suggestions and give his blessing according to the person's needs. If a medical problem arose, he would urge the sufferer to consult an experienced doctor or ask for a second opinion. In reciprocity, the love and devotion the Boyaner chassidim bore to their Rebbe was limitless. The following is an illustration:

It happened when Soviet Russia was still allowing outsiders to visit the country. Two of my graduate students, a married couple (the Drs. Grant), visited Kiev for the purpose of *kiruv*. On the first day of Succos, they attended the Great Shul, sharing their *machzor* with the local congregants who had none. The old *gabbai*, R' Pinchos, greeted them and asked where they were from. They answered that they were from New York. The *gabbai* inquired as to whether they had heard of the Boyaner Rebbe in New York, and they replied: "The Rebbe's son-in-law is our teacher." Trembling with emotion and weeping, R' Pinchos searched in his breast pocket, took out a picture of the Rebbe and, kissing it, showed it to them.

R' BARUCH BARZEL, A MAN IN HIS 90'S FROM SAFED, WAS A CHASSID WHO was well known for his communal leadership and his exquisite per-

EMOTIONAL ATTACHMENT
formance of song and dance on Lag BaOmer in Meron, at the grave of R' Shimon bar Yochai. He and his wife spent their last years in an old age home in Raanana. When the author of these lines and his wife visited the elderly chassid and identified ourselves, he jumped up from his bed, and with ecstatic joy pronounced the *shehecheyanu* blessing, "for the happy occasion granted to him to see the Rebbe's children ..."

THE REBBE FIRMLY BELIEVED THAT THE PATH OF CHASSIDUS IS THE

I AM A CHASSID
safest and most effective medium of faith for the preservation of the burning torch of Torah and mitzvos, and the safest means for combating igno-

rance, assimilation and alienation. He interpreted the verse in *Tehillim* 86:2, שָׁמְרָה נַפְשִׁי כִּי חָסִיד אָנִי, *Guard my soul because I am a chassid*, in the following way: "It is a protection for your soul if you wish your children to follow the correct path. Do not say that once there were chassidim. Rather say, 'I am a chassid.' I belong to those who walk the path of Chassidus for the preservation of Judaism."

THE FOLLOWING STORY WAS RELATED BY THE SKULENER REBBE, A CLOSE friend and admirer of the Boyaner Rebbe. While he was still resid-

A LOST WAGER
ing in Vienna, a distinguished-looking stranger entered the Boyaner Rebbe's *beis midrash* and humbly asked to be allowed to be the *shaliach tzibbur*, since he had *yahrzeit* that day. Permission was granted to him, but no sooner had he begun reciting the prayers, the Rebbe emerged from his room next door, walked up to the *amud* (lectern) and asked the man why he was there. "I am a *chiyuv* (one who is obligated to lead the service)," the man explained. "But who says I am obliged to listen to you?" retorted the Rebbe. Hearing this, the stranger walked right out of the *beis midrash*. In reality, the stranger was an *apikores* — a confirmed heretic — in disguise, who had wagered a large sum of money with his friends that he could mislead the Rebbe by posing as a pious Jew. The individual's bet cost him a pretty penny and he ended up the laughingstock of his friends.

ON SEVERAL OCCASIONS, AMERICAN-BORN, ASSIMILATED PARENTS EXPRESSED radical opposition to the Rebbe's efforts to bring their children to the

THE REBBE'S BERACHAH
way of Chassidus. We recall the case of a young man who, under the influence of the Rebbe, had chosen to lead a religious life. One day, he approached the Rebbe with tears in his eyes, telling him that his father had threatened that if he didn't give up his newly adopted "*shtetl* lifestyle" he would have him declared insane by a psychiatrist and placed in a mental insti-

tution. The Rebbe calmed the young man and promised him to resolve the problem in his favor. Soon after, the father visited the Rebbe and, with tears in his eyes, related to the Rebbe that his second son had just come down with a severe mental illness and was now a patient in the same hospital in which the father had earlier threatened to place his chassidic son. Realizing that this bore all the signs of a Divine judgment, he begged the Rebbe for a blessing that his son would recover, and pledged to stop mistreating his older son. The Rebbe's blessing was fulfilled. The mentally troubled son recovered and the entire family subsequently returned to Judaism and became ardent Boyaner chassidim.

AN AMERICAN WAS TOURING IN JERUSALEM AND, WHILE VISITING THE Mount of Olives, asked the tour guide to show him the grave of the

RUACH HAKODESH Boyaner Rebbe. When the guide showed him the grave on the summit of the mountain, the tourist burst into tears and started to recite

Tehillim. Asked about his relationship to the Boyaner Rebbe, he ex-

The Boyaner Rebbe speaking at an Agudah convention; on his left is R' Eliezer Silver, on his right is R' Mendel Chodorov

plained, sobbing: "My father used to live in downtown New York, on the Lower East Side. Once, while he was visiting the Rebbe's house, the Rebbe suddenly shouted, 'Run back home and bring your little boy indoors at once.' My father rushed home and, finding his little boy playing in the courtyard, grabbed him and brought him into the house. At that very moment a heavy branch broke off from the tree and fell exactly on the spot where the little boy had been playing only seconds earlier."

R' Nochum Dov of Boyan, the present Boyaner Rebbe

And the American concluded, "I am that boy who was saved. How can I not get excited and not pray at the Rebbe's grave?"

IT WAS THE REBBE'S ACHIEVEMENT TO HAVE UNITED THE REMNANTS OF the Rizhin-Boyan survivors of the Holocaust, although the great majority of chassidim had perished, together with entire communities of loyal adherents, as was the case in Poland, Hungary, Galicia, Ukraine, Romania and other regions.

AN INTERPERSONAL APPROACH

In the bustling metropolis of New York the Rebbe's *beis midrash* functioned as a haven and center of Torah and Chassidus. And while the Rebbe was sitting in his small *kleizel* (private room), somehow he magically attracted youth searching for meaning and substance in their lives. His adherents, young and old, considered him their spiritual mentor, a giant in Chassidus and in action, inspiring *chessed* and majestic grace.

The late Lubavitcher Rebbe quoted the Boyaner Rebbe, who said in the name of the Rizhiner his great-grandfather, "Just as one mitzvah leads to another mitzvah, so does one state of *simchah* lead to another."

The Rebbe always extolled humility, which he himself practiced to the letter. He interpreted the Gemara (*Sotah* 5), "A *talmid chacham* should possess an eighth of an eighth of pride": The idea is that, first of all, a person has to become a *talmid chacham*. For before he knows that he really is a *talmid chacham*, he surely cannot rely upon the above statement of our Sages to be prideful. Even if he is a real *talmid chacham*, however, I think the Sages meant that *he should become exalted in the ways of Hashem* (cf. *II Chronicles* 17:6).

WHEN THE REBBE VISITED SAFED, A YOUNG MAN WAS DESIGNATED TO attend to all his needs. At dawn, the man heard a noise coming from

REFUSING ASSISTANCE

the Rebbe's room, which was adjacent to his. Rushing into the room, he found the Rebbe moving his bed, from beside to the wall to the middle of the room. Shocked, he asked the Rebbe why he had moved

the bed. The Rebbe answered, "At midnight it became very cold, and so, because of my arthritis, I was forced to move the bed away from the cold wall to the middle of the room. Now, I am returning the bed to its original place." The young man asked the Rebbe why he had not called him to move the heavy bed. The Rebbe answered that he saw no reason to ask him for he was capable of doing it himself.

From r. to l. The Boyaner Rebbe (r.) with R' Moshe Feinstein and R' Aaron Kotler at a chupah

SAID THE BOYANER REBBE OF NEW YORK: "ALTHOUGH ONE HAS SINS,

IN DEFENSE OF THE JEWS every Jew possesses a part of Hashem in him which is flawless. Therefore, *He (Hashem) has not beheld iniquity in Yaakov* (*Bamidbar* 23:21). This verse can justly be applied to the generation of today."

WHILE ATTENDING A CONVENTION OF AGUDAS ISRAEL, THE REBBE WAS called to the Torah for *revi'i*, the fourth *aliyah*. The third *aliyah* had

ALPHABETICAL ORDER been given to Mr. Louis Septimus, a prominent communal leader. Unknown to the *gabbaim*, the third *aliyah* was customarily given to the Boyaner Rebbe.

The chassidim were very upset with the error. It came to the ear of the Rebbe, who summoned them and said, "*Nisht kushe, nisht kushe* (not a problem, not a problem). In the Hebrew alphabet the letter *samech* (for Septimus) comes before the letter *fei* (for Friedman)."

The Boyaner Rebbe dancing at a Hachnosas Sefer Torah

EPILOGUE

AFTER FIFTEEN PRAYFUL YEARS OF WAITING, THE JOYOUS DAY OF hope and expection arrived. Boyaner chassidim were looking forward to Chanukah, the day when the new Boyaner Rebbe would be inaugurated in the traditional manner to carry on the Boyaner dynasty.

The young man assuming leadership had been unanimously elected to this most awesome position, but he resisted. What he really wanted was to join a kollel and devote himself to Torah study, but there was irresistible moral pressure on him to accept the position. Such great Rebbes and Rabbonim as the Gerrer Rebbe the Beis Yisroel, Rav Moshe Feinstein and the Lubavitcher Rebbe urged him to accept. His parents did not wish to intervene, but chassidim and leaders in the Jewish community did not stop pressuring his parents to prevail upon their son. This was a generation after the

Holocaust, in which more than three quarters of Boyaner Chassidim perished. Finally he agreed, ending fifteen years of spiritual frustration and exceptional loyalty of the chassidim, who lived with hope that Boyan would not come to an end. His followers rallied around the new Boyaner Rebbe, joining ranks around the tree of Rizhin. The new Rebbe followed in the footsteps of his revered grandfather, adding innovations and helping his chassidim with *kiruv*, guidance and direction.

A great deal of his success is due to the Rizhiner Yeshivah, which had been led by his grandfather, the previous Rebbe, whose lifestyle was unique. Assuming the presidency of the Yeshivah the new Rebbe became the leader and mentor of thousands of chassidim. Thus, the *berachah* given by his great-grandfather, Reb Sholom Shachna of Prohobisht, was fulfilled. The golden chain of Rizhin would be continued *ein keitz*, without end, until the arrival of *Mashiach*.

The present Rebbe extended his influence by building new yeshivos and kollelim, in Eretz Yisrael, Europe, and the United States, to memorialize and eternalize the descendants of the House of Rizhin. The Rizhiner Yeshivah plays a central role in the advanced education and high standards of Jewish scholarship and education. *Batei midrash* are sprouting in such new

R' Nochum Dov Brayer, the present Boyaner Rebbe

yishuvim as Betar, Ramot, and Shuafat, all of them extensions of the Rebbe's initiative.

The charismatic Rebbe is fully involved in the lifestyle of his chassidim, who revere him with wholehearted love. He directs all spiritual gatherings and festive encounters, such as *tischim,* toward the constant process of growth and development. The success of and respect enjoyed by these institutions and activities augur to the expanding influence of Boyan in Jerusalem and overseas. A vibrant Boyan is developing under the leadership of a young Rebbe, who is a worthy successor to the many generations of Rizhin. After the Holocaust, *Od Boyan Chai,* Boyan is still alive.

In truth, it has been a long, but successful journey from Rizhin to Jerusalem.

Yeshivah Tiferes Yisroel of Rizhin in Jerusalem